| DATE DUE | | | |
|---|---|---|---|
| Fall 77 Freedman Reserve | | | |
| OCT 10 '77 | | | |
| OCT 13 '77 | | | |
| U.C. Spring '78 Freedman Reserve | | | |
| NOV 5 '83 | | | |

# SOCIETAL BEHAVIOR:
# NEW AND UNIQUE RIGHTS
# OF THE PERSON

# SOCIETAL BEHAVIOR: NEW AND UNIQUE RIGHTS OF THE PERSON

*By*

**WARREN FREEDMAN, A.B., LL.B.**
*Member of the New York and U.S. Supreme Court Bars*

CHARLES C THOMAS • PUBLISHER
*Springfield • Illinois • U.S.A.*

*Published and Distributed Throughout the World by*
CHARLES C THOMAS • PUBLISHER
BANNERSTONE HOUSE
301-327 East Lawrence Avenue, Springfield, Illinois, U.S.A.
NATCHEZ PLANTATION HOUSE
735 North Atlantic Boulevard, Fort Lauderdale, Florida, U.S.A.

This book is protected by copyright. No part of it may be reproduced in any manner without written permission from the publisher.

© *1965, by* CHARLES C THOMAS • PUBLISHER
Library of Congress Catalog Card Number: 65-19289

*With THOMAS BOOKS careful attention is given to all details of manufacturing and design. It is the Publisher's desire to present books that are satisfactory as to their physical qualities and artistic possibilities and appropriate for their particular use. THOMAS BOOKS will be true to those laws of quality that assure a good name and good will.*

340
F875s

*Printed in the United States of America*

# PREFACE

IN THE CHAOTIC GROWTH of modern society, the individual is being coerced, conformed, and threatened in new and unique ways. The legal background to today's (and tomorrow's) headlines puts the spotlight on these new and unique rights of the individual in his struggle against other individuals, in his struggle against institutions. To understand these problems, the essential legal analysis of decided cases plays an important role . . . but only insofar as whetting the appetite for study, research, and clear-thinking. The reader is exposed to the impact of laws and court cases only to the extent that such information is necessary for focusing upon these new and unique rights of the individual in modern society.

The law of torts describes socially-imposed private duties upon the individual which, in the light of changing social experiences, are necessary to promote the common welfare of society. Since a *duty* presupposes a *right,* the individual in society gains cherished *rights* measured by security and even peace of mind, by the legal recognition of *duties* which society imposes. Fortunately, our courts have not always been hampered by legal precedents and restrictive legislation in carving out new and unique rights of the person based upon this *duty-right* relationship. The modern law of torts is a dynamic concept as are the headlines in modern life; thus, *it is our inquiry as to whether this dynamism in the law is equal to the task of measuring the social value of individual rights amid ever-changing economic, political, and social conditions.* Tortious wrongs, whether intentionally or negligently committed, are made "right," not by the fixity of rules and logical systemization, but by the social desirability of blending the interests of the individual and society in a harmonious balance.

These twelve chapters view *those* new and unique rights of the person which, in the author's opinion, well illustrate the changing concepts of individual needs in our society in a dramatic portrayal of "human interest." The treatment of these selected topics is purposefully not complete nor intended to be exhaustive of the subject matter; but is designed to foster intelligent appraisal of the legal and social structure of our society in which the individual lives.

Professor Warren Seavey of Harvard Law School in his book, *Cogitations on Torts,* called upon his fifty years of teaching tort law, and nobly declared:—

> "Some think of the law of torts as the law of wrongs; it might better be said to be a law for the creation and protection of rights. Its function has continuously been to mark out new areas for the protection of human interests. It is not restricted, as are the rules of property, to developing rules for the transfer of things from one person to another, nor as are the rules of contracts or associations to the regulation of business transactions. While constitutional law protects primarily against legislation which impairs basic interests, the law of torts has given protection against harmful conduct to the entire range of human interests, not always completely and sometimes poorly, but on the whole effectively . . . . .
>
> "The law of torts has a further distinction. It is here that we can best realize that law is not static but dynamic; that it grows and expands to meet changing economic and social conditions. It is here that the judges have been and should be most free from the shackles of stare decisis; it is here that we can best see how the judges, beginning with the simple idea of giving protection against physical interference with persons or things, have created a vast network of rules by which all human interests have been given protection. This they have done without having the legislative background which is the basis of modern civil law, and largely without legislative aid. As the subject exists today, its principles as well as its rules are the product of judges. They have been successful in proportion as they have met the needs of successive generations."

Indeed, this mobility in the law of torts has been in the direction of extending liability by staking out new and unique rights necessary for protection of the individual. In New York, for example, the courts have delineated a *"prima facie"* tort doctrine to speed relief to the injured party who suffers harm as the result of the "infliction of intentional harm, resulting in damage, without excuse or justification by an act or a series of acts which otherwise would be lawful" (*Ruza v. Ruza*, 146 N.Y.S.2d 808, 1955). Consequential and punitive damages are frequently allowed the injured person, because there is a lack of justification for the tort, which fails to serve the welfare or interests of society. Courts endeavor to satisfy a maximum of human wants with the minimum of sacrifice of other human wants.

A passing word on "judicial precedent" — i.e., a rule of law established in earlier cases and binding upon courts today. Fortunately, the English doctrine of legal precedents whereby the House of Lords is absolutely bound by its own prior decisions, and every court is absolutely bound by decisions of all superior courts — has never found root in the United States. We respect judicial precedents, not because they have been made, but because their wisdom commends them to the court *per se*. However, no judge in the United States would ignore or overrule deliberately a given judicial precedent, merely for the sake of being arbitrary. Indeed, the goal is to attain justice in the particular case by attaining it within the pattern of law. The legal order is always a system of compromises, and it is the duty of the judge to resolve the litigation within the framework of individual needs and societal welfare. Justice J. I. Shapiro of the New York Supreme Court, Queens County, expressed it well:

> "The tradition of a dynamic law adapting itself to changing needs is a proud mainstay of our judicial system. Previous interpretations which are not in harmony with modern conditions of life should not be *woodenly* applied merely for the sake of record consistency. The perpetuation of a fiction which has outlived its usefulness and the adherence to which can only bring about an unjust result, is not required by either law or common sense" (*Siegel & Hodges v. Hodges*, 9/23/59).

W. F.

# CONTENTS

|   | Page |
|---|---|
| *Preface* | v |

*Chapter*
I. THE RIGHT OF PRIVACY: THE INDIVIDUAL IN SOCIETY ..... 3
    Definition and Characterization of "Privacy" ........ 3
    Statutory Recognition of the Right of Privacy ........ 5
    The Right of Privacy in the Absence of Statute ....... 8
    The Public Figure and the Dissemination of News .... 9
    Defamation and the Right of Privacy ................ 12
    The Personal Right of Privacy ...................... 13
    Signatures and the Right of Privacy ................ 14
    Photographs and the Right of Privacy .............. 16
    Immoral and Criminal Portrayals and the Right of Privacy ....................................... 18
    Fictionalization and the Right of Privacy ........... 19
    Old News and the Right of Privacy ................. 20
    Improper Debt Collection and the Right of Privacy ... 22
    Physicians and the Patient's Right of Privacy ........ 23
    Autopsy and the Right of Privacy ................... 26
    Privacy — Impinged Upon by Recent Scientific Developments ....................................... 27
    The United Nations and the Right of Privacy ........ 28
    Selected Bibliography ............................. 29
    Questions for Review ............................. 29
II. ALIENATION OF AFFECTIONS AND FAMILIAL PEACE ........ 31
    The Family as a Group ............................ 31

| Chapter | Page |
|---|---|
| Interference with Relational Interests | 31 |
| Loss of Consortium as a Measure of Damage | 34 |
| The Child's Loss of Consortium | 37 |
| Two "Classical" Cases of Alienation of Affections | 37 |
| Statutory Changes in New York and Other States | 38 |
| Testimonial Compulsion and the Husband-Wife Relationship | 39 |
| Domestic Tranquility in England | 42 |
| Support of Dependents Generally | 43 |
| The Marriage Contract | 45 |
|     The Common Law Marriage | 47 |
|     First-cousin Marriages | 47 |
| Personal Injuries Within the Family | 48 |
|     Suits by the Minor Child Against His Parent | 50 |
|     Suits Between Spouses | 53 |
|     "Conditions" For Invoking the Family Immunity Doctrine | 55 |
|     Abolition of the Family Immunity Doctrine | 56 |
|     Conflict of Laws in Intra-family Tort Liability | 57 |
|     The New York Insurance Dilemma | 58 |
| Parents' Liability for Misconduct of Children | 59 |
| Selected Bibliography | 61 |
| Questions for Review | 61 |
| III. HARMS TO UNBORN CHILDREN: RECOVERY FOR PRENATAL INJURIES | 63 |
| The Traditional Legal View of "Entity" | 63 |
| Recovery for Prenatal Injuries — The Majority View Today | 66 |
| Denial of Recovery for Prenatal Injuries — The Minority View Today | 69 |
| Denial of Recovery for Wrongful Death of the Unborn Viable Child | 71 |
| Causal Relation Between Injury and Act of Negligence | 71 |
| Separability of Child from Moment of Conception | 73 |

| Chapter | Page |
|---|---|
| Environmental Stress and Hereditary Influences as Causes of Prenatal Injury | 74 |
| Criminal Abortion: The Legal "Entity" of the Unborn Child | 75 |
| Selected Bibliography | 76 |
| Questions for Review | 76 |
| IV. SELF-INCRIMINATION AND THE FIFTH AMENDMENT: A PERSPECTIVE OF OUR TIMES | 77 |
| The Historical Background | 77 |
| The "Presumptive Guilt" Theory | 79 |
| The "Presumptive Innocence" Theory | 80 |
| "Loyalty Oath Affidavits" | 81 |
| Some "Qualifications" of the Privilege Against Self-incrimination | 83 |
| Congressional Committees and the Fifth Amendment | 84 |
| The Slochower Case | 85 |
| The Watkins Case | 87 |
| The Barenblatt Case | 88 |
| The Presser Case | 90 |
| The McPhaul Case | 91 |
| The Wilkinson and Braden Cases | 91 |
| Federal Government Employment and the Fifth Amendment | 93 |
| The Greene Case | 93 |
| The Vitarelli Case | 94 |
| The Brawner Case | 94 |
| The Communist Party Cases | 95 |
| State Legislatives Inquiries and the Fifth Amendment | 98 |
| The Sweezy Case | 98 |
| The Uphaus Case | 99 |
| The Malloy Case | 101 |
| Local Government Investigations and the Fifth Amendment | 103 |
| The Lerner Case | 103 |

| Chapter | Page |
|---|---|
| The Nostrand Case | 104 |
| Grand Jury Proceedings and the Fifth Amendment | 105 |
| The Steuding Case | 105 |
| The Curcio Case | 106 |
| The Halperin Case | 106 |
| The Reina Case | 107 |
| Civil Cases and the Fifth Amendment | 107 |
| Disbarment Proceedings and the Fifth Amendment | 108 |
| The Konigsberg Case | 109 |
| The Anastaplo Case | 110 |
| The Cohen Case | 111 |
| Deportation Hearings and the Fifth Amendment | 112 |
| School Board Hearings and the Fifth Amendment | 114 |
| The Jencks Case and Inspection of the Evidence | 115 |
| Motives for "Taking the Fifth" | 117 |
| Waiver of the Privilege Against Self-incrimination | 118 |
| Corporate Entity and the Fifth Amendment | 120 |
| Federal Immunity Statutes and the Fifth Amendment | 121 |
| The Ullmann Case | 122 |
| The Brown Case | 123 |
| State Immunity Statutes and the Fifth Amendment | 124 |
| The Knapp Case | 124 |
| The Mills Case | 125 |
| The Cioffi and Stein Case | 125 |
| The Raley Case | 126 |
| State Immunity and Federal Immunity Under the Fifth Amendment | 126 |
| Scientific Evidence and the Fifth Amendment | 128 |
| The Breithaupt Case | 128 |
| Double Jeopardy and the Fifth Amendment | 129 |
| The Bartkus Case | 129 |
| The Sabella and La Cascia Case | 130 |
| The Forman Case | 131 |
| Other Cases on "Double Jeopardy" | 132 |

| Chapter | Page |
|---|---|
| Selected Bibliography | 132 |
| Questions for Review | 133 |
| V. SOCIAL UTILITY ASPECTS OF LIBEL AND SLANDER LAW | 135 |
| Introduction to Defamation | 135 |
| The Nature of the Legal Remedy for Defamation | 136 |
| Property Rights, Personality, and Employment Opportunities Under Attack | 139 |
| The Right of Privacy and Defamation | 141 |
| Product Defamation | 141 |
| Defamation of Personality | 142 |
| Libel by Will or Testament | 147 |
| "Hidden Libels" and Innuendoes | 147 |
| Privilege to Defame: Absolute and Qualified Privileges | 150 |
| Truth: An Absolute Defense to Defamation? | 151 |
| Privilege of the Press: The Right to Fair Comment | 152 |
| The Sensational, Exposé Magazine | 155 |
| The Newspaper Reporter's Privileged Communication | 156 |
| Defamation by Radio and Television | 159 |
| Protection of Public Officials from Liability for Defamation | 161 |
| Immunity of Legislators from Defamation Liability | 164 |
| Group Libel and Group Slander | 175 |
| Selected Bibliography | 179 |
| Questions for Review | 179 |
| VI. CORPORATE MERGERS AND ACQUISITIONS: PATTERNS OF ECONOMIC CONCENTRATION | 181 |
| Our American Economy Generally | 181 |
| A Short History of the Merger Movement: "The Urge to Merge" | 182 |
| The Role of the Federal Trade Commission in Mergers | 183 |
| The Role of the U. S. Department of Justice in Mergers | 185 |
| The Problems of Merger: "Line of Commerce," "Relevant Market," and "Competitive Impact" | 187 |

| Chapter | Page |
|---|---|
| Types of Mergers: Horizontal, Vertical, and Conglomerate | 190 |
| Selected Recent Cases: "Pillsbury" and "duPont-General Motors" | 191 |
| Other Selected Merger-Acquisitions Cases | 195 |
|     Bethlehem Steel and Youngstown Sheet and Tube Co. | 195 |
|     Cuban-American Sugar Co. | 196 |
|     Chrysler Corporation | 197 |
|     Federal Trade Commission Cases | 197 |
| Bigness! Is it Illegal Under the Anti-trust Laws? | 198 |
| Selected Bibliography | 199 |
| Questions for Review | 199 |
| **VII. ANTI-TRUST LAW: THE BUSINESS OF SPORTS** | 201 |
| "Trade or Commerce" and Sports | 201 |
| The Business of Baseball | 203 |
|     "Inside Baseball": How It Operates | 206 |
|     Other Baseball Problems and Practices | 207 |
| The Business of Football | 209 |
| The Business of Boxing | 212 |
| The Business of Wrestling | 214 |
| The Business of Basketball | 215 |
| The Business of Horse-Racing | 216 |
| Legislative Proposals for Exemption of Professional Teams from the Anti-trust Laws | 216 |
| Selected Bibliography | 217 |
| Questions for Review | 217 |
| **VIII. GAMBLING—LOTTERIES, BINGO, AND THE PUBLIC INTEREST** | 218 |
| The Historical Background of the Lottery | 218 |
| "Lottery" Defined | 220 |
| New York's Attack Upon Lotteries and Gambling | 223 |
| Merchandising by Lottery Devices | 224 |
|     Trading Stamps as Gift Enterprise | 226 |
| Lotteries and the Federal Communications Commission | 227 |
| Bingo or Lotto by Referendum in New York | 228 |

| Chapter | Page |
|---|---|
| The Status of Gambling in England | 230 |
| Selected Bibliography | 231 |
| Questions for Review | 231 |
| **IX. ADOPTION AND SOCIETY: THE LEGAL CREATION OF A FAMILY** | 233 |
| "Adoption" Defined | 233 |
| Questionable Adoption Practices | 234 |
| A Capsule History of Adoption Practices | 236 |
| Deficiencies in Present-day Adoption Statutes | 237 |
| Aims of Adoption | 238 |
| Classification of Adoptions and Procedures | 238 |
| Religious Groupings Under the New York Statute | 239 |
| The True Foundling: What Religion? | 240 |
| The Constitutional Issue of Religious-grouping | 240 |
| Enforcement of Pre-nuptial Agreements to Rear Child in Particular Religion | 241 |
| The Religious Choice in Adoptions | 242 |
| Adoption Procedures in New York | 244 |
| Investigation of Prospective Parents | 244 |
| Initial Placement of Child in Private Adoptions | 245 |
| The Inheritance Rights of the Adopted Child in New York | 247 |
| The Statistics of Adoption | 247 |
| The "Black Market" for Adoption of Babies | 248 |
| Termination of Parental Rights Over the Child | 249 |
| Termination of Parental Rights by Foster Parents | 250 |
| Judicial Determination of Termination of Parental Rights | 251 |
| Selected Bibliography | 253 |
| Questions for Review | 253 |
| **X. THE RIGHT TO TRAVEL: PASSPORTS, DEPORTATION, AND FREEDOM** | 254 |
| Travel: A Constitutional Right? | 254 |
| A Short History of the Right to Travel | 255 |
| Some Problems with Passports | 257 |

| Chapter | Page |
|---|---|
| The Rockwell Kent Case | 258 |
| The 1958 Legislative Attack Upon the Right to Travel | 262 |
| The "Worthy" Chronicle: Area Travel Restrictions | 262 |
| The Ban on Communist Travel Abroad | 265 |
| A Report of a Bar Association on Freedom to Travel | 266 |
| Travel by Aliens: Deportation and/or Dentention | 270 |
| Deportation: Travel Away from the U. S. | 271 |
| Detention: "No Travel" | 274 |
| Visas and the "Right to Exclude" Aliens | 275 |
| Selected Bibliography | 278 |
| Questions for Review | 278 |
| XI. SELECTED CRIMES AGAINST INSTITUTIONS: SOCIAL AND CRIMINAL WRONGS | 280 |
| Extortion | 280 |
| Blackmail | 282 |
| Perjury | 284 |
| Forgery | 284 |
| Plagiarism | 286 |
| Bribery | 287 |
| Unlawful Detention of Person by an Institution | 288 |
| Deceptive Practices in the Broadcasting Industries | 290 |
| Selected Bibliography | 292 |
| Questions for Review | 292 |
| XII. GOVERNMENTAL REGULATION OF THE INSURANCE INDUSTRY | 293 |
| The Nature of the Business of Insurance | 293 |
| Insurance Is or Is Not "Commerce" (1868-1944) | 296 |
| A Short History of Rate-making or Price-fixing | 296 |
| Insurance Is "Commerce" (1944) | 297 |
| Aftermath of the South Eastern Underwriters Association Case | 299 |
| Jurisdiction of the Federal Trade Commission | 300 |
| The American Hospital Case | 303 |
| F.T.C. Conflict Resolved — 1958 and 1960 | 306 |
| The Travelers Health Association Case | 307 |

| Chapter | Page |
|---|---|
| Aviation Insurance | 310 |
| Boycotts and Restraints: Jurisdiction of the U. S. Department of Justice | 310 |
| The Future of Regulation | 313 |
| Selected Bibliography | 313 |
| Questions for Review | 314 |
| Index | 315 |

# SOCIETAL BEHAVIOR: NEW AND UNIQUE RIGHTS OF THE PERSON

# Chapter I

# THE RIGHT OF PRIVACY: THE INDIVIDUAL IN SOCIETY

### Definition and Characterization of "Privacy"

IN DECEMBER 1890, the *Harvard Law Review* published an article written by Louis Brandeis and Samuel Warren as a protest against the undue newspaper publicity given to the private social affairs of Mrs. Warren. This seventy-five year old article entitled "The Right of Privacy" has been so widely quoted by lawyers, judges, social psychologists and sociologists that the following pertinent excerpts are worthy of note:

> " . . . . the right to life has come to mean the right to enjoy life—the right to be let alone . . . . Recent inventions and business methods call attention to the next step which must be taken for the protection of the person . . . . The intensity and complexity of life, attendant upon advancing civilization, have rendered necessary some retreat from the world, and man, under the refining influence of culture, has become more sensitive to publicity, so that solitude and privacy have become more essential to the individual . . . .
>
> "The common law secures to each individual the right of determining, ordinarily, to what extent his thoughts, sentiments, and emotions shall be communicated to others . . . . The existence of this right does not depend upon the particular method of expression adopted . . . . Neither does the existence of the right depend upon the nature or value of the thought or emotion, nor upon the excellence of the means of expression . . . . In every case, the individual is entitled to decide whether that which is his shall be given to the public . . . .
>
> "A man records in a letter to his son, or in his diary, that he did not dine with his wife on a certain day. No one into whose hands those papers fall could publish them to the world . . . . What is the thing which is protected? Surely, not the intellect-

ual act of recording the fact that the husband did not dine with his wife, but that fact itself . . . .

" . . . . if privacy is once recognized as a right entitled to legal protection, the interposition of the courts cannot depend upon the particular nature of the injuries resulting . . . . It is like the right not to be assaulted or beaten, the right not to be imprisoned, the right not to be maliciously prosecuted, the right not to be defamed . . . . . there inheres the quality of being owned or possessed—and . . . . there may be some propriety in speaking of those rights as property . . . . The principle which protects . . . . is in reality not the principle of private property, but that of an inviolate personality.

" . . . . the rights, so protected, whatever their exact nature, are not rights arising from contract or from special trust, but are rights as against the world . . . . If the invasion of privacy constitutes legal injuria, the elements for demanding redress exist, since already the value of mental suffering, caused by an act wrongful in itself, is recognized as a basis for compensation . . . .

"The right to privacy does not prohibit any publication of matter which is of public general interest . . . .

"The right of privacy does not prohibit the communication of any matter though in its nature private, when the publication is made under circumstances which would render it a privileged communication according to the law of libel and slander . . . .

"The law would probably not grant any redress for the invasion of privacy by oral publication in the absence of special damage . . . .

"The right of privacy ceases upon the publication of the facts by the individual or with his consent . . . .

"The truth of the matter published does not afford a defense . . . . The absence of 'malice' in the publisher does not afford a defense . . . .

" . . . . the protection of society must come mainly through a recognition of the rights of the individual . . . . Shall the courts thus close the front entrance to constituted authority, and open wide the back door to idle or prurient curiosity?"

Thus, the right of privacy is the inherent right of a person to be left alone in the conduct of their private affairs. It includes the unwarranted appropriation or exploitation of one's personality, the publicizing of one's private affairs with which the public has no legitimate concern, etc., in such a manner as to outrage or cause mental suffering, shame, or humiliation to a person of ordinary sensibilities. As a society, we are not yet capable of sealing ourselves hermetically from the probers of gossip, scandal, and commercial exploitation; and, therefore, we must anticipate and await frequent invasions and intrusions upon "privacy." In *Bradley v. Cowles Magazines, Inc.* (168 N.E.2d 64) the Illinois Appellate Court surmised:

> "Guaranty of the right of privacy is not a guaranty of hermetic seclusion. We live in a society geared in the opposite direction; a society that makes public demands and imposes public duties . . . . "

Yet, "the right to privacy (or personality) is a part of the right to liberty and the pursuit of happiness, which recognizes that the individual does not exist solely for the state or society, but has inalienable rights which cannot be taken from him so long as he behaves properly" (*Barber v. Time Inc.*, 159 S.W.2d 291).

## Statutory Recognition of the Right of Privacy

Although a majority of states have recognized a right of privacy as an inherent, inalienable right of the individual, it has been necessary, in a number of states such as Texas, Nebraska, Rhode Island, Wisconsin, and New York, to enact legislation. After New York, in 1902, in *Roberson v. Rochester Folding Box Co.* (171 N.Y. 538) had refused to recognize the right of privacy, appropriate legislation was enacted prohibiting the use "for advertising purposes or for the purposes of trade" of the name, portrait, or picture of any living person, without his prior written consent. (Sections 50 and 51 of the New York Civil Rights Law). Both criminal and civil liability are imposed in New York for violation of the statutes. A survey of recent New York decisions is in order:—

> In *Lahr v. Adell Chemical Co.*, the well-known stage, screen and radio star, Bert Lahr, brought suit against the manufac-

turer of a detergent "Lestoil" alleging, among other causes of action, invasion of his right of privacy. Specifically, he contended that his distinctive voice and original style of vocal comic delivery which had made him widely known and readily recognizable as a unique and extraordinary comic character, was imitated by the defendant in advertising its product on television, to wit: a cartoon film of a duck with a voice imitating Bert Lahr, so that the television audience believed the voice was Lahr's. Lahr argued that this was a misappropriation of his creative talent and vocal delivery, and a trading upon his fame and renown, to the extent that his reputation was damaged because it appeared that he had been reduced to giving anonymous commercials! But the First U.S. Court of Appeals on March 12, 1962, held that the allegations did *not* state a cause of action for invasion of Lahr's right of privacy:

"Any rights resulting from the special New York statute, sometimes called the right of privacy statute, flow from the use, for commercial purposes, of a party's 'name, portrait or picture' . . . . Plaintiff's claim, here, at best, is that, though the picture was that of a duck, the voice was the 'name' which he enlarges to 'identify' of the plaintiff. The statute is very specific. If the Legislature intended that whenever an anonymous speaker extolled a commercial product a cause of action arose (and criminal penalties could be imposed) if anyone could claim the voice was mistaken as his, it should have used a phrase of more general import. In the absence of any New York authority 'name' can be given no such catholic connotation."

In *Lomax v. New Broadcasting Co.*, decided by the New York Appellate Division, 1st Dept., on April 1, 1963, an announcer and interviewer sued the radio station for which she worked, alleging the use of her name and photograph in advertising, without her permission, in connection with a sponsor's products. She had complained about her employer's practice early in the course of employment, and was told to resign if she did not like the practice. She therefore cooperated fully in the use of her name and photograph. The Court held that her oral consent was not necessarily a complete defense under the statute, but only in mitigation of damages.

In *Hill v. Erskine* (240 N.Y.S. 2nd 286), the plaintiffs, husband and wife, with their children were held captive in their home for nineteen hours by three escaped convicts. About six months later a novel entitled *The Desperate Hours* was published that dealt with a family held as hostages in their home by three escaped convicts. Later a play and a motion picture were produced that were based upon the novel. In 1955 (three years after the event), when the fictional play opened and when the plaintiffs had moved to another state and had sought to forget about their experience, an article was published in defendant's magazine in which the plaintiffs' name was used. This magazine article stated that many would recall the plaintiffs' "desperate ordeal," and the novel which was "inspired by the family's experience," and the play where one now "can see the story re-enacted," and "next year will see it in his movie." The New York Appellate Division, 1st Dept., on May 14, 1963, held that the conclusion was inescapable that the purpose was to advertise the play and to increase the circulation of the defendant's magazine; hence, there was a violation of plaintiffs' right of privacy. (Jury verdict of $175,000. affirmed).

In *Youssoupoff v. Columbia Broadcasting System* the plaintiff was a member of the former Russian royal family, and in 1916 had admittedly murdered the Russian monk Rasputin. Plaintiff had written two books in which he described the plot and the details of the killing of Rasputin who had an evil influence upon the Czarina and through her upon the Czar. CBS broadcast a dramatic sketch or play entitled *If I Should Die* in which an actor impersonated the plaintiff. Every effort was made by CBS to adhere to historical facts surrounding the death of Rasputin. The New York Supreme Court, New York County, on June 24, 1963, found no invasion of the right of privacy:

> "The privilege to use a person's name or photograph in portrayals of current news or of past events of legitimate public or general interest does not . . . . extend 'to commercialization of . . . personality through a form of treatment distinct from the designation of news or information' . . . . The portrayal of the plaintiff by the actor who impersonated him in the broadcast . . . . (did not) in any way . . . injure in the slightest plaintiff's character or reputation . . . . the effect on the reviewer is no different from the effect produced by the reading of plaintiff's own books on the subject of the conspiracy and its consummation."

In *Selsman v. Universal Photo Books,* decided by the New York Appellate Division, 1st Dept., on March 21, 1963, the infant plaintiff, an actress and model, was employed in the Walt Disney film entitled *The Light in the Forest.* A number of on-location pictures were taken with Minox cameras, which pictures were acquired from Disney by Kling which delivered the photographs to its advertising agency, and the photographs after publication were made available to defendant which published the Minox Manual. One photograph shows the plaintiff focusing a Minox camera. The Court declared that the use of plaintiff's photograph without her written consent to advertise the Minox camera was an invasion of her right of privacy.

## The Right of Privacy in the Absence of Statute

In Indiana (*Voelker v. Tyndall,* 75 N.E.2d 548, 1947), the doctrine of the right of privacy was said to be well established, derived from natural law and guaranteed by Federal and State constitutions, so that as between man and man, it must be respected. In New Jersey (*McGovern v. Van Riper,* 43 A.2d 514, 1945), the right of privacy was described as "immutable and absolute, transcends the power of any authority to change or abolish it." And in *Harris v. United States* (331 U.S. 145), the U. S. Supreme Court, in 1947, declared that "the rights of privacy and personal security protected by the Fourth Amendment . . . . are to be regarded as of the very essence of constitutional liberty; and the guarantee of them is as important and as imperative as are guarantees of the fundamental rights of the individual citizen."

On the other hand, Nebraska (*Brunson v. Ranks Army Store,* 73 N.W.2d 803, 1955) and Wisconsin (*Yoeckel v. Samonig,* 75 N.W.2d 925, 1956) have flatly declared that there was no common law right of action for invasion of privacy. In the *Yoeckel* case, a tavern operator had invaded the privacy of the ladies' restroom and taken a picture of a patron of the tavern which picture was presumably circulated for amusement among other patrons. The Wisconsin court found no invasion of any right of privacy, *in the absence of statute.*

Where the right of privacy is not founded upon statute, it

seems that the plaintiff has a better chance to succeed. In *Barber v. Time, Inc., supra,* the Missouri court, in 1942, delineated the issues involved in a hospital situation where the plaintiff was being treated for a continuous and ravenous appetite. She was interviewed by news reporters who tried to persuade her to consent to the publication of an article on her illness; but she protested any publicity. Nevertheless, under the heading "Medicine" the defendant magazine published an article entitled "Starving Glutton" and gave an account of the plaintiff's symptoms, as she had told them to her physician at the hospital, together with her photograph in bed in a long-sleeved hospital gown. The court upheld a verdict in her favor for invasion of right of privacy:

> "Certainly plaintiff's picture conveyed no medical information. While the plaintiff's ailment may have been a matter of some public interest because unusual, certainly the person who suffered this ailment was not . . . ."

The Missouri court held that her right of privacy must include the right to withhold her identity in any publication.

In Connecticut, in *Korn v. Rennison* (156 A.2d 476, 1959), plaintiff's photograph was used for advertising purposes without her permission. The court readily found an invasion of her right of privacy: "The common law is not static and its protecting arm does not become immobilized from lack of precedent."

### The Public Figure and the Dissemination of News

It is axiomatic that a person who possesses news interest is exposed to publicity and, therefore, the "public figure" (and occasionally even the little known person) becomes the object of a publication. The issue is whether the particular publication legitimately gratifies the interest of the public in news, or transcends it and indefensibly exploits the situation. Generally, the courts will extend rather than curtail the privilege to publicize truly newsworthy items, as perhaps illustrated by *Goelet v Confidential, Inc.* (5 A.D.2d 226). Here a famous husband and wife complained of an article in the defendant magazine portraying intimate details of their lives, accompanied by photographs. The

New York court found no invasion of the statutory right of privacy because:—

> "While the article sub judice is a lurid and spicy delineation of the activities of plaintiffs' it obviously is not fictionalized nor is it a treatment of public figures distinct from its dissemination of news or information . . . "

The court refused to pass judgment on the reading habits of the American public (which apparently enjoyed the sort of news purveyed by *Confidential* magazine), nor take judicial notice that the magazine's very nature and reputation was to capitalize on sensational intimate articles concerning prominent individuals. But there was no commercialization of personality, and so the demands of a free press must prevail over the sensibilities of the plaintiffs.

In *Dallesandro v. Henry Holt & Co.* (7 N.Y.2d 735), the New York court, in 1960, considered the question whether a picture on the cover of a book constituted a violation of Section 51 of the Civil Rights Law. The book, *Waterfront Priest* detailed the vigorous crusade of Father Corridan to combat the incidence of gambling and terrorism in the New York waterfront. The defendant publisher snapped a picture of the plaintiff, a longshoreman, engaged in conversation with Father Corridan. The court dismissed the complaint because the illustration had a direct relationship to the news about a public figure, and could not be classified as a direct or disguised form of advertising.

Arlene Dahl, the motion picture actress, in an action against Columbia Pictures Corporation (166 N.Y.S.2d 708, aff. 7 A.D.2d 769) could not object to artistic sketches, drawings and designs intended to publicize and spotlight a cinematic production in which she was a performer. Since she had consented to the display of her likeness for publicity and advertising exploitation, the promotional operations were held not to deviate from the theme or scenes of the film.

A sombre situation was presented in the Pennsylvania case of *Jenkins v. Dell Publishing Co.* (251 F.2d 447, C.A.3, 1958). In 1953, a man was killed by a gang of teen-aged youths, and the family of the murdered man permitted a newspaper photographer to take pictures upon the understanding that the pictures were to be used for a newspaper story. Thereafter, the newspaper, without the knowledge or consent of the family, sold the pictures to World Wide Photos which in turn sold it to the defendant for *Front Page Detective* magazine. In 1954, defendant published a factually accurate account of the homicide under the title "Heartbreak House," naming the persons concerned and illustrating the story with the photographs of the family. The appellate court declared that since the homicide was an item of current news, the publication did not infringe upon the right of privacy of the plaintiffs. The court agreed that the article was "not an intellectual or educational publication and would hardly be characterized as appealing to 'elevated tastes';" however, the court found "nothing in it which could fairly be characteristic as disgusting or indecent or appealing to depraved tastes.' " The dissenting opinion rested on the ground that the use made of the photographs exceeded the limits imposed when the plaintiffs consented to pose for the photographs.

In Spring 1961, two Delaware newspapers, commenting on suggested legislation making punishment of whipping mandatory in certain cases, named the plaintiff as the last person to be sentenced to whipping in 1952. The plaintiff, claiming reformation and a good family life, contended that the publication of his name and the fact of his humiliating punishment violated his right to privacy. In *Barbieri v. News Journal Co.* (189 A.2d 773), the Delaware Supreme Court, in 1963, disagreed, declaring that a person accused or convicted of crime cannot escape public notice, and cannot reacquire his right of privacy merely by the passage of time. Moreover, the subject matter of the publication, i.e., the use of corporal punishment to deter crime, was of wide, public interest in Delaware in 1961:

> "It was a legitimate subject of public interest, and the plaintiff connection with it — the last man to have suffered the penalty — had a real bearing on the matter."

The well-known actress Shirley Booth sued Curtis Publishing Co., in 1962, for unauthorized use of her photograph taken at a particular resort in Jamaica where she was vacationing. *Holiday* magazine did a series on the resort, and Miss Booth did not object at the time, except for one color photograph showing her in the water up to her neck, wearing a brimmed, high-crowned street hat of straw. The photograph was published in the magazine about a year later. The New York Appellate Division, First Dept., in 1962, found no invasion of her right of privacy, for even a republication of the photograph was "no more than a necessary and logical extension of the privileged or exempt publication of news content..."

### Defamation and the Right of Privacy

In *Cason v. Baskin* (155 Fla. 198, 1944), the defendant author published her autobiography in a book *Cross Creek,* and therein she described the plaintiff by name and retold incidents in which the plaintiff participated. Except for the revelation that the plaintiff indulged in profanity, the book portrayed the plaintiff in a favorable light. The Florida court upheld the complaint for breach of her right of privacy, pointing out that the public interest in the defendant-author, born of her eminence in the literary world, did not entitle her to project the plaintiff into the limelight, nor "destroy the right of privacy" accorded to the plaintiff. Admittedly, the defendant had skirted close to the limits of defamation as well.

In *Bennett v. Norban* (151 A.2d 476), the Pennsylvania court, in 1959, faced a lawsuit by a prospective purchaser suing the owner of a self-service store because of her indignity at being stopped without cause and searched on the way out of the store. The assistant manager had put his hand on plaintiff's shoulder, blocked her path, and reached into two pockets on the sides of her dress, and had taken her purse and peered into it. The court ruled that not only was the entire incident suffered by the plaintiff slanderous, but also invaded her right of privacy. Indeed, an action for defamation is closely allied to an action for invasion of privacy, although in the former, the action must be grounded upon real injury to reputation; the action for invasion of privacy does not require that the plaintiff suffer ridicule or contempt. Both actions seek to compensate for injuries to feelings, and individual pride is the prime motivator of such suits.

In the *Almy* case (387 P.2d 372), the Washington Supreme Court, in 1964, refused to find a physician and his wife liable for inflicting "great mental pain, embarrassment and anguish" in the course of negotiating the adoption of a child. When a patient, about to give birth, informed her physician that she intended to offer the child for adoption, she insisted that the parents selected for her child must not have adopted any other child in the recent past. The physician found a couple he thought suitable, and arrangements were made for adoption. However, when the prospective father and mother took the child, they declared that they were in the process of adopting another infant. The mother thereupon sought to retrieve her baby, and asked the physician to help her. After the baby was returned, the couple, frustrated in their adoption efforts, filed suit against the physician and his wife, alleging invasion of their right of privacy, and also charged slander arising from a telephone conversation in which the physician's wife allegedly told the would-be mother that she was "unfit, selfish, mean and didn't have the right to have any children, let alone two children." The court held that when a couple apply for the adoption of a child, they automatically waive their right to privacy; the physician had a duty to probe "the private lives and affairs of the parties" before recommending the couple as fit parents. The court found the telephone remarks as not slanderous since they were not heard by a third party and, therefore, could not be considered as damaging to the plaintiffs.

### The Personal Right of Privacy

As a personal right, privacy is said to end with the death of the individual, as illustrated in *Schumann v. Loews, Inc.* (144 N.Y.S. 2d 27). Here the descendants of the famous composer, Robert Schumann, complained of a motion picture portraying his life, including his mental illness during his later years. The New York court, in 1955, denied recovery of invasion of right of privacy because the right had terminated upon the composer's death. Similarly, in *Kelly v. Johnson Publishing Co.* (325 P.2d 659), the California court, in 1958, held that the surviving sisters of a deceased prize fighter had no cause of action for the publication of a story about their brother who had captured the welterweight boxing title in 1931, and had "wound up a deep-sodden derelict on the shadowy San Francisco waterfront where one morning his knife-scarred body was fished from the Bay." Nor, does the publication of the picture of the body of a child who has met violent death under circumstances creating legitimate public interest give the parents a cause of action for violation of privacy, despite the obvious mental anguish inflicted upon them, *Kelly v. Post Publishing Co.,* (327 Mass. 275, 1951).

In *Bradley v. Cowles Magazines* (168 N.E.2d 64), a mother's right-of-privacy suit, based on the magazine's articles concerning the murder of her fourteen-year-old son, was dismissed by the Illinois Appellate Court in 1960. The court emphasized that the "right of privacy is not a guaranty of hermitic seclusion," but must be defined against the current background of social custom and habit. Indeed, the right of privacy was personal to the deceased son and did not transfer to his mother.

And, in *Runyon v. United States* (281 F.2d 590), the Second U. S. Court of Appeals, in 1960, affirmed the long-standing judicial doctrine that the right of privacy doctrine applies exclusively to a living person, and may not be resorted to by heirs and personal representatives of the deceased. The Court also declared that a son of Damon Runyon does not possess the legal title of copyright to the name or life story of a departed father.

### Signatures and the Right of Privacy

In states where the right of privacy is not derived from statute, it has readily been held that the right of privacy is invaded by signing a person's name to a communication without his consent. In *Hinish v. Meier & Frank Co.* (113 P.2d 438), the plaintiff's full name and address were, without his consent, signed by the defendant-employer, to a telegram to the Governor, urging the veto of a law which would have adversely affected the business of the defendant. The Oregon court, in 1941, sustained the right of privacy violated by the unauthorized signature: "We should not be deterred by fear of being accused of judicial legislation. Much of our law is judge-made, and there are those who think it is the best law."

In *Kerby v. Hal Roach Studios* (53 Cal. App.2d 207), the defendants, in order to popularize a motion picture being exhibited in Los Angeles, prepared a breezy letter written in a feminine script, addressed to "Dearest," and inviting the recipient to meet the writer in front of Warner's Theatre. The letter ended: "Just look for a girl with a gleam in her eye, a smile on her lips, and mischief on her mind! Fondly, Your ectoplasmic playmate, Marion Kerby." The letter, reproduced mechanically on pink stationery and enclosed in pink envelopes, was mailed to 1,000 male householders selected by a mailing agency. The plaintiff, Marion Kerby, an actress, concert singer and monologist of repute, lived in Los Angeles and was the only person of that name listed in the city and telephone directories. Marion Kerby was also the name of the principal feminine fictional character in the movie. The California court, in 1942, stated that the plaintiff's right of privacy had been invaded by the unauthorized use of her name and signature.

And in *Harms v. Miami Daily News, Inc.* (127 So.2d 715) the newspaper published an article: "Wanna hear a sexy voice? Call . . . and ask for Louise." Plaintiff Louise was the person referred to, and she worked for the newspaper. The Florida court, in 1961, held that employment in a business office did not render her a public personage permitting journalistic comment and did not make out any relinquishment of her right of privacy. The stating of her Christian name without surname was still sufficient identification of her "signature."

On the other hand, in a state like New York, where the right of privacy exists only by virtue of the statute, there is less likelihood that "signature" will spell out invasion of privacy. An incidental, disparaging remark about a public gymnasium in a motion picture is not actionable in New York. In *The Country Girl*, one of its main actors recited that he could repair to "Stillman's Gym and get a punch-drunk fighter;" In *Stillman v. Paramount Pictures Corp.* (147 N.Y.S.2d 504, aff. 2 A.D.2d 18), it was held that the sentence could *not* spell out a scheme to promote the film by utilization of the plaintiff's name or signature for its renowned physical quarters. Similarly, in *Moglen v. Varsity Pajamas* (113 A.D.2d 114), the New York court, in 1961, held that there could be no cause of action for violation of the right of privacy in favor of a tennis player because the defendants had made a fabric in which there was reproduced, as part of a patchwork pattern, a portion of a newspaper account of a tennis match in which the plaintiff played and lost:

> "It would not be easy to conceive any 'use' of plaintiff's name that could be more incidental, or so entirely pointless for 'advertising purposes' or for the 'purposes of trade' than the use made of it by defendants on the fabric . . "

And, in *Siegel v. Esquire Magazine* (157 N.Y.S.2d 246), plaintiff's photograph was used to embellish an article entitled "The Miracle of Face Planning." The court, in 1957, repudiated the claim that the picture was inserted to spur an active trade campaign; the article was denominated as newsworthy in the field of medical development.

### Photographs and the Right of Privacy

Recovery for invasion of privacy was denied in *Oma v. Hillman Publications, Inc.* (281 A.D. 240), because the New York court, in 1953, found that the use of a photograph of the plaintiff was fully justified. *Pageant* magazine ran a sensational article on the corruption and degradation of progressional boxing entitled "Let's Abolish Boxing." On the back cover was the photograph of Lee Oma, a well-known boxer, and the photograph included his name and this inscription: "Tycoon—this man can make $25,000, on a single deal, but it might cost him his life. Why? See page 24." The court ruled that, as a public figure in the news, Oma and Oma's photograph were directly related to the discussion, and its publication was not for purposes of trade or advertising:

> "It is immaterial that its manner of use and placement was designed to sell the article so that it might be paid for and read. We are dealing here with a matter of the highest public interest, printed comment on public affairs, and the lines may not be drawn so tight as to imperil more than we protect."

The dissenting justices thought the photograph had no relation to the article but was plainly designed to catch the eye and advertise the magazine and article.

On the other hand, in *Metzger v. Dell Publishing Co.* (203 Misc. 182), in 1955, recovery for invasion of right of privacy was allowed. The defendant had illustrated an article entitled "Gang Boy" published in its magazine *Front Page Detective,* with a photograph of the plaintiffs who happened to be standing together in front of a place of employment. The New York court held that the plaintiffs had no connection at all with the subject matter of the article:

> "So far as these plaintiffs are concerned, the article is fiction, pure and simple, and nothing but fiction . . . . The fact that it is legitimate to discuss the existence of gangs and gangsters does not make it legitimate to drag these plaintiffs into the discussion."

And, in *Leverton v. Curtis Publishing Co.* (192 F.2d 974, 1951), the federal court in Pennsylvania treated a publication of a photograph of the plaintiff as a "frightful example of pedestrian carelessness." The *Saturday Evening Post* had, twenty months after an accident involving a child struck by an automobile, published a photograph of the child being lifted to her feet by a woman bystander; the photograph depicted the plaintiff child's face as distorted by pain or terror, and with her hair and clothing disarranged. (The picture had initially been published in an Alabama newspaper on the day after the auto accident.) The *Post* article on traffic accidents emphasized pedestrian carelessness under the title "They Ask to Be Killed," illustrated by the photograph of the plaintiff. The court stated that the defendant had no right to use the photograph which was a needless exploitation of her accident, and had therefore invaded her privacy.

In *Flores v. Mosler Safe Co.* (7 A.D.2d 226), a New York newspaper had published a three-column photograph of a burning building captioned "2 Men Searching for Keys Start Broadway Loft Fire." The news story beneath the picture described the circumstances of the fire and identified the plaintiff by name, residence, and occupation as one of the two men shown in the photograph. Mosler Safe Co. reproduced the photograph and news story, adding certain advertising material which pointed out the "dangerous risk" of keeping business records in inadequate safes.

The New York court, in 1959, said that a newspaper item may not be reproduced "bodily" in an advertisement of defendant's products, and held that the use of plaintiff's photograph, without his permission, for advertising and trade purposes was an invasion of his right of privacy.

**Immoral and Criminal Portrayals and the Right of Privacy**

Highly inflammatory reporting on sexual, criminal, and wayward demeanor has resulted in opening the floodgate of suits. In *Garner v. Triangle Publications* (97 F. Supp. 546, 1951), the magazine made derogatory allusions about the plaintiff's role in the slaying of a husband (the other plaintiff's) and their unusual closeness to each other. The federal court in New York did not view the spicy headlines and racy comments as a factual report on a newsworthy report on an event of public value. While the characters in the article were public figures, their true position could not be perverted by fictional or novelized representation. The court stated that even veracious comments of sensationally intimate or peculiarly personal import would not be legally sanctioned, if they outraged the community's notions of decency. Hence, plaintiff's right of privacy was invaded by the improper portrayal.

But in *Vogel v. Hearst Corporation* (116 N.Y.S.2d 905), in 1952, the New York court held that the photographs of two college girls used in connection with a collegiate lecture on marriage, were not used to advertize the defendant's magazine, and hence did not violate their privacy under the New York statute. It is obvious that most literary media are published for profit, and the New York statute does not cover that aspect if conscious trade or advertising motivation is not the crucial factor in reproduction or story.

In *Russell v. Marboro Books* (183 N.Y.S.2d 8), in 1959, a professional model of high moral standing had unconditionally consented to the sale, transfer, assignment and use of her photograph for trade and advertising purposes. The negative had been used to illustrate Marboro's educational books. However, a seller of bed sheets secured the photograph and distorted it so as to make the plaintiff appear in a compromising, romantic pose. The court declared that the gross distortion had the effect of terminating the original consent. And, in *Norris v. Moskin Stores, Inc.* (123 So.2d 321), a female agent of defendant store, to whom plaintiff was in debt, called plaintiff's wife and sister-in-law and posed as an "acquaintance" of plaintiff "in trouble," and was surprised to discover plaintiff was married, etc.—apparently, a scheme to coerce plaintiff into paying the debt. As a result of such "pressure," plaintiff's wife left home, and plaintiff's character was injured. The Alabama court, in 1961, declared that the principle of privacy extended to an intrusion into plaintiff's private seclusion, and that defendant's efforts to collect a debt exceeded the bounds of reasonable action since the agent's actions were wholly unrelated to actual debt collection.

### Fictionalization and the Right of Privacy

Broadly speaking, the use of an individual's photograph or personality in a work of fiction is forbidden by the New York statute on right of privacy. Our society has grown accustomed to the statement in books and motion pictures that any resemblance to actual persons is purely coincidental. But such disclaimer did not deter one who had been a member of the same company in the army with the author of the novel *From Here to Eternity*, a work of fiction dealing with happenings at an army post in Hawaii, just before Pearl Harbor, from instituting a criminal prosecution against the book publisher and the producer of a motion picture based on the story. In *People v. Chas. Scribner & Sons* (205 Misc. 818), the complainant was Joseph Anthony Maggio whose name resembled the fictional character in the book "Angelo Maggio." The New York City magistrate pointed out that since there was no positive identification of the complainant with the fictional character, the complainant's name was not used without his consent, and no criminal action for invasion of right of privacy could stand. The 1954 decision affirmed that it was within the bounds of legal propriety to employ any nomenclature in a work of fiction as long as there was no description or characterization of personal, public, and familial facts which would identify the character to the reader: "It is obvious that there is always the possibility that, no matter what name is used, there is always some living person with that name."

Similarly, in *James v. Screen Gems, Inc.* (344 P.2d 799), the California court held that an invasion of privacy of a third person was not actionable by his relatives due to a fictionalized movie and television show of the life of Jesse James, Jr., son of Jesse James, the outlaw. The undesired publicity brought to the son's widow was not compensable since it was not directed toward her, and "only as an incident to that (movie and TV show) . . . was is claimed that plaintiff's privacy had been invaded. Neither reason nor authority indicates that there should be an extension of liability to cover such a situation. Such a rule would open the courts to persons whose only relation to the asserted wrong is that they are related to the victim of the wrongdoer . . ."

## Old News and the Right of Privacy

While the publication of current news items does not generally involve violation of the right of privacy, a different result often pertains to the subsequent publication of former newsworthy items. In *Sidis v. F. R. Publishing Corp.* (113 F.2d 806), *The New Yorker* Magazine, in 1937, published a biographical sketch of the plaintiff who, as a child prodigy, had attracted much public attention over twenty-five years earlier when he taught mathematics at Harvard as a child of eight! The federal court, in 1940, held that, since the natural desire of the public to know what had become of the prodigy made the biography a subject of *current* interest, the publication was not in violation of the right of privacy under the New York statute.

In *Bernstein v. National Broadcasting Co.* (129 F. Supp. 817), the District of Columbia court similarly found no invasion of the right of privacy. Plaintiff had been convicted of bank robbery in Minnesota, in 1919, and after serving some years in prison, had been paroled and later pardoned. In 1933, he was convicted of first degree murder in the District of Columbia and sentenced to death by electrocution. The conviction was affirmed on appeal, although plaintiff consistently protested his innocence and claimed he was the victim of mistaken identity. Through the efforts of a committee working in his behalf and, in part, as the result of the labors of Martha Strayer, a reporter on the *Washington Daily News,* his sentence was commuted, in 1935, to life imprisonment and, in 1945, he received a Presidential pardon. Between the time of his trial and his conditional release, in 1940, his story had been given much publicity; a detective story magazine carried an article on his case and, in 1948, a fictionalized version using the true name of reporter Martha Strayer was given on a radio program. The facts of this fictionalized version were so similar to the true facts that plaintiff and others identified the story as his story. Plaintiff was in government employment and leading a normal law-abiding life, in January 1952, when NBC telecast live a sponsored television program "The Big Story" which was a fictionalized dramatization of plaintiff's murder, conviction, and pardon. The telecast lauded the efforts of Martha Strayer to secure plaintiff's commutation, and, with her consent, used her true name. Plaintiff's consent was not obtained, and his name was not used either in the program or in press releases. Though the televised story purported to be fiction, and there were minor discrepancies between its incidents and those which had actually taken place, it was, on the whole, sufficiently close to the truth to enable one already familiar with plaintiff's history to connect him with it, despite the omission of plaintiff's name. Before the telecast, the plaintiff sent NBC a written request not to produce the program. The court granted summary judgment to NBC, finding no invasion of privacy, and the appellate court in 1956 affirmed (232 F.2d 369).

A contrary view imposing liability for republicizing events of past interest, i.e., old news, is illustrated by *Melvin v. Reid* (112 Cal. App. 285). Plaintiff, at one time a prostitute, had, in 1918, been tried for murder and was acquitted; she then abandoned her former life, married, and took her place in respectable society. In 1925, defendants produced a motion picture *The Red Kimono* which used plaintiff's true maiden name and featured unsavory incidents of her past. The court, in 1931, decided that the use of plaintiff's name and the statement in advertisements that the story of the film was taken from true incidents in the life of the woman bearing that maiden name, violated her constitutional right to pursue and obtain happiness!

In *Ettore v. Philco Television Broadcast Corp.* (126 F. Supp. 143, 1954), the court barred the plaintiff professional boxer from recovering any damages for invasion of his right of privacy when the defendant reproduced on television a 1935 match with Joe Louis. The court stated that "old news" was of legitimate public interest, and no prohibition on the use of the public event film was warranted.

## Improper Debt Collection and Right of Privacy

The decisional law of most jurisdictions recognize an action for invasion of the right of privacy by a debtor in harassment situations. Creditors are entitled to pursue "extra judicially" the collection of outstanding debts, since time and cost factors often weigh heavily against resort to formal court action. But such efforts cannot be given unbridled license at the expense of legitimate rights of debtors, and courts step in to protect debtors from over-zealous collection activities. In *Santiesteban v. Goodyear Tire & Rubber Co.,* the plaintiff, a country club employee, alleged that the installment-plan seller of some tires and tubes had removed them from plaintiff's car in the country club parking lot, although plaintiff was current in his payments. The Fifth U. S. Court of Appeals on July 24, 1962, declared that Florida would permit an action based on debtor harassment as an invasion of the right of privacy. On almost identical facts, the Maryland Supreme Court in *Carr v. Watkins* (177 A.2d 841), held that "oppression of a debtor by a creditor in attempting to collect even a just debt may be an invasion of privacy." In *Housh v. Peth* (133 N.E.2d 340), the Ohio court found that there had been a campaign of harassment and an actionable invasion of right of privacy, although generally the writing of letters to an employer advising him of the debt of his employee and requesting the employer's assistance or cooperation is not an invasion of the privacy of the employee. In *Gouldman-Taber Pontiac v. Zerbst* (100 S.E.2d 881), the Georgia court pointed out that such a letter "was not giving to the general public information concerning a private matter in which it had, or could have no legitimate interest, since an employer has a natural and proper interest in the debts of his employees."

In *Biederman's of Springfield, Inc. v. Wright* (322 S.W.2d 892), the Missouri court, in 1959, ruled that oral publication of the debt invaded the debtor's privacy. The creditor had brought the action for balance of account of purchased merchandise, and defendant counterclaimed for invasion of right of privacy. The court noted that plaintiffs' agent appeared in a cafe where defendant wife worked as a waitress, that he followed her around the restaurant stating in a loud voice that she and her husband had refused to pay their bills, and that they were deadbeats; he stated that he intended to get them both fired. The court held that declaiming such degrading things in loud, threatening manner humiliated the defendants in public, and invaded their right of privacy.

## Physicians and the Patient's Right of Privacy

The physician's ethical duty to keep secret all confidential information obtained from his patient is founded upon the Hippocratic Oath adopted by the American Medical Association. Professional secrecy is based also upon the sacredness of the doctor-patient relationship. The instances of a patient's right of privacy involve either intrusion upon his physical solitude or seclusion, or publication by the doctor of offensive private information about his patient. In *DeMay v. Roberts* (9 N.W. 146), a Michigan court, in 1881, permitted a patient to recover damages (for shame and mortification) from the doctor who brought an unmarried layman with him, when attending the plaintiff at the birth of her child. But in *Simonsen v. Swenson* (177 N.W. 831), a Nebraska court, in 1920, considered the issue of whether a patient's right of privacy was involved when his doctor disclosed to a third party details about the patient's physical and mental condition. The doctor had informed the owner of a hotel where the patient was staying that the patient was suffering from a contagious disease! The disclosure was held to be legally justified, and no invasion of right of privacy was found. The patient's right to secrecy is not absolute, but must bow to more important social interests, as in *Berry v. Moench* (331 P.2d 814), where the Utah court, in 1958, held it permissible for the doctor to disclose to another doctor his psychiatric evaluation of his patient who was about to marry the patient, even though the information eventually reached the girl.

Of the various defenses to a patient's privacy action against his physician, the following are paramount: (a) consent of the patient to the disclosure is an absolute defense, provided the patient fully understands all the relevant circumstances and the doctor does not exceed the scope of the consent; (b) doctor is required by statute to disclose information to designated public officials where he finds patient is suffering from certain highly contagious diseases or where the patient has committed a crime and (c) overriding competing interests may force disclosure such as protecting others endangered by patient's condition, or serving various interests of society as in advancing medical science. [Note the sampling of A.M.A. forms hereinafter.]

Form 20

### AUTHORITY TO ADMIT OBSERVERS

PATIENT'S NAME _____ AGE \_\_\_\_ DATE _____

I hereby grant authority to Dr. _____ and to

_____ Hospital to permit the presence of such observers as they may deem fit to admit in addition to physicians and hospital personnel, while I am undergoing (operative surgery) (childbirth), examination and treatment.

Signed_____

Witness_____."

Form 21.

## CONSENT TO TAKING OF PHOTOGRAPHS

In connection with the medical services which I am received from Dr. \_\_\_\_\_

_____, I consent that photographs may be taken of me or parts of my body, under the following conditions: (1) The photographs may be taken only with the consent of my physician or surgeon and under such conditions and at such times as may be approved by him. (2) The photographs shall be taken by my physician or by a competent photographer, approved by my physician. (3) These photographs shall be used for medical records only, unless, in the judgment of my physician, medical research, education, or science will be benefitted by their use. In that event I agree that they may be used for such purposes, provided that my identity is not revealed by the photographs or by descriptive texts accompanying them.

_____ M.D.    _____
                                                (Patient)


_____    _____
         Witness                      (Parent or Legal Guardian)

Form 22.

## CONSENT TO PUBLICATION OF PHOTOGRAPHS

PATIENT _____ PLACE _____ DATE _____

1. I hereby authorize Dr. _____ and such assistants, photographers, and technicians as he may engage for this purpose, to take such photographs of me as he may desire before, during, and after the operation which is to be performed upon me on or

about _____ 19\_\_\_\_, and to permit such photographs to be published and republished in professional journals and medical books or to be used for any other purpose which he may deem fit in the interest of medical education, knowledge or research.

2. Authority is further given to permit the modification or retouching of the aforementioned photographs, and to the publication of information relating to my case, either separately or in connection with the publication of the photographs taken of me.

3. Although I give permission to the publication of all details and photographs concerning my case, it is specifically understood that I will not be identified by name.

Signed_____

Witness_____

Form 23.

### CONSENT TO TELEVISING OF OPERATION

PATIENT _____ PLACE _____ DATE _____

In the interest of medical education and knowledge, I hereby consent to the televising of the operation which is scheduled to be performed upon me on or about _____ 19___. I hereby authorize Dr. _____ _____ and the _____ Hospital to admit to the operating room, the cameramen and technicians who are to participate in the televising of this operation, in addition to the usual hospital staff.

Signed_____

Witness_____

Form 24.

### CONSENT TO TAKING OF MOTION PICTURES OF OPERATION

PATIENT _____ PLACE _____ DATE _____

1. I hereby consent to the taking of motion pictures of the operation which is scheduled to be performed upon me on or about _____ 19___. I authorize Dr. _____ and the _____ Hospital to admit to the operating room the cameraman and technicians who will participate in the filming of this operation.

2. I hereby and forever waive all rights that I may have to any claims for payment or royalties in connection with any exhibition, televising, or other showing of this motion picture film, regardless of whether such exhibition, televising, or other showing is under philanthropic, commercial, institutional, or private sponsorship, and irrespective of whether a fee of admission or film rental is charged.

3. I grant this consent as a voluntary contribution in the interest of medical education and knowledge and subject only to the condition that I will not be identified by name in this motion picture film.

Signed_____

Witness_____

## Autopsy and the Right of Privacy

After the death of a patient, his right of privacy terminates but his right to freedom from interference automatically passes in a modified form to his spouse or to his next of kin, and any unauthorized interference with his dead body exposes the offender to a suit for damages by the person entitled to its custody. One who participates in an autopsy to which the surviving spouse or next of kin has not consented and which is not authorized by law is also subject to criminal prosecution.

Generally, the person entitled to possession of a body for purposes of burial is entitled to authorize an autopsy upon it to determine the cause of death. There are statutes in some states which provide for the order of the right to control of a dead body. The law has not undertaken to fix the relative rights of persons of equal degree of kinship, i.e., the relative rights of several children or of several brothers and sisters, and so on. Generally, it will be found that some one of a given group of children or brothers or sisters will be at the place of death and will assume charge of the body, and it is to such that application should be made for permission to perform an autopsy. The person who has the right to authorize an autopsy has the right to state the limits within which the autopsy shall be performed. All autopsies must be performed in a manner which shows decent respect for the body and for the privacy and feelings of the survivors.

In all jurisdictions, the coroner or medical examiner has legal authority to perform autopsies with respect to deaths due to other than natural causes. When death is due to violence or casuality or there is reasonable ground to believe that death had been caused in an unnatural manner, the right to custody of the dead body vests immediately and supremely in the coroner or medical examiner.

### Privacy—Impinged Upon by Recent Scientific Developments

The extent to which recent scientific developments threaten the balance between the needs of society and government for information and the right of the individual for privacy, is a timely subject deserving our immediate concern. Among these trends in a changing technology which impinge upon areas of individual privacy are the following: laser beams and their utility for eavesdropping on conversations; closed-circuit, concealed television surveillance; micro-miniaturized radio transmitters which can be hidden in tiny objects of common use; lie-detector tests, including those that might be administered without the individual's knowledge; subliminal and subaudial projection of messages to audiences on radio, television, and motion pictures; drugs that might be administered to unlock secrets of persons without their awareness; brain-wave recordings which increase the prospects of learning an individual's emotions and attitudes; personality-tests that delve into the recesses of attitudes, beliefs, and behavior; and the increasing pace of computer processing of information about millions of individuals.

Mr. Vance Packard, in his 1964 book, *The Naked Society* (David McKay Co., Inc.) explores "the recent, enormous growth in methods for observing, examining, controlling, and exchanging information about people." He points to some of the ways in which modern society tends to put individual freedom, diversity, and dignity under pressure; and he describes uses and abuses committed in the name of national security, loyalty, suitability for employment, education, good health, law enforcement, or simply prurient satisfactions. Packard concludes that "privacy is becoming harder and harder to attain, surveillance more and more pervasive;" and that the "individual is at bay" today with a last desperate opportunity to take a stand for his privacy and dignity, his creativity and freedom. Packard's book underscores two major forces now at work in our society to diminish privacy which is a central part of our ethics as a nation: (a) the scientific advances (referred to above), and (b) the growth of power centers ("big business," "big government," "big education") which can profoundly alter the level of tolerance and humanity so vital to dignity and decency of life. It is frightening to lose privacy to a powerful government or boss as much as it is to lose an element of privacy by having it trumpeted without compassion wherever the electronic word can reach. It is Packard's contention that we must conduct a wide-ranging and uncompromising attack on a number of practices which, aided by recent scientific developments, have tended to deface contemporary life.

### The United Nations and the Right of Privacy

On November 14, 1960, the U. N. General Assembly's Social Committee approved a covenant declaring a person's right to protection of law against interference with his "privacy, family, home, or correspondence." Although none of the ninety-nine nations on the Committee voted against the covenant, the United States, Great Britain, and Cuba abstained! (The U. S. delegation feared that the covenant went beyond prevailing law, and therefore the covenant would have to go before Congress as a treaty for approval.)

### Selected Bibliography

*Insurance Law Journal,* October 1962, p. 618.
*Ravich v. Kling,* 187 N.Y.S.2d, 272, 1959.
*Wilk v. Andrea Radio Corp.,* 200 N.Y.S.2d 522, 1960.
*Inderbitzen v. Lane Hospital,* 12 P2d 744, Calif., 1932.
*Haggard v. Shaw,* 112 S.E.2d 286, Ga., 1959.
*Sharkey v. NBC,* 93 F. Supp. 986, 1950.
*Hill v. Hayes,* 207 N.Y.S.2d 901, 1960.
*Annerino v. Dell Publishing Co.,* 149 N.E.2d 761, Ill., 1958.
*Sellers v. Henry,* 329 S.W.2d 214, Ky., 1959.
*Shor v. Billingsley,* 4 Misc.2d 857, N.Y., 1956.
*Buzinski v. Doall Co.,* 175 N.E.2d 577, Ill., 1961.
*Sullivan v. Ed Sullivan Radio & T.V., Inc.,* 1 A.D.2d 602, 1956.
*Jansen v. Hilo Packing Co.,* 202 Misc. 900, N.Y., 1952.
*Fleischer v. WPIX, Inc.,* 213 N.Y.S.2d 632, 1961.

### Questions for Review

1. If Brandeis and Warren had not written their famed article in 1890, would there have been a "right of privacy?"
2. Is proof of mental harm or suffering necessary to sustain an invasion of privacy?
3. Why have so few states legislated on the subject of privacy? Could there be a federal statute on the subject?
4. Can there be an invasion of privacy in New York, in the absence of advertising or selling a product or name? Explain.
5. Should a "public figure" have greater or lesser respect for his or her right of privacy? Are politicians, movie stars, presidents of large corporations and notorious criminals all in the same category?
6. Are there differences between an action for defamation and privacy? Which is easier to prove?
7. Why is the right of privacy necessarily "personal?" Should it be changed by legislation?

8. How does a motion picture producer guard against suits for privacy based upon his choice of a name for its "star" in a given film?
9. Is there a difference between the use of a person's name, signature, and photograph insofar as right of privacy is concerned?
10. When, if at all, should news be suppressed if it involves disclosure of a private person's intimate affairs? Where is the line for "freedom of the press" to be drawn?
11. Can one write a novel about fictional characters, and avoid a lawsuit for invasion of privacy if the characters' names turn out to be *real* people?
12. How does an autopsy involve the right of privacy?

## Chapter II

## ALIENATION OF AFFECTIONS AND FAMILIAL PEACE

### The Family as a Group

To ascertain the problems conjured up by alienation of affections in our present-day society, the family must be examined as the vortex of many interests including legal, social, ethical, religious, and moral. The law and the social sciences do not have much difficulty recognizing the family as a species of a small group of common concern, although just what use each is to make of the other is still not entirely clear to either. The law is moving in the direction of utilizing the services of social science in the administration of the laws of domestic relations centering about the family. Social science, in turn, has recognized that it must deal with the *real* problems arising out of the limitations of these laws on family welfare. Inevitably, certain values are expressed by the law: if the law has little to do directly about power and authority within the family, it does nevertheless regulate these matters in other ways, indirectly, such as, for example, by its power of testamentary disposition, its power over living trusts preserving the power of control over a business, etc. Social science, therefore, must make a comprehensive analysis of the family in which it takes for granted the law's classification of the family as *the* important social group.

### Interference with Relational Interests

Legal recognition of interference with the relational interest of the individual in his familial surroundings, such as by deprivation of love and affection, loss of society, companionship, or consortium, or loss of comfort or loss of support, have been all of recent origin. Early court decisions under the English common law protected the relationship of parent and child, for example, only insofar as the parent suffered pecuniary loss or property loss by another's act which interfered with that parent's relationship to his child. In *Pickle v. Page* (225 A.D. 454), the grandparents were unsuccessful in their suit against the mother for kidnapping their grandchild; the mother had taken the child out of New York under authority of an Ohio divorce decree. The New York court declared that only where the parents (or grandparents) had a right to the pecuniary services of the child would the court protect their rights in the personality of the child! But there was a protectable interest in the chastity of a female child which is related to family honor, self-respect, mental comfort, and supposedly pecuniary value. In *Heck v. Schupp* (394 Ill. 296), a soldier, upon his return from military service, sued a "civilian" who had carried on an illicit affair with his wife while he was overseas, and thus had destroyed her affection for him. The Illinois Supreme Court held that "every member of the family . . . (has) a right to protect the family relationship," and granted monetary judgment in favor of the soldier. Even more significant was *Johnson v. Luhman* (330 Ill. App. 598), where suit was filed by five minor children against a woman who allegedly had enticed their father away from the home, thus depriving the minor children of his support, parental care, guidance, and affection. The Illinois court opined:

> "The children are presently regarded more as responsible individuals than as subservient charges, and there are both criminal and civil statutes protecting them from physical abuse and neglect. While they generally contribute only companionship and inspiration to the family circle, they are entitled to both the tangible incidents of family life, such as food, clothing, and shelter, and to the intangible though equally significant elements of affection, moral support, and guidance from both of the parents."

The court concluded that the minor children "have a right to protect their relationship with their parents and are properly entitled to seek damages from one who has destroyed their family unit."

An early New York case, *Heermance v. James* (47 Bar 120), in 1866, added the element of mischief or design as a basis for suit for alienation of affections. The defendant paramour was accused of "contriving and wickedly and unjustly intending to injure plaintiff, and to deprive him of the affections, comfort, fellowship, society, and assistance of Rachel, his wife." The defendant had allegedly "by false insinuations against the plaintiff, and by other insidious wiles so prejudiced and poisoned the mind of said Rachel against the plaintiff" that Rachel filed an action for divorce or separation. The New York court found for the plaintiff because the defendant's acts were "done mischievously, designedly, and wickedly and with intent to produce the consequences that ensued."

Injunctive relief has even been granted to halt interference with the relational interest, as in the 1958 Alabama decision in *Latham v. Karger* (103 So.2d 337). Here the second woman was enjoined from alienating the affections of the plaintiff's husband, not to protect property rights or pecuniary values, but simply to safeguard personal rights encompassed within the family entity.

Domestic tranquillity as a protected interest was somewhat battered by the remarkable decision of the Tennessee appellate court in *Graham v. Smith* (330 S.W.2d 573). In 1960, the mother of a sixteen-year-old daughter seduced by a thirty-eight-year-old owner of a gambling house, was awarded the sum of $20,000, although the mother's own reputation was "bad," according to the testimony of several witnesses. The court upheld the award as compensation for interference with a protected relational interest, to wit, that of mother and daughter.

In Vermont, in August 1959, the Meaders and Clappers were involved in an unusual suit for interference with the relational interests of each other. Mrs. Meader, mother of four children, and Mr. Clapper were sued by their respective spouses after abandoning their respective homes to live with each other. Judgment in the sum of $5,000 was awarded Mr. Meader against Mr. Clapper, and $3,000 in favor of Mrs. Clapper against Mrs. Meader. Since neither of the defendant spouses could pay the judgments, they were jailed under an old Vermont law that permitted a person to be jailed indefinitely until he discharged the financial debt. According to the *New York Times* of April 30, 1960, "the publicity given the case brought cash contributions that enabled them to engage legal aid." Furthermore, "each of the defendants had been allowed to leave the jail on numerous occasions for hunting excursion, a visit to Mr. Clapper's dying mother, a birthday party, and shopping trips for jail supplies. . . . Both Mr. Clapper and Mrs. Meader have worked in the jail kitchen. They do cooking, laundry, and housekeeping chores for inmates, and have also painted six rooms in the sheriff's quarters." Presumably, the "couple" raised the necessary money to pay the judgments and were released from jail!

### Loss of Consortium as a Measure of Damage

"Consortium" is defined as "the conjugal fellowship of husband and wife, and the right of each to the company, cooperation, and aid of the other in every conjugal relationship," *Pratt v. Daly* (104 P.2d 147, Ariz., 1940). In English common law the husband had a right to recover damages for loss of his wife's consortium when she was injured due to the negligence of another person; but the wife was *not* granted the corresponding right when the husband was injured. This anomaly was explained as follows: (a) the wife was the husband's inferior, and only he had a property right in consortium; (b) the wife could not sue unless she joined her husband in the suit, and then he was entitled to the proceeds of the lawsuit, and (c) the husband was entitled to the wife's services, but she was not entitled to his services, and consortium was incidental to the right of services. The enactment of the Married Women's Property Acts in the several states removed procedural barriers to suits by married women but, prior to 1950, there was not a single appellate court in the United States that had recognized the wife's right of consortium!

The right of consortium was examined in its historical context and its applicability to modern concepts questioned in 1950 by the federal court in the District of Columbia in *Hitaffer v. Argonne* (183 F.2d 811, cert. den 340 U.S. 852). Noting that wedlock conferred upon both spouses the legal right to the conjugal society of the other, the Court held that, as in any tort, an unjustifiable interference with that interest was actionable. The tort that injured the husband also breached a duty owed to the wife and was the proximate cause of her loss and damage. Furthermore, the right of consortium was not limited to services, but is a right that contains many elements independent of services such as companionship, sexual relations, comfort, and the like. The wife's recovery was measured by the loss she suffered, and it did not duplicate his loss, which was measured by his injury, loss of earnings, and disbursements.

As a result of the *Hitaffer* decision, at least ten states overruled prior decisions and recognized the wife's right of consortium, to wit: Arkansas (*Missouri Pacific Transp. Co. v. Miller,* 299 S.W.2d 41, 1957); Delaware (*Yoner v. Adams,* 167 A.2d 717, 1961); Georgia (*Brown v. Georgia-Tennessee Coaches,* 77 S.E.2d 24, 1953); Illinois (*Dini v. Naiditch,* 170 N.E.2d 881, 1960); Iowa (*Acuff v. Schmitt,* 78 N.W.2d 480, 1956); Missouri (*Novak v. Kansas City Transit, Inc.,* 365 S.W.2d 539, 1963); Michigan (*Montgomery v. Stephan,* 101 N.W.2d 227, 1960); Nebraska (*Cooney v. Moomaw,* 109 F. Supp. 448, 1953); South Dakota (*Hoekstra v. Hegeland,* 98 N.W.2d 669, 1959); and New Jersey (*Alfone v. Newark Frame Umbrella Co.,* 80 A.2d 589, 1951). California reacted to the *Hitaffer* case by denying the action in favor of the husband, hitherto recognized, on the grounds that the right was an anachronism left over from feudalism and should be interred (*West v. City of San Diego,* 353 P.2d 929, 1960. A *majority* of states have retained the old rule based on the compulsion to follow the precedent of past decisions.

The husband's right to consortium is, of course, taken for granted. In *Parker v. Gordon* the Massachusetts court, in 1949, faced the usual "triangle," when Gordon, upon returning from overseas during World War II, as a soldier, found his wife had engaged in an amatory dalliance with one Parker. In the days that followed, his wife remained at Gordon's table, but shunned his bed. He divorced her and then sued Parker for breaking up the marriage. Since adultery was not proved at the trial and since his wife had not quit the Gordon household, there was a serious question as to whether an action for interference with relational interest would stand up. Judge Magruder awarded Gordon the sum of $5,000:

> "If the defendant's course of love-making, with the purpose of disrupting the marital relationship, has the effect of inducing a married woman to refuse sexual relations with her husband, there has been a tortious deprivation of an essential right of the consortium . . . . "

New York does *not* recognize a wife's right to consortium, as evidenced by the New York Appellate Division, First Dept., ruling on March 7, 1961, in *Gottlieb v. American Airlanes, Inc.* that the wife cannot recover damages for the "loss of her husband's consortium as a result of injuries suffered by him when he was a passenger in an airplane . . . . which crashed upon landing." In contrast Illinois, in *Dini v. Naiditch, supra,* held that the husband's right to the conjugal society of his wife is no greater than hers, and that invasion of the wife's conjugal interests merits the same protection of the law as the invasion of the husband's conjugal interests. However, the next year, Illinois, in *Knierim v. Izzo* (174 N.E.2d 157, 1961), held that the widow's action for causing death of her husband covers her mental and emotional suffering, and should not include loss of consortium! In *Hoekstra v. Helgeland, supra,* the South Dakota Supreme Court allowed the wife to recover for loss of consortium, but limited the damages to the time from the injury until her husband's death, thus refusing the wife's contention that she could recover in excess of the $20,000 limitation in South Dakota for wrongful death. Thus, the wife's recovery was based upon loss of "society, companionship, conjugal affections, and the assistance of the other," but did not include the loss of financial support from her husband, which was part of her husband's estate claim.

In Michigan, in *Montgomery v. Stephan, supra,* the court solemnized: "Were we to rule upon precedent alone, we would have no trouble with this case. We would simply tell the woman to be gone, and take her shattered husband with her. . . . . Legally, today, the wife stands on a par with her husband. The obstacles to the wife's (court) action were judge-invented and they are herewith judge-destroyed."

### The Child's Loss of Consortium

In the majority of states where the wife is deprived of her loss of consortium, the child does not fare any better. In *Feneff v. New York Central* (89 N.E. 436, 1909), the Massachusetts court ruled that "minor children of an injured father who is legally bound to furnish them with support may suffer indirectly from his injury . . . yet it was never held that . . . a minor child could recover for the consequences of a father's disability against one who had negligently injured him." In *Morrow v. Yannantuono* (273 N.Y. 912), the plaintiff child living with his parents was obviously deprived of motherly affection, comfort and love by the defendant who enticed his mother away from home and "harbored her." The child also alleged that his own reputation was damaged by the act of the paramour. But the highest New York court, in 1934, dismissed his complaint, finding no loss of consortium, merely shame, which was not compensable. The Court opined that only the plaintiff's father had a sufficient, enforceable right to protect the child's interest. Also, if the plaintiff were permitted to recover, then all his brothers and sisters could sue, thereby creating a multiplicity of suits which would be a harassment of the tortfeasor.

### Two "Classical" Cases of Alienation of Affections

Plaintiff brought suit against defendant for alienating the affections of his lawfully wedded spouse in that defendant cohabited with his wife. Defendant admitted the allegation, but defended upon the ground that he had no knowledge of the woman's relationship to plaintiff (or to himself?). The Greek court ruled: "The defendant Oedipus will not be excused from liability after recklessly and wantonly entering the connubial state with his mother, the wife of his father Laius, without due investigation of either the marital or blood status of his purported spouse."

And, in a similar fictional case, plaintiff appointed defendant as his agent to arrange a marriage between himself and one Priscilla. However, defendant, instead of talking for his principal, Miles Standish, talked faster for himself, and made off with the said Priscilla. The Puritan court held that John Alden had willfully breached his fiduciary duty, and alienated the affections of Priscilla for Miles Standish!

### Statutory Changes in New York and Other States

Like many other States, New York has, by statute, abolished actions for alienation of affections, criminal conversation, seduction, and breach of promise to marry, upon the grounds of general public policy to discourage such suits which are customarily fraught with fraud. However, courts, in necessary situations and in order to do justice, have recognized actions "for deceit in fraudulently inducing the woman to enter into a void marriage." In *Friedman v. Libin,* the plaintiff woman was allegedly induced to marry decedent by his representation that he was not then married, and she lived with him as his wife until his death ten years later. His representation was, in fact, false: he had a living wife and children. At some time during the ten-year period, she learned the truth, but continued to live with him. The New York Supreme Court, Bronx County, in November 1956, specifically held that the action for deceit was not barred in New York because fraud had induced the promise to marry!

Illinois, as indicated in *Siegall v. Solomon* (166 N.E.2d 5, 1960), has upheld a statutory limitation on damages recoverable for alienation of affections:

> "Actions for alienation of affections are considered as incident to, or as arising from, the marriage relation, and are likewise subject to the basic power of the legislature to enact reasonable police regulations for the public welfare .... The 1947 statute, limiting the damages recoverable to actual and compensating damages only if it has acted in the public interest ... (in not allowing punitive damages). Such a regulation ... does not infringe upon any rights arising from the marriage contract."

In *Albert v. McGrath* (278 F.2d 16), the District of Columbia court held that a Washington, D. C. woman was liable to a Maryland wife for alienation of the affections of the wife's husband, despite the fact that Maryland had by statute abolished actions for alienation of affections. The court simply applied the law of the District of Columbia which had not abolished the action, for the misconduct took place in Washington, D. C.

## Testimonial Compulsion and the Husband-Wife Relationship

Familial peace prompted the U. S. Supreme Court, in 1958, in *United States v. Hawkins* (358 U.S. 74), to adhere to an ancient rule that wives may not testify, even voluntarily, against their husbands. Here, the defendant was convicted of transporting a seventeen-year-old girl from Arkansas to Oklahoma, to engage in prostitution. He was sentenced to five years in jail upon the testimony of his own wife, from whom he was separated; his wife had allegedly given the young girl the necessary instructions from her husband to enable the young girl to engage in prostitution. Mr. Justice Black voided Hawkins' conviction and ordered Hawkins to be retried without his wife as a witness against him. According to Mr. Justice Black, having a wife give adverse testimony, would "be likely to destroy almost any marriage;" and therefore:

> "The basic reason the law has refused to pit wife against husband, or husband against wife, in a trial where life or liberty is at stake, was a belief that such a policy is necessary to foster family peace, not only for the benefit of husband, wife, and children, but for the benefit of the public as well. Such a belief has never been unreasonable and is not new. Moreover, it is difficult to see how family harmony is less disturbed by a wife's voluntary testimony against her husband than by her compelled testimony. In truth, it seems probable that much more bitterness would be engendered by voluntary testimony than by that which is compelled . . . . Adverse testimony given in criminal proceedings would, we think, be likely to destroy almost any marriage."

The Court continued its dissertation:

> " . . . . there is still a widespread belief, grounded on present conditions, that the law should not force or encourage testimony which might alienate husband and wife, or further inflame existing domestic differences . . . . The mere presence of

a wife as a witness against her husband, in a case of this kind, would most likely impress jurors adversely. When to this there is added her sworn testimony that she was a prostitute, both before and after marriage, we cannot be sure that her evidence, though in part cumulative, did not tip the scales against petitioner on the close and vital issue of whether his prime motivation in making the interstate trip was immoral . . . At least, use of the wife's testimony was a strong suggestion to the jury that petitioner was probably the kind of a man to whom such a purpose would have been perfectly natural."

Mr. Justice Black would have allowed the wife to testify against her husband, if her husband offered no objection, which was exceedingly unlikely; the rule enunciated is that the privilege is that of the accused, not of the witness! The court concluded that it would not support any distinction between compelled and voluntary testimony!

However, two years later, on May 16, 1960, the U. S. Supreme Court in *U. S. v Wyatt* (362 U.S. 525), took a contrary position by a six to three vote, and held that a wife might be compelled to testify against her husband when he was charged with having taken her across state lines for purposes of prostitution. Wyatt was convicted of taking Mary Byrd from Georgia to Alabama where she and he asked a hotel bellboy to get her engagements as a prostitute. Afterwards, the two were reported to have been married, and at Wyatt's trial, she claimed the privilege against testifying, but the trial court compelled her to testify against her husband. Mr. Justice Harlan reasoned that when the wife was the victim of the crime, the husband had no privilege to prevent her from testifying. She could be compelled to testify against her will, although she may voluntarily testify against her husband. The Court pointed out that Congress had assumed that many women were "too weak to resist" subjugation by men: "The act (Mann Act) reflects the supposition that the women with whom it sought to deal often had no will of their own, and must be protected against themselves." The dissenting opinions of Chief Justice Warren and Justices Black and Douglas accepted the majority's view that a husband whose offense was against his wife had no right to keep her from testifying; but the dissenters thought the wife retained a privilege and could not be compelled to be a witness. Chief Justice Warren attacked what he termed the majority's assumption that Mrs. Wyatt was "somehow mesmerized by him" and had no will of her own: "The evidence in point of fact strongly suggests that the wife played a managerial role in the sordid enterprise which formed the basis for the prosecution."

It is of interest to note that only a small minority of states have enacted statutes which make the wife competent to testify in a prosecution against her husband for pandering or white slavery, when she is the female involved, and only a few states make her testimony compellable as well as competent. See *Maine Rev. Stats.,* 1954, Ch. 134, Sec. 22; *Oregon Comp. Laws Ann.,* 1940, Sec. 23-921; *Utah Code Ann.,* 1943, Sec. 103-51-14; *Virginia Code,* 1950, Sec. 18-97; and *West Virginia Code Ann.,* 1955, Secs. 6062, 6063.

On June 27, 1960, about one month after the decision in the *Wyatt* case was handed down, the U. S. Supreme Court in the *Dege* case ruled that a husband and wife could be prosecuted for conspiracy to violate federal law, thereby overruling old precedents that the spouses are a single entity incapable of conspiring with one another. Husband and wife were charged with conspiring to smuggle parakeets from Mexico in violation of federal law. Mr. Justice Frankfurter stated that the indivisibility of man and wife rested legally on doubtful interpretations of an English case decided in the year 1365: "It is revolting to have no better reason for a rule of law than that it was so laid down in the time of Henry IV. It is still more revolting if the ground upon which it was laid down had vanished long since, and the rule simply persists from blind imitation of the past." The dissenters led by Chief Justice Warren argued that a wife may easily join in a criminal venture solely out of loyalty to her husband, and Congress rather than the court, should take the step against "the solidarity and confidential relationship of marriage." The six to three majority opinion would allow testimonial compulsion by one spouse against the other.

On June 9, 1961, the highest New York court ruled that New

York's statutory privilege regarding husband-wife communications did not prevent a wife from testifying in her husband's criminal trial that she saw him and some of his friends in the kitchen of their home with firearms, *New York v. Melski* (10 N.Y.2d 78). The defendant was convicted of grand larceny in the second degree for the theft of some guns and ammunition from a sporting goods store. At the trial, and over his objection, the wife gave incriminating testimony; two of the participants related the entry of the wife into the kitchen. Judge Burke affirmed the admission of the wife's testimony on the basis that the communication to her was not confidential, and that, therefore, her testimony was not barred by the New York statute which required communications from one spouse to the other to be confidential in order to be privileged. Judge Burke pointed out that the wife had walked in on the kitchen scene unexpectedly and that under those circumstances it could not be said that the husband made a "disclosure" in confidence to her! In addition, the communication was made in the presence of third parties and the husband had himself related the incident in a statement to police officers! Thus, under these circumstances, the public policy to promote confidence between husband and wife would not have been served by excluding the wife's testimony. The three dissenters of the seven-judge panel felt that the communication was confidential by its very nature since the kitchen meeting was obviously a secret one and the communication to the wife "of its purpose and significance was essentially confidential." The dissenting opinion concluded:

> "Proof of the defendant's guilt is strong, but much stronger is our public policy . . . . Founded on the 'sanctities of the marriage relation' the rule as to non-disclosure is to be 'strictly construed,' and an error in relation to it is not technical but affects 'the substantial rights of the defendant.'"

### Domestic Tranquility in England

The 1959 English case of *Lilley v. Lilley* (3 W.L.R. 306) raised several novel questions of familial harmony, support, and mental illness, with overtones of testimony by one spouse against the other. The wife commenced proceedings by taking out a summons against her husband alleging that he had been guilty of willful neglect to maintain her; but the magistrate dismissed the complaint upon finding that the husband had not been guilty of matrimonial misconduct and that the wife had, in fact, deserted him. The evidence showed that the wife was a severe neurotic. On appeal, the judgment was affirmed, although the court held that there could be no desertion by the wife because as a victim of neurosis, she was not capable of making a rational decision to desert her husband! The wife again appealed to the English Court of Appeal, contending that her husband was obliged to maintain her although she could not live under his roof. The Court determined that a separation which had been forced upon the parties by mental illness did not constitute desertion; and the husband is under a duty to support his wife, even though she is in a mental hospital!

Thus, it would appear that, in England, a husband must remain bound to a woman for life, even though she had left him because of an unshakeable, neurotic determination never to see him!

### Support of Dependents Generally

In the interest of protecting the family relationship and familial peace, a Uniform Support of Dependents Law was drafted with provisions for reciprocal enforcement in other states. In 1949, New York, for example, enacted such a statute:

*"Persons Legally Liable for Support of Dependents:* For the purpose of this Act, the following persons in one state are declared to be liable for the support of dependents residing or found in the same state or in another state having substantially similar or reciprocal laws, and, if possessed of sufficient means or able to earn such means, may be required to pay for such support a fair and reasonable sum, as may be determined by the court having jurisdiction of the respondent in a proceeding instituted under this Act:

(a) husband liable for support of his wife;

(b) father liable for support of his child or children under seventeen years of age;

(c) mother liable for support of her child or children under seventeen years of age, whenever the father of such child or children is dead, or cannot be found, or is incapable of supporting such child or children;
(d) parents severally liable for support of their child or children seventeen years of age or older, whenever such child or children are unable to maintain himself or is likely to become a public charge;
(e) wife liable for support of her husband if he is incapable of supporting himself;
(f) adult person liable for support of his or her parent or parents;
(g) grandparent liable for support of his or her grandchild or grandchildren."

This New York statute was declared constitutional in 1956, in *Landes v. Landes* (1 N.Y.2d 358). The petitioning mother sought support for her twelve and one-half year-old daughter, both residing in California, from her husband residing in New York. It appeared that the mother had secured custody of the dependent child pursuant to a California divorce decree which did not provide support for either the child or mother. After her remarriage, she instituted proceedings under the California Uniform Reciprocal Enforcement of Support Act. (A transcript of these proceedings were remitted by the California court to the New York court). The father appeared and argued that California law placed primary responsibility for the support of the minor upon the person having custody of the minor; furthermore, the second husband in California was better able to provide for the child. After a hearing, the New York court ordered the father to pay twenty dollars weekly for the support and maintenance of his daughter in California. The highest New York court affirmed and upheld the constitutionality of the Act:

"Enforcement of proceedings to compel the support of dependent minor children within and without the state is primarily of local concern to the states. Both at common law and by statute, New York has always treated the husband as absolutely responsible in keeping with his ability for the support of his dependent minor child or children .... and there is no doubt whatever that neither divorce or remarriage, nor the fact that the mother has legal custody of the child or children, terminates that liability . . . and this may be enforced regardless of residence . . . . "

"Reciprocal enforcement of a support order aimed at this primary parental obligation may not be avoided or excused by resort to the immunities privileges clause of the federal constitution . . "

The court held that the reciprocal provisions of the Act was "clearly not the result of an agreement or compact requiring the consent of Congress;" nor does the statute "inhibit in any way the constitutional safeguards erected to assure due process to one charged with crime (the reciprocal enforcement of support being quasi-criminal in nature)."

Reciprocal support of dependents statutes have been enacted and held constitutional in North Carolina (*Mahan v. Read,* 240 N.C. 641); Kentucky (*Duncan v. Smith,* 262 S.W.2d 373); Maryland (*Commonwealth v. Warren,* 204 Md. 467); (*Freeman v. Freeman,* 226 La. 410); Connecticut (*Procter v. Sachner,* 143 Conn. 9); Pennsylvania (*Commonwealth v. Shaffer,* 175 Pa. Super. 100); and California (*Smith v. Smith,* 270 P.2d 713).

## The Marriage Contract

While marriage is a contract between two persons, it is also a status vitally affecting the public welfare; and, as a social institution, is subject to regulation by public authority. The state is a party at interest in every marriage contract, and the preservation of the marital relation is essential to the public welfare. Legislatures of the various states have enacted procedures which proscribe and regulate the entry into the marital relationship. In addition to civil ceremonies, the parties are generally required to obtain health certificates stating that they are free from contagious diseases as a prerequisite to the issuance of the marriage license. Courts have the power to declare marriages null and void, or to grant the parties legal separation or divorce.

In *Edwards v. Huntting,* the New York Supreme Court, Nassau County, on January 13, 1960, dissolved a marriage between a seventy-nine-year-old husband and a sixty-three-year-old wife who were married in 1957. Two years later, the husband was declared incompetent to manage himself and his affairs by reason of imbecility. The wife sought to have the marriage declared null and void because the husband was, at the time of the marriage, a lunatic, mentally incapable of understanding the nature, effect and consequence of marriage. The court noted that the husband "was habitually wetting and soiling his bedclothes and his underwear," as well as substantiating testimony of two psychiatrists. On the other hand, in *App v. App,* the New York Supreme Court, Queens County, on April 28, 1960, refused to annul a marriage:

> "It is repugnant to this court's concept of the marriage contract, and contrary to the public policy of this state, to require a wife to promise to raise a family, maintain a home, and seek employment . . . . "

The validity of marriage of minors by justices of the peace was judicially examined by the New York Appellate Division, 2nd Dept., in *People v. Heine* (12 A.D.2d 36). The lower court had dismissed an indictment for bigamy upon the basis that the marriage was not valid; but the court reversed:

> "A result other than the one recommended is not only legally incorrect but socially undesirable. To hold this marriage void is to countenance attempts at trial marriages . . . . "

The New York Court of Appeals affirmed, in 1961 (9 N.Y.2d 925), although under Section 11 (5) of the New York Domestic Relations Law, a justice of the peace was without authority to solemnize a marriage where either party was under the age of twenty-one. The court held the statute to be merely "directory" and not affecting the validity of the marriage.

The marriage contract itself was paramount in the mind of the New York Legislature which abolished in New York such actions as alienation of affections, criminal conversation, seduction, and breach of contract to marry. The Legislature sought to preserve and protect the marriage contract from such actions:

> " . . . . having been subjected to grave abuses, causing extreme annoyance, embarrassment, humiliation, and pecuniary damage

to many persons wholly innocent and free of any wrongdoing, who were merely victims of circumstances, and such remedies having been exercised by unscrupulous persons for their unjust enrichment, and such remedies having furnished vehicles for the commission or attempted commission of a crime, and in many cases having resulted in the perpetration of frauds . . . "

## *The Common Law Marriage*

A common law marriage, recognized in perhaps eighteen states, is a civil contract which is completely consummated *per verba praesenti,* even though not followed by cohabitation. An agreement or consent to become husband and wife immediately at the time of the agreement or consent is necessary. Some states accept as a common law marriage mutual promises to marry in the future, followed by sexual intercourse.

The desirability of recognizing common law marriages is predicated upon the need for legitimizing the children and sanctioning the status of the bona fide widow. Obviously, the religious segment of the community regarding marriage as a sacrament and sex as a sin have bitterly contested recognition of such marriages.

## *First-cousin Marriages*

In most states, a marriage between first cousins constitutes incest and is null and void, although the Ohio Supreme Court, in 1958, in *Mazzolini v. Mazzolini* (168 Ohio St. 357), ruled that the Ohio statute which provided that persons "not nearer of kin than second cousins" may marry, did not render a marriage of first cousins void; the three dissenting judges commented that the decision created a situation which made "a mockery of the marriage statute." At common law, first cousin marriages were valid, so that it takes a statute to change the prevailing law and make such marriages void.

First-cousin marriages are said to be undesirable because they very often result in a deficient and degenerate offspring. The afflictions most commonly ascribed to consanguineous marriages are sterility, idiocy, insanity, deaf-mutism, albinism, hemophelia, and even baldness. When a near-kin marriage takes place, there is a union of similar heredities; recessive genes come into expression in such situations, i.e., recessive characters, hitherto latent in the stock, are rendered homozygous, and the child of the marriage may exhibit the undesirable character.

On the other hand, the history of consanguineous marriages, it can be argued, produced no woeful consequences:—the pharaohs of ancient Egypt practiced brother-sister marriage, Cleopatra was the child of a brother-sister union; Abraham married his half-sister Sarah, Jacob married his first cousins Rachel and Leah, and Moses was the offspring of a nephew-aunt marriage; and, in recent times, Abraham Lincoln and the four sons of Charles Darwin were the progeny of first cousin marriages. Most European countries today allow such first cousin marriages, although the number of such marriages probably does not exceed 1 per cent of all marriages.

Whether or not first cousin marriages are detrimental to family stability is an open question. Family solidarity and maintenance of moral values are decidedly the goals to be attained.

### Personal Injuries Within the Family

Because marriage merged the legal identity of husband and wife, neither spouse could sue the other at common law. Even after passage of the Married Women's Acts, by the several states, most courts banned suits between each other for personal injuries inflicted by one spouse upon the other. Implicit here is the quest for familial peace—and courts took similar positions in banning suits for personal injuries between one family member and another. Nurtured by the thought that intra-family litigation endangers domestic bliss and that family harmony will turn to ashes in the flames of family litigation, and that the family exchequer will be depleted by such insurrectionary lawsuits, the courts have deemed intra-family suits not to be in the public interest. There has also been the argument that recognition of such suits for personal injuries between family members will promote conspiracy or collusion to defraud an insurance company insuring the interest of the tortfeasor. Illustrative of this concept of parental and family "immunity" is the 1957 Pennsylvania decision in

*Parks v. Parks* (390 Pa. 287) : plaintiff, a six-year-old minor, sustained personal injuries in an accident which occurred while she was riding as a passenger in an automobile owned by her father and operated by her mother. The mother was insured under a liability insurance policy issued to the father. The defense was based upon Pennsylvania law that a parent is immune from personal injury actions by an unemancipated minor child. The Pennsylvania Supreme Court upheld the decision on grounds of public policy since the injuries to the minor child did not arise out of the exercise of parental discipline and control. In contrast is the 1958 decision, in Connecticut, in *Silverman v. Silverman* (145 A.2d 826) which allowed the action for personal injuries by an unemancipated child for willful or wanton misconduct of the parent: the wife was permitted to recover from her husband for harm negligently inflicted upon her by her eighteen-year-old unemancipated minor child driving the "family car." The mother, while driving to the hospital to see her husband, had an auto accident in which the driver of the other vehicle was her eighteen-year-old son. The mother recovered judgment against her husband for the negligence of the son; another injured son (in the auto with his mother) recovered against both his father and the eighteen-year-old brother driving the other vehicle. The court cited an old Connecticut case *(Stickney v. Epstein,* 123 A. 1) to the effect that "the head of the family who maintains a motor vehicle for the general use and convenience of his family is liable for the negligence of a member of the family having general authority to drive it, if it is being used as a family car."

In *Sullivan v. Christiensen* (191 N.Y.2d 625), the New York court, in 1959, declared that a child could recover from his father's employer for injuries the child received as a result of his own father's negligence, even though, in a suit against his father, in New York, the child would have to prove willful and wanton negligence. Justice Meyer cogently stated:

> "Insurance coverage is now required, and that coverage protects both the corporation and the parent-employee. It is therefore improbable that domestic tranquility will be disturbed, at least not unless a recovery in excess of policy limits is had. If

there is any conflict between the two, the more recent legislative policy requiring insurance in order to provide compensation for negligent automobile injury would have to be upheld against the older judge-made, and somewhat outmoded policy concerning domestic tranquility."

And, in *Decker v. Decker* (193 N.Y.2d 431), a nine-year-old child was permitted to sue his father for harm resulting from wanton misconduct of his father. His intoxicated father had fallen asleep at the wheel of the automobile and, in the resulting accident, the child suffered traumatic amputation of the left leg. The New York court, in 1959, granted the child a $20,000 recovery.

But, on April 27, 1961, the New York Court of Appeals, in *Badigian v. Badigian* (9 N.Y.2d 472), seemingly reversed this trend, and held that an unemancipated minor child had no right of action against his father for injuries that were not willfully caused! Here a three-year-old son released the brakes of the family car which the father had left unlocked in a parking lot. The child was injured when he tried to jump from the moving car. The decision of the court left the automobile liability insurance funds intact. A strong dissent by Judge Fuld emotionalized that "the pains (of the child) must be endured for the peace and welfare of the family is something of a mockery:"

> "If the present decision were necessary to preserve the integrity of the family, I would subscribe to it. But I do not believe that it is . . . . A parent who by negligence injures his minor child surely commits a civil 'wrong' in the sense that there is neither lawful right nor privilege to inflict the injury . . . "

### Suits by the Minor Child Against His Parent

The right of a minor child to maintain an action, with regard to contract or real property, has been settled for many years, but the child's right to sue his parent for negligently-caused injuries is *not* recognized by a majority of states today. The "beginning" was in 1891, in *Hewlett v. George* (9 So. 885), when the Mississippi court declared that a mother was harmless for wrongfully causing her unemancipated minor daughter to be confined in an insane asylum. The decision was based upon the family concept of reciprocal rights and duties; the parent was obligated to support guide, and control the child, and the child was bound to obey, aid, and comfort his elders and was subject to parental discipline for nonperformance. Parental breach or abuse of authority was held to be rectifiable by criminal proceedings only. Hence, there was no need to disrupt the "peace of society, and of families" by permitting a minor to sue his parent for negligence. Twelve years later, in Tennessee, in *McKelvey v. McKelvey* (77 S.W. 664), the court again refused a child's action against his father and stepmother for excessively beating him. And, in *Roller v. Roller* (79 P. 788), the Washington court, in 1905, dismissed an action for rape against the father who had previously been convicted of the crime against his daughter. Although shocked by the nature of the act, and impressed with the daughter's argument that the family harmony concept had already been shattered, the court declined to depart from the archaic rule. Indeed, uncompensated torts are very capricious devices for fostering family unity and buttressing parental discipline! The truth is that most intra-family suits are brought because the defendant is insured, and the family peace and pocketbook are strengthened, not depleted, by such suits.

The trend against such restrictions began to change, in a few states, as crying need for justice was heard. One of the most compelling cases was *Mahnke v. Moore* (77 A.2d 923), decided by a Maryland court in 1951. Here the unemancipated minor child was forced by her father to witness the murder of her mother under horrifying circumstances; the minor child of the age of five was kept for a week with the corpse, and then forced to watch her father commit suicide. The child was spattered with blood. In an action brought against her father's estate for the child's severe emotional disturbance and resulting illness, the appellate court ruled that the father's acts "show complete abandonment of the parental relation," and therefore the illegitimate child could maintain the action! Indeed, the interest in preserving domestic tranquility and securing parental control must not be blindly enforced where the result is to protect a depraved and wantonly malicious parent!

It has been held, in a few states, that the immunity from suit by a member of the family expires upon the death of the protected party, and does not extend to the decedent's estate. In *Brennecke v. Kilpatrick* (336 S.W.2d 68), the Missouri Supreme Court, in 1960, ruled that the mother's death "terminates the family relationship and there is no longer in existence a relationship within the reasonable contemplation of the doctrine (of family immunity)." A six-year-old child was permitted to sue her mother's estate for her own injuries caused by the mother's negligence. In Pennsylvania, the courts have allowed an action by a child based upon the Pennsylvania Death Statute under which a minor child can share in compensation payable where negligence caused his parent's death (*Minkin v. Minkin*, 7 A.2d 461, 1939). But in *Parks vs. Parks, supra,* Pennsylvania reverted to the traditional argument of public policy to deny recovery by an unemancipated minor child against his mother in 1957! In his dissent, Justice Musmanno opined: "It is simply preposterous to say that an automobile owner who carries insurance to indemnify children who may be injured through his negligence intends to protect all children except the fruit of his own loins . . ."

In a 1959 Missouri court decision, *Wirth v. Wirth* (322 S.W.2d 745), a nineteen-year-old minor was permitted to sue her father for injury resulting from his negligent operation of an automobile because the court found that the daughter was "emancipated" at the time of the accident! In contrast, in *De Lay v. De Lay* (337 P.2d 1057), the Washington court, in 1959, ruled that the injured child, although living with his aunt and uncle rather than with his father, was not emancipated and, therefore, could not sue his father for the latter's negligence!

Although the New York rule limits the action by the child against his parent to instances where the parent was willfully and wantonly negligent (*Cannon v. Cannon*, 287 N.Y. 425), recovery has been permitted upon the basis of "an infringement on a property right . . . . although predicated on negligence." In *Becker v. Rieck* (188 N.Y.S.2d 724, 1959), one brother was injured while a passenger in a car driven by brother Charles; the father sued Charles for loss of services and medical expenses incurred as the result of his brother's injury. The court allowed recovery to the father because the injured brother "can recover not only damages for personal injuries but future medical expenses as well." Moreover, "this action is to recover for pecuniary loss by a parent." There appears little difficulty in suits by brother against brother, even though both are unemancipated; see *Herrell v. Haney* (341 S.W.2d 574), in which the Tennessee court, in 1960, rejected in a brother-brother suit the family immunity defense, for the next of kin of the deceased brother happened to be the parents.

## Suits Between Spouses

The ban against suits between spouses, especially for prenuptial torts, is illustrated by *Benevides v. Kelly* (157 A.2d 821). In this 1960 Rhode Island case, the wife sued her husband for injuries sustained in an auto accident prior to their marriage. She contended that the Married Women's Acts abrogated the common law rule of inter-spousal immunity from suit, particularly where there was insurance coverage. The court responded:

> "It is settled in this jurisdiction that the courts will follow the common law to the extent that it remains applicable in given circumstances unless such law is modified by statute . . ."

Even death does not terminate the husband-wife suit immunity. A wife's complaint against her husband's administrator for the husband's willful injury to her before his death, was dismissed by the Illinois court in *Heckendorn v. First National Bank* (166 N.E.2d 571):

> "The legislature created a statutory disability during the lifetime of the parties. Its intent was to prevent a cause of action from coming into being. If a cause of action could not exist in favor of the wife and against the tortfeasor-husband, it could not survive his death . . . . The majority of the jurisdictions within the United States are in accord with our view . . . . "

Nevertheless, the doctrine of family immunity is in retreat, particularly where the wrong is willful and aggravated. In *Landy v. Landy,* the New Jersey Supreme Court on May 8, 1961, held that a widow may maintain an action against her deceased husband's estate for injuries resulting from an auto collision which was caused by his negligence. Though one spouse could not sue the other in tort, the negligent infliction of injury here was a wrongful act demanding compensation. In *Goode v. Martins* (361 P.2d 941), the Washington court, in 1961, permitted the injured wife to maintain an action against her husband for a sexual assault committed while the spouses were legally separated; the husband ruptured her cyst, causing profuse hemorrhaging and loss of her only ovary. The court ruled the common law rule of immunity was waived by the *intentional* tort; the notion about disruption of family harmony was irrelevant because divorce proceedings had already begun and the tort itself demonstrated the irreconcilable differences.

The factor of insurance coverage has imprudently been permitted to sanction and to bar such suits between spouses for personal injuries. In *Prince v. Prince*, the Tennessee Supreme Court, on July 27, 1959, held that a wife could not maintain an action against her husband for injuries resulting from his negligence in operating an automobile in which she was a passenger. Although the husband was covered by a liability insurance policy, the court ruled that such policies are indemnity policies and if an action cannot be maintained against the insured, there is nothing to indemnify! In *Emory v. Emory* (289 P.2d 218), the California court, in 1955, in a sister-brother, parent-child lawsuit opined:

> "Moreover, although defendants' statement that the existence of insurance, of which there is no evidence in the present case, 'gives no cause of action where one did not exist before' is correct, by the same token the more possibility of fraud or collusion because of possible existence of liability insurance does not warrant immunity from liability where it would otherwise exist. . . . The fact that there may be greater opportunity for fraud or collusion in one class of cases than another does not warrant courts in closing doors to all cases of that class. Courts must depend upon the efficacy of the judicial process to ferret out the meritorious from the fraudulent in particular cases."

Where the husband is injured on the job, the wife may sue the employer, and the husband-wife immunity is not available as a defense for the employer, *Kowaleski v. Kowaleski* (Oregon Supreme Court, April 19, 1961). In *Eule v. Eule Motor Sales* (170 A.2d 241), the plaintiff-wife was a passenger in a partnership auto operated negligently by her husband; the New Jersey court, in 1961, held that she may sue her husband's partnership upon analogy to actions against employer for negligence of employee-husband. The court declared that it was of no matter that the partnership asset of the husband, of direct value to him, could be reached, or that his private assets could be tapped if partnership assets were insufficient.

## *"Conditions" for Invoking the Family Immunity Doctrine*

It is submitted that the "family immunity" doctrine should be invoked only if all three of the following "conditions" are met: (a) there must be a marital or parent-child relationship between the person injured and the defendant; (b) the injury must arise out of conduct which occurs due to the marital or parent-child relationship, i.e., in the conduct of "family business," as society reasonably expects, in such situations as where the injury resulted from a mother's preparations for family dinner, a father's act of shoveling snow from the walk of their house, or perhaps the husband's attempts at making house repairs and (c) the defendant's conduct must be consistent with the reasonable performance of the marital or family duties. The following illustration is pertinent: assume that a father, while intoxicated, runs his auto into a building, and that a son he was driving to school is injured. From these stated facts, it is fairly clear that the father was negligent and that he would be liable to a stranger injured under these circumstances. However, the father might be protected under the family immunity doctrine in a suit by his son, if the above three "conditions" are present: the first requirement is met since a parental relationship exists between the plaintiff and defendant; the second requirement is met in that the injury occurred while the father was acting in furtherance of a parental purpose, i.e., driving his son to school; however, the third requirement is *not* met, for the jury would find that an intoxicated father driving his son to school did not conduct himself in a manner consistent with the parental relationship! (For a comparable case, see *Henderson v. Henderson,* 169 N.Y.S.2d 106, 1957.)

Where the family immunity doctrine does not protect family harmony, the reason for its existence fails. The mere initiation of the suit by the child or spouse indicates a lack of family harmony. The fact of the negligent injury indicates that the parent or spouse has failed to fulfill his duty where suit is brought in good faith. If there is collusion between the parties, the family harmony is not worthwhile being retained or protected.

### Abolition of the Family Immunity Doctrine

Judge Fuld of the New York Court of Appeals in his dissent in the *Badigian* case, *supra,* in 1961, criticized the "doctrine" in these terms:

> "A rule which so incongruously shield conceded wrongdoing bears a heavy burden of justification . . . "

Nevertheless, a majority of states have not taken seriously the burden of explanation or justification for retention of the "family immunity" doctrine. Collusion between spouses and/or members of the family is not a persuasive argument, for such fraud contemplates the commission of a crime (obtaining money under false pretenses) and is punishable as a crime. It is no more a deterrent by being made a factor in a civil suit for compensation; the opportunity for collusion between family members in actions involving a property right has not deterred the courts from permitting such litigation. The possibility that some people may act dishonestly does not seem to justify the complete denial of tort actions between members of the family.

In *Midkiff v. Midkiff* (113 S.E.2d 875), the Virginia court, in 1960, solemnized: "The aim of the law is to deal with realities, and where there is no reason for a rule, one cannot be assumed to exist. . . . Courts should not immunize tortfeasors because of the possibility of fraud or collusion. It is more important to protect an infant in his person than to avoid the possibility of fraud and collusion by denial of such protection."

Nevertheless, it can be argued that abolition of the family immunity doctrine might create as much injustice as it seeks to eliminate. Members of the family do owe legal as well as moral obligations to each other, and their relationship tends naturally to bring the members into constant contact with each other. Therefore, it seems unjust and unwise to decide arbitrarily that members of the family must observe the same standards of conduct toward one another that they are required to observe toward other persons. Recognizing the undeniable fact that even the best of people are at times careless, it would seem that a *limited* degree of immunity should be allowed to protect members of the family against certain types of conduct which would otherwise be recognized as tortious.

## *Conflicts of Laws in Intra-family Tort Liability*

Although a majority of states do not permit intra-family suits, the applicable state law is not always clear, as evidenced by *Haumschild v. Continental Casualty Co.,* (95 N.W.2d 814) in which the Wisconsin Supreme Court, in 1959, grappled with the problem. The parties were married and lived in Wisconsin when plaintiff was injured in California, while riding in a truck driven by her husband. Suit was brought in Wisconsin where there is no tort immunity between husband and wife; under California law there is tort immunity, though not among the rest of the family. The trial court dismissed the action, ruling that the immunity question was a substantive matter governed by California law. But the highest Wisconsin court reversed, declaring that the law of the domicile, i.e., Wisconsin, should apply in determining capacity to sue based upon family relationship! (The decision departed from the rule of the Restatement of Conflict of Laws, adopted to establish uniformity in the field.)

However, most States cling to the idea that spousal or intra-family immunity is a substantive question governed by law of the place of injury (*Bissonnette v. Bissonnette,* 142 A.2d 527, Conn., 1958). In the *Emory* case, *supra,* California announced that the law of the domicile controls all questions of intra-family immunity, on the ground that the domicile is the state most vitally concerned with the problem! Under this rule, parent's liability will not change each time he crosses the border of a traditional state into a reform jurisdiction. There is, however, a constitutional question as to whether a state can refuse to enforce a defense vested under the law of the place of the tort. Matters of defense which are regarded as substantive are treated as rights vested in the defendant and hence to be governed by the place of the wrong. The rule providing that the law of the domicile should control will result in a more equitable distribution of insurance losses. The ability to bring such action be determined by the law under which the premiums, based on the incidence of such suits, are more readily calculable by the parent's liability insurer, it is argued.

## *The New York Insurance Dilemma*

Under Section 167 of the New York Insurance Law, there is the provision that "no policy shall be deemed to insure against any liability of an insured because of death of or injuries to his or her spouse or because of injury to, or destruction of property of his or her spouse unless express provision relating specifically thereto is included in the policy." And, under Section 57 of the New York Domestic Relations Law, action between husband and wife for personal injuries and property damage is sanctioned. Nevertheless, a spouse can successfully sue her husband for personal injuries, and the insurance carrier for the husband cannot recoup its payment from the husband or the husband's corporation, *Ulanoff v. Croyden Shirt Co.* (174 N.Y.S.2d 357, 1958).

In *New Amsterdam Casualty Co. v. Stecker* (3 N.Y.2d 1) the New York Court of Appeals, in 1957, held that Section 167 excluded protection for inter-spouse liability arising out of an accident occurring in New York or in any other state. However, in *Maryland Casualty Co. v. Jacek* (156 F. Supp. 43, 1957), the court held the wife had a statutory cause of action in New York where the accident occurred (the insurance policy was issued in New Jersey where the wife lived); and the husband was protected and entitled to a defense under the contract, by reason of the fact that New Jersey had no legislation similar to that of New York. It thus appears that compulsory automobile liability insurance dictates against any immunity doctrine, for tranquil domesticity of the home is not disturbed by interspouse litigation.

**Parents' Liability for Misconduct of Children**

At common law, a parent, as such, is not vicariously liable for the torts of his minor child. Dissatisfaction with this rule, due to increase of juvenile delinquency and the use of automobiles by minors, manifested itself, and the need for a change prompted State Legislatures to enact laws imposing vicarious liability upon parents for the torts of their children. Approximately twenty states, including Nebraska, have held the parent liable for the child's willful destruction of property, but in *Connors v. Pantana* (86 N.W.2d 367, 1957), a four-year-old child burned down a garage while playing with matches, and because the child could not be guilty of such a crime as a matter of law, the court held that the parents could not be civilly liable. New York has vetoed such legislation upon the grounds that the economic burden of the liability would fall most heavily upon the low income family and increase family tension.

Liability for the tort of the child may be based upon the negligence of the parent himself, as where the parent entrusts a gun to an inexperienced child, *Stoelting v. Hauck* (159 A.2d 385, 1960). Many states have criminal statutes making it a misdemeanor to permit a minor to have a gun; violation of this statute has generally been held to be negligence *per se*, chargeable to the parent in civil cases for damages. A parent is not guilty of negligence *per se* in entrusting to his child a toy capable of inflicting injury, unless he is aware or should have been aware that the child would use the toy improperly, *Joseph v. Peterson* (160 N.E.2d 420, Ohio, 1959). Then, a parent has a special power of control over the conduct of his child which becomes a duty to exercise for the protection of others; to render the parent liable for breach of this duty, the parent must have knowledge of his child's propensity for misbehavior and must have an opportunity to correct such propensity, *Preston v. Duncan* (349 P.2d 605, Washington 1960).

In 1953, the plaintiff, a four-year-old boy, visited the home of his playmate, the defendant, also age four, who procured a cigarette lighter from his parent's home and used it to ignite papers on the floor of his parent's parked automobile. The infant plaintiff sustained severe burns, and commenced suit against the infant defendant and his parents. Nine years later, in 1962, after trial, jury verdicts were against the defendant mother for almost $4,400, but in favor of the infant defendant and his father. In *Marks v. Thompson* (18 A.D.2d 731, aff. 13 N.Y.2d 1029, 1963), the cause of action was ordered dismissed:

> "Insofar as her actual and immediate supervision of the child at play is concerned, the record supports no finding of negligence (on the part of the defendant mother). To the extent that the verdict may rest on possession of the lighter, in a place accessible to the child, it is unwarranted, as applying a standard of care considerably higher than that ordinarily accounted reasonable. The lighter was in a category not essentially different from that of such household articles and appliances in constant daily use as matches, stoves, and cutlery—to select random examples—which possess some potential danger but are commonly and necessarily exposed for ready use."

On the other hand, "parents may be held liable for the dangerous habits of their minor children causing injuries and damages to others, when (a) the parent has opportunity and ability to control the child; (b) the parent has knowledge or in the exercise of due care should have knowledge of the child's habit, propensity or tendency to commit specific wrongful acts; (c) the specific acts would normally be expected to cause injury to others, and (d) the parent fails to exercise reasonable means of controlling or restraining the child," *Bocock v. Rose* (373 S.W.2d 441). Here, the Tennessee court, in 1963, dealt with the parents of nineteen-year-old boys who had assaulted without cause or provocation the plaintiff, a college student.

When parents furnished their ten-year-old daughter with a power lawn mower and she negligently injured another child, the parents were held liable, *Herrin v. Lamar* (126 S.E.2d 454, Georgia, 1962). A mother who abetted children in a practical joke which caused the infant plaintiff to be frightened and injured was liable, *Langford v. Shu* (128 S.E.2d 210, North Carolina, 1962). And, the parents of a fifteen-year-old psychotic boy who shot a deputy sheriff with a rifle and ammunition that they had left accessible in the home, were held liable for the act of their son in *May v. Goulding* (111 N.W.2d 862, Michigan, 1961).

The constitutionality of such statutes imposing liability upon parents for the negligent acts of their children seems to be assured. In *Kelly v. Williams* (346 S.W.2d 434), the Texas statute which imposed liability for malicious and willful destruction of property by any minor child was upheld, in 1961, as a reasonable restriction on parents for their offending minor children. Indeed, the courts and legislatures are determined to make the parent responsible for the tortious, anti-social acts of their children.

## Selected Bibliography

*Milde v. Leigh,* 28 N.W.2d 530, North Dakota, 1959.
Vol. 28 *University of Kansas City Law Review* 183, Summer, 1960.
*Grindstaff v. Watts,* 119 S.E.2d 784, North Carolina, 1961.
*Cwik v. Zylstra,* 155 A.2d 277, New Jersey, 1959.
*Morin v. Le Tourneau,* 156 A.2d 131, New Hampshire, 1959.
*Buttrum v. Buttrum,* 105 S.E.2d 510, Georgia, 1958.
*Schweinkhoff v. Farmers Mutual Auto Ins. Co.,* 104 N.W.2d 154, Wisconsin, 1960.
*Burdick v. Nawrocki,* 154 A.2d 242, Connecticut, 1959.
*United States v. Wooldridge,* 10 U.S. CMA 510, 1959.
Vol. 33 *Tulane Law Review* 884.
*Parker v. Hoefer,* 2 N.Y. 2d 612, 1957.
*Neuberg v. Bobowicz,* 401 Pa. 146, 1960.
*Smith v. United Construction Workers,* 122 So.2d 153, Alabama, 1960.

## Questions for Review

1. Why did courts in the early days insist upon finding some *property interest* before recognizing interference with relational interests?
2. Why does a court have an interest in domestic tranquility, apart from deciding that issue in a particular case?
3. Define "consortium." Why was the wife's right to consortium not recognized in the U.S. until 1950?

4. Is there a difference between a child's loss of support and his loss of consortium?
5. Why have states like New York abolished actions for alienation of affections and for breach of promise to marry?
6. Explain how testimonial compulsion of one spouse against another weakens familial peace and harmony. Which spouse has the privilege?
7. If a communication between husband and wife is basically privileged (like that of a lawyer and client), why can a court compel one spouse to testify against another?
8. Did you agree with the decision of the English court in *Lilley v. Lilley?* Why?
9. How do reciprocal support-of-dependents statutes operate? What is the purpose of such legislation? Do they contribute to family unity?
10. Should the state or the church have exclusive control over the marriage contract? Is there room for both agencies to exercise control?
11. Define "common law marriage." Should it be abolished?
12. Why are first-cousin marriages undesirable?
13. Other than *legal* grounds, why should we not recognize personal injury suits within a family? Does the existence of a liability insurance policy alter your answer?
14. Would a "family immunity" doctrine result in a substantial decrease in premium rates for automobile liability insurance?
15. Does prosecution for criminal wrong solve the problem of a father's negligence which injured his son? Why?
16. Is it more important for an unemancipated child to be given the right to sue for parental torts than an emancipated child? Explain.
17. What is the New York rule on parental liability to the child?
18. If one spouse is employed by the other in a business enterprise, does the "family immunity" doctrine apply to personal injuries?
19. What is meant by "conflicts of law?" How can uniformity be achieved?
20. What are the criteria for determining when a parent should be liable for the civil wrongs of his child? Does such a rule promote familial peace?

## Chapter III

## HARMS TO UNBORN CHILDREN: RECOVERY FOR PRENATAL INJURIES

### The Traditional Legal View of "Entity"

TRADITIONALLY, the courts have been reluctant to recognize any rights or privileges of an unborn child, and particularly has this been true with respect to injuries received before birth, due to the negligence of some person or persons. There are many practical considerations for not recognizing harms to unborn children as the basis for legal liability, aside from the argument that the unborn child had no "legal existence" at the time of the injury: (a) the injury is not very common or usual or readily foreseeable; (b) there is no pressing social need to give the unborn child compensation for its injuries because the child, if alive, may achieve its place in society; (c) recognition of harms to unborn children may encourage fictitious claims in court for remote, speculative damages; (d) imposition of liability upon the person or persons negligently causing the injury would not deter the number of such unfortunate injuries to unborn children; (e) the mother bearing the child may herself have been contributorily negligent, so that any recovery for the benefit of the infant would be based upon "liability without fault;" and (f) it is extremely difficult, if not impossible, to prove, even by a preponderance of the evidence, the causal relationship between an injury to an unborn child and the particular act or acts of negligence.

One of the leading cases supporting the conclusion that a person who negligently causes harm to an unborn child is *not* liable to such child for the resulting harm was *Drobner v. Peters* (232 N.Y. 220), decided by the highest New York court, in 1921. A pregnant woman stepped into an uncovered hole in defendant's sidewalk, and her infant, born prematurely, died eleven days later, presumably from the injuries sustained by his mother. The New York Court of Appeals determined that the child was, at the time of the injury, part of the mother, not severed until birth, subsequent to the accident; and hence the dead child had no legal existence, and no suit could be brought in its behalf. In other words, there was no legally foreseeable duty of care by the third party or tortfeasor to the unborn child. As a fetus (after the end of the third month of gestation) and even as a viable fetus sufficiently developed (after perhaps seven months) for extra-uterine survival, no legal rights existed for the benefit of the unborn child.

In 1884, Mr. Justice Oliver Wendell Holmes, as a member of the Supreme Judicial Court of Massachusetts, decided *Dietrich v. Northampton* (138 Mass. 14). Suit was brought by the administrator of the child's estate for the death of the child as a result of a premature delivery necessitated by the defendant's negligence. At the time of the accident, the mother was five months pregnant, and the accident forced out the fetus which survived only ten to fifteen minutes after being born. Mr. Justice Holmes refused recovery for the death of the child, because the unborn child was part of the mother at the time of injury and, furthermore, any damage to the child would have been conjectural:

> "If we assume, irrespective of precedent, that a man might owe a civil duty and incur a conditional, prospective liability in tort to one not yet in being, and if we should assume also that causing an infant to be born prematurely stands on the same footing as wounding or poisoning, we should then be confronted by the question raised by the defendant, whether an infant dying before it was able to live separated from its mother could be said to have become a person recognized by the law as capable of having a locus standi in court."

Mr. Justice Holmes obviously answered his own queries in the negative, finding no legal liability upon the part of the defendant.

Sixteen years later, in 1900, the Illinois Supreme Court, in *Allaire v. St. Luke's Hospital* (184 Ill. 359), also refused to recognize the right of an unborn child, injured within ten days prior to birth, to bring suit. The accident happened while the infant's mother was being transported in a hospital elevator which struck a projection in the elevator shaft. According to the Illinois court:

> "That a child before birth is, in fact, a part of the mother and is only severed from her at birth, cannot, we think, be successfully disputed. The doctrine of the civil law and the ecclesiastical and admiralty courts, therefore, that an unborn child may be regarded as *in esse* for some purposes when for its benefit, is a mere legal fiction, which, so far as we have been able to discover, has not been indulged in by courts of common law to the extent of allowing an action by an infant for injuries occasioned before its birth . . . "

It is of interest to note the distinction here drawn by the Illinois court between a *viable* i.e., capable of living apart from its mother if prematurely born, and a *non-viable* child, because just twenty-four years later, in 1924, a Pennsylvania court in *Kine v. Zuckerman* (4 Pa. D & C 227) allowed a *viable* child to sue for injuries sustained while in its mother's womb. The subsequent years revealed a growing judicial recognition that natural justice and the inherent right of the injured infant to recover for injuries were morally necessary! It was argued that where a wrong was committed, there must be a remedy to right the wrong! And, in December 1951, the New York Court of Appeals in *Woods v. Lancet* (303 N.Y. 356) *reversed* its thirty-year old decision in *Drobner v. Peters, supra:*

> "To deny the infant relief in this case is not only a harsh result, but its effect is to do reverence to an outmoded, time-worn fiction not founded on fact and within common knowledge untrue and unjustified."

The highest New York court upheld the complaint which alleged that, while the infant plaintiff was in its ninth month in his mother's womb, the negligence of the defendant caused the infant to be born in a maimed condition. Judge Desmond declared that the "precise question" was whether New York should "bring the common law of this state . . . into accord with justice? . . . . We should make the law conform to right . . . We act in the finest common-law tradition when we adapt and alter decisional law to produce common-sense justice."

In January 1960, the Supreme Court of New Jersey, in *Smith v. Brennan* (157 A.2d 497), also discarded the immunity for prenatal injury and expressly held that it was for the court, not the legislature, to reexamine and reject the archaic doctrine which had precluded recovery for such injuries. Ohio has recently permitted recovery for prenatal injuries to a viable child even when the child is born dead; in *Stidham v. Ashmore* (190 Ohio App. 431), the court, in 1959, opined:

> "The test of the existence of that right (for wrongful death) is that the injury 'would have entitled the party injured to maintain an action and recover damages if death had not ensued.' If death had not ensued, the child in our present case would have been entitled to maintain an action. We are unable to reconcile the two propositions, that if the death occurred after birth there is a cause of action, but that if it occurred before death there is none . . . . "

On the other hand, the Commonwealth of Massachusetts still retains the viability doctrine, *Keyes v. Construction Service, Inc.* (165 N.E.2d 912, 1960): the action was not maintainable for prenatal injuries including four hours of pain and suffering by the viable child *which subsequently died*. This view is decidedly a minority position among those States which have expressed themselves on the question.

### Recovery for Prenatal Injuries—The Majority View Today

In recent years, a considerable body of authoritative court decisions has accumulated in perhaps twenty-four states allowing recovery by a child for prenatal injury: California: *Scott v. McPheeters* (33 Cal. App.2d 629); Connecticut: *Tursi v. New England Windsor Co.* (111 A.2d 14); Delaware: *Worgan v. Greggo & Ferrara, Inc.* (128 A.2d 557); District of Columbia: *Bonbrest v. Kotz* (65 F. Supp. 138); Georgia: *Tucker v. Howard Carmichael & Sons* (208 Ga. 201); Illinois: *Amann v. Faidy* (415 Ill. 422); Iowa: *Wendt v. Lillo* (182 F. Supp. 56); Louisiana: *Cooper v. Blanck* (72 So.2d 116); Kansas: *Hale v. Manion* (368 P.2d 1); Kentucky: *Mitchell v. Couch* (285 S.W.2d 901); Maryland: *Damasasiewicz v. Gorsuch* (197 Md. 417); Massachusetts: *Keyes v.*

*Construction Service, Inc. supra;* Michigan: *La Blue v. Specker* (100 N.W.2d 445); Minnesota: *Verkennes v. Corniea* (38 N.W.-2d 838); Mississippi: *Rainey v. Horn* (72 So.2d 434); Missouri: *Steggall v. Morris* (288 S.W.2d 577); Ohio: *Williams v. Marion Rapid Transit Co.,* (152 Ohio St. 114); New Jersey: *Smith v. Brennan, supra;* New York: *Woods v. Lancet, supra;* New Hampshire: *Bennett v. Hymers* (147 A.2d 108); Oregon: *Mallison v. Pomeroy* (291 P.2d 225); Pennsylvania: *Sinkler v. Kneale* (164 A.2d 93); South Carolina: *Sox v. United States* (187 F. Supp. 465); Tennessee: *Shousha v. Matthews Drivurself Service, Inc.* (358 S.W.2d 471); and Wisconsin: *Puhl v. Milwaukee Auto Ins. Co.* (99 N.W.2d 163).

In the *Puhl* case, *supra,* the issue revolved about a Mongoloid child whose mother was injured in an automobile accident when she was twelve weeks pregnant. Plaintiff's physician testified that "Mongolism could be caused by a lack of oxygen to the fetus about the thirteenth week of pregnancy, and . . . . that it was his opinion to a reasonable medical certainty that the accident caused . . . (the child) to be born a Mongoloid." It was argued by experts that lack of oxygen to the fetus would damage formation of the brain tissue or cells, resulting in a deformed brain and an abnormal development. Experts for the defendant contended that there was no known specific cause of Mongolism. Although the Wisconsin court held the evidence was insufficient to establish that the Mongoloid condition of the child was caused by injuries sustained by her mother in the automobile accident, the court recognized that the unborn child was deserving of legal protection, even in the pre-viable period, and therefore rejected viability as a condition of the law's protection of the child in the womb.

Pennsylvania, in 1960, in *Sinkler v. Kneale, supra,* expressly overruled *Berlin v. J. C. Penney Co.* (16 A.2d 28, 1940) and allowed recovery for prenatal injuries. The complaint had alleged that the mother was driving her automobile which was struck from the rear by defendant's negligently-driven automobile. She was then one-month pregnant with the infant plaintiff which was subsequently born Mongoloid as the alleged result of the prenatal injuries. The Pennsylvania court declared that the "real catalyst of the problem is the current state of medical knowledge on the point of the separate existence of the foetus," and medical knowledge now supports the postulate that mother and child are two separate and distinct entities. Thus, the court reasoned, the traditional objection to maintenance of the action (that the tortious injury was to the mother rather than to the unborn child) no longer had validity. Specifically, the court held that the child had a separate existence from the moment of conception—and the question of viability of the child had "little to do with the basic right to recover." Six judges voted for recovery, the lone dissent basing his opinion upon the desirability of decreasing the number of negligence cases "swamping our courts!" Justice Bok and the Pennsylvania Supreme Court solemnly opined that suit by the unborn child was one of medical proof and of legal causation.

In the 1961 Illinois case, *Daley v. Meier* (178 N.E.2d 691), the mother was approximately one-month pregnant when she was injured by defendant in an automobile accident. She alleged that as a result of such injuries her child was born with subnormal mental faculties, did not develop normally, and would require medical care throughout its life. The court declared: "It is our conclusion that an infant who was born alive and survives can maintain an action to recover for prenatal injuries, medically provable as resulting from the negligence of another, even if it had not reached the state of a viable fetus at the time of the injury."

South Carolina, in *Hall v. Murphy* (113 S.E.2d 790), in 1960, also ruled that a viable child who suffers a negligently caused prenatal injury may bring an action after birth: "We think the reasons assigned by the courts for holding that a child after birth may not maintain an action for prenatal injuries are unsound, illogical, and unjust. We need not be concerned about lack of precedent. There is now plenty."

And, in New Hampshire, in the *Bennett* case, *supra,* the court squarely held that a child may recover for prenatal injuries whether or not the injuries were sustained while the fetus was viable or nonviable. Thus, the legal personality was deemed to have begun from the moment of conception! Accordingly, the court explained:

"It is not our intention to engage in an abstruse and technical discussion of the exact moment when conception occurs and the life of the new being starts. However, it seems to us that if an infant is born alive and survives, bearing physical or mental injuries medically provable to have been incurred by it while *en ventre sa mere,* it is being oblivious to reality to say that the mother alone was injured by the tortious act and not the child . . . . We adopt the opinion that the fetus from the time of conception becomes a separate organism and remains so throughout its life . . . We hold therefore that an infant born alive can maintain an action to recover for prenatal injuries inflicted upon it by the tort of another, even it it had not reached the state of a viable fetus at the time of injury. We so decide because we see no logical reason for not extending the protection of the law of torts to it and are impressed by the harshness of the opposite result."

## Denial of Recovery for Prenatal Injuries—The Minority View Today

Standing somewhat aloof are those five states which still refuse to recognize the unborn child's right to sue for prenatal injuries: Alabama: *Stanford v. St. Louis-San Francisco Ry. Co.* (214 Ala. 611); Nebraska: *Drabbels v. Skelly Oil Co.,* (50 N.W.2d 299); Oklahoma: *Howell v. Rushing* (261 P.2d 217); Rhode Island: *Gorman v. Budlong* (23 R.I. 169); and Texas: *Jordan v. Magnolia Coca Cola Btling Co.* (78 S.W.2d 944). The "heartache" of this minority rule against recovery for prenatal injuries is well illustrated by the *Jordan* case, *supra.* Here an eight-month pregnant mother was negligently knocked down by defendant's automobile, and she gave birth prematurely to twins. One baby was so badly bruised that he died nineteen days after birth. The Texas court refused recovery for injuries to the dead child, contending that the defendant motorist had no legally recognized duty of care to an unborn child:

"The argument finally made in support of a right of recovery is that we have here a wrong and an injury, and there should be a remedy. But the law can only be administered in accordance with defined rules and settled principles. Otherwise, there would be no standard of conduct. Because of the necessity for a standard, injuries often are suffered for which no relief can be granted. The task is not to undertake in the particular case to do justice in the abstract, but to ascertain whether in accordance with sound principles of the law of torts there is liability . . . . The existence of duty and breach of duty constitute in the law of negligence the foundation of liability . . . . Did the defendant owe a duty to the unborn child? We think, that, tested by the knowledge, experience and conduct of the ordinary prudent man, it 'owed no duty of care to the unborn child in the present case, apart from the duty to avoid injuring the mother . . . . ' Good reason is found for denial of the right of recovery in the fact that in many cases it would be impossible to establish, except by speculation or conjecture, that the death or condition of the child was proximately caused by the injury. But far worse than the indulgence of such speculation and conjecture and the insurmountable difficulty of satisfactorily proving viability, there would follow in the wake of this character of litigation many fictitious claims, with false testimony in their support, which defendants would always find difficult and often impossible to refute. These considerations we think outweigh the denial of justice in the abstract to the meritorious case."

In Ireland, Justice O'Brien, in *Walker v. Great Northern Railway of Ireland* (28 L.R. Ir. 69), similarly concluded that the law contained no principle out of which the right to maintain such action could be developed by anything short of the legislature:

"The pity of it is as novel as the case—that an innocent infant comes into the world with the cruel seal upon it of another's fault, and has to bear a burden of infirmity and ignominy throughout the whole passage of life. It is no wonder therefore that sympathy for helplessness and undeserved misfortune has led to what is literally a kind of creative boldness in litigation. But there are instances in the law where rules of right are found upon the inherent and inevitable difficulty or impossibility of proof. And it is easy to see on what a boundless sea of speculation in evidence this new idea would launch us. What a field would be opened to extravagance of testimony, already great enough—if Science could carry her lamp, not over certain in its light where people have their eyes, into the unseen laboratory of nature—could profess to reveal the causes and things that are hidden there . . . . . The law is in some respects a stream that gathers accretions with time from new relations and conditions. But is is also a landmark that forbids advance on defined rights and engagements . . . . "

## Denial of Recovery for Wrongful Death of the Unborn Viable Child

Since a wrongful death action may generally be maintained only in circumstances under which the deceased child might have had an action if it survived, it is necessary for a court to decide first that the child could have sued for prenatal injuries had it been born alive. A majority of courts have denied recovery for wrongful death of an unborn viable child, as illustrated the following decisions: Alabama: *Stanford v. St. Louis-San Francisco Ry. Co., supra;* California: *Norman v. Murphy* (268 P.2d 178); Nebraska: *Drabbels v. Skelly Oil Co., supra;* New York: *In Re Logan* (156 N.Y.S.2d 49, aff. 144 N.E.2d 644); Oklahoma: *Howell v. Rushing, supra;* Rhode Island: *Gorman v. Budlong, supra;* and Texas: *Magnolia Coca Cola Btling. Co. v. Jordan, supra.*

The minority rule is embraced by an ever-growing number of states, however, as illustrated by *Hale v. Manion* (368 P.2d 1), in 1962, when the Kansas Supreme Court declared that parents may maintain an action for wrongful death of their viable unborn child resulting from the negligent acts of the defendant. The nature of the injuries to the child was not detailed except that the mother bled, cramped, and delivered a perfectly-formed child one week later "which did not survive birth," allegedly because the automobile accident had caused placental disruption which led to expulsion and death of the child. The court determined that since the child was in a viable state at the time of accident, the action was proper. Two judges dissented, protesting that the cause of action should be created by legislative enactment if at all, and not by judicial determination.

## Causal Relation Between Injury and Act of Negligence

The inherent difficulty of proof of causal relation between the prenatal injury and the defendant's act of negligence is perhaps made evident by the distinction between a "medical" and a "legal" cause of the prenatal injury. The former may be defined as the immediate pathological cause, proved beyond a reasonable doubt, and given a narrow meaning, as a distinct possibility; and the latter or "legal" cause may be defined as the nearest cause in time to the given injury but not the immediate cause necessarily, proved only by a preponderance of the evidence, given a broad meaning as a distinct probability. Certainly medical authority is not unanimous about even the medical cause of a given injury, and courts are equally disturbed about lack of certainty in finding the legal cause of a prenatal injury. For example, birthmarks have been held *not* to have been caused by the fright of the mother, *Young v. Atlanta Railway Co.* (39 Ga. App. 761), but x-rays have been held to produce permanent injury to an unborn child when x-rays are negligently administered during the mother's pregnancy, *Smith v. Luckhardt* (19 N.E.2d 446). Negligent use of forceps during delivery can produce brain damage and paralysis in the child, *Scott v. McPheeters, supra*. But a child born without hands was held *not* to have sustained the defect or injury as a result of the tortious, prenatal injury, *Kine v. Zuckerman, supra*. Epilepsy was held to have resulted from a serious head injury to the child during the mother's pregnancy, *Lipp v. Milwaukee Electric R & L Co.* (164 Wis. 272).

The federal court decision in *Pan American Casualty Co. v. Reed* (240 F.2d 336, Louisiana, 1957) illustrates the difficulty of proof of medical causation: the plaintiff was approximately seven and one-half months pregnant at the time of the automobile accident. Prior thereto, she had experienced some bleeding accompanied by irregular pains, and her physician diagnosed same as "false labor." Subsequently, the pains began again, occurring at irregular intervals, and on the advice of the physician plaintiff and her husband left for the hospital in a car driven by plaintiff's mother. The car went out of control, careened into a ditch, and came to rest on its side. Plaintiff and her husband were taken to the hospital by a passing motorist, and shortly thereafter plaintiff gave birth to an apparently normal child which died forty-six hours later of atelectasis, i.e., a failure of the lungs. At the trial, there was medical testimony that from all signs the birth had been normal; there was no evidence of damage to the placenta or of excessive bleeding. Two expert witnesses, in response to hypothetical questions, indicated that premature birth often resulted from such automobile accidents, although atelectasis was a common cause of death of premature infants. None of the medical witnesses completely ruled out trauma as a possible cause of the infant's death. The jury brought in a verdict for the plaintiff, and the Fifth U.S. Court of Appeals affirmed that there had been no error in allowing the evidence as to medical causation to go to the jury:

> "We hold that is the right of the infant to start in life that results from nature's scheme of granting a nine months' period of gestation is shown to have been violently interfered with by the negligent act of another, and it is shown, as it has been here, that such interference substantially increased the chances of death from the defect that actually caused death, then the jury may attribute the fact of death to the negligent act that caused the premature death . . . . "

There are, of course, many "exotic" causes recognized by medical science as responsible for prenatal injuries, but generally legal proof leaves must to be desired, as, for example, German measles (responsible for anomalies in heart, eyes, ears, and nervous system where the mother is exposed); radiation (responsible for mental retardation and other congenital defects as the result of radiation of the mother); and drug administration (responsible for various congenital defects).

### Separability of Child from Moment of Conception

The most advanced, liberal position on the right of the unborn child has been taken by New York, in *Kelly v. Gregory* (125 N.Y.S.2d 693), in 1954. The court declared that legal separability of the child from its mother takes place at conception and, therefore, after birth, the child has a right to recover for injuries received at any period of his prenatal life. Medical testimony established the fact that the child born two months prematurely had been weakened and otherwise debilitated by the defendant's act of negligence. The New Hampshire decision, *Poliquin v. MacDonald* (135 A.2d 249) refused to go as far as New York, and limited recovery to a viable child born alive: "If a child can live separate and apart from the mother, even though she die, it does not seem logical to say that the injury was wholly that of the mother and not of the chold. . . . A fetus having reached that period of prenatal maturity where it is capable of independent life apart from its mother is a person . . ." But the Georgia Supreme Court in *Hornbuckle v. Plantation Pipe Line Co.* (93 S.E.2d 727) followed the New York view on separability from the moment of conception, and allowed recovery for pre-viable, prenatal harm. Previously in *Porter v. Lassiter* (87 S.E.2d 100) the Georgia court had allowed a mother to recover for the death of the unborn child who had been conceived only one and one-half months before the accident and who had died following a miscarriage three months later. Ingeniously, the court held that the cause of action arose, not on the date of the automobile accident, but on the date of the death of the unborn child!

## Environmental Stress and Hereditary Influences as Causes of Prenatal Injury

Prenatal injury and its cause has received the attention of the American Medical Association. In the July 14 and December 29, 1954 and March 2, 1957 issues of the Journal of the American Medical Association, two eminent medical specialists Dr. Theodore H. Ingalls and Dr. N. Fraser, took opposing positions on the cause of prenatal injuries. Dr. Ingalls favored environmental stresses and strains, and not hereditary defects, as the cause of prenatal defects; he contended that the mechanism was stress producing promptly and directly hypoxia in the unborn child which tends to produce teratogenic defects. Dr. Ingalls argued that the stress of injury may be a final common path for certain other maternal-placental diseases which likewise contribute to defective development of unborn children. On the other hand, Dr. Fraser favored the hereditary influences in determining the constitutional reaction of the pregnant woman to stress. He contended that any consideration of stress partaking in the role of developmental defects in babies should specify exactly how the adrenocortical mechanism of the unborn child is involved. Dr. Ingalls, several years later, was an expert witness for an injured plaintiff in *Meyers v. Mohr.* (148 N.Y.S.2d 487, 1955), and testified that the child was mentally deformed as a result of an automobile accident sustained by her mother some two years previous. At the time of the accident, the mother was five-months pregnant, and the impact of the defendant's car propelled her car 300 feet down the road into a pole. The jury returned a $15,000 verdict!

## Criminal Abortion: The Legal "Entity" of the Unborn Child

> "If men strive and hurt a woman with child so that her fruit depart from her, and yet no mischief follow, he shall surely be punished . . . . and he shall pay as the judges determine."
> (*Exodus, Ch. 21, 22-26*)

In the criminal field, there has been no conceptual difficulty about recognition of the legal "entity" of an unborn child. The killing of an unborn child is homicide under Sections 189 and 294 of the New York Penal Law, for example. Although the practice of abortion goes back to earliest recorded history, its emergence as a crime is a comparatively recent development; in some societies, abortion laws reflect a desire to foster population growth, although Plato and Aristotle recommended abortion as a desirable method of limiting population. In Rome, during the pagan empire, abortion received only mild social disapproval, but with the advent of Christian emperors came the first unqualified condemnation of the practice in the Western World. The Christian church established abortion as a crime against the unborn fetus, for which the penalty was death. Voltaire, Rousseau, and other reformers succeeded in obtaining abolition of such an extreme penalty and, in 1803, the first abortion statute was enacted in England. Today's abortion laws are designed to protect the mother's health, but the severity of the crime has fostered clandestine operations under non-aseptic conditions, and the mother's health has suffered. Although it has been estimated that there are perhaps two million abortions performed annually, all but an insignificant number of these abortion cases go unprosecuted! A majority of abortions are performed on married women! The problem of unenforcement of abortion laws might be resolved by statutory reform liberalizing the offense, and by elimination of the reasons for procuring the abortion.

## Selected Bibliography

*Nugent v. Brooklyn Heights Railway Co.,* 139 N.Y.2d 367.
*Thelluson v. Woodford,* 31 Eng. Rep. 117, 1799.
*Williams v. American Employers Ins. Co.,* 103 So.2d 568, 1958, 10 A.L.R.2d 1059.
*Stewart v. Rudner,* 84 N.W.2d 816, Mich., 1957.
*Raphann v. Armstrong,* 141 A.2d 525, Md., 1958.
Statute 43 George III, Chapter 58, 1803.
*State v. Cox,* 197 Wash. 67, 1938.
*Insurance Law Journal,* November, 1962, pp. 687-695.

## Questions for Review

1. Is there, in fact, a pressing social need for giving compensation for harm to unborn children? Would payment to the parent suffice?
2. What single factor brought about the change in judicial thinking favoring compensation for prenatal injuries to the child? How would you explain the 1951 New York decision in *Woods v. Lancet?*
3. Is Mongoloidism or Mongolism a contributing or resulting factor in prenatal injuries? How is the relative state of medical knowledge relevant?
4. Is *viability* of an unborn child a fact readily ascertainable? Why do some states limit recovery for wrongful death involving viable children?
5. Can the medical and legal causes of prenatal injury differ? Which controls?
6. What arguments can be mustered against recognition of the separability of the child from moment of conception?
7. Why are environmental stresses as important as hereditary factors in ascertaining the *legal* cause of prenatal injuries?
8. Why was the legal "entity" of the unborn child irrelevant in cases of criminal abortion?
9. Is making abortion a criminal offense a true deterrent?
10. Are abortion laws designed to protect the mother's health? Why?

*Chapter IV*

## SELF-INCRIMINATION AND THE FIFTH AMENDMENT: A PERSPECTIVE OF OUR TIMES

### The Historical Background

*"No person . . . . shall be compelled in any criminal case to be a witness against himself . . . "*

*Fifth Amendment to the Constitution*

THERE IS THE POPULAR TALE, somewhat supported in fact, about an Englishman called John Lilburne who was so cantankerous a person that it was said that "if all the world was empty of all but John Lilburne, Lilburne would quarrel with John and John with Lilburne." One day, in the year 1637, he was brought before the Star Chamber in England, charged with importing heretical and seditious books. Lilburne refused to take the oath to answer truthfully and accordingly was whipped and pilloried. Some four years later, when the famous Long Parliament abolished the Star Chamber, it upheld Lilburne's right to refuse to testify against himself, i.e., it gave credence to the privilege against self-incrimination!

A historical examination of the American antecedents of the privilege against self-incrimination under the Fifth Amendment to the U.S. Constitution is further revealing. The American colonists were well aware of the cruel injustice in the use of judicial torture to elicit evidence, but only the State of Virginia included the privilege against self-incrimination in its constitution. The Virginia provision drafted by George Mason covered all prosecutions whether judicial, legislative, or executive, so long as those transactions were either "capital or criminal." The States of Massachusetts, Maryland, New Hampshire, North Carolina, and Pennsylvania enacted the Virginia language, and eventually the Virginia provision on August 17, 1789, almost verbatim, was adopted by the U.S. Congress, and approved as part of the Bill of Rights in the U.S. Constitution on December 15, 1791, except for the amended language confining the privilege against self-incrimination to criminal cases, the work-product of James Madison, later President of the United States.

Probably the first court decision on the privilege against self-incrimination arose in 1807, when Aaron Burr was prosecuted for treason in a trial presided over by later Chief Justice John Marshall of the U.S. Supreme Court. Burr's secretary, having been questioned by the grand jury concerning the authorship of a certain Burr message, refused to answer upon the ground of the privilege against self-incrimination. In his opinion, "Judge" Marshall stated:

> "It is a well settled maxim of law that no man is bound to incriminate himself. This maxim forms an exception to the general rule which declares that every person is compellable to bar testimony in a court of justice . . . If the question be of such description that an answer to it, may or may not incriminate the witness, according to the purport of that answer, it must rest with himself, who alone could tell what it would be, to answer the question or not. If, in such case, he says upon his oath that his answer would incriminate himself, the Court can demand no other testimony of the fact."

Despite this solemn pronouncement, Burr's secretary was ordered to answer the particular questions, probably because the privilege belonged to Burr and not to the secretary. Note that neither the court nor Burr's secretary specifically invoked the Fifth Amendment which had been adopted by the U.S. Congress some sixteen years previous!

The modern "doctrine" as to the Fifth Amendment was announced in 1892, by the U.S. Supreme Court, in *Counselman v. Hitchcock* (142 U.S. 547), when it was declared that the privilege against self-incrimination was available not only to defendants in criminal cases, but also to witnesses in criminal cases. But the court regarded the privilege merely as a rule of evidence, and not as an integral substantive right which was immune or impregnable from any alteration or even abolition by Congress. Years later, Mr. Justice Cardozo expressed the same view of the privilege against self-incrimination:

## Self-incrimination and the Fifth Amendment

"It is not of the very essence of ordered liberty . . . Few would maintain that a fair and enlightened system of justice would be impossible without it . . . No doubt there would remain the need to give protection against torture, physical or mental . . . . . . ." (302 U.S. 325, 326).

Indeed, the privilege embodied in the Fifth Amendment, because it is *not* a fundamental right within the privileges and immunities clause of the U.S. Constitution, is *not* binding on the states as an element of due process of law within the Fourteenth Amendment, *Adamson v. California* (342 U.S. 46, 1947) and *Twining v. New Jersey* (211 U.S. 78, 1908). Yet the deep solicitude for civil liberties have prompted the courts to interpret the simple words, "no person . . . . shall be compelled in any criminal case to be a witness against himself," with great care and study even in purely state proceedings.

### The "Presumptive Guilt" Theory

The Fifth Amendment has been invoked for diverse purposes, including the blocking of anti-trust legislation, the defeating of reform movements in local government, the covering up of embezzlements by faithless fiduciaries, and the like—long before the 1950's, when adverse public reaction or moral blame fell upon any person who "took" the privilege against self-incrimination. In the 1950's, public anger, confusion, and controversy greeted anyone invoking the privilege, innocent and guilty alike, when they refused to answer questions upon the ground that their answer would tend to incriminate them. As a result, the "presumptive guilt" theory was born, i.e., the public is entitled to mistrust a person who takes the Fifth! Such an opinion of "presumptive guilt" received the approval of President Eisenhower in his March 27, 1957, press conference: "I must say I probably share the common reaction: if a man has to go to the Fifth Amendment there must be something he does not want to tell."

Professor Sidney Hook in his book, *Common Sense and the Fifth Amendment,* supported the view that the failure of a person to speak by invocation of the privilege against self-incrimination "establishes some presumption of guilt with respect to the question at issue." Professor Hook argued that, while such invocation of the privilege does not constitute conclusive evidence of guilt, the evidence of guilt is sufficient to be further evaluated in light of all other available evidence. He implied that if an innocent man is accused, he will normally cry out and speak rather than refuse to answer; unfortunately, the privilege had been a "shield for the innocent as well as a shelter for the guilty." Professor Hook recognized that invocation of the privilege, in the 1950's and 1960's, was bound to injure the reputations of persons presumptively guilty; but he had apparently little sympathy for persons guilty only of youthful errors or follies committed many years ago. He overlooked the fact that little public indignation attaches to the accused in a criminal court where the accused is relieved from testifying, and his failure to do so does not permit any comment nor even an inference of guilt!

Advocates of "presumptive guilt" by invocation of the Fifth Amendment contend that there is no social utility in the suppression of the truth and prefer that a person bear witness to a crime which he has committed. Professor John Wigmore in his monumental treatise, *Law of Evidence* (1940) examined the claim of exemption from the "general duty to give what testimony one is capable of giving:"

> "This contribution is not to be regarded as a gratuity, or a courtesy, or an ill-requited favor. It is a duty, not to be grudged or evaded. Whoever is impelled to evade or resent it should retire from the society of organized and civilized communities, and become a hermit. He who will live by society must let society live by him when it requires to . . . . "

Professor Wigmore believed that society has a "right" to one's testimony, that all society potentially is involved in each individual case because the vital process of justice must continue unceasingly. Presumptively, he would concur in the "presumptive guilt" theory of the Fifth Amendment.

### The "Presumptive Innocence" Theory

In contrast to the "presumptive guilt" theory, there is the fundamental right of a person to be presumed to be innocent until his guilt is proved. According to Dean Erwin Griswold, then of

Harvard Law School in his book, *The Fifth Amendment Today*, there is a "presumptive innocence" which is not rebutted simply by invocation of the privilege against self-incrimination, because the embodiment of the privilege is "one of the great landmarks in man's struggle to make himself civilized." Society benefits through the compulsion which is exerted upon prosecuting officials to prove their cases by external evidence rather than by confessions extracted from suspects. O. John Rogge, former Assistant Attorney General in charge of the Criminal Division of the U.S. Dept. of Justice, in his 1960 book, *The First and the Fifth*, wrote that an individual, as to any accusation which may tend to incriminate him, should have an absolute right to remain silent!

### *"Loyalty Oath Affidavits"*

In 1958, Congress enacted the National Defense Education Act (72 Stat. 1581-1605) under which Section (f) reads:

> "No part of any funds appropriated or otherwise made available for expenditure under authority of this Act shall be used to make payments or loans to any individual unless such individual (1) has executed and filed with the Commissioner an affidavit that he does not believe in, and is not a member of and does not support any organization that believes in or teaches the overthrow of the United States Government by force or violence or by any illegal or unconstitutional methods, and (2) has taken and subscribed to an oath or affirmation in the following form:—"I do solemnly swear (or affirm) that I will bear true faith and allegiance to the United States of America and will support and defend the Constitution and laws of the United States against all its enemies, foreign and domestic."

President A Whitney Griswold of Yale University on December 13, 1959, took issue with the "loyalty oath" requirements by serving notice that Yale was withdrawing from the program establishing or expanding upon loan funds for needy students. According to the *New York Times,* Dean Griswold stated:

> "The negative affidavit . . . . partakes of the nature of the oppressive religious and political test-oaths of history which were used as a means of exercising control over the educational process by church or state. The universities of the free world,

especially those of England and the United States, have taken the lead in resisting and doing away with such oaths."

Harvard's President Nathan M. Pusey also spelled out his objections to the "loyalty oaths," according to the *New York Times*:

"This provision is discriminatory since it singles out students alone in our population, and, among student, the neediest, as subjects for special distrust . . . . The disclaimer affidavit represents an affront to freedom of belief and conscience. As a kind of test-oath substituting an implied threat of coercion for persuasion in the realm of ideas, it seems counter to the philosophical principles on which our national strength has been built . . . . It also seems to many to imply interference on the part of government in an area of administration which belongs properly without restriction to free institutions of higher learning . . . "

Other objections to the "loyalty oath" requirement may be summarized as follows: it is futile, as no Communist would hesitate to take the oath, and any Communist can be prosecuted under the Smith Act, and the phrasing requiring a student to swear "that he does not believe in" is contrary to the First Amendment guaranteeing freedom of thought.

State requirements that public employees swear that they are not "subversive persons" was struck down by the U.S. Supreme Court on June 1, 1964, as unconstitutionally vague. Upon the same ground, the Court held unconstitutional a Washington State teachers' oath designed to "promote respect for the flag and the institutions of the United States, reverence for law and order, and undivided allegiance to the Government." Sixty-four employees of the University of Washington, ranging from full professors to typists, had challenged the two oaths required by state statutes passed in 1931 and 1955, the former making teachers swear to promote respect for government institutions and the latter providing an oath that one is not a "subversive person," nor one who "commits, attempts to commit or advocates, abets, advises or teaches, by any means, any person to commit any act intended to overthrow, destroy, or alter the constitutional form of the Government of the United States or the State of Washington." Mr. Justice White, speaking for the seven to two majority, declared that the 1955 law might condemn a man for giving some advice that led a third or fourth person to try to alter constitutional government:

> "Is it subversive activity to attend international conventions of mathematicians and exchange views with scholars from communist countries? .... What about the editor of a scholarly journal who analyzes and criticizes the manuscripts of communist scholars submitted for publication? .... Could one support the repeal of the 22nd Amendment (limiting a President to two terms) or participation by this country in a world government? .... "

The oath required by the 1931 law was subject to similar uncertainties, according to Mr. Justice White, particularly such indefinite terms as governmental "institutions" and "respect for the flag:"

> "The oath may prevent a professor from criticizing the Supreme Court or the institution of judicial review. Or it might be deemed to proscribe advocating the abolition, for example, of the Civil Rights Commission, the House Committee on Un-American Activities, or foreign aid .... "

In essence, the court found both oaths so vague in language as to give those who take them no fair guide to what they may be swearing. Mr. Justice Clark, in his dissent, accused the majority of having dreamed up a parade of horribles that could not really happen: "To so interpret the language of the act is to extract more sunbeams from cucumbers than did Gulliver's mad scientist. And to conjure up such ridiculous questions, the answers to which we all know or should know are in the negative, is to build up a whimsical and farcical straw man which is not only grim but Grimm" (see *Nostrand v. Little,* 362 U.S. 474, 1960).

## Some "Qualifications" of the Privilege Against Self-incrimination

An analysis of the privilege against self-incrimination, as delineated in court decisions, reveals the following qualifications:

1. The privilege was designed for the protection of the individual and not for the benefit of any group or other persons. An individual invoking the privilege must invoke it for

himself. It is not a "right" against self-incrimination, but a privilege which must be affirmatively claimed at the time the person refuses to testify. There is no requirement that the person be warned or advised of his privilege against self-incrimination, even under notions of fair play, *United States v. Parker* (C.A.7, 1957). An individual cannot, in the absence of an immunity statute, claim that he should not have been subsequently convicted of a federal crime based upon his earlier testimony, unless he had based his refusal upon the known willingness of prosecuting officials to proceed against him. Nor can a witness refuse to testify at all *before* any questions are asked of him.

2. The availability of the privilege is limited to criminal proceedings, although in the *Counselman* case, *supra,* it was stated that the privilege could be employed in other proceedings. In *Nusbaum v. Newark Morning Ledger Co.* (165 A.2d 177), in 1960, the Supreme Court of New Jersey permitted a witness in a *civil* suit to invoke the privilege because the answers could be a link in a chain to prosecution for violation of the Smith Act which makes it a crime to conspire to teach or advocate the forcible overthrow of the Government.

3. Since an individual cannot be compelled to incriminate himself, it seems clear that he is not required to prove that his answer will, in fact, incriminate himself, because in the course of such proof, incriminating facts would be clearly disclosed! Courts have been conscious of this dichotomy and have not required a person to reveal the sources from which evidence could be obtained, which might subsequently incriminate that person. Similarly, it has been held that an individual is not required to answer that which falls into the realm of ideas or in the area of opinion, *Watkins v. United States* (77 S.Ct. 1184).

**Congressional Committees and the Fifth Amendment**

The privilege against self-incrimination *in action* can be shown not only in its application to State legislative inquiries, grand jury proceedings, civil cases, disbarment proceedings, deportation hearings, school board hearings, and the like, but also in its application to Congressional committees. The inference of guilt (or of innocence) should be drawn in the context of the enveloping pattern of the factual background.

## *The Slochower Case*

The right of Congress to legislate and to compel testimony in pursuance of an investigation leading to legislation is not questioned, but a troublesome problem arises where the federal inquiry touches upon the employment of a state or city employee, such as a teacher. Harry Slochower, an associate professor at Brooklyn College with twenty-seven years' experience as a college teacher, was called in 1952 before an open hearing of the Internal Security Subcommittee of the U.S. Senate Committee on the Judiciary, which was investigating allegedly subversive influences in the American educational system. Slochower denied that he was at the time a member of the Communist Party, but refused to answer questions relating to such membership in 1940 and 1941, on the ground that his answers would tend to incriminate him. (It had been alleged in testimony given before the Rapp-Coudert Committee of the New York Legislature, in 1942, that Slochower had been a Communist party member.) Shortly thereafter, Professor Slochower was suspended by Brooklyn College and his position declared vacant, pursuant to Section 903 of the Charter of the City of New York for his refusal to answer "any question regarding 'official conduct.'" Slochower brought suit for reinstatement but relief was denied by the New York courts, and he appealed to the U.S. Supreme Court (350 U.S. 551). In a five to four decision the highest court, in 1956, *reversed* the New York courts, and held that New York, in regulating a teacher's employment, had acted arbitrarily and discriminatorily in violation of the Fourteenth Amendment. Mr. Justice Clark condemned the "practice of imputing a sinister meaning" to Slochower's exercise of the privilege against self-incrimination which

> "would be reduced to a hollow mockery if its exercise could be taken as equivalent either to a confession of guilt or a conclusive presumption of perjury .... The privilege serves to

protect the innocent who otherwise might be ensnared by ambiguous circumstances."

The court found that the New York City statute operated to discharge every city employee (including a college professor) who invoked the privilege since "the questions asked are taken as confessed and made the basis of the discharge." Furthermore, the dismissal was based upon a federal inquiry not directed at the "official conduct of city employees;" nor were the questions "wholly related to his college functions."

The dissent by Mr. Justice Reed upheld the right of a local community to demand that its teachers fully disclose information relating to their official conduct. Mr. Justice Harlan's dissent opined that Slochower's continued employment would jeopardize public confidence in New York City's school system. However, both the majority and minority opinions agreed that no unfavorable moral inference should be drawn from Slochower's invocation of the privilege against self-incrimination.

On authority of the *Slochower* case, the California Supreme Court, in *Board of Education v. Mass* (304 P.2d 1015), required the local school board to afford another hearing to a school teacher who had been dismissed for failure to tell a Congressional committee whether he was a past or present member of the Communist party.

But, in 1960, the U.S. Supreme Court sharply restricted the significance of its prior decision in the *Slochower* case by holding, in *Nelson and Globe v. Los Angeles County* (362 U.C. 1), that a state or local government may dismiss employees who refuse to answer questions about alleged subversive activities before a Congressional committee. At issue was a California statute making it a "duty" of all public employees to answer such questions before a state or federal investigating body. Anyone failing to answer "on any ground whatsoever" was deemed "guilty of insubordination" and "shall be suspended and dismissed." Both employees were social workers and had invoked the Fifth Amendment before the House Committee on Un-American Activities. In a five to three decision, Mr. Justice Clark (who wrote the opinion in the *Slochower* case) ruled that the *Slochower* case had involved a "built-in inference of guilt, derived solely from a Fifth Amendment claim (which) we held to be arbitrary and unreasonable. But the test here, rather than being the invocation of any constitutional privilege, is the failure of the employee to answer.... California has not predicted discharge on any built-in inference of guilt in its statute, but solely on employee insubordination for failure to give information which we have held the state has a legitimate interest in securing." The *New York Times* editorial of March 2, 1960, called the decision "regrettable":

> "What Senator Jenner was unable to achieve the Supreme Court has now virtually accomplished on its own . . . . (The unlamented, Supreme Court ripper bill proposed some years ago by former Senator Jenner included a provision designed, as Senator Jenner frankly stated, to overrule the court's 1956 decision in the case of Harry Slochower) . . . . . The distinction without a difference was seized upon by the majority to distinguish . . . . If a state or city is wise enough to avoid putting the term 'self-incrimination' explicitly in the law, it is free to punish employees who exercise a privilege granted to them as individuals by the United States Constitution . . . . "

## *The Watkins Case*

In the summer of 1957, the U.S. Supreme Court struck a bold blow against indiscriminate Congressional investigations. In the *Watkins* case (77 S.Ct. 1184), the conviction of a labor leader who not only "took" the Fifth Amendment but was allegedly in violation of a federal contempt statute making it crime to refuse "to answer any question pertinent to the question under inquiry," was *reversed* as the Court imposed numerous judicial curbs on the investigative powers and procedures of Congressional commitees. Chief Justice Warren stated flatly that there is "no Congressional power to expose for the sake of exposure," especially "where the predominant result can only be an invasion of the private rights of individuals." He declared that the decisions of these committees "can lead to ruthless exposure of private lives in order to gather data that is neither desired by Congress nor useful to it." Investigations conducted solely for personal aggrandizement of investigators were indefensible; Congress was at fault for failure to spell out the jurisdiction of the investigating committee and the purpose of its inquiry. Furthermore, Watkins was deemed not adequately informed of the pertinency of the questions asked, and thus he was "not accorded a fair opportunity to determine whether he was within his rights in refusing to answer." Chief Justice Warren wrote:

> "Fundamental fairness demands that no witness be compelled to make such a determination . . . . unless the subject matter has been made to appear with indisputable clarity . . . He must decide at the time the questions are propounded whether or not to answer . . . . A person compelled to make this choice is entitled to have knowledge of that subject to which the interrogation is deemed pertinent . . . . with explicitness and clarity."

In his concurring opinion, Mr. Justice Frankfurter pointed out that the "actual scope of the inquiry . . . . and the relevance of the questions to that inquiry, must be shown to have been luminous at the time when asked, and not left, at best, in cloudiness." The lone dissent by Mr. Justice Clark accused the court of substituting itself "as the grand inquisitor and supervisor of Congressional investigations." It is submitted that the dissent is but an abdication of the court's duty and power to hold a coordinate branch of government within its constitutional bounds by insisting that the basic rights of the individual citizen are the primary and ultimate concern of our system of government. (Some of the sting of the *Watkins* case was "surgically removed" by the U.S. Supreme Court in *Flaxer v. United States* (358 U.S. 147), when a contempt conviction of a Senate committee witness who was given ten days to produce union membership lists was *reversed*.)

### The Barenblatt Case

Another case softening the impact of the *Watkins* decision involved a member of the Vassar College faculty, Professor Barenblatt, who had relied, not on the Fifth Amendment, but upon a prepared memorandum which based his refusal to answer questions upon the "First, Ninth, and Tenth Amendments, the prohibition against bills of attainder, and the doctrine of separation of powers." The House Committee certified his refusal to answer questions to the U.S. Attorney who in turn brought contempt proceedings. The case was tried without a jury, and Barenblatt was found guilty. The U.S. Supreme Court in a five to four decision affirmed the conviction (360 U.S. 109), and declared that the House Committee had pervasive authority to conduct investigations of this type. Barenblatt contended that the questions put to him were not pertinent to the investigation of Communist infiltration into the field of education; but the court replied that he was aware of the Committee's purposes but had not timely raised his objection. Furthermore,

> "We conclude that the balance between the individual and the governmental interests here at stake must be struck in favor of the latter."

In a dissenting opinion (in which Chief Justice Warren and Mr. Justice Douglas joined), Mr. Justice Black argued that Rule XI creating the Committee authorized such a sweeping and indiscriminating compulsory examination that it violated due process, that compelling Barenblatt to answer abridged his freedom of speech and association, and finally that the Committee's proceedings were an attempt to stigmatize and punish witnesses considered to be guilty of Communist affiliations, and thus amounted to a usurpation of the judicial function by a committee of the legislative branch:

> "Ultimately all the questions in this case boil down to one— whether we as people will try fearfully and futilely to preserve democracy by adopting totalitarian methods, or whether in accordance with our traditions and our Constitution we will have the confidence and courage to be free."

Exactly forty years previous, in 1919, Mr. Justice Holmes of the U.S. Supreme Court in the *Schenck* case (249 U.S. 47) had enunciated the "clear and present danger" rule, which is implicit in evaluating the mouthings of agitators and even the refusals of educated citizens to answer questions before Congressional committees. In the *Schenck* case, the defendants were convicted of obstructing recruiting during World War I by sending circulars to draftees urging resistance to conscription. The majority of the court affirmed the convictions, although Mr. Justice Holmes in his dissent agreed that free speech had its limitations: "The most stringent protection of free speech would not protect a person in falsely shouting 'fire' in a theatre, and causing a panic." However, such "clear and present danger" does not exist if there is time to avert the impending evil by resorting to rational processes. In the 1941 decision, *Bridges v. United States* (314 U.S. 252), this formula was approved: "What finally emerges from the 'clear and present danger' cases is a working principle that the substantial evil must be extremely serious and the degree of imminence extremely high before utterance can be punished." Thus, today the question remains, when does the refusal to answer questions before the Congressional committee become a "clear and present danger" to established institutions?

### *The Presser Case*

In 1958, the Senate Select Committee on Improper Activities in the Labor or Management Field was investigating an alleged misappropriation of funds belonging to the teamsters' union. It issued a subpoena to William Presser, a teamster official in Ohio, to testify and produce his personal financial records for an indicated period. Before appearing as a witness he delivered to the Committee's staff at Cleveland certain books and documents relating to his personal affairs. Thereafter, the Committee heard evidence indicating that Presser had not furnished all the material sought, but had destroyed some of the personal records he had in his possession at the time he was served with subpoena. When he appeared as a witness, the Committee sought to ascertain from him whether, after service of the subpoena, he had destroyed some of the records called for, or had fully complied with the subpoena. Presser refused to answer the questions and was cited for contempt of Congress; subsequently, he was found guilty by the federal court, imprisoned for two months and fined $100. On appeal, his conviction was affirmed by the U.S. Court of Appeals for the District of Columbia in 1960. The court held that Presser's conviction was proper because he had subjected himself to cross-examination by answering the previous questions and, therefore, could not refuse to answer the question about destruction of his records. He could have refused to answer the question whether he had complied with the subpoena, but by answering that question as he did, he subjected himself to cross-examination as to how he had complied. Presser *waived* his privilege against self-incrimination about destruction of his personal records.

## The McPhaul Case

A subpoena was issued commanding McPhaul to produce certain records of the Civil Rights Congress before a subcommittee of the House Committee on Un-American Activities. He appeared before the subcommittee in Detroit but refused "to answer . . . any question which deals with the possession or custody of the books and records called for in the subpoena." He then asserted his privilege against self-incrimination. He was indicted for contempt and found guilty by a jury. His conviction was affirmed by the U.S. Court of Appeals, and also by the U.S. Supreme Court in 1960 (364 U.S. 372). Mr. Justice Whittaker stated that, while McPhaul could not be punished for failure to produce records that he did not have, in this case, he never had claimed that the records did not exist or that they were not in his possession or control. The evidence of the subcommitee's reasonable basis for believing that McPhaul could produce the records in question, coupled with the evidence of his failure even to suggest to the subcommittee his inability to produce those records, clearly supported an inference that he could have produced them. The Court rejected his argument that he could rely upon his plea of self-incrimination or that the evidence was insufficient to show that the records called for were pertinent to the inquiry.

Mr. Justice Douglas wrote a dissenting opinion in which Chief Justice Warren, and Justices Black and Brennan joined, to wit: there was no evidence that McPhaul was an officer of the Civil Rights Congress, or that he was in possession of any of its records. The dissent also argued that it was improper to shift the burden of proof to McPhaul.

## The Wilkinson and Braden Cases

On February 27, 1961, the U.S. Supreme Court, by a five to four vote, affirmed contempt convictions of the House Un-American Activities Committee against Wilkinson and Braden who had refused to testify about possible Communist affiliations. The court found that the Committee had a legitimate legislative purpose, including the right to investigate its own critics: "We can find nothing to indicate that it was the intent of Congress to immunize from interrogation all those (and there are many) who are opposed to the existence of the Un-American Activities Committee." Mr. Justice Stewart, however, concluded that circumstances "do not necessarily lead to the conclusion that the subcommittee's intent was personal prosecution . . . . It is not for us to speculate as to the motivations of individual members of the subcommittee."

The four dissenters charged that the court majority of five had opened the way for the House Committee to intimidate its critics by investigating them. Mr. Justice Black accused the majority of following "a constitutional doctrine that is steadily sacrificing individual control . . . . It is already past the time when people who recognize and cherish the life-giving and life-preserving qualities of the freedoms protected by the Bill of Rights can afford to sit complacently by while those freedoms are being destroyed by sophistry and dialectics." With great passion Mr. Justice Black declared:

> "There are not many people in our society who will have the courage to speak out against such a formidable opponent. If the present trend continues, this already small number will necessarily dwindle as their ranks are thinned by the jails . . . Government by consent will disappear to be replaced by government by intimidation because some people are afraid that this country cannot survive unless Congress has the power to set aside the freedoms of the First Amendment at will. I can only reiterate my firm conviction that these people are tragically wrong. This country was not built by men who were afraid and it cannot be preserved by such men."

Mr. Justice Brennan in his dissent stated that "the dominant purpose" of calling Wilkinson was "not to gather information in aid of law-making" but to harass him because he was one of its critics. Mr. Justice Douglas echoed this sentiment: "If Wilkinson is to go to jail for criticizing the Un-American Activities Committee, I can think of a number of newspaper editors who should join him there."

## Federal Government Employment and the Fifth Amendment

The federal government, under Executive Order 10450 issued by President Eisenhower, on April 27, 1953, discharged employees suspected of disloyalty. The Executive Order provided that "a refusal by the individual, upon ground of constitutional privilege against self-incrimination, to testify before a Congressional committee regarding charges of his alleged disloyalty or other conduct" was a factor to be considered in determining whether he should be employed in the federal service (Section 8[a][8]).

### The Greene Case

The entire federal security program received a 1959 battering from the U.S. Supreme Court in *Greene v. McElroy* (360 U.S. 474). Greene, an aeronautical engineer, lost his $18,000 a year job as vice-president of an engineering concern under contract to the federal government, because Greene's security clearance had been withdrawn by the Government. On the basis of his former wife's testimony (from whom he was divorced in 1947) he was "frozen" out of the position in which he had worked for six years on classified, aeronautical matters. Chief Justice Warren wrote the eight to one decision extolling the virtues of confrontation of witnesses against an accused and the legal necessity for the right of cross-examination. It was evident that the industrial security program of the federal government required *less* use of confidential informants and *more* use of live witnesses to confront the accused and be cross-examined, in turn:

> "They must be made explicitly not only to assure that individuals are not deprived of cherished rights under procedures not actually authorized, but also because explicit action, especially in areas of doubtful constitutionality, requires careful and purposeful consideration by those responsible for enacting and implementing our laws . . . . "

The lone dissent by Mr. Justice Clark opined that no one had "a constitutional right to have access to the government's military secrets." But it is submitted that the lone dissent foolishly endeavored to remove the cloud over the employee loyalty program of the federal government, overlooking the constitutional necessity for confrontation and cross-examination! Indeed, what is vital is "disclosure of witnesses" which does not require disclosure of defense or other military secrets. Where a valuable right such as employment by the federal government or by a contractor doing business with the federal government is in issue, it should not be taken away without a hearing, including such essentials of fairness as adequate notice of the charges and full confrontation and cross-examination.

### The Vitarelli Case

In support of the Interior Department's dismissal of Vitarelli for security reasons, the Government argued that the meager hearings accorded him by the Department's security officer and hearing board were more than his due. But in *Vitarelli v. Seaton* (359 U.S. 535), in 1958, the U.S. Supreme Court held that his 1954 dismissal was invalid; the five to four decision declared that he was entitled to reinstatement because the Department's own regulations were not followed in the mistaken belief that an employee in a non-sensitive position was not entitled to the same procedural safeguards as an employee in a sensitive position. Vitarelli had been fired a second time in 1956, when he received a discharge notice omitting all reference to any statute, order, or regulation relating to security discharges. It was on this point that the dissent of Mr. Justice Frankfurter seized: "I cannot join in an unreal interpretation which attributes to governmental action the empty meaning of confetti throwing."

### The Brawner Case

On June 19, 1961, the U.S. Supreme Court, by a five to four vote, upheld the government's right to dismiss a "security risk" employed by a contractor at a naval installation without notice or right of hearing. Rachel Brawner was a cook employed by a restaurant concessionaire at a naval gun factory. In 1956, the factory's security officer withdrew her security badge, and she was dismissed from her employment. In response to the query whether the security officer could deny her access to the naval installation, the court declared:

"It cannot be doubted that both the Legislative and Executive branches are wholly legitimate potential sources of such explicit authority. The control of access to a military base is clearly within the constitutional powers granted to both Congress and the President."

And, as to the query whether this exclusion deprived Mrs. Brawner of any constitutional right, the court opined:

"The Fifth Amendment does not require a trial-type hearing in every conceivable case of government impairment of private interest . . . . Where it has been possible to characterize that private interest as mere privilege subject to the Executive's plenary power, it has traditionally been held that notice and hearing are not constitutionally required . . . This case . . . involves the Government's dispatch of its own internal affairs . . . It has become a settled principle that Government employment, in the absence of Legislation, can be revoked at the will of the appointing officer."

## *The Communist Party Cases*

On June 5, 1961, the U.S. Supreme Court in *Communist Party v. Subversive Activities Control Board* (367 U.S. 1) upheld two of the federal government's major legislative weapons against Communism within the United States. The Court by five to four vote sustained a section of the Internal Security Act of 1950 requiring "Communist-action" organizations to register with the Government. It also found constitutional the clause of the Smith Act of 1940 that made it a crime to be an active member of a group or party advocating the violent overthrow of the government. The majority opinion refused to consider the argument that, by the mere act of signing a registration, officers of the party would identify themselves and make themselves liable to punishment under the Smith Act, in open violation of the privilege against self-incrimination under the Fifth Amendment. Mr. Justice Frankfurter opined:

"When existing government is menaced by a world-wide integrated movement which employs every combination of possible means, peaceful and violent, domestic and foreign, overt and clandestine, to destroy the Government itself—the legislative judgment as to how that threat may best be met consistently with the safeguarding of personal freedom is not to be set aside merely because the judgment of judges would, in the first instance, have chosen other methods."

He rejected the argument that approval of registration here might allow Congress to make "any group which pursues unpopular political objectives" register: "Nothing we decide here remotely carries such an implication."

Mr. Justices Brennan and Douglas, in separate opinions, dissented because the Court did not uphold the contention that making the officers sign the registration statement would violate their Fifth Amendment rights. Mr. Justice Douglas went further and stated that the Fifth Amendment also barred forced disclosure of member's names by the party. (The majority had indicated that the registration statement had to include the names of all members and officers within the past year and a financial statement.) Chief Justice Warren thought the majority should not have reached constitutional questions; the subversive board's order should be set aside because of procedural flaws in its hearing and because it had used incorrect evidentiary standards. He said, however, that since the majority rejected these non-constitutional arguments, he joined Mr. Justice Brennan in finding a violation of the Fifth Amendment in compelling the officers' signing of the registration statement.

Mr. Justice Black considered the Act as a whole, including all the penalties on the party and its members. He found it unconstitutional for a variety of reasons, including as an act of outlawry, a bill of attainder, a denial of due process, and a violation of the First Amendment. He concluded that it was impossible to read the Internal Security Act as a whole without concluding that it was a devious attempt to ban the Communist Party:

> "The first banning of an association because it advocates hated ideas—whether that association be called a political party or not—marks a fateful moment in the history of a free country . . . . "

The net effect of the Court's five to four decision was to require the Communist Party to file a bare statement that it was registering. Party officers could refuse to sign the statement on the basis of the Fifth Amendment, but this defect in the regulations was soon cured by an amendment allowing an innocent agent, who could not possibly be incriminated, to sign the form, without any testimonial immunity being granted to the reporting agent. Later, in *United States v. Communist Party,* the U.S. District Court for the District of Columbia fined the Communist party $120,000 "for failure to register as an agent of the Soviet Union." The court instructed the jury "to disregard the defense contention that the registration statute infringed the party's constitutional privilege against self-incrimination," and declared that the Fifth Amendment "does not apply to organizations but 'only to living human beings.'" It seems clear that the court, by construing the regulations as granting a testimonial immunity to the reporting agent or allowing the agent to claim the privilege against self-incrimination on behalf of the party members and officers, could have avoided weakening the impact of the Fifth Amendment. On December 17, 1963, the U.S. Court of Appeals for the District of Columbia *reversed* the conviction of the Communist Party on the ground that the government had failed to prove that the party could obtain an innocent agent, holding that because identity alone is an incriminating fact, it would not follow the usual presumption that an organization can always find an agent or even an attorney to act for it!

On the same day, June 5, 1961, when the U.S. Supreme Court decided the *Subversive Activities Control Board* case, *supra,* Mr. Justice Harlan examined, in the *Noto* and *Scales* cases, the requirement under the Smith Act of active membership in a group or party advocating the violent overthrow of the government. In the *Noto* case, he declared that the Act covered only advocacy, i.e., "incitement to action," not advocacy of the "mere abstract doctrine of forcible overthrow." In the *Scales* case, the various requirements of active membership, not nominal or passive membership, and of personal, "specific intent to bring about violent overthrow" were met; in the *Noto* case the evidence was insufficient. Mr. Justice Douglas dissented in the *Scales* case with these words:

"Nothing but beliefs are on trial in this case. They are unpopular and to most of us revolting. But they are nonetheless ideas or dogmas or faith within the broad framework of the First Amendment. What we lose by majority vote today may be reclaimed at a future time when the fear of advocacy, dissent and non-conformity no longer cast a shadow over us."

### State Legislatives Inquiries and the Fifth Amendment

In the same charged atmosphere, several State legislative investigations were conducted which matched the eagerness of the Congressional committees, but, as is evident below, the courts were perhaps somewhat more vigilant in barring inroads upon the Fifth Amendment in state proceedings.

#### *The Sweezy Case*

A one-man legislative committee in the State of New Hampshire was the bone of contention in *Sweezy v. State of New Hampshire* (354 U.S. 234) where the U.S. Supreme Court reversed the contempt conviction of a college professor who refused to answer questions of the State Attorney General about the content of his lectures and his friends' activities on behalf of the political causes of the Progressive Party. Professor Sweezy had denied that he had been a member of the Communist Party. Chief Justice Warren deplored the one-man legislative committee for failure to separate the power of legislative inquiry from the responsibility to direct the use of that power. Merely to summon a witness and compel him against his will to disclose the nature of past expressions and past associations, he declared, "is a measure of governmental interference . . . . an invasion of petitioner's liberties in the areas of academic freedom and political expression—areas in which Government should be extremely reticent to tread." Chief Justice Warren opined:

"No one should underestimate the vital role in a democracy that is played by those who guide and train our youth. To impose any straight-jacket upon the intellectual leaders in our colleges and universities would imperil the future of our nation."

In a concurring opinion, Mr. Justice Frankfurter asserted:

> "Progress in the natural science is not remotely confined to findings made in the laboratory. Insights into the mysteries of nature are born of hypothesis and speculation. The more so is this true in the pursuit of understanding, in the groping endeavors of what are called the social sciences, the concern of which is man and society . . . . For society's good—if understanding be an essential need of society—inquiries into these problems, speculations about them, stimulation in others of reflection upon them, must be left as unfettered as possible. Political power must abstain from intrusion into this activity of freedom, pursued in the interest of wise government and the people's well-being, except for reasons that are exigent and obviously compelling."

Both opinions expressed the belief that the State of New Hampshire had not given exigent and compelling reasons for the inquiries, especially since Professor Sweezy had sworn that he never, during lectures at the University of New Hampshire or anywhere else, had advocated the overthrow of the government by force or violence.

In a separate concurring opinion, Mr. Justice Harlan declared the need to protect the "right of a citizen to political privacy:"

> "The inviolability of privacy belonging to a citizen's political loyalties has so overwhelming an importance to the well-being of our kind of society that it cannot be constitutionally encroached upon on the basis of so meager a countervailing interest of the states as may be argumentatively found in the remote, shadowy threat to the security of New Hampshire allegedly presented in the origins and contributing elements of the Progressive party . . . . "

The dissents of Mr. Justices Clark and Burton were based upon the state's right to control its own subversive activity without federal interference!

### The Uphaus Case

In another New Hampshire case, the U.S. Supreme Court, in 1959, took a decidedly different stand and upheld the sentence for contempt imposed on Willard Uphaus (360 U.S. 72). Uphaus, executive director of the New Hampshire World Friendship Center, Inc., which operated a summer camp at Albany, N. H., declined to produce documents demanded by the same New Hampshire Attorney General during an investigation of subversive activities. Uphaus denied that he had ever been a Communist, and asserted that to produce the camp registration list, his correspondence with guest speakers, and the names of non-administrative employees, would make him a "contemptible informer." The New Hampshire Supreme Court held that the State Attorney General's order to produce such data did not violate Uphaus' constitutional rights, and the U.S. Supreme Court agreed, in an opinion by Mr. Justice Clark (who had dissented in the *Sweezy* case) who pointed out that "the academic and political freedoms" in the *Sweezy* case were "not present here in the same degree." A summer camp "is neither a university nor a political party;" moreover, ample evidence of a connection between the summer camp and subversive activities was present:

> "The investigation was therefore undertaken in the interest of self-preservation, 'the ultimate value of any society' . . . . This government interest outweighs individual rights in an associational privacy which, however, real in other circumstances were here tenuous at best."

The dissenters (Mr. Justices Brennan, Black, Douglas, and Chief Justice Warren) were convinced that the only purpose of this investigation was "exposure for exposure's sake":

> "It was logical that the adverse effects of unwanted publicity —of exposure—as concomitants of the exercise of the investigatory power, should come to be recognized, in certain circumstances, as invading protected freedoms and offending constitutional inhibitions upon governmental actions. For, in an era of mass communications and mass opinion, and of international tensions and domestic anxiety, exposure and group identification by the state of those holding unpopular and dissident views are fraught with such serious consequences for the individual as inevitably to inhibit seriously the expression of views which the Constitution intended to make free . . . . "

On October 12, 1959, the U.S. Supreme Court refused to reconsider its earlier five to four decision, and Dr. Uphaus was ordered to jail until he decided to "talk." The *New York Times,* of the next day, quoted Dr. Uphaus to the effect that the decision against him "may mean a life sentence" because he held it "morally wrong" to name "innocent people" who had come to his camp "simply to enjoy a vacation and to work for peace." However, the power of a state to proceed with prosecutions (for sedition, for example), against the state itself, under the Smith Act had been previously upheld by the court in *Pennsylvania v. Nelson* (350 U.S. 497).

## The Malloy Case

On June 15, 1964, the U.S. Supreme Court extended the protections of the Fifth Amendment to state proceedings as well as federal proceedings, in *Malloy v. Hogan,* overturning a precedent made fifty-six years ago. Malloy was convicted on a betting charge in 1959, and drew a ninety-day jail sentence and a $500 fine. In 1961, he was called to testify before an inquiry into gambling and other illegality in Hartford County, Connecticut, where he had previously been convicted. He was asked questions about his arrest and about whether he knew a John Bergoti, apparently a suspect of some kind. Malloy refused to answer, invoking the Fifth Amendment. He did not explain how answers to those questions might incriminate him. He persisted in silence even after he was told that the statute of limitations had run out on any gambling activities as early as 1959. The Connecticut Supreme Court of Errors ruled that he had not properly invoked the privilege against self-incrimination; and that his mere assertion that he might be incriminated, without giving some reason, was not enough to avoid answering such apparently innocent questions. In a five to four decision, the U.S. Supreme Court *reversed* and, in an opinion written by Mr. Justice Brennan, declared that the earlier 1908 decision of the court that the Fifth Amendment privilege against self-incrimination did not extend to state proceedings, had been undercut by more recent judicial determinations, including those throwing out coerced confessions as being denials of due process under the Fourteenth Amendment! Mr. Justice Brennan also noted the court's recent decisions applying to the states the rules requiring free counsel for the poor and excluding illegally seized evidence. He rejected a request by Connecticut that, if the Fifth Amendment be held now to cover the states, the states be allowed a less stringent standard in applying it:

> "The Fourteenth Amendment secures against states' invasion the same privileges that the Fifth Amendment guarantees against federal infringement—the right of a person to remain silent unless he chooses to speak in the unfettered exercise of his own will."

A dissent by Mr. Justice Harlan, joined by Mr. Justice Clark, objected specially to the insistence that the privilege against self-incrimination be applied to the states with exactly the same standards that have obtained in federal proceedings:

> "The reasoning behind the Court's decision carries extremely mischievous, if not dangerous, consequences for our federal system in the realm of criminal law enforcement . . . . This Court now (has decided) that the Fourteenth Amendment makes the Fifth's privilege against self-incrimination applicable to the states (and that) the federal standard justifying a claim of this privilege likewise applies to the states . . . . .
>
> "The ultimate result is compelled uniformity, which is inconsistent with the purpose of our federal system and which is achieved either by encroachment on the states' sovereign powers or by dilution in federal law-enforcement of the specific protections found in the Bill of Rights."

Mr. Justice Harlan stated that he would agree, for example, that if a state gave no protection to its citizens against being made to testify, that would deny due process; but the State of Connecticut, he said, had given Malloy ample protection here. He warned in his dissent that the majority's decision could lead to "incorporation" of all the other constitutional limits on federal criminal procedure, among which is the guarantee of indictment by a grand jury which most states have dispensed with!

Specifically, the "federal standard" referred to in Mr. Justice Brennan's opinion, commands that "no person shall be compelled in any criminal case to be a witness against himself." The general standard of the states is that a mere claim of self-incrimination is *not* sufficient, and it is up to the trial judge to determine if there is reasonable ground to apprehend danger of criminal liability from the accused's being required to answer. The dissent of Mr. Justice White in which Mr. Justice Stewart joined, argued that Malloy had not given sufficient reason for fearing incrimination under the general standard of the State.

## Local Government Investigations and the Fifth Amendment

In the field of local governmental loyalty investigations, there has been as much agitation as in state and federal investigations, though perhaps the emotional impact here was more intense, though unwarranted.

### *The Lerner Case*

A municipal subway employee refused to answer certain questions in a 1954 hearing before the New York City Commissioner of Investigation (which questions pertained to whether or not he was then a member of the Communist Party). He was dismissed from his employment, and the New York Court of Appeals, in 1957, upheld the dismissal (2 N.Y.2d 335). The highest New York court distinguished the *Slochower* case, *supra,* on the ground that Lerner was not discharged for invoking the Fifth Amendment, but for creating a doubt as to his trustworthiness and reliability; Lerner's refusal to testify was held to be "reasonable grounds" for his discharge. In 1953, the New York Transit Authority had been classified as a "security agency" by the New York Civil Service Commission, acting pursuant to and under a New York statute. Lerner's job as a subway conductor therefore involved a security risk. (The dissent of Judge Fuld regarded the New York court's determination in this regard "as a submission to unreasoning fear rather than a rational basis for administrative action.")

On June 30, 1958, the U.S. Supreme Court by a five to four vote affirmed Lerner's dismissal upon the basis of "doubt" concerning his trustworthiness and reliability (357 U.S. 468). Mr. Justice Harlan said that Lerner was not dismissed because of any inference that he was a Communist, but because he refused to answer a relevant question put by his employer. Mr. Justice

Frankfurter stressed the fact that Lerner was discharged because his employer had sought to satisfy itself of his dependability and had been balked in its inquiries. But the dissenting opinion of Chief Justice Warren held that the *Lerner* case was bound by the determination in the *Slochower* case, for Lerner's plea of the Fifth Amendment was "inextricably involved" in his employer's decision to discharge him, which was an invalid ground for dismissal of a public employee. Mr. Justice Douglas also dissented: "I would allow no inference of wrongdoing to flow from the invocation of any constitutional right." And Mr. Justice Black similarly dissented because the majority "refuses to pierce the transparent denials that each of these employees was publicly branded disloyal."

## The Nostrand Case

In the State of Washington, in *Nostrand v. Little,* the constitutionality of a state statute requiring every public employee to subscribe to an oath that he is not a member of the Communist Party or any other subversive organization, was tested. On May 2, 1960, the U.S. Supreme Court remanded the case (362 U.S. 474) in order to allow the highest Washington court to determine whether the state statute afforded a hearing at which the employee could explain or defend his refusal to take the oath. In its *per curiam* opinion the court pointed out that the Washington court had recently overturned an ordinance because it established a presumption of guilt without affording the accused a hearing. Mr. Justice Douglas, joined by Mr. Justice Black, argued that the remand was "a useless act," because a hearing could serve no function under the statute which provided that refusal to take the oath "on any grounds" was cause for "immediate termination" of employment.

In 1961, the Washington Supreme Court held that certain University of Washington professors who were contesting the constitutionality of the public employee loyalty oath, were *not* entitled to a hearing *per se,* but that they had a right to a hearing pursuant to the University's tenure regulations. In the absence of such tenure provisions, there could be no hearing on the issue of refusal to take the oath; there was no violation of due process because the professors did not have a vested right to public employment:

> "If he signs the affidavit, that is the end of the matter. If he declines to sign, the employee is subject to immediate discharge."

However, this procedure did not apply to the professors in the instant case because they had tenure rights and were entitled to a hearing under the rules and regulations of the University.

## Grand Jury Proceedings and the Fifth Amendment

A grand jury investigation is but the first step in a criminal case, the issue before the grand jury being whether or not a particular criminal proceeding should be continued or terminated. Invoking the Fifth Amendment before the grand jury has been a common pastime.

### *The Steuding Case*

A public official in New York was subpoenaed to appear before a grand jury. Without claiming his privilege against self-incrimination, after he was fully informed of his right to do so, he answered the propounded questions. Thereafter, the extraordinary grand jury returned an indictment against him. His motion to dismiss the indictment was founded upon the claim of self-incrimination in violation of Article I, Section 6 of the New York Constitution. In *People v. Steuding* (6 N.Y.2d 214), in 1959, the highest New York court affirmed a dismissal of the indictment:

> "The protection from indictment and from use of any incriminating testimony given by the defendant results automatically from the violation of the constitutional privilege, and the right and protection thus accorded by the Constitution may not be taken away . . . . "

Section 2447 of the New York Penal Law which prescribed the method by which immunity may be conferred upon "witnesses" was deemed inapplicable to defendants or "targets of investigation."

### The Curcio Case

In *Curcio v. United States* (77 S.Ct. 1145), the U.S. Supreme Court upheld the refusal of a labor leader to answer questions about the whereabouts of union records which he had failed to produce in response to a grand jury subpoena. In drawing a distinction between the custodian of corporate records who is not protected by the constitutional privilege against self-incrimination, the court held that Curcio's answers to questions would disclose the identity of persons who had the missing union records and hence incriminate them! But it is submitted that Curcio here misused the Fifth Amendment to avoid identifying others and not necessarily to protect himself, which is the very purpose of his privilege against self-incrimination! The U.S. Supreme Court had, seventy years previously, written:

> "Every good citizen is bound to aid in the enforcement of the law, and has no right to permit himself, under the pretext of sheltering his own good name, to be made the tool of others who are desirous of seeking shelter behind his privilege" (*Brown v. Walker*, 161 U.S. 591).

### The Halperin Case

Shortly before the *Curcio* decision, the U.S. Supreme Court examined the claim of Max Halperin, a New York attorney, who was subpoenaed by a Brooklyn grand jury investigating corruption in federal income tax matters. Halperin refused to answer the grand jury questions upon his privilege against self-incrimination. At his trial, the prosecuting attorney was permitted to draw from him this fact, and the trial judge's charge to the jury also referred to Halperin's questionable truthfulness and trustworthiness as a witness. The U.S. Supreme Court ruled this was "prejudicial error" which had deprived Halperin of the protection of the Fifth Amendment (353 U.S. 391). In his concurring opinion, Mr. Justice Black opined:

> "I can think of no special circumstance that would justify use of a constitutional privilege to discredit or convict a person who asserts it. The value of these constitutional privileges is

largely destroyed if persons can be penalized for relying on them . . . "

In ordering a new trial, the Court held it was "quite consistent with innocence for him to refuse to provide evidence which would be used by the government in building its incriminating chain. For many innocent men who know they are about to be indicted will refuse to help create a case against themselves . . . "

## *The Reina Case*

Reina was serving a five-year sentence for a federal narcotics offense when he was subpoenaed by a federal grand jury. A number of questions were asked him concerning his crime, particularly as to the persons involved with him and their activities in smuggling narcotics into the United States from Europe. Reina invoked the Fifth Amendment, and the U.S. Attorney obtained a court order directing him to answer; but he still refused to testify. He was adjudged guilty of criminal contempt (170 F. Supp. 592) and the conviction was affirmed by the Second U.S. Court of Appeals (273 F.2d 234). The U.S. Supreme Court, in 1960, affirmed the conviction (364 U.S. 507), declaring that one who has been convicted of a crime may not as a condition of his testifying require that he receive a pardon or amnesty as to the unserved portion of his sentence. (Congress may in order to compel testimony concerning narcotics violations authorize the granting of immunity from state as well as federal prosecution, which was done here.)

## Civil Cases and the Fifth Amendment

In civil litigation between private parties, the failure of a person to answer or deny in court (or out of court) conduct or acts which give rise to civil liability is generally deemed to be affirmative evidence of that conduct or acts. The invocation of the Fifth Amendment would not seem to be applicable to noncriminal cases, but the courts have not always so construed the privilege against self-incrimination. In *Berner v. Schlesinger*, the New York Supreme Court, Nassau County, on April 28, 1958, held that "as to the two matters concerning which the debtor refused to testify on constitutional grounds (Fifth Amendment) the debtor will not be compelled to testify. If an answer may tend to accuse a person of a crime he may not be required to furnish 'a single link in a chain of facts capable of being used to his detriment or peril.' "

In *Travelers Fire Insurance Co. v. Wright,* decided by the Oklahoma Supreme Court on February 25, 1958, recovery was sought upon two insurance policies. The carrier defended upon the ground that plaintiff's property was deliberately destroyed with the intent of cheating and defrauding the carrier. The court reversed a $20,000 jury verdict, and pointed out that if a witness is called to testify in a civil trial and invokes the privilege against self-incrimination, and his claim of privilege is upheld, his testimony is as unavailable as if he were dead! If the witness indicates that his claim of the privilege is based on fear of prosecution for lack of good faith or truthfulness in his prior testimony, he should not be compelled to testify, according to the Oklahoma court.

In contrast, however, is *Levine v. Bornstein* (174 N.Y.S.2d 574) where the New York court granted a motion dismissing the complaint because the plaintiff, by his claim of the privilege against self-incrimination, had deprived the defendant of the right to develop an affirmative defense which might well destroy the plaintiff's action. In the pre-trial examination, the plaintiff had refused to give details of his claim on the ground that his answers might tend to incriminate him.

### Disbarment Proceedings and the Fifth Amendment

Lawyers have also "taken" the Fifth Amendment under diverse circumstances. Of the 305 individuals claiming the privilege, in 1953, before Congressional committees, for example, fourteen were attorneys (*Cong Rec.,* 3/31/54). Actions for disbarment have often resulted, particularly when the attorney had refused to attend a hearing before his own bar association, although mere refusal to testify was not *ipso facto* the basis for disbarment. Some state bar associations simply "suspended" lawyers who "took" the Fifth Amendment until the bar association had the opportunity to hold a hearing. However, suspension was practically as disastrous economically and professionally as disbarment! It would seem all such measures are much too severe punishment, for ordinary professional disciplines of bench and bar are preferred over public trials.

## The Konigsberg Case

Individuals who invoke the Fifth Amendment in proceedings for admission to the bar have received protection from the U.S. Supreme Court, as illustrated by the *Konigsberg* case (353 U.S. 252). Here, the applicant who passed the California bar exams was suspected of having a background of Communist Party membership. The California State Committee of Bar Examiners refused to approve his application upon the grounds that he had failed to prove he was a person of good moral character and did not advocate the overthrow of the government by unconstitutional means. Specifically, Konigsberg had refused to answer questions about his political affiliations and beliefs. The court noted that he had proved his moral character from forty-two persons who knew him, including a Catholic priest, a Jewish rabbi, lawyers, doctors, professors, and businessmen; and concluded that the evidence tending to indicate Communist leanings, i.e., the testimony of one ex-Communist that Konigsberg attended meetings of the Communist Party in 1941, and had criticized certain public officials in newspaper editorials, was *not* sufficient to justify a finding that Konigsberg had failed to show a good moral character or that he advocated overthrow of the government by unlawful means. Mr. Justice Black, speaking for the six to three majority, declared that the term "good moral character" is unusually ambiguous:

> "It can be defined in an almost unlimited number of ways, for any definition will necessarily reflect the attitudes, experiences, and prejudices of the definer. Such a vague qualification, which is easily adapted to fit personal views and predilections, can be a dangerous instrument for arbitrary and discriminatory denial of the right to practice law . . . . Obviously, the state could not draw unfavorable inferences as to his truthfulness, candor or his moral character in general, if his refusal to answer was based on a belief that the United States Constitution pro-

hibited the type of inquiries which the Committee was making
. . . . A bar composed of lawyers of good character is a worthy
objective but it is unnecessary to sacrifice vital freedoms in
order to obtain that goal . . . . "

On remand, the California Supreme Court referred the case back to the State Bar Committee which held a hearing and warned Konigsberg that his refusal to answer material questions would constitute an independent ground for refusing to certify him for admission to the California bar. Konigsberg refused to answer questions concerning membership in the Communist Party, and the California Supreme Court upheld the Committee (344 P2d 77), basing the denial of certification upon his refusal to answer "material" questions: "That inquiry as to membership in that Party is relevant and material in determining whether the proscribed advocacy (overthrow of government by unlawful means) exists."

On April 24, 1961, the U.S. Supreme Court ruled that the State of California was entitled to get its questions answered in order to make the whole process of inquiry feasible (366 U.S. 36). Mr. Justice Harlan did not state that mere admission of Communist Party membership would be enough to exclude a man from becoming a lawyer, but that the state could judge whether Konigsberg's present views made him unfit! Mr. Justice Brennan dissented on the ground that the burden of proof that Konigsberg did not advocate violent overthrow had been unconstitutionally put on him; three other justices dissented on the basis that the earlier decision had disposed of the case.

### *The Anastaplo Case*

In Illinois, Anastaplo was refused admission to the bar, although he had passed the bar examination in 1950, because he refused to answer questions of the Illinois Supreme Court's Character and Fitness Committee as to his Communist Party membership. But he did state that he believed in the abstract in the doctrine of the overthrow of government by force, and saw nothing contradictory between Party membership and the attorney's oath to support the constitutions. The Committee concluded that his refusal to asnwer questions precluded the Committee from judging his ability to take the oath in good conscience. The Illinois Supreme Court upheld the Committee's refusal to certify him (3 Ill.2d 471) and the U.S. Supreme Court denied an appeal (348 U.S. 946).

In 1956, after the U.S. Supreme Court decided the *Konigsberg* case, *supra,* Anastaplo filed a supplementary petition, and the court directed the committee to give him another hearing. He continued his refusal to answer questions about possible Communist affiliations, and the Illinois committee adhered to its earlier position. The Illinois court affirmed again, in 1959, on the ground of Anastaplo's refusal to answer material and pertinent questions. On April 24, 1961, the U.S. Supreme Court also affirmed (366 U.S. 82) and rejected Anastaplo's contention that he was "lulled into a false sense of security" by statements from members of the committee that refusal to answer would not automatically operate to exclude him from the bar. The court said that he had been repeatedly warned that failure to answer "could and might" result in non-admission; therefore, the "basic and only reason" for denial of his certification as an attorney was his refusal to cooperate with the Committee.

## *The Cohen Case*

The disbarment of an attorney, not because he invoked the privilege against self-incrimination, but because he failed to discharge an obligation and responsibility which he owed to the New York court and thus showed he was unfit to continue to be a member of the legal profession, was upheld, *Cohen v. Hurley.* The attorney Cohen was required by subpoena to testify and to produce records in a judicial inquiry into illegal and unethical practices by attorneys in the procurement and prosecution of negligence cases. He invoked the Fifth Amendment. The New York Appellate Division, 2nd Dept., on December 31, 1959, held that it is the duty of an attorney to aid the court in such an inquiry, to obey its rules and orders, to respond to all relevant questions put by the court, and to refrain from any act which may thwart the inquiry or impede the administration of justice. The constitutional privilege against self-incrimination does not protect an attorney from disbarment, which is not a punishment for wrongdoing, but simply the means of removing from the legal profession one who is unfit to be engaged in the practice of law.

On April 1, 1960, the New York Court of Appeals affirmed the disbarment, holding that Cohen was under an obligation to give his full cooperation in a judicial inquiry and investigation, and his refusal to answer questions was a breach of his duty as an officer of the court (7 N.Y.2d 488). On June 24, 1961, the U.S. Supreme Court ruled that Cohen was properly disbarred, because there was no arbitrary denial of due process since Cohen had been duly warned of the consequences of his refusal to answer the material questions (366 U.S. 117):

> "We do not hold that lawyers, because of their special status in society, can therefore be deprived of constitutional rights assured to others, but only, as in all cases of this kind, that what procedures are fair, what state process is constitutionally due, what distinctions are consistent with the right to equal protection, all depend upon the particular situation presented . . . . "

But Mr. Justice Black, joined by Chief Justice Warren and Mr. Justice Douglas, wrote a vigorous dissent, arguing that the majority's theory "constitutes nothing less than a denial to lawyers of both due process and equal protection" since it separated lawyers into a special group with special burdens not borne by others. Mr. Justice Douglas dissented upon the ground that the court was "downgrading" the Fifth Amendment, and that there was no exception in that amendment for lawyers anymore than for others.

## Deportation Hearings and the Fifth Amendment

The widespread belief that the Fifth Amendment situation detracted from the power of the government to combat Communism, was certainly not true in the usual deportation hearing. In the *Bonetti* case (356 U.S. 691), the highest Court dealt with an alien who entered the United States in 1923, left the Communist Party in 1936, departed from the United States in 1937, and returned in 1938, disclosing his past Communist Party membership. Under the pertinent statute, an alien was deportable if he had been a Communist at any time after "entry" into the United

## Self-incrimination and the Fifth Amendment 113

States. The question centered about whether his "entry" was 1923 or 1938, and the court determined that deportability depended upon whether he was a Communist *since* his 1938 entry when he was not a Communist! Mr. Justice Whittaker pointed out the novel facts of this case would not set a precedent whereby Communists could neutralize their records by leaving the country and returning!

In *United States v. Witkovich* (353 U.S. 194), an alien refused to answer a large number of questions asked by the Attorney General as to his association with various groups and persons (such as "Do you know the editor of Narodni Glasnik?" "Do you know Anton Minerich?" "Are you now a member of the Communist Party, U.S.A.?" and "Have you attended any meetings at the Chopin Cultural Center?"). The lower federal court held these questions were outside the Attorney General's authority under the statute: the alien could only be questioned to elicit "such information as is necessary to enable the Attorney General to be certain that the alien is holding himself in readiness to answer the call to be deported when it comes." The U.S. Supreme Court affirmed against the government because the power of interrogation and supervision is aimed at the "availability for deportation," and the information solicited by the questions would only "serve as a basis for confining an alien's activities."

The U.S. Supreme Court, in *Truax v. Raich* (239 U.S. 33), had solemnly declared that all the guarantees under the Fifth Amendment apply equally to aliens and to all persons within our borders. An order of deportation is not equivalent to a finding that the person has been especially dangerous, as compared with a non-deportable member of the population, and most certainly it represented no findings as to the alien's current propensities. But an alien is deportable for crimes involving moral turpitude committed at any time after entry; membership in the Communist Party at any time after entry, even where the alien has no knowledge of its aim of violence or was "duped into joining," is ground for deportation, *Galvan v. Press* (347 U.S. 522) and *Niukkanen v. McAlexander* (362 U.S. 390).

In *Kimm v. Rosenberg* (363 U.S. 405), the petitioner invoked the Fifth Amendment when asked if he was a member of the Communist Party, and was ordered to be deported to Korea. Neither the Board of Immigration Appeals nor the U.S. Court of Appeals supported him in seeking suspension of the order of deportation. In 1960, the U.S. Supreme Court affirmed, upon the ground that the burden of proof on non-membership in the Communist Party was upon him because party membership constituted an absolute disqualification for suspension. Of the four dissenting opinions Mr. Justice Douglas argued that, in effect, the majority of five Justices was allowing invocation of the Fifth Amendment to serve as proof that an alien lacked the "good moral character" he must have to be eligible for suspension of the deportation order: invocation of the privilege against self-incrimination is a neutral act and consistent with innocence as with guilt!

### School Board Hearings and the Fifth Amendment

In the *Beilan* case (357 U.S. 399), the highest court, by a five to four vote, resolved the question of the status of a Pennsylvania school teacher who was discharged as "incompetent" when he refused to answer the school superintendent's question about his Communist activities. Beilan had been called in to the superintendent's office and told that he would be asked one question, and that he could then decide whether he wished to answer other questions of the same type. The question asked was whether or not he had been the Press Director of the Professional Section of the Communist Political Association in 1944. When Beilan appeared at a later meeting, he declined to answer the question or any other questions "similar to it" or "questions about political or religious beliefs." He was warned that the affair was "very serious," and that "failure to answer the questions might lead to his dismissal." The school board thereupon conducted a hearing upon the charge that Beilan's refusal to answer constituted "incompetency" under Section 1122 of the Pennsylvania Public School Code of 1949. Beilan was discharged, and each appeal through various administrative and judicial tribunals did not change the result. In 1958, the U.S. Supreme Court similarly affirmed his dismissal:

> "By engaging to teach in the public schools (he) did not give up his right to freedom of belief, speech or association. He

did, however, undertake obligations of frankness, candor and cooperation in answering inquiries made of him by his employing Board examining into this fitness to serve it as a public school teacher . . . The question asked of (him) by his superintendent was relevant to the issue of . . . fitness and suitability to serve as a teacher. . . . The Board based its dismissal upon (his) refusal to answer any inquiry about his relevant activities—not upon those activities themselves. It took care to charge (him) with incompetency, and not with disloyalty. It found him insubordinate and lacking in frankness and candor . . . . . "

The dissenting opinion of Mr. Justices Douglas and Black "would allow no inference of wrongdoing to flow from the invocation of any constitutional right . . . . When we make the belief of the citizen the basis of government action, we move toward the concept of total security (which) is possible only in a totalitarian regime."

On the other hand, in *Shelton v. Tucker* (364 U.S. 479), in 1960, the highest court declared an Arkansas statute which required every teacher in the public school system to file an affidavit listing without limitation every organization to which he had belonged or regularly contributed during the past five years, to be invalid. The court opined that compelling a teacher to so disclose impaired his freedom of association:

"Even though the governmental purpose be legitimate and substantial, the purpose cannot be pursued by means that broadly stifle fundamental personal liberties when the end can be more narrowly achieved."

### The Jencks Case and Inspection of the Evidence

In June 1957, in the *Jencks* case (353 U.S. 657), the U.S. Supreme Court demonstrated great concern for the protection and preservation of the individual right of an accused to force the government to produce documents relative to testimony of its witnesses against the individual (who may also have pleaded the Fifth Amendment). Jencks, a New Mexico labor organizer, was accused of lying when he filed a non-communist affidavit under the Taft-Hartley Act. Among the government witnesses were two paid informers, Harvey Matusow (who later recanted) and Ford who had submitted written as well as oral reports on Jencks to the FBI and the Justice Department. The lower courts ruled that Jencks was not entitled to inspect these reports because he had not laid a preliminary foundation of inconsistency between the contents of those reports and the testimony of the witnesses! But the U.S. Supreme Court declared that Jencks had a right to see the reports in an effort to show a conflict between the witnesses' testimony in court and the reports previously written. Furthermore, Jencks should be permitted to cross-examine witnesses on these reports. The government refused to produce the reports, and the lower court subsequently dismissed the case against Jencks.

Within three months, Congress enacted Public Law 269 (18 U.S.C. 3500) giving the trial judge the discretion and ultimate decision whether government reports should be available to the defense. The law, nullifying the *Jencks* decision, provided that no discovery could be allowed of statements or reports of the government until the witness had actually testified for the government on direct examination. In August 1958, the statute was held not applicable to the minutes of a federal grand jury, *United States v. Spanglet* (258 F.2d 338); the defendant was denied the right to examine the grand jury testimony of the government's major witness against him. Two weeks later, the same Second U.S. Court of Appeals, in the *Palermo* case (258 F.2d 397), declared that the statute was "the exclusive standard in this field and controls the procedure;" defendant convicted of income tax evasion was desirous of obtaining a written memorandum prepared by the I.R.S. agents sometime after a conference with a witness who subsequently testified for the government. The court similarly held that Palermo was not entitled to the statement because it was not a "substantially verbatim recital," the statement being merely a summary of the agent's recollection. The U.S. Supreme Court agreed (360 U.S. 343):

> "The act's major concern is with limiting and regulating defense access to government papers, and it is designed to deny such access to those statements which . . . . do not relate to the subject matter of the witness' testimony. It would indeed de-

feat his design to hold that the defense may see statements in order to argue whether it should be allowed to see them."

And in *Campbell and Lester v. United States* (365 U.S. 85) the highest court, in 1961, reviewed a prosecution for bank robbery in which a government witness who identified a defendant as one of the robbers, stated on cross-examination that he had "told the story" to a government agent who took down what he had said and read it back to him. The prosecutor stated that he had no such paper, only an "interview-report" prepared after the meeting. The court declared that the government agent who prepared the "interview report" should have been called as a witness by the trial judge to ascertain whether there was such a paper as the witness described and, if there was and if the report was not that paper, what became of it. Thus, error was committed for failure to verify the existence or non-existence of the report.

## Motives for "Taking the Fifth"

Professor Daniel H. Pollitt of the University of North Carolina Law School in the June 1958 issue of *Pennsylvania Law Review* reported on the results of his personal survey of 120 witnesses (out of 368) who during 1953 and 1954 "took the Fifth Amendment" before a Congressional committee inquiring into Communist Party membership. His questionnaire was designed to elicit what possible motives could justify the individual in keeping his silence at the expense of "cloaking his guilt." Professor Pollitt's three lines of injury were: (a) how did background data tend to support inferences of guilt or innocence; (b) how severe was the public condemnation, and (c) what reasons were given for refusing to answer. His conclusion was simply that there was no basis for the term, "Fifth Amendment Communist" since most witnesses did so for reasons apart from fear of incrimination, thus weakening the very fiber of the argument that the withheld answer was adverse to the interest of the witness "taking the Fifth." According to Professor Pollitt, the following "reasons" were assigned by these witnesses for pleading the Fifth Amendment, in the order of priority: (a) belief that the question infringed upon the witness' freedom of speech, association, or conscience; (b) fear that answering a particular question would "waive" the right to refuse to answer questions concerning the identity of others; (c) fear of perjury indictment if questions are answered in the negative; (d) desire to protect the integrity of the Fifth Amendment or to support the position of others who had relied upon it; (e) belief that reliance on the Fifth Amendment is the only safe way to refuse to cooperate with the committee; (f) belief that the question is not pertinent to the committee's business; (g) fear that answering a particular question would "waive" the right to plead the Fifth Amendment when asked other questions about own activities; (h) fear that an answer would cause public humiliation, economic hardship, or social ostracism; and (i) other and miscellaneous reasons, including the Sixth, Ninth, and Tenth Amendment, and the due process clause of the Fourteenth Amendment.

It is thus evident that few if any witnesses invoked the Fifth Amendment upon the necessary legal grounds.

### Waiver of the Privilege Against Self-incrimination

Under certain conditions and circumstances, the privilege against self-incrimination may be waived. By answering preliminary questions as to name and address, a person may find that he has waived his privilege if what he will say cannot incriminate him anymore than what he had already said. But mere admission of membership in the Communist Party does not constitute a waiver of the privilege to refuse to give details as to Communist activities and association (*Nelson v. United States,* 103 F. Supp. 215, 1952).

In *Brown v. United States* (356 U.S. 148), the U.S. Supreme Court held, in a five to four decision, that Mrs. Brown, in a civil denaturalization proceeding, had waived her privilege against self-incrimination once she took the stand in her own behalf. She had been charged with fraudulently obtaining her citizenship, in 1946, by falsely swearing that she was attached to the principles of the Constitution and that she was not at that time, nor had she been for ten years a member of the Communist Party or any organization teaching the overthrow of the government by unlawful means. At the hearing, she was called as a witness by the government and denied party membership prior to 1946, although she admitted having once been a member of the Young Communist League. She thereupon claimed the privilege as to questions concerning party membership or activities and association which were unlimited in time or directed to the period after 1946. She later took the stand as a witness in her own behalf, and reaffirmed the truthfulness of the statements contained in her application for naturalization. She also stated that she had never been a member of a subversive organization, nor had she ever taught or advocated overthrow of the government. On cross-examination, when the government sought to question her as to her Communist activities after 1946, she refused to answer upon the basis of the privilege against self-incrimination. The federal district court ruled that by taking the stand in her own defense, she waived the privilege, and ordered her to answer. The U.S. Court of Appeals affirmed the conviction for contempt (234 F.2d 140), and the U.S. Supreme Court likewise affirmed:

> "Such a voluntary witness has no choice, after weighing the advantage of the privilege against self-incrimination against the advantage of putting her version of the facts and her reliability as a witness not to testify at all. She cannot reasonably claim the Fifth Amendment gives her only this choice, but, if she elects to testify, an immunity from cross-examination on matters she has herself put in dispute. It would make of the Fifth Amendment not only a human safeguard against judicially coerced self-disclosure, but a positive invitation to mutilate the truth a party offers to tell . . ."

The dissent of Mr. Justice Black argued that the rule of waiver relied upon by the five-judge majority should be confined to criminal cases where an accused's failure to take the stand may not be adversely commented upon by the prosecutor or judge. To apply the criminal law waiver rule here placed the defendant in a dilemma: if she testifies voluntarily, she can be made to give incriminating evidence against herself; but if she does not testify, her silence can be used against her since the failure of a party to testify in a civil action may be freely commented upon by the adversary. Mr. Justice Brennan dissented upon the ground that refusal to answer questions cannot be considered as contempt when the witness believes that the Fifth Amendment affords a privilege to refuse to answer.

In *United States v. Cleary,* the Second U.S. Court of Appeals, in March 1959, reviewed the dismissal of an indictment of the defendant for thefts from the U.S. mail and for conspiracy to commit mail thefts. Cleary, after arrest and in response to a subpoena, appeared before a grand jury; although he was warned of his rights, he testified at length deeply incriminating himself. He was in dicted but the district court (164 F. Supp. 328) dismissed the indictment contending that his testimony was improperly received unless it could be found that at that time he had *waived his* privilege against self-incrimination with full knowledge of the protection the privilege afforded him. The district court felt that Cleary did not fully understand his rights, but the appellate court ruled that his testimony was completely voluntary for he has been explicitly advised before he testified and had been similarly advised on four earlier occasions since his arrest that he need not answer any incriminating question:

> "Appearing before a grand jury is not in itself an unduly coercive situation . . . . And there are no additional facts here to indicate coercion. That he was nervous and confused during his testimony—a not unusual reaction of a witness—is not sufficient to render the testimony involuntary . . . . We do not see that the circumstances under which appellee's indictment was procured reveal the slightest injustice to him or afford any basis for believing that he will not receive a fair trial in due course."

### Corporate Entity and the Fifth Amendment

The privilege against self-incrimination belongs to an individual and not to a corporate entity. In *Hale v. Henkel* (210 U.S. 43) the highest court declared that "corporations under state law are subject to the state's visitorial power to inspect corporate records to prevent violations of corporate charters," and this so-called visitorial powers doctrine predominates over any privilege against self-incrimination. The reasoning of the U.S. Supreme Court was that "the federal system" requires that powers such as commerce and taxation, delegated by the states under the Constitution to the federal government, "include state visitorial power over corporations" to facilitate effective national government. Thus, the corporation is denied the *federal* privilege against self-incrimination under the Fifth Amendment guarantees to any "person." In this case, the defendant was an officer of an incorporated association who refused to obey a subpoena to produce corporate records in his custody because "their compulsory production would violate both his and the corporation's constitutional privileges against self-incrimination." Since the grand jury had subpoenaed the *officer* rather than the *corporation,* the court held that, even if corporations enjoy the privilege, this was not a proper case for its invocation.

Relying upon the *Hale* case, the U.S. Supreme Court in *United States v. White* (322 U.S. 694) denied an officer of an *unincorporated* labor union both the Fourth and Fifth Amendment privileges interposed against a grand jury subpoena. The court held that no association could claim the privilege if—

> " . . . one can fairly say under all the circumstances that a particular type of organization has a character so impersonal in the scope of its membership and activities that it cannot be said to embody or represent the purely private and personal interests of its constituents, but rather to embody their common or group interests only."

But even the limited privilege granted in the *White* case was contracted by cases such as *Shapiro v. United States* (335 U.S. 1) in which the required records doctrine was invented. Gradually one department of government after another have required that documents be filed or maintained. The government then has asserted a right to inspect the documents and has maintained it can do so free from both the Fourth and Fifth Amendment privileges.

### Federal Immunity Statutes and the Fifth Amendment

To meet the problem of the Fifth Amendment in criminal prosecutions, a practice of exchanging amnesty for information was long ago established. The first immunity law was adopted by Congress over one hundred years ago, in order to fill the gap between private privilege and public need for information. Immunity statutes have been enacted in several states, and thereby raised another problem: whether or not a witness can refuse to testify because the federal or state immunity does not extend to possible prosecution in the other jurisdiction. Congress had preempted certain areas involving national security and national defense so that such federal immunity ordinarily encompasses state immunity, and a federal witness once given immunity, could not be prosecuted for that crime involving national security and national defense, either by the state or by the federal government. But once a person is "immunized" he must testify, and the social order cannot be deprived of his testimony. The extent of the immunity granted must be equally as broad as the protection the witness would have under the Fifth Amendment. If he is to be forced to convict himself of a given crime, his immunity must cover in *all* courts that specific crime.

### *The Ullmann Case*

Ullmann was called by a federal grand jury and asked about his knowledge of espionage activities and participation in the Communist Party. He refused to answer upon the Fifth Amendment, and pursuant to the 1954 federal immunity statute, the federal district court ordered him to answer. Upon his refusal, he was found guilty of contempt of court and sentenced to six months in jail. In 1956, the U.S. Supreme Court (360 U.S. 422), in a seven to two decision, upheld the federal immunity statute as not abridging the constitutional privilege against self-incrimination. Mr. Justice Frankfurter dismissed Ullmann's argument that "because the impact of the disabilities imposed by federal and state authorities and the public in general—such as loss of job, expulsion from labor unions, state registration and investigation statutes, passport eligibility, and general public opprobrium—is so oppressive that the statute does not give him true immunity":

> "The immunity granted need only remove those sanctions which generate the fear justifying invocation of the privilege: 'The interdiction of the Fifth Amendment operates only where a witness is asked to incriminate himself—in other words, to give testimony which may possibly expose him to a criminal charge. But if the criminality has already been taken away the Amendment ceases to apply' .... Here since the Immunity Act pro-

tects a witness who is compelled to answer to the extent of his constitutional immunity, he has, of course, when a particular sanction is sought to be imposed against him, the right to claim that it is criminal in nature."

The court also ruled that the federal immunity act had prohibited effectively state prosecutions of federal witnesses for those offenses about which they were compelled to testify in the federal proceedings.

Able dissents by Mr. Justices Douglas and Black argued that "the right of silence created by the Fifth Amendment is beyond the reach of Congress"; also, the federal immunity statute did not protect against loss of important citizenship rights. The privilege against self-incrimination was originally given, according to Mr. Justice Douglas, to protect "the conscience and dignity of the individual, as well as his safety and security, against the compulsion of government." Therefore, the privilege must protect the accused against infamy and its resulting loss of office, dignity and face—which are as effective a punishment as a fine or imprisonment. Mr. Justice Douglas declared that other social consequences not involving potential criminal punishment necessarily result from ordering Ullmann to speak: an answer may tend to degrade a person or subject him to public scorn and infamy, or an answer may result in loss of employment and other economic consequences.

### The Brown Case

In 1959, the U.S. Supreme Court dealt with a defendant who, in the words of Mr. Justice Stewart, was "grasping at straws" in contending that the federal immunity statute did not give him full immunity from prosecution if he testified. In conducting an investigation of possible violations of the Interstate Commerce Act, the federal grand jury had asked the defendant certain questions which he refused to answer. When brought before the federal district court, he was assured by the court that the statute granted him full immunity from prosecution; after a second refusal, he was held in contempt and sentenced to fifteen months in jail. In *Brown v. United States* (359 U.S. 41), the highest court by a five to four decision upheld the contempt conviction, pointing out that the statute was not ambiguous and clearly bestowed an immunity co-extensive with the scope of the privilege against self-incrimination.

## State Immunity Statutes and the Fifth Amendment

### The Knapp Case

In a six to three decision, in *Knapp v. Schweitzer* (357 U.S. 371), the highest court dealt with a witness before a New York grand jury who refused to testify on the ground that his answer might incriminate him, and who was thereupon offered immunity from prosecution for any transaction concerning which he gave an answer. Knapp, a partner in a New York manufacturing firm, was subpoenaed to appear before the grand jury conducting an inquiry into alleged bribery of labor representatives, conspiracy, and extortion. Knapp refused to answer questions about certain wage negotiations and, under New York statute, was granted immunity from state prosecution. But Knapp refused to answer, alleging that the immunity did not protect him against federal prosecution. His conviction was affirmed by all New York courts, and the U.S. Supreme Court, in 1958, declared that Knapp did not have the right to refuse to answer because the Fifth Amendment imposed no restriction on the states and, furthermore, the privilege against self-incrimination does not impair the power of New York to require disclosure in exchange for immunity from state prosecution. To allow Knapp's plea because he might still be exposed to federal prosecution would mean that every witness before a state grand jury proceeding would feel free to block such vitally important proceedings. (The court agreed that if a federal officer were a party to the compulsion of testimony by the state authorities, the Fifth Amendment would come into play.)

The dissent of Mr. Justice Black, joined by Mr. Justice Douglas, felt that the majority view created a situation "where a person can be whipsawed into incriminating himself under both state and federal law, even though there is a privilege against self-incrimination."

## The Mills Case

On the heels of the *Knapp* case came *Mills v. Louisiana* (360 U.S. 230) which delineated the problem of testimony in a state court which the federal government sought to use as the basis for a charge of violation of federal law. Mills was summoned before a state grand jury and interrogated about bribery of public officials and income tax evasion; at the same time, he was under investigation by the Internal Revenue Service. He refused to answer on the privilege against self-incrimination, but was ordered to answer and the Louisiana Supreme Court refused to grant relief. The U.S. Supreme Court also affirmed *per curiam* without an opinion, but the dissenters led by Chief Justice Warren (with Mr. Justices Black and Douglas) argued that the case was one of collaboration between federal and state officials, and that the majority view "means that a person can be convicted of a federal crime on the basis of testimony which he is compelled to give in a state investigation. This opens vast opportunities for calculated efforts by state and federal officials working together to force a disclosure in a state proceeding and to convict on the basis of that disclosure in a federal proceeding." (And in the *Bonanno* decision, the U.S. District Court in New York on October 7, 1959, held that evidence obtained in the course of an investigation by a state agency under a grant of immunity, was admissible in a federal prosecution!)

## The Cioffi and Stein Case

In New York, two attorneys, Cioffi and Stein, refused to testify before the grand jury investigating charges of conspiracy, though both men were told by the district attorney that neither was a prospective defendant or target of investigation. Immunity as provided by New York Law was offered, but each attorney refused to answer whether he was ever employed by a certain law firm under investigation. On appeal, the New York Court of Appeals (8 N.Y.2d 220), in 1960, affirmed the contempts because they had been given "complete immunity as to any and all crimes to which their testimony related."

## The Raley Case

On the other hand, the State of Ohio relied upon its witness-immunity statute as the basis for a contempt conviction of witnesses in *Raley v. Ohio* (360 U.S. 423) for refusing on self-incrimination grounds to answer certain questions after the Ohio agency had assured them that the privilege against self-incrimination was available. The U.S. Supreme Court reversed and held that this state action was a type of "entrapment" that violated the due process clause of the Fourteenth Amendment.

The failure of a Virginia legislative committee on racial activities to clearly inform a recalcitrant witness of the purpose of the inquiry and the pertinency of the questions concerning his activities in racial integration groups, was held to invalidate the contempt conviction after the witness invoked the Fifth Amendment in *Scull v. Virginia* (359 U.S. 353).

## State Immunity and Federal Immunity Under the Fifth Amendment

In 1944, in *Feldman v. United States* (322 U.S. 487), it was held that testimony first compelled in a state proceeding does *not* give immunity to a subsequent prosecution in a federal court on the basis of that testimony. And, in the 1947 case of *Adamson v. California* (332 U.S. 46), the highest court, by a five to four vote declared that the Fifth Amendment did *not* apply to state proceedings, although Mr. Justice Black, after searching the history of the Fourteenth Amendment, made a powerful argument for the privilege against self-incrimination to be applied in state proceedings. The immunity hassle centered about the fact that a state could not grant federal immunity nor immunity beyond its geographical jurisdiction. The states found difficulty in extracting vital testimony without the benefit of a satisfactory immunity statute. The *Knapp* decision, *supra*, in 1958, was not a reassuring solution to the problem.

On June 15, 1964, the U.S. Supreme Court, in *Murphy v. Waterfront Commission*, overruled its 1944 decision in the *Feldman* case and rejected the logic of the *Knapp* case that the federal government could compel testimony by granting immunity only from federal, not state, prosecution. The case arose from proceedings of the New York Waterfront Commission which had subpoenaed Murphy and Moody, two officials of I.L.A. to testify about a work stoppage in Hoboken, N. J. When Murphy and Moody said that they might incriminate themselves, they were granted immunity from prosecution by New York and New Jersey. But they still refused to testify because they feared federal prosecution, and so were held in contempt. A *unanimous* court ordered the commission to proceed and compel testimony, and at the same time prohibited the federal government from thereafter using in its prosecutions testimony compelled in state prosecutions in return for a grant of state immunity. Mr. Justice Goldberg stated that it was erroneous to regard the federal and state governments as being in separate compartments as far as protecting citizens from testifying against themselves. He quoted an 1828 opinion by Chief Justice Marshall who had held that the protection against self-incrimination must be good against all sovereignties:

> "There is no continuing legal vitality to, or historical justification for, the rule that one jurisdiction within our federal structure may compel a witness to give testimony which could be used to convict him of a crime in another . . .
> 
> "We hold that the constitutional privilege protects a state witness against self-incrimination under federal as well as state law, and a federal witness against incrimination under state as well as federal law."

Mr. Justice Harlan, joined by Mr. Justice Clark, rejected the history and constitutional logic of the court, but they favored overruling the 1944 *Feldman* case and prohibiting the federal use of compelled state testimony in the exercise of the U.S. Supreme Court's supervisory power over federal courts: "Increasing interaction between state and federal governments speaks strongly against permitting federal officials to make prosecutional use of testimony which a state has compelled when that same testimony could not constitutionally have been compelled by the federal government and then used against the witness." It will indeed be interesting to watch future developments of the new doctrine.

## Scientific Evidence and the Fifth Amendment

The application of the Fifth Amendment has also been judicially discussed with respect to the introduction of scientific evidence in the courtroom. Voice identification, speedometers, lie detectors, radar speed-detection devices, writing exemplars, intoxication and blood testing, and the like have been the subject of intense litigation. Despite the logical conclusion that such scientific evidence does often tend to incriminate, the introduction of such scientific evidence in court has not been denied. In the *Harper case* (115 Cal. App.2d 776) the California court refused to extend the privilege against self-incrimination to cover physical evidence in the form of handwriting samples which police officers had extracted from the accused for comparison with a signature on an incriminating document; specifically, handwriting samples were held not to be "unwilling testimonial disclosure." Yet the conviction of the defendant was in part in reliance upon this incriminating handwriting. Similarly compelled conduct, such as fingerprinting and blood testing for alcoholic content, have been delineated as negative conduct not pertaining to the veracity of the accused and therefore not protected by the Fifth Amendment. In *People v. Simons,* an indictment was obtained through "compulsory self-incrimination of the defendant by the use of wire-tap recording used as evidence" (made by a duly executed court order). The County Court of Queens County, New York, on December 3, 1959, denied a motion to dismiss the indictment. But in the *Taylor* case (213 S.C. 330), the South Carolina Supreme Court refused to admit into evidence a voice recording of the defendant who had permitted a witness to identify him. Since the voice identification also determined the veracity of the accused, which was being used to convict him of the crime, the court held that the voice identification definitely violated the defendant's privilege against self-incrimination!

### The Breithaupt Case

In *Breithaupt v. Abram* (352 U.S. 432), the highest court ruled on the problem of the constitutionality of taking a sample of a person's blood while he was unconscious after an automobile accident. The blood was then analyzed by a laboratory of skilled technicians who determined that he was intoxicated at the time of the accident. The court pointed out that such tests have become routine in modern life since they are commonly used for those going into the military service and for those applying for marriage licenses. The person's right to have his person held inviolable was far outweighed by the importance of blood tests as a means of detecting drunken driving. The dissenting opinion of Chief Justice Warren (joined in by Mr. Justices Black and Douglas) contended that involuntary blood testing was unconstitutional upon the authority of an earlier *Rochin* case (342 U.S. 165) that condemned the forcible use of a stomach pump to retrieve narcotic pills swallowed by the accused. Mr. Justice Douglas also argued that any form of compulsion to compel people to furnish evidence against themselves should be outlawed!

The coercive apsect of much of this scientific evidence, particularly drunkometer tests and urinary analyses, shocks the judicial sense of justice and fair play. But some such restraint is necessary in today's society, and the Fifth Amendment application to testimony from the lips of the accused is preferable. Protection of privacy is important, but it is better safeguarded by suits between private parties in non-criminal cases.

## Double Jeopardy and the Fifth Amendment

In the absence of effective immunity statutes (at least before the 1964 decision in the *Murphy* case, *supra*), it was likely that a man might be subjected to both federal and state prosecution for the same criminal act. The Fifth Amendment also contains the following clause: "Nor shall any person be subject for the same offense to be twice put in jeopardy of life or limb." This clause in simple terms precluded "double jeopardy."

### *The Bartkus Case*

The defendant was acquitted by a federal court jury, in 1953, on the charge of robbing an Illinois bank. Later, he was prosecuted in an Illinois court for the same bank robbery and given a life sentence under the Illinois habitual-criminal statute. In a five to four decision, the U.S. Supreme Court upheld the second trial and conviction in March 1959, rejecting the argument that a state prosecution after a federal acquittal was not due process of law guaranteed under the Fourteenth Amendment. Mr. Justice Frankfurter opined that (a) the due process clause has never been interpreted to include a flat bar against double jeopardy; and that the states are free under the Constitution to retry prisoners in ways barred to the federal government by the Fifth Amendment, and (b) the basic concepts of Federalism, i.e., coexistence of both federal and state governments, would be violated by barring successive prosecutions by the federal and state governments. If the law were otherwise, Mr. Justice Frankfurter pointed out, the federal government could prevent any state prosecution by trying the man first in any case where one act violated both state and federal statutes:

> "The result would be a shocking and untoward deprivation of the historic right and obligation of the States to maintain peace and order within their confines . . . . Precedent, experience, and reason all support the conclusion that Alfonse Bartkus has not been deprived of due process of law. The Anglo-American system of law is based not upon transcendental revelation but upon the conscience of society ascertained as best as it may be by a tribunal disciplined for the task and environed by the best safeguards for disinterestedness and detachment."

Mr. Justice Black dissented upon the ground that the federal trial barred any subsequent state prosecution, and warned: "After today, prosecutors who lose cases will be quick to try to arrange second trials in another jurisdiction . . . . Similar examples are not hard to find in lands torn by revolution or crushed by dictatorship." Mr. Justice Brennan, in a separate dissent, opined that federal officials had connived in the subsequent state prosecution of Bartkus making it "in effect, a second federal prosecution."

### The Sabella and La Cascia Case

On the other hand, the Second U.S. Court of Appeals on November 13, 1959, in *United States v. Sabella and La Cascia,* ruled that the defendants may not be later tried for the same crime under another statute in which the same act was also made a crime. The defendants had been put in double jeopardy within the meaning of the provision in the Fifth Amendment that no person shall "be subject for the same offense to be twice put in jeopardy of life or limb." The defendants had been in the narcotics trade allegedly selling heroin. According to Judge Friendly:

> "The Fifth Amendment guarantees that when the government has proceeded to judgment on a certain fact situation, there can be no further prosecution of that fact situation alone. The defendant may not later be tried again on that same fact situation, where no significant additional fact need be proved, even though he be charged under a different statute. He may not again be compelled to endure the ordeal of criminal prosecution and the stigma of conviction. These are the plain and well understood commands of the Fifth Amendment in forbidding double jeopardy. Here there was one sale of narcotics. The government should have but one opportunity to prosecute on that transaction . . . . "

## *The Forman Case*

The U.S. Supreme Court held, in *Forman v. United States* (361 U.S. 416), that the double jeopardy rule had no application. The petitioner and one Seijas were convicted of conspiracy to evade the individual income tax of Seijas and his wife. The case was submitted to the jury on a charge directing that the petitioner should be acquitted unless the jury found that there was a subsidiary conspiracy, continuing to within six years of the indictment, to conceal the attempt to evade taxes. The U.S. Court of Appeals reversed and remanded with instructions to enter a judgment of acquittal. However, on rehearing, the U.S. Court of Appeals held that the case might have been tried on an alternative theory that certain of the acts charged in the indictment which took place in 1948, 1951, and 1952 could well have been in furtherance of the conspiracy to evade taxes and not merely to further a conspiracy to conceal the evasion. The highest court in affirming pointed out that when one seeks a reversal of his conviction, "there is no double jeopardy upon a new trial." The Court rejected the petitioner's argument that his right to acquittal "matured" then the Court of Appeals entered its first order: "The original opinion was entirely interlocutory and no mandate was ever issued thereon. It never became final and was subject to further action on rehearing."

### Other Cases on "Double Jeopardy"

In New York, *People v. Fennell,* the Appellate Division, 1st Dept., on March 15, 1960, held that a defendant's acquittal on the trial of a charge of disorderly conduct was not a defense to a prosecution for assault with which he had been separately charged at the same time and which arose from the same occurrence but the proof of which required evidence of different facts:

> "While a defendant may not be placed in jeopardy twice for the same offense . . . . it does not follow that a person may not be convicted of several crimes arising out of the same incident. If the crimes are separate and distinct as a matter of law, a defendant may be convicted of each, although the facts may be closely related."

Similarly, in *United States v. Gori,* the Second U.S. Court of Appeals on July 22, 1960, held that an accused had not been put in jeopardy when the district judge during the district attorney's interrogation of the witness and without the request or consent of the accused, declared a mistrial either for the purpose of protecting the rights of the accused or to punish the district attorney for what the judge regarded as disobedience. The proceedings which were thus terminated did not bar putting the accused on trial anew.

### Selected Bibliography

*Dennis v. United States,* 341 U.S. 494, 1951.
*Service v. Dulles,* 354 U.S. 363, 1957.
*Cole v. Young,* 351 U.S. 536, 1957.
*United States v. Rosenberg,* 245 F.2d 870, aff'g 360 U.S. 367, 1958.
*Pittsburgh Plate Glass Co. v. United States,* 360 U.S. 395, 1958.
*United States v. Tomaiolo,* 280 F.2d 411.
*In Re Summers,* 325 U.S. 573.
*Roviaro v. United States,* 353 U.S. 53, 1957.
Vol. 50 *American Bar Association Journal* 497, May 1964.

*Black v. Cutter Laboratories,* 351 U.S. 292, 1957.
*Grunewald v. United States,* 353 U.S. 391, 1957.

## Questions for Review

1. Why had so few states, in colonial days, enacted provisions in their constitutions about the privilege against self-incrimination? Explain the historical background to our Fifth Amendment.
2. Is the "privilege" available to both defendants and to witnesses in a criminal proceeding? Is the "privilege" an integral, substantive right?
3. Is the presumptive *guilt* theory of the "privilege" a logical or a moral involvement? Is this theory applicable to any ordinary criminal trial where the defendant remains silent?
4. What is the inherent "wrong" in the loyalty oath affidavits required for educational benefits under the National Defense Education Act of 1958?
5. Why is the "privilege" personal, belonging to the individual and not to a *group* of persons? Must an individual *prove* his contention that he will be incriminated by his testimony?
6. Is the *Slochower* decision consistent with the "presumptive innocence" theory?
7. Does a state or a city have a constitutional right to discharge its public employees for merely invoking the "privilege?" Does a private employer have the same right? Explain.
8. Is the doctrine of separation of powers between judicial, legislative, and executive a necessary involvement in the U.S. Supreme Court's decisions on the privilege against self-incrimination? Explain.
9. Are the decisions in the *Barenblatt* and *Slochower* cases consistent with each other? Was there a "clear and present danger" to established institutions in both decisions?
10. Why are confrontation of witnesses against the accused and the right of cross-examination necessary procedural safeguards in every case where the individual invokes the Fifth Amendment?
11. What is the innate "wrong" in one-man legislative committee investigation? Can the "defect" be cured?
12. Does the Fifth Amendment "privilege" today extend to citizens in state court proceedings? Explain what happens to the trial judge's discretion as to the invocation of the privilege.

13. Is the "privilege" available in a *civil* matter between two or more private parties?
14. As an officer of the court, should an attorney be held to a higher standard than the ordinary citizen in invoking the Fifth Amendment? Is disbarment an effective deterrent?
15. Is an alien entitled to invoke the "privilege" in the same manner as a citizen? Explain.
16. May a public school teacher be discharged simply for invoking the "privilege?" Why is conduct, demeanor and other criteria for employment an integral part of the procedure?
17. Why should an accused be entitled to inspect the government's records against him? Was Public Law 269, of 1957, constitutional in limiting access to such government records?
18. Is waiver of the "privilege" a common fact in situations where the Fifth Amendment has been invoked? When does a waiver amount to coercion?
19. Should a "corporation" be entitled to "take the Fifth?" Would it hamper regulation of business?
20. What is an "immunity statute?" How does it bridge the gap between a private privilege and a public need for information?
21. Can the states give "immunity" from prosecution? Is *federal* "immunity" preferable and why?
22. What is the significance of the *Murphy* decision by the U.S. Supreme Court on June 15, 1964?
23. Why has scientific evidence which incriminates a person not been barred by the Fifth Amendment? Is there a difference between testimonial compulsion and a blood-alcohol test result?
24. What is meant by "double jeopardy" under the Fifth Amendment? Does a state conviction bar a subsequent federal or another state conviction? Explain.

# Chapter V

# SOCIAL UTILITY ASPECTS OF LIBEL AND SLANDER LAW

### Introduction to Defamation

THE LAW OF DEFAMATION involves libel, which is written or published, and slander, which is oral or spoken; in addition, there is criminal libel which is written defamation and involves the protection of the public interest. The legitimate social ends of regulating individual conduct and of solving, in part, practical human problems in society are served by recognition of the legal limits of defamation. An individual's interest in his reputation (the privilege not to be defamed) must be reconciled with the interests of society in the free exchange of opinions and ideas. Freedom of speech and freedom of the press, guaranteed under the First Amendment, are basic to our democratic society; but the right to persuade, to form minorities, or to seek equality of status or employment, for example, are not absolute, for such freedom to act or speak or write must not infringe upon the privacy of others who similarly are entitled to the enjoyment of these basic liberties. The law of defamation seeks to protect the interest of the individual whose reputation has been or is about to be harmed by another's untrue and unprivileged accusation. In *Speed v. Johnson Publishing Co.*, the New York City Court, New York County, on March 30, 1961, tersely set forth the applicable principles:

> "The defamation is actionable, without allegation or proof of special damages, if it tends to expose a person to hatred, contempt, or aversion, or to induce an evil or unsavory opinion of him in the minds of a substantial number of the community, even though it may impute no moral turpitude to him . . . . A false accusation which dishonors or discredits a person in the

estimate of the public or his friends and acquaintances, or has a reasonable tendency to do so is libelous . . . . "

"It has been held that matter is defamatory if it tends to make a person shunned or avoided . . . . or if it tends to induce an evil opinion of him in the minds of right-thinking persons and to deprive him of their confidence and friendly intercourse in society . . . .

"The law of defamation is concerned only with injuries to one's reputation . . . . and a communication is defamatory if it tends . . . . to deter third persons from associating with him . . . . or to diminish his respectability or to change his position in society for the worse . . . . "

Here, the New York court held that the publication—"Sam Cooke, whose record, 'You Send Me' is a juke box hit, is romancing Connie Pitts who sings with the Daniel Singers, a gospel group" —was defamatory, because the statement did not mention that Connie Pitts was "a married woman and a mother, many of whose social and professional contacts center around church and religious groups where the matter published would particularly injure her reputation and tend to expose her to contempt." The statement attacking her personality was, of course, false, and she recovered for her injury to her reputation.

On the other hand, in *Rudolph v. E. W. Scripps Co.* (169 N.E.2d 300) the Ohio appellate court, in 1959, found that the false newspaper headline, "Building Condemned, "Fourteen Homeless" did not defame the building owner and house painter:

"To make the words actionable because of their effect upon one's business or office, they must be said with deference to something connected with such business or office. There are many reasons why a house could be condemned without reflecting upon the owner's reputation, and such words in themselves do not adversely affect the plaintiff in his occupation."

### The Nature of the Legal Remedy for Defamation

The remedy afforded by the law of libel and slander entitles the person defamed to recover from the defamer the monetary damages suffered thereby. The victim of the defamation in his private lawsuit against the defamer must generally prove that the defendant-defamer (a) acted with malice; (b) uttered or published specific defamatory remarks which designated the plaintiff; (c) defamed in the presence of other persons; (d) defamed falsely and (e) uttered or published a defamation calculated to produce (and which did produce) a particular adverse reaction in a substantial number of respectable or right-thinking persons who heard or read the defamation.

This latter requirement of a sizeable and moral segment of the community to attest to the defamation is not always capable of definitiveness or certainty. Mr. Justice Oliver Wendell Holmes once defined a "word" as "not a crystal, transparent and unchanged; it is the skin of living thought and may vary greatly in color and content according to the circumstances and the time in which the word is used." Therefore, it must be appreciated that a "word" which is defamatory today may well be a "word" of praise tomorrow! But, despite the vagueness of the standard of what constitutes defamation, the judgment of a substantial number of respectable citizens of the community is the preferred gauge of liability!

Some courts which are vigilant in protecting the individual's reputation are apt to broaden the limits of the libel or slander, and permit great latitude to the victim of the defamation. The degree of proof required may vary from state to state and even be dependent upon the identity of the person defamed! Still other courts encourage freedom of discussion in those areas where society's interest is paramount, and strictly require the plaintiff to prove his defamatory injury perhaps even beyond a reasonable doubt!

Where the slanderous or libelous remark is of a particularly serious and substantial nature, the court may deem the remark to be *slander per se* or *libel per se*, and presume general damages resulted without requiring proof of actual damages sustained by the victim of the defamation. A defamation which imputes to the victim the commission of a serious crime, or certain loathesome diseases, unchastity (for a woman), or adversity directly affecting the victim's business, trade or profession, are examples of the defamation *per se* variety, as illustrated by the following cases:—

*Gersten v. Newark Morning Ledger Co.* (145 A.2d 56) —The New Jersey Superior Court in 1958 held that it was libelous *per se* for the defendant to publish falsely that the township attorney was having "wife trouble" and that he was being sued for divorce. The court opined that "a substantial segment of the respectable population" regarded divorce as "disgraceful and even sinful," and therefore the plaintiff's reputation in his legal profession was injured.

*Thompson v. Upton* (146 A.2d 880) —The Maryland Court of Appeals in 1958 found that statements in a nasty letter written by a disgruntled citizen to the mayor were libelous *per se*. The defendant's letter stated in part: "As nearly as I can determine, your tin-horn cop sits in nearby concealment sipping beer until he sees a car parked over twelve minutes at a defective meter . . . then sneaks over, places a ticket on the car, and then hustles back to his beer. I can smell skunk perfume a long way, and this definitely smells like a racket, whether to raise money for the police, or to divert trade to the shopping center across Baltimore Blvd." The defendant claimed the whole thing was a joke, but the Court took a serious attitude and held that the letter imputed qualities to the policeman which would make him unfit to serve, warrant his discharge, and even subject him to public scorn and ridicule.

*Texas Plastics Co. v. Roto-Lith, Ltd.* (250 E.2d 844) : The Fifth U.S. Court of Appeals found that calling a businessman falsely "a cheap chiseller" and "a crook" was slanderous *per se*.

*Grein v. La Poma* (340 P.2d 766) : The Washington court, in 1959, ruled that the oral charge that the plaintiffs were "Communists" was slanderous *per se*.

In contrast, in the following cases, the court found no defamation *per se:*—

*Reoux v. Glens Falls Post Co.* (18 Misc.2d 1097) : The New York court, in 1959, held that calling the plaintiff "contumacious" (i.e., stubborn) was not defamatory *per se*.

*Surdi v. Dallmar* (—N.Y.S.2d—) : The New York Supreme Court, Suffolk County, in March 1959, examined the following spoken statement: "The only reason you (the plaintiff) are for the auditorium is that you will get the electrical contract. You know damn well you've got it all sewed up." The court ruled the statement was not slanderous *per se* "in the setting and under the circumstances" in which the words were uttered.

*Adler v. Lois* (–N.Y.S.2d–) : The New York Supreme Court, New York County, in April 1959, ruled that the following words uttered to a policeman were not slanderous *per se*. "He (the plaintiff) is wanted by the FBI. If you come quickly you can pick him up." The court declared that these words "without further allegation of extrinsic facts alleging a specific crime involving moral turpitude" were not actionable.

## Property Rights, Personality, and Employment Opportunities Under Attack

Attacks upon property rights, personality, and employment opportunities have figured most prominently in defamation actions. Libelous matter, rather than slander, has been the media, because as Judge Cardozo so concisely put it, in *Ostrowe v. Lee* (256 N.Y. 36, 1939) : "What gives the sting to the writing is its permanence of form. The spoken word dissolves, but the written one abides and perpetuates the scandal." A majority of courts have deemed libel actionable without the necessity of proof that any damages have actually occurred, so that most libels are deemed to be libels *per se.*

The New York Appellate Division, 2nd Dept., on December 15, 1959, in the *Group Health Insurance, Inc.* case, which allegedly involved unnecessary medical treatment, held that charges that the plaintiff physician "rendered services in a particular case which were not required in accordance with accepted standards of medical practice or medical care" were not libelous *per se,* and therefore the complaint was properly dismissed:

> "The language complained of does not charge appellant with malpractice, as there is no statement, express or implied, that the patient was injured by plaintiff's treatment . . . Neither does that language impute such a charge of general professional, ignorance, want of skill, or carelessness, as to be defamatory *per se."*

In *Clevenger v. Baker, Voorhis & Co.,* the highest New York court on July 8, 1960, opined that the defendant publisher had libeled the plaintiff, a legal writer and editor, by publishing a legal treatise with his name on it, which treatise gave the erroneous impression that he had revised and edited it. Furthermore, it was shown that the treatise contained numerous errors which were attributed to him by lawyers using the treatise. The court ruled that plaintiff's reputation as a legal writer and editor was consequently damaged by the libel.

A different result pertained in *Steward v. World Wide Automobile Corp.*, in which Mr. Justice Shapiro of the New York Supreme Court, Queens County, on July 10, 1959, wrote a lengthy opinion on the following utterances:

> "He (meaning the plaintiff) has a police record as long as your arm; he has been arrested many times, and is a notorious character . . . . his name is upon every police blotter in Long Island . . . "

Plaintiff alleged that these words "were circulated amongst the automobile trade . . . calculated and intended they would . . . injure his reputation, credit, good name, and business standing, and was a factor in the loss of his position." The court specifically ruled that these utterances were not slander *per se* because they did *not* (a) impute some loathesome or offensive disease to the plaintiff; (b) charge plaintiff with a crime involving moral turpitude, nor (c) attack him in relation to his business or trade. Furthermore, the court opined that "one who utters a slander . . . is not responsible for its voluntary and unjustifiable repetition, without his authority or request, by others over whom he has no control who thereby make themselves liable to the person injured." However, there was no slander *per se* nor evidence of any *prima facie* tort.

In *Teichner v. Bellan,* the New York Appellate Division, Fourth Dept., in February 1959, reviewed a libel action in which the plaintiff-physician sent defendant's account to a credit bureau for collection. In response to the credit bureau's letter, the defendant debtor charged the plaintiff with assault, unethical, illegal, despicable and unprofessional conduct. The court initially ruled that there was a "publication" of the defamatory matter, even though the credit bureau was the agent of the plaintiff; but finally held that the defendant had *a qualified privilege* created by the demand for payment of the bill to set forth his reasons for nonpayment. Furthermore, defendant's statement was made without malice, according to the Court, and therefore not actionable.

### The Right of Privacy and Defamation

Many people prize above all else their reputation, and seek recompense for any attack upon their personality, whether defamatory or simply an interference with their right to be left alone. A 1960 English case, *Cassidy v. The Daily Mirror,* aptly illustrates: "General Corrigan" was accompanying a certain young lady to the races when approached by a reporter; he innocently remarked that "you may say that we are engaged." The plaintiff, Mrs. Cassidy and the wife of "General Corrigan" was annoyed, to say the least, and sued the newspaper. Mr. Justice Scrutton allowed her damages for the injury to her interest in her reputation, though the newspaper neither knew that he (or it) was dealing in defamatory matters, nor that there was a plaintiff wife!

In *Hewitt v. Wasek* (35 Misc. 2d 946) the New York court, in 1962, held that the words "affair with a married man" were not defamatory *per se*. The plaintiff was a married woman, but the court ruled that "an affair between married people during any particular period or at any given time does not necessarily involve sexual intimacy." In contrast was *Deshotel v. Thistlethwaite* (121 So.2d 222) in which the Louisiana court, in 1960, declared that a newspaper was liable for falsely charging an attorney (running for Congress) with refusal to fly and taking off his wings during Naval air service in Korea. The fact was that the plaintiff had merely asked for a transfer to legal officer duties, but the imputation of the libel was otherwise.

Thus, a set of facts which give rise to defamatory utterances or statements may not be actionable either as libel or slander; the plaintiff may also recover upon the basis of an invasion of right of privacy under the common law of the state.

### Product Defamation

Like a person or personality, a product may be defamed or disparaged so as to cause damages which demand relief. In *Harwood Pharmacal Co. v. National Broadcasting Co.,* the New

York Supreme Court, New York County, in March 1959, examined the following utterance over television as defaming or disparaging a product: "*Snooze*, the new aid for sleep. *Snooze* is full of all kinds of habit-forming drugs. Nothing short of a hospital cure will make you stop taking *Snooze*. You'll feel like a run-down hound dog and lose weight." The court held the statement was a "misrepresentation" of plaintiff's product of such a nature as to "constitute a fraud upon the public." The highest New York court on April 20, 1961, affirmed, despite the contention of NBC that the performer on the Jack Paar Show who uttered the defamation of product was totally unaware that *Snooze* was other than a fictitious product!

On the other hand, in *Drug Research Corp. v. Curtis Publishing Co.* (7 N.Y.2d 435) the highest New York court, in 1960, held that a magazine article in which it was charged that there are mail frauds in the sale of plaintiff's weight-reducing pills, did *not* libel the product. The court found that the manufacturer's name was not specifically mentioned in the magazine article, and that nothing was written therein as to plaintiff's integrity or business methods. Furthermore, if the article were regarded as a libel of the drug product, the manufacturer had not proved special damages. (In *Le Dans, Ltd. v. Daley* the New York Appellate Division on May 24, 1960, held that an allegation of special damages was not necessary when extrinsic facts otherwise identified the plaintiff!)

## Defamation of Personality

Elizabeth and Eddie Fisher, prominent screen personalities, in 1960, as husband and wife, brought a libel action against Dell Publishing Co., charging that the front cover and table of contents of its *Modern Screen* magazine was so worded as to lead readers to believe that the two plaintiffs had had sexual relations while each of them was married to someone else. Also, it was alleged that the publication implied that Elizabeth Frances Taylor was illegitimate. The New York Supreme Court, New York County, on May 2, 1961, first struck out, on procedural grounds, certain allegations of the complaint, and then declared that the "grievance" of the plaintiffs "can only be that the publication imputed adultery to them by intimating that the child was actually Eddie Fisher's although he was married at the time to someone other than the child's mother . . . . The imputation of illegitimacy can only affect the child. It does not add to the defamation of the plaintiffs, which must rest solely upon the imputation of adultery . . . . "

The plaintiffs thereupon amended the complaint to allege the defamation of personality, but subsequently the case was settled out of court!

In the height of a political campaign, defamation of personality is frequently committed and with the resulting lawsuit. In *Iannucci v. Von Hagen*, the New York Supreme Court, Westchester County, on January 14, 1960, observed that the defendant "in soliciting and obtaining signatures of voters to his own designating petition as a candidate for political office," stated to voters that plaintiff was "fired," "discharged," and "thrown out" of the Police Department of the City of Yonkers, where plaintiff previously served. The court, however, dismissed the action upon finding that the words were not slanderous *per se,* and furthermore there was no proof that plaintiff had thereby suffered any special damages:—"Conceivably, a disparagement may cause injury to plaintiff and yet not be actionable." In truth, the court sought to give the contestants in a political campaign the utmost freedom of speech, and to overlook what otherwise might be regarded as defamation of personality. In *Brewer v. Powell Savory Corp.*, the New York Supreme Court, Queens County, in August 1958, examined a newspaper article which related that plaintiff favored picketing a prominent statesman. Plaintiff alleged that as the result of this false statement (along with a report on how the idea was killed "stone cold dead") his good name and reputation had been injured; and, in addition, he suffered special damage in being later denied designation as district political leader. But the court opined:

"While there is some colorful language in the article and its general tone is hardly complimentary to the plaintiff, it is far from defamatory . . . . The language used was not libelous."

The older decisions such as *Post Publishing Co. v. Hallam* (59

Fed. 530), in 1893, were far more protective of the personality from defamation:

> "The danger that honorable and worthy men may be driven from politics and public service by allowing too great latitude in attacks on their characters outweighs any benefit that might occasionally accrue to the public from charges of corruption that are true in fact, but incapable of legal proof. The freedom of the press is not in danger from the enforcement of the rule we uphold . . . "

The majority view, to the contrary, regards it as of paramount importance that there be free discussion among the voters of the merits of a candidate for office, without fear of paralyzing lawsuits. Thus, a candidate for public office who offers himself to the voters must accept a diminution in his interest of personality.

A novel New York case, *Shenkman v. O'Malley,* in 1956, illustrates the defense of "fair comment" on matters of public interest which otherwise might have been defamatory of the personality of a reputable Brooklyn physician. Plaintiff performed a delicate nerve operation on the injured hand of Roy Campanella, star catcher of the then Brooklyn Dodgers professional baseball team. His bill for medical services amounting to $9,500 was presented to defendant—owner of the Dodgers, but was unpaid. Suit was commenced, and simultaneously, plaintiff publicly announced that his bill was not paid either by Campanella or the Dodgers! Defendant responded by issuing a statement to the press that (a) Dr. Shenkman's fee was exorbitant; (b) the operation was probably unnecessary; (c) other doctors agreed that an earlier operation had been successful and (d) Dr. Shenkman thought he was operating on Campanella's bankroll rather than on his hand. The New York Appellate Division, First Dept., declared that "medical treatment of such players, especially in reference to their capacity to play, is . . . a matter of general comment and interest. This aspect of the defenses, therefore, requires no further discussion." However, the court held that the defendant's comment (particularly to the effect that Dr. Shenkman consciously engaged in an unnecessary operation for the purpose of obtaining an unjustified professional fee) was not based upon facts truly stated, but upon the opinions of others, and therefore the defense of fair comment (on a matter of general comment and interest) was *not* applicable. Any other determination, said the court would wrongly

> "justify endless repetition of defamatory matter, no matter how false, simply because the defamatory matter or its supporting basis, was the product of widespread—even expert—opinion or prejudice."

Defendant O'Malley's reasonable reliance on such expert opinion was no defense, although it would negative malice and therefore mitigate the damages. Furthermore, O'Malley's response to Dr. Shenkman's statement of nonpayment for medical services was excessive and went beyond the provocation. The court also dismissed O'Malley's defense of a qualified privilege to defame where it served to protect his business interest.

Mr. Quentin Reynolds brought a successful libel action in New York against Westbrook Pegler who seemed to have a penchant for writing the wrong things all the time! And, Fulton Lewis, Jr., another newspaper columnist, was held to have libelled, in a nationwide broadcast on January 6, 1956, one Pearl Wanamaker, former Superintendent of Public Instruction in the State of Washington. It seems that Lewis referred to the woman as having a brother, he alleged, who had "ducked" behind the Iron Curtain and renounced his American citizenship. The columnist also criticized Mrs. Wanamaker's role in the 1955 White House Conference on Education, and discussed her reversal of the suspension of a Tacoma school counselor who had refused to answer questions posed by the House Un-American Activities Committee. A federal court jury, in 1959, awarded Mrs. Wanamaker the sum of $145,000 in damages! The Court (173 F. Supp. 126) approved the award without any additional sum for punitive damages.

In *MacLeod v. Tribune Publishing Co.* (343 P.2d 36), the California court examined a published article in the defendant newspaper which stated that another newspaper, characterized as a mouthpiece of the Communist Party, had carried a list of recommendations including the name of the plaintiff who was a candidate for political office. He contended that the article defamed his personality, and the court agreed that the only reasonable interpretation of the article was that the so-called Communist paper itself recommended plaintiff for election! In *Lawson v. New York Post Corp.*, the New York Supreme Court examined the following article published by the defendant-newspaper: ". . . It was the penalty for being, in the description of Diana Lawson who hunts quiz show candidates for some of the top shows, 'an ideal daytime quiz show couple.' Her description: they come from Indiana. The boy is twenty-six, the girl twenty-four; they are white and Protestant, and have two kids." The court held the statement to be defamatory of the plaintiff who had a position "in an extremely sensitive industry." The statement "imports selectivity by exclusion upon an improper basis, and directly affecting her business and reputation. . . . The use of the word 'ideal' stamps plaintiff's position and attitude toward the contestant and the viewing public. It circumscribes clear and derogatory limits to the operation of her function in the industry." However, on appeal, the New York Appellate Division, 1st Dept., on April 20, 1960, *reversed:*

> "As a matter of law, the statement is not susceptible of this defamatory meaning . . . . It suggested merely that the plaintiff was of the view that, perhaps because of nationwide audience identification, candidates having the stated characteristics are generally more acceptable."

Defamation of personality may be privileged, as in *Galvin v. New York New Haven & H Ry Co.* (168 N.E.2d 262), where the privilege was based upon the superior duty of an employee to his employer. But the Massachusetts court, in 1960, held that the privilege was lost because it was abused "by an unnecessary, unreasonable, or excessive publication of the defamatory matter." Railroad police had seen the plaintiff-employee carrying packages to his car at night, and accused him loudly and repeatedly before fifty or sixty truck drivers after provocatively demanding that he open his car. On the other hand, in *Dopsovic v. Stork Restaurant* a waiter allegedly shouted in the presence of other patrons: "This is the man who walked out of here about two months ago without paying his $11 bill," and "You were sitting right at that end of the bar with two women and your wife was not one of them." Plaintiff charged that the statements accused him of a punishable crime, but the New York Supreme Court on October 4, 1960, found that the words did not defame, although admittedly the accusations were made loudly and embarrassingly.

Defamation of personality by an assistant Attorney General of the State of New York confers no immunity upon the State, *Goodyear Products Co. v. State of New York* (21 Misc. 2d 725). Here a newspaper reporter was told by the assistant Attorney General about the claimant's alleged reprehensible conduct of its business, and the court ruled that the privilege or immunity applied only to "official reports and communications by or to the executive head of a department of government." The words uttered by the assistant Attorney General were not in the nature of an official report; there was "no moral or legal duty to advise a newspaper reporter."

### Libel by Will or Testament

Since one should not speak ill of the dead, should the dead be permitted to write ill of the living? The issue of defamation by will or testament was delineated in *Brown v. DuFrey* (1 N.Y.2d 190) where the plaintiff was awarded $5,000 from the decedent's estate. But in a Pennsylvania case, *Nagle v. Nagle* (316 Pa. 507), the libel was deemed to be privileged as part of a judicial proceeding:—"The rule which makes the pleadings in a judicial proceeding absolutely privileged may properly be applied to a will." A court is within its power to strike out defamatory portions of a will as it did in *Matter of Bomar* (18 N.Y.S. 214).

### "Hidden Libels" and Innuendoes

Defamation, whether in the form of libel or slander, is frequently not spelled out, but takes the form of an implied or indirect attack upon a person's reputation. Insinuation and innuendo, sarcasm and irony, sensational exposeés and "hidden libels" are examples of potential defamation by implication. In *Grant v. Readers Digest* (151 F.2d 733), a Massachusetts lawyer was described in a magazine article as "a legislative representative for the Massachusetts Communist Party." The Second U. S. Court of Appeal, in 1945, *reversed* the trial court's dismissal of the complaint for libel and declared that, although the statement did not say that Grant was a member of the Communist Party, a jury could properly find that the statement implied that Grant was in general sympathy with the objects and methods of the Communist Party. The court opined that such defamatory words affected "right-thinking people" and caused them "to regard plaintiff with scorn, aversion, or hostility." Furthermore, Grant, as a lawyer performing a public service, was entitled to have a jury "appraise how far he should be indemnified" for the libelous statement about his reputation.

The New York Court of Appeals, in January 1959, commented in *Tracy v. Newsday, Inc.* (5 N.Y.2d 134) about the "hidden libel" in a situation involving a police instructor and criminologist whom the defendant newspaper identified as the man who aided a sex pervert "in jumping his bail and assisted him to escape the consequences of his alleged criminal actions." But the court held that the statement was *not* defamatory:

> "The admitted purpose of an innuendo is to explain matter that is insufficiently expressed. Its office is to point out the libelous meaning of the words used. If the article is not susceptible of a libelous meaning" then innuendo cannot make it libelous . . . . The innuendo therefore may not enlarge upon the meaning of the words so as to convey a meaning that is not expressed . . . . Standing alone, these statements obviously are not defamatory. It is unfair to conclude that the article either states or implies anything that could subject the respondent to contempt, aversion, or induce any unsavory opinion or affect him in his calling."

Still another instance of potential libel was the *Time* magazine article, in 1957, in the *Berkson* case:

> "Bombs Away. The 'Mad Bomber' who has been busily planting home-made bombs around New York has given the city's newspapers one of the best homemade stories in years. No paper has matched the space or the big black headlines that Hearst's Journal-American has given the case. By last week,

after the Journal received a surprisingly frank letter from the bomber and had the chance to score the most sensational beat on the story to date, Scripps-Howard's World-Telegram snatched the story away. When the Journal received the crudely printed letter (signature F.P.), it decided to withhold the story from police and aim for the jackpot: the bomber's surrender. Instead of printing the letter, the Journal ran a wily item in its Personal column intimating that it would 'help' the bomber if he gave himself up. The ad caught the eye of World-Telegram managing editor Richard Starnes who guessed immediately that the Journal had received a letter from the bomber, checked out his hunch, and broke a Page One story on the bomber's 'new letter to a New York newspaper, hinting that he may declare at least a temporary truce.' Three days later when most other New York newspapers had printed the story, the Journal-American's account finally appeared under an eight-column banner. The Mad Bomber's letter contained more clues to his identity than police had unearthed in years. Among the disclosures: he had spent 'most of my adult life in bed;' two of the bombs he had deposited last year had not yet been found; he named three former New York State officials who he said would 'know all.' The Journal gave the bomber's letter to police who were able to eliminate hundreds of questioned signatures and narrow the search—as the press noted proudly—down to 'forty-two suspects who are being followed night and day.' But at week's end, the bomber was still at large—or in bed."

The New York Appellate Division, First Dept., on June 25, 1959, declared that the magazine article could *not* be read as charging the plaintiffs with a crime or with obstructing public authority. Plaintiffs argued that they were charged with being accessories to the crime because they aided the offender "with intent that he may avoid or escape from arrest." The court opined:

> "No possible pleading of construction or innuendo can convert this publication into a charge of such a crime . . . . The article infers, and indeed states expressly, that the newspaper was activated by a desire itself to capture the criminal . . . . There is nothing defamatory in this; what is published is not criminal and it is not disgraceful; nor does it meet any of the common criteria by which a libel is tested."

## Privilege to Defame: Absolute and Qualified Privileges

The social ends achieved by the law of defamation are made more palatable by recognition that under certain circumstances the defamer may be privileged to defame. Privileged defamations fall into two categories: (a) those *absolutely* immune from responsibility without regard to the defamer's purpose, motive, or reasonableness of his conduct—such as in judicial and legislative proceedings, proceedings of executive public officers charged with important public responsibility, publications made with the defamed victim's consent, or communications between husband and wife, and (b) those *qualifiedly* or conditionally privileged, based upon the good motives and reasonable behavior of the defamer such as (1) publications made to protect or advance a legitimate and important interest of the defamer; (2) publications made to protect or advance the interest of the victim or other person where under ordinary social standards a reasonable person would believe himself under a legal or moral obligation to speak or write: (3) communications between persons having a common interest; (4) publications made to proper officials in the public interest; (5) fair criticism or fair comment upon matters of public interest or public concern and (6) reports of proceedings of public interest or public concern. The *qualified* or conditional privilege can be forfeited, however, by excessive and improper publication such as under circumstances when a reasonable man would have no grounds for a belief in the truth of the defamation.

The *absolute* privilege inherent in the communication between husband and wife was delineated in *Poppe v. Poppe* (3 N.Y.2d 312). The wife brought an action for separation founded upon abandonment, and the husband defended upon the ground of her cruel and inhuman treatment. She objected to his testimony upon the basis of the New York statute barring disclosure of confidential communications between spouses. The trial court allowed the husband to testify that his wife had boasted to him of repeated, illicit sexual relations with another man with whom she planned to elope. On appeal, the New York Court of Appeals, in 1957, affirmed and refused to recognize his testimony as absolutely privileged because the New York statute was designed to protect and strengthen the marital bond by giving protection only to those communications between husband and wife which were prompted by the affection, confidence, and loyalty engendered by the marital relationship. Thus, absolute privilege to defame was not recognized because "the disclosure related, it is evident, not to the confession of a penitent wife confiding to her husband the story of her wrongdoing, but to a defiant declaration of misconduct and of an intention to persist therein and go away with another man."

In *Crawford & Co. v. Graves* (100 S.E.2d 714) the Virginia court, in 1957, declared that the defendant had exceeded the scope of his *qualified* privilege in the performance of his insurance adjusting duties. It seems that he had tried to induce the insured to switch to an orthopedic surgeon to treat an injury instead of a chiropodist whom the insured had hired. The defendant stated that the chiropodist "is not the type of a doctor for this work. He is a doctor for ingrowing toenails, flat feet, and fallen arches." The court upheld the action for slander, as did the Maryland Appellate Court in *Simon v. Robinson* (154 A.2d 911) where a libel *per se* was found: in a dispute between a builder and contractor, one letter stated that "funds were fraudulently diverted and converted for his own use from the above building project to one in which it now appears you are a partner." The defendant's claim of a *qualified* privilege because the parties were engaged in a common interest or duty was rejected, and the libel was upheld.

## Truth: An Absolute Defense to Defamation?

Truth is the *best* defense to any civil action for defamation, although several states have, by statute, limited the defense of truth by requiring proof of good motives and justifiable ends. An interesting case pointing out the difficulties of establishing the defense is *Stephens v. Columbia Pictures Corp.*, decided by the Second U. S. Court of Appeals in 1957. The plaintiff, an employee of Columbia, was authorized to make disbursements which were customarily later reimbursed to him. In 1952, he retained certain Columbia monies as an offset against another claim which he allegedly had against Columbia. The defendant corporation reported this matter in a sworn proof of loss to its insurance carrier as "a misappropriation . . . with intent to fraudulently deprive. . . ." There was also a letter containing similar defamatory statements by Columbia's insurance manager to the insurance brokerage firm. The plaintiff Stephens thereupon sued in libel, and Columbia defended upon the ground of truth. The court held that "to establish the defense of truth . . . the facts proved in justification must substantiate *all* of the defamatory matter charged;" and Columbia could not prove Stephen's *intent to defraud*, so the defense of truth was rejected by the court. Columbia's other defense of *qualified* privilege to publish such defamation was also refuted by Columbia's malice which the court held had destroyed the qualified privilege to report its loss to its insurance carrier: "The evidence was sufficient to sustain a finding of reckless disregard of the plaintiff's rights."

In *Singer v. News Syndicate Co.*, the New York Supreme Court, New York County, on January 13, 1959, examined a newspaper's defense of truth to its article which accused the plaintiff of being responsible for the imprisonment of her former husband because of "fresh arrears accruing while he was in jail." The court considered the absolute defense of truth, and opined that only a trial would decide "whether the justifying facts have the meaning which plaintiff claims to be the meaning of the article" (If truth were an absolute defense here, no subsequent trial of the issues would have been necessary.)

### Privilege of the Press: The Right to Fair Comment

The right of a newspaper to gather and disseminate information and to comment fairly upon such information has been restricted by the courts which draw a strict line between what is private and what is public. The invasion of a person's privacy is a recognized injury, for matters which are solely a private person's concern should not be exposed to the public. In *MacRae v. Afro-American Co.* (172 F. Supp. 184, USDC ED Pa., 1959) it was held that the newspaper's *false* report that the plaintiff had helped bring about her daughter's suicide entitled the plaintiff to $30,000 compensatory damages. Plaintiff was the wife of a university dean and the newspaper report falsely stated that she was displeased with her daughter's grades and had told her daughter not to come home from the university unless her grades improved, thereby causing her daughter to be suicidally despondent. The newspaper had exceeded the bounds of fair comment upon a matter which was not necessarily a matter of public concern. (No plea of freedom of press was evidently raised in defense of the libel.)

The press has a "right" to publish opinions based upon facts which are of public concern; but this "right" is forfeitable should the article be published falsely or with actual malice. Some courts have defined "malice" in terms of a wrongful act done intentionally without just cause or excuse, and have required the defamed person to prove malice without the benefit of any inference from the publication itself. In Pennsylvania, a constitutional provision requires proof that a publication concerning official conduct of public officials be "maliciously or negligently made" before a defamed person can recover from the press. Undoubtedly, such a Pennsylvania restriction is designed to liberalize comment by the press on matters of public concern. In the *Swallow* case (8 Pa. Super. 580), an 1898 Pennsylvania court upheld the newspaper's defense to libel by finding evidence that due care was exercised in investigating the matter before publication. Fifty-two years later, in the *McAndrew* case (364 Pa. 504), the failure of a newspaper to verify facts secured in a telephone conversation with leaders of one political party was held to be negligent, but the court opined that the published facts, though carelessly reported, were in fact *not* defamatory!

The New York case, *Hogan v. New York Times* (U.S.C.A.2, February 8, 1963), by contrast, resulted in libel judgments for two policemen against the newspaper for depicting a dice-game raid in which they participated as following "the script of a Keystone Comedy." The libelous article told of a raid conducted by the Stamford, Connecticut, police on a street-corner dice game. It was rewritten and embellished with satiric humor from a story in the local newspaper after the *New York Times* correspondent had made a few telephone calls to check the story, but the correspondent had failed to find anyone who knew anything about it. The defendant newspaper's account which appeared on its front page under a headline "Dice Raid in Stamford Follows The Script of a Keystone Comedy," contained apparently false statements that the players picked up by the police escaped, that some of them were recaptured after chase and scuffle, that one policeman struck another with his nightstick while aiming at one of the players, and that four nightsticks were lost in the furor. The federal court held that the sole purpose of the publication was to amuse the readers at the policemen's expense: "That the *New York Times,* a newspaper of international pre-eminence, devoted to extensive reporting of important current events, should find the raid of an open-air crap game in Stamford to constitute news fit to print—and on the front page at that—is quite enough evidence by itself." The court concluded that the jury was warranted in finding reckless disregard for the truth from the slap-dash manner in which the story was checked, and upheld jury verdicts of $6,020 and $6,125 for the two policemen.

In a magazine article concerning the Russian spy, Rudolph Abel, there were photographs depicting Abel's activities in the guise of a law-abiding American citizen and showing how he was regarded by his neighbors who were unaware that he was a spy. One photograph of the plaintiff contained the following legend beneath: "His admirer, Frank Gambuzza, a radio dealer who sold Abel some parts for a wireless receiver, praised the Russian for his electronic know-how." In *Gambuzza v. Time Incorporated,* the New York Supreme Court, New York County, on April 23, 1963, opined that the word "admirer" must be read in the context of the entire legend, and the article accompanying the photographs must also be read as a whole. Thus fairly read, the publication cannot be regarded as libelous *per se* without proof of special damages.

In *England and Bower v. Daily Gazette Co.* (104 S.E.2d 306), the West Virginia court, in 1958, examined the defendant newspaper's editorial which stated that the plaintiffs, who were legislators and in the insurance business, had been alloted fire insurance policies on state property through the executive branch of the state government. A libel suit was commenced upon the basis of the insinuations accompanying these factual statements, the gist of which was that insurance business was alloted to the plaintiffs for the purpose of "buying" their political support. The editorial charged:

> "They are the governor's marionettes on the Senate and House floors, and the jump when ordered to . . . like Kukla Fran and Ollie of television fame. It's easy to see that they've sold their votes and sold out their constituents—for a price. They're more dedicated to their own creature comforts than to the comforts and welfare of the folks back home."

In affirming judgments of $5,000 and $8,000, the West Virginia Supreme Court of Appeals conceded that the newspaper was qualifiedly privileged to make fair comment, but held that the newspaper had lost the privilege because of the excesses, abuses, and false imputations of the editorial. The vehement and violent nature of the accusations coupled with the absence of any substantial proof destroyed the privilege of fair comment.

Similarly, an advertisement in a newspaper suggesting that a named legislator running for reelection was the corrupt tool of utilities was libelous in *Purvis v. Bremer's Inc.* (344 P.2d 705, 1959).

Newspapers, however, are frequently protected by statute, as in New York, which bars a civil action for publication of a fair and true report of any judicial proceeding, legislative hearing, or other official meeting. Yet in *Fischer v. Post Standard Co.* (217 N.Y.S.2d 947), a 1961 newspaper story of the conduct of a pretrial examination by the district attorney using such terms as "Star Chamber," "Iron Curtain," and inferences of police brutality, was deemed to be libelous and not fair comment.

## *The Sensational, Exposé Magazine*

Courts have traditionally favored the right of free discussion by the press, and have held such publication libelous only where it exceeded all bounds of reasonableness and fair comment. The sensational, exposé magazine, which distorts the basic facts of a story about a public personality by important omissions and by suggestive and salacious titles embellished by photographs, poses a different problem, particularly in those states where proof of *pecuniary* loss is required if the libelous matter is not otherwise libel *per se*. These scandal magazines frequently impute that the celebrity has engaged in immoral, indecent, and perverted sex conduct. As a public personality, the victims are not entitled to protection of their privacy, and it is difficult to prove pecuniary loss from such publication. Indeed, freedom from emotional stress and strain, which freedom is invaded intentionally and with reckless disregard of the celebrity's personal honor, self-respect and human dignity, should be protected. Only a barbarous society demands a sacrifice of these human sensibilities in favor of such irresponsible freedom of the press. A sensational, scandalous magazine by indulging in such vicious defamation has forfeited its right of free expression. No constitutional purpose is served by needlessly besmirching reputations (even of the public personality), nor by allowing such magazines to exploit commercially the propensities of the reading public.

### *The Newspaper Reporter's Privileged Communication*

In November 1957, the privileged communication between a newspaper reporter and the source of the news item was *not* recognized by the U. S. District Court in New York City, in the course of a libel action brought by actress Judy Garland against the Columbia Broadcasting System. One Marie Torre, television-radio columnist for the *New York Herald Tribune,* quoted in her January 10, 1957 column, certain allegedly defamatory statements about Miss Garland from an unidentified CBS executive. Defendant C.B.S. subpoenaed Miss Torre who refused to disclose the source of her news item. Judge Sylvester Ryan ordered her held in criminal contempt of court, and sentenced her to ten days in jail, although she was released on her own recognizance pending her appeal to the U. S. Court of Appeal. Specifically Judge Ryan had asked Miss Torre: "What is the name of the network executive mentioned and referred to in your article?"

Miss Torre replied: "For the reasons stated in the papers submitted to your honor, I must respectfully decline."

Judge Ryan then stated: "Miss Torre, I direct you to make

answer at this moment. It is my duty to advise you that in the event of your refusal to do so, I shall be obligated to adjudge you in criminal contempt of this court. I now direct you to answer the question."

Miss Torre responded: "For reasons previously stated, your honor, I must respectfully decline."

Judge Ryan then stated: "Miss Torre, I adjudge you in criminal contempt of this court. . . . You are committed for a term of ten days. You may sit down. . . . I understand that you feel you are right in the position you are taking and I sympathize with that position. However, I rule as a matter of law that it is a position . . . that . . . has no legal support. . . . I think we should have noted upon the record that Miss Torre's demeanor is entirely respectful to the court and is not intended as a personal affront of the dignity of the court. However, she takes a position which makes impossible the functioning of the court. . . . The processes of the court must be obeyed, and we may not have witnesses who have been subpoenaed in cases, notwithstanding the high motives which may prompt their actions, interfere with the judicial process." The November 14, 1957 editorial of the *New York Herald Tribune* stated that it "will push" the case "as far as it can possibly be pushed;" and that the issue was

> " . . . whether a newspaper reporter can be sent to jail for refusing to divulge the sources of information given in confidence. The still bigger question involved is whether the First Amendment guaranteeing the freedom of the press to print all the news it can gather also protects the right of reporters to gather the news."

Ten months later, in September 1958, the U. S. Court of Appeals for the Second Circuit affirmed Miss Torre's conviction. Mr. Justice Potter Stewart (now a member of the U. S. Supreme Court) accepted "the hypothesis that compulsory disclosures of a journalist's confidential sources of information may entail an abridgement of press freedom by imposing some limitation upon the availability of news." But he opined:

> "Freedom of the press, precious and vital though it is to a free society is not an absolute. What must be determined is

whether the interest to be served by compelling the testimony of the witness in the present case justifies some impairment of this First Amendment freedom."

Mr. Justice Stewart found a "paramount public interest in the fair administration of justice," and he held that, in this case, the right of the press was less central to democratic values than the right of the citizen to compel testimony in his behalf in court:

> "We are not dealing here with the use of the judicial process to force a wholesale disclosure of a newspaper's confidential source of news, nor with a case where the identity of the news source is of doubtful relevance or materiality."

In Miss Torre's case, Mr. Justice Stewart said, to let her escape testifying "would poorly serve the cause of justice."

Counsel for Miss Garland, in his U. S. Supreme Court brief, called Miss Torre a retailer of "gossip" who was not entitled to the protection of the First Amendment by printing libelous statements of others without identifying them. But on December 8, 1958, the highest court refused to review the contempt conviction of Miss Torre, and she chose to go to jail rather than reveal her news source. She spent ten days in a New York City jail, and was released with an understanding that she would talk! (It is significant to point out the possibility that nobody may even have said what is alleged by Judy Garland to have been said; also, if something was said, that in and of itself is not proof of the truth of the statement; and finally it is unjust to wreck the presumption of innocence without allowing CBS the opportunity to defend itself.) On January 10, 1961, it was publicly announced that Judy Garland had withdrawn her suit against CBS "with prejudice" and without costs to either party. Thus, the words of Mr. Justice Stewart bear repetition:

> "Freedom of the press, hard-won over the centuries by men of courage, is basic to a free society. But basic too are courts of justice armed with the power to discover truth. The concept that it is the duty of a witness to testify in a court of law has roots as deep as the guarantee of a free press."

The newspaperman's refusal to disclose his sources of information has generally been punished by our courts which have refused to recognize a journalist's "privilege" to decline. In *Appeal of Goodfader,* the Supreme Court of Hawaii, on November 3, 1961, conceded that the First Amendment is calculated to preserve an untrammeled press as a vital source of public information; but the court declared that freedom of the press is not absolute and is not itself sufficient to protect against divulging news sources. Whether in any particular case an asserted right to conceal a news source should prevail, depends upon weighing and balancing the supposed right against the purposes which would be defeated by losing the testimony. In this case, the Hawaii court ruled that the revelation of the newspaperman's source was vital to the plaintiff's case because it would provide the identity of a possible witness to support the conspiracy theory against the plaintiff.

## Defamation by Radio and Television

Another social aspect of defamatory utterances is found in the communications media of radio and television. Under Section 315 of the Federal Communications Act of 1934, all political candidates for public office must be allotted "equal opportunities" for broadcasting and/or televising. The Act, as amended in 1952 and 1959, states that the broadcaster is to have no power of censorship over the material broadcast. During the 1956 elections in North Dakota, there were three candidates vying for the U. S. Senate seat. Television station WDAY carried telecasts of two of the candidates, and the third thereupon demanded equal time. In a subsequent telecast by the third candidate, he declared that both of his opponents "take orders from Communist-controlled Democrat Farmers Union," that the Democrat Farmers Union program "would establish a Communist Farmers Union soviet right here in North Dakota." The Farmers Educational and Cooperative Union brought suit for libel against WDAY, but the North Dakota Supreme Court ruled that the plaintiff had no action for libel since WDAY was obliged by law to transmit the telecast. (89 N.W.2d 102, April 1958) The court noted that the federal government had pre-empted the field of such communication, and opined:

"We cannot believe that it was the intent of Congress to compel a station to broadcast libelous statements and at the same time subject it to the risk of defending actions for damages."

On appeal to the U. S. Supreme Court, the decision was affirmed by a vote of 5-4 on June 29, 1959 (360 US 525). The majority opinion by Mr. Justice Black held that Section 315 of the Federal Communications Act superseded state laws against libel, and "whatever adverse inference may be drawn from the failure of Congress to legislate an express immunity (from libel) is offset by its refusal to permit stations to avoid liability by censoring broadcasts." The court opinion conceded that the decision which a broadcasting station would have to make if it attempted to remove libelous matter "is far from easy. . . . Quite possibly if a station were held responsible for the broadcast of libelous material, all remarks faintly objectionable would be excluded, out of an excess of caution. Moreover, if any censorship were permissible a station so inclined could intentionally inhibit a candidate's legitimate presentation under the guise of lawful censorship of libelous matter."

The minority view expressed by Mr. Justice Frankfurter argued that "due regard for the principle of separation of powers limiting this court's functions and respect for the binding principle of federalism, leaving to the states authority not withdrawn by the Constitution or absorbed by Congress, are more compelling considerations than avoidance of a hardship legally imposed." He pointed out that since defamation was an intentional tort, there was a "solid likelihood" that North Dakota courts could be relied on to reach the conclusion that in the face of a compulsory broadcast WDAY lacked the necessary intent to communicate the defamation, and therefore the station's conduct was not tortious.

Thus, the absolute privilege accorded in the WDAY case is an immunity arising from the personal appearance of the candidate. This immunity, however, does not extend to speeches made on behalf of a candidate by another (*Felix v. Westinghouse Radio Stations, Inc.,* 186 E.2d 1, 1950); but it does extend to utterances by the candidate which are completely unrelated to his candidacy, because to limit the content of the candidate's remarks would be censorship prohibited under Section 315. Of course, the candidate himself is not immune from personal liability for his libelous remarks and he is generally solvent and can afford to pay for his indiscretions.

Legislation requiring proof of actual damages, in libel actions based upon broadcasting, has been enacted in almost twenty states, in an attempt to minimize the liability of the broadcaster in those instances not covered by Section 315 (see Arizona Revised Statutes, Title 12, Section 652; Nebraska Revised Statutes, Section 86.603, and Wyoming Compiled Statutes Annotated, Section 3-8205, for example).

**Protection of Public Officials from Liability for Defamation**

Perhaps it should naturally follow that if we "immunize," in the public interest, the radio and television stations from liability for defamation by political candidates, then why not "immunize" all government officials who can be and who are sued for defamation while acting in the public interest? The *Barr* and *Howard* cases decided by the U. S. Supreme Court pose and answer the problem of the "qualified privilege" to defame.

William G. Barr, acting director of the Office of Rent Stabilization, in 1953, in Washington, was sued by two former employees for his statement in a press release that these two workers would be fired! The U. S. District Court jury awarded the employees $8700 in damages. The U. S. Court of Appeal for the District of Columbia upheld the verdict (256 F.2d 890), but it was ordered by the U. S. Supreme Court (79 S. Ct. 1335) to consider whether Barr had a "qualified privilege," which the appellate court promptly did find, and ordered another jury trial on the issue whether Barr had lost his qualified privilege because of possible malicious intent. On June 29, 1959, the U. S. Supreme Court (360 U.S. 564) formally declared that Barr as an official of the federal government was *absolutely immune* from libel or slander for public statements on policies committed to his charge, and for reports forwarded to members of Congress. In the five to four decision, Mr. Justice Harlan wrote that the immunity of governmental officials is not limited to Cabinet members but extends to subordinates several levels below:

> "We think that under these circumstances, a publicly expressed statement of the position of the agency head announcing personnel action which he planned to take in reference to charges so widely disseminated to the public, was an appropriate exercise of that discretion which an officer of that rank must possess if the public service is to function effectively. It would be an unduly restrictive view of the scope of the duties of a policy-making executive official to hold that a public statement of the agency policy in respect to matters of wide public interest and concern is not action in the line of duty . . . . The privilege is not a badge or emolument of exalted office, but an expression of a policy designed to aid in the effective functioning of government."

The dissenting opinion of Chief Justice Warren felt that the majority opinion "purports to launch this court on a balancing process in order to reconcile the interest of the public in obtaining fearless executive performance and the interest of the individual in having redress for defamation." This dissent in which Mr. Justice Douglas joined continued:

> "Even accepting for the moment that these are the proper interests to be balanced, the ultimate disposition is not the result of a balance. On the one hand, the principal opinion sets up a vague standard under which no government employee can tell with any certainty whether he will receive absolute immunity for his acts. On the other hand, it has not given the slightest consideration to the interest of the individual who is defamed. It is a complete annihilation of his interest."

The *Howard* case revolved about Admiral W. E. Howard, Jr., the Commander of the Boston Naval Shipyard who wrote to the Chief of the Bureau of Ships as to his reasons for withdrawing recognition from the Federal Employees Veterans Association representing organized employees at the Yard. Copies of Howard's letter went to Massachusetts' members of Congress. Two officers of the Association filed a million dollar libel suit against Howard, but the federal court found that Admiral Howard had an *absolute* privilege in reporting to his superior officers, but only a *qualified* privilege in reporting to Congressmen! The appeal by the defendant and the government was based upon the belief that the ruling would seriously hamper the flow of official information from the executive to the legislative branch of government. Also, the government deplored the actuality of a jury trial on the motives of government officials in taking that official action. The U. S. Supreme Court (360 U.S. 593), in 1959, by a six to three vote, upheld the *absolute* immunity for military officers in the performance of their duties. Shortly thereafter, the U. S. Department of Justice issued a memorandum for all departments and agencies of the executive branch of the federal government, setting forth guiding principles for all personnel, among which are the following:

"It is not the title but the duties of the office which clothes the official with immunity from civil defamation suits.

"The privilege does not apply to defamatory statements unrelated to official duties . . . . No government official should assume that these (court) decisions give him full and complete protection against actions for defamation.

"Act with an awareness of the vital importance of avoiding unnecessary injury to any person."

On November 10, 1960, the U. S. Court of Appeals for the Seventh Circuit in *Sauber v. Gliedman* similarly held that the plaintiff, a former District Director of Internal Revenue had no cause of action against a special assistant Attorney General who was prosecuting him under an indictment charging conspiracy to defraud the United States of income taxes. At a press conference, the defendant announced that his job was to conduct work preparatory to trial to seek "possible further corruption," and declared: "When you have a man who was District Director indicted for conspiracy to defraud the U. S. government, it doesn't take a genius to see something is wrong. This is not a witch hunt and it should be good for employee morale because and awful cloud has been hanging over the Chicago office." The court declared that the test of privilege is the relation of the conduct complained of to the matters committed to the defendant's official control and supervision; but warned that this immunity or absolute privilege did not mean that any official would be immune to governmental or professional sanctions if he were guilty of official irresponsibility. Thus, the defamation was privileged because the greater interest was free communication, i.e., complete candor about matters of public importance.

### Immunity of Legislators from Defamation Liability

Protection of persons from defamation by legislators in Congressional hearings has frequently resulted in citizens being cowed by threats of untrammeled and privileged denunciation by ambitious legislators and by the partisan interests they represent. In 1950, a small group of U. S. Senators, headed by Senator Margaret Smith of Maine, vehemently protested against the wave of character assasination by certain legislators riding "the four horsemen of calumny, fear, ignorance, bigotry and smear." The paralyzing fear of ignominious defamations in legislative halls was first noted in 1834, by Mr. Justice Story of the U.S. Supreme Court:

> "No man ought to have a right to defame others under color of a performance of the duties of his office. And if he does so in the actual discharge of his duties in Congress, that furnishes no reason why he should be enabled, through the medium of the press to destroy the reputation and invade the repose of other citizens. It is neither within the scope of his duty nor in the furtherance of public rights or public policy. Every citizen has as good a right to be protected by the laws from malignant scandal and false charges and defamatory imputations, as a member of Congress has to utter them . . . . If it were otherwise a man's character might be taken away without the possibility of redress, either by malice or indiscretion, or overweening self-conceit of a member of Congress." (*Story's Commentaries on the Constitution of the United States,* Vol. 3, p. 632).

This immunity of Congressmen is based upon Section 6, Clause 1, Article I of the United States Constitution:

> "Senators and Representatives shall . . . . in all cases, except Treason, Felony, and Breach of the Peace, be privileged from Arrest during their Attendance at the Session of their respec-

tive Houses, and in going to and returning from the same; *and for any Speech or Debate in either House they shall not be questioned in any other Place."* (Italics added)

The first part of this clause, as to privilege from arrest, has, however, generally been construed so as not to place any serious personal wrong done by a United States Senator or Representative to a private citizen beyond the effective reach of the court. In 1934 Senator Huey P. Long was required to accept service of a civil process in an action for libel after he had allegedly distributed in public copies of his Senate speech defamatory of a private citizen *(Long v. Ansell,* 293 U. S. 76). On the other hand, the protection given by the latter part of this clause has been held applicable to oral and written reports presented in either house, to resolutions offered, to the act of voting, and generally to every other act resulting from the nature and in the execution of the office [*Kilbourn v. Thompson,* 103 US 204].

At English common law, this immunity of members of legislative bodies (as well as their agents, informers or witnesses) for acts or words in performance of legislative duties, regardless of purpose, motive, or reasonableness of conduct, was deemed indispensable to government. Legislative immunity as to defamatory statements was early recognized in this country as *absolute,* as long as the defamation had some relationship to the business of the legislature [*Coffin v. Coffin,* 4 Mass. 1] Some thirty years ago, United States Senator James Couzens, of Michigan, fell into certain tax difficulties with the Bureau of Internal Revenue regarding his sale of capital stock of the Ford Motor Company. Cochran, a Washington tax consultant, was consulted, and undoubtedly the relationship was most unsatisfactory, for Senator Couzens, shortly thereafter, in the course of a speech in the Senate, stated that Cochran "knew the inside tax game," was allegedly a close friend of an employee of the Bureau of Internal Revenue, and had allegedly offered to arrange to have the tax case settled for a fee of $1,500,000! Cochran then brought an action for slander, but the Court of Appeals of District of Columbia dismissed the suit for want of jurisdiction, declaring that a United

States Senator is "absolutely privileged and not subject to be questioned in any other place." [*Cochran v. Couzens*, 42 F.2d 783]. More recently in *Barsky v. United States* [167 F.2d 241, cert den 334 U.S. 843] a federal court opined that the basis of this drastic rule of absolute immunity of governmental officials, congressional and administrative, from liability for damage done by their acts or speech, even though knowingly false or wrong, is the overbalancing of the individual harm by the public necessity for untrammelled freedom of legislative and administrative activity, within the respective powers of legislature and the executive. Therefore, in order to allow the peoples' representatives to execute the function of their office without fear of prosecution, civil or criminal, this immunity has been universally accepted.

Insofar as state legislative proceedings are concerned, note the 1951 case, *Tenney v. Brandhove* [341 U.S. 367], decided by the United States Supreme Court, in which a witness before the California Legislative Committee on Un-American Activities sought damages for injury to reputation by members of that Committee. Action was brought under the civil rights statutes [28 U.S.C. 43 and 47 [3]] which were enacted in 1871 to enforce the Fourteenth Amendment. Plaintiff Brandhove had allegedly circulated a petition among members of the California Legislature to urge them to cut off further funds for the Tenney Committee when the Committee took action itself with certain allegedly scurrilous, sensational charges against the plaintiff. The court held that these civil rights statutes were not intended to make State legislators personally liable for damages to a witness injured by a committee exercising legislative power. A vigorous dissent by Mr. Justice Douglas took the position that

" . . . when a committee perverts its powers, brings down on an individual the whole weight of government for an illegal or corrupt purpose, the reason for the immunity ends. It was indeed the purpose of this civil rights legislation to secure federal rights against invasion by officers and agents of the states."

In the majority opinion, Mr. Justice Frankfurter pointed out that "self-discipline and the voters must be the ultimate reliance for discouraging or correcting such abuses."

## Social Utility Aspects of Libel and Slander Law 167

The need for such congressional immunity has been further emphasized in the avowed aim of the House Committee on Un-American Activities:

" . . . to permit the greatest court in the world — the court of American public opinion — to render a continuing verdict on all of its public officials and to evaluate the merit of many in public life." *(Interim Report, re Communist Espionage in U. S. Government, 80th Cong., 2nd Sess., p. 1-2 [1948].)*

Obviously, this committee and Congressmen, generally, are the important molders of American public opinion. Exaggerated charges and pronouncement of judgment without supporting evidence can inflict such personal and financial disaster upon an accused that no subsequently-formed public opinion can aid him. Indeed, ruthless exploitations which make the accusation so sensational that later revelation of the truth seems drab, dull and unnewsworthy, by comparison, can completely overcome the public notion that an accused has a basic constitutional right to be heard, to defend himself, and not to be tried in committee, in newspapers, or on radio or television. Under the aegis of the immunity, a Congressman can get desirable national publicity to build up his own political personality; an unscrupulous Congressman can readily impute unworthy or unpatriotic motives to anyone, by innuendo or as an outright accusation, without offering one shred of evidence in support of such charges. Look at the background of *one* of these typical "purveyors" of fear and intimidation: there were at his death such still *unanswered questions* concerning his activities as an indictment for federal income tax evasion; near disbarment as a lawyer for violating the code of ethics; his sponsorship of legislation to save from execution Nazi SS men convicted of killing 350 unarmed American P.O.W.'s; his wilful destruction of official records; receipt of $10,000 from a corporation almost entirely subsidized by agencies under the jurisdiction of Congressional committees of which he was a member; diversion of funds publicly solicited to fight Communism; use of close associates and members of his family to secrete income and to indulge in stock speculations; and his granting while a judge of two-day divorces to accommodate people who had contributed to his political campaign! These very *questions* which the public was entitled to have answered, were raised by the Subcommittee on Privileges and Elections of the United States Senate Committee on Rules and Administration. Despite every opportunity to appear, answer and defend against these charges, this member of Congress contented himself with harassing the subcommittee and then barring full distribution of their written report. Had one of his accusers been so contemptuous of congressional procedure, the late Senator Joseph R. McCarthy of Wisconsin would have certainly labeled him an enemy or traitor and heaped upon him every opprobrium at his command!

McCarthyism, as a term of opprobrium, resulted from the antics of the late U. S. Senator from Wisconsin and from the widespread publicity given his defamatory remarks in the press. One such example was *Coleman v. Newark Star Ledger* decided by the New Jersey Supreme Court on March 9, 1959. The plaintiff charged that the defendant newspaper published defamatory remarks made by Senator McCarthy at a Fort Monmouth, N. J., press conference in 1953. The court upheld the qualified privilege of the newspaper in printing defamatory statements made by members of Congress outside congressional hearing rooms when the statements concerned Congress, provided no malice was intended. Justice Heher, in dismissing the $600,000 libel suit, wrote:

> "It cannot be that evidence adduced and information acquired in the course of an executive session of a congressional investigating committee are sealed against public disclosure for all time, save as unprivileged communications subjecting the members of the committee to the risk of suit. When the judicial process is invoked, it is for the jury to say whether the privilege is abused, unless there be an absolute privilege in the circumstances irrespective of malice."

Justice Heher said that if Senator McCarthy's remarks were "fairly" reported by the defendant without malice, they were necessarily privileged. In fact, the Senator testified at the trial of the suit that his statements were accurately reported by the defendant. Thus, according to the court:

> "The jury could have found, as it no doubt did find, that the communication was honestly made in the pursuit of what was reasonably conceived to be a public responsibility, an exercise of the basic right of freedom of speech and of press. Here the evidence of a committee-authorized publication stood uncontradicted; and even if the proofs be open to contradictory interpretations, then the issue was within the exclusive province of the jury."

The lone dissent by Chief Justice Weintraub pointed out that the Senator's remarks in respect to the secret hearing were not privileged because the entire testimony at that session had not been made public:

> "I do not understand the majority to find an absolute privilege beyond the precincts of the House and committee room. The reason for the immunity is fully served by an immunity thus localized, and I see no need to expand it. The fact that the session was secret is, in my view, sufficient to deny a privilege. The privilege which the majority opinion establishes is, in my view, an invitation to irresponsibility."

Chief Justice Weintraub accused Senator McCarthy of pursuing an "unfair and unreasonable" course in his statements at the close of the secret hearing:

> "The majority places the privilege upon the Senator's duty and the public's right to know. I find neither element. It is not the duty of a Senator to investigate and prosecute violations of law. That role is constitutionally reserved to the grand jury and members of the Executive Branch."

(It should be noted that the *Coleman* case overlooked the fact that plaintiff, a radar expert at Fort Monmouth, was suspended as an alleged security risk in 1952, but ultimately reinstated by court order. The two articles by the newspaper were published in October and December 1953, some time after the plaintiff actually lost his employment.)

A legislator's privilege against defamation applies also to libelous statements inserted into the Congressional Record, though not delivered in the halls of Congress, *McGovern v. Martz* (182 F. Supp. 343, 1960).

Agents, investigators and willing witnesses, employed or otherwise available to virulent Senators and Congressmen, sometimes seek to use an anti-subversive drive as an instrument for their own particular brand of subversion of American ideals. In this orgy of dirty politics, professional informers have frequently been given the public spotlight to turn their own sordid pasts into a lucrative present. Lists of "men without faces" have been flouted before the public, not to establish facts, as in a court of law, but for the accuser to make personal headlines in newspapers, on radio and television. Embittered, unprincipled masters of the black technique of villainy, they have unfortunately employed congressional immunity as a license for character assassination.

Since defamation of character before legislative proceedings is still personally and financially a grievous wrong, it is submitted that some redress should be given against such irresponsible exercise of governmental power or immunity. It is submitted that legislative reform of procedure, or self-discipline by members of Congress, is not a feasible solution due to the general fear that any restrictions or limitations upon the actions or conduct of legislators will interfere with the legislative process. On February 10, 1953, the late Senator Estes Kefauver of Tennessee introduced a bill to help protect persons accused in Congress or by congressional committees by requiring that the accused (a) be notified in advance of any defamatory material under study; (b) then be given an opportunity to present rebuttal evidence to be read on the floor of Congress or published in the Congressional Record; (c) be allowed to have counsel appear with him; (d) be permitted to file questions to be asked the accusing witnesses and (c) be allowed to make a complete statement at conclusion of the evidence. But the bill never reached the floor of Congress!

Seldom, if ever, does the accusor repeat, without shelter of immunity, the charges made under immunity. Of course, statements made to the F.B.I. concerning activities or conduct of government employees, or of any citizen, are privileged communications. (*Foltz v. Moore-McCormack Lines, Inc.*, 189 F.2d

537); but publicity-seeking accusers are not content to disclose quietly their accusations to the F.B.I. Therefore, to truly equalize the position of accuser and accused, and to give redress to justified grievances, a more militant measure is necessary.

A distinguished federal district court judge, the Hon. Leon R. Yankwich, in commenting about the Federal Tort Claims Act, of 1946, in which the United States waived its sovereign immunity so as to indemnify citizens, "for injury or loss of property or personal injury or death caused by the negligent or wrongful act or omission of any employee of the government while acting within the scope of his office or employment, under circumstances where the United States, if a private citizen, would be liable to the claimant in accordance with the law of the place where the act or omission occurred" stated his views in terms of this problem of immunity of congressional speech:

> "There is as much reason for holding the government responsible for the reckless slander of an innocent person by our legislative agents as there is for holding the government responsible for the reckless driving of a postal employee. The wrong committed in both instances is a tort" (99 *Univ. of Penna. L. Rev.,* pp. 960-977, 1951).

This theory of government liability for the wrongs perpetrated by its employees or agents can be legally expressed as the doctrine of respondeat superior, "let the higher respond." Like private corporations or private employers, government should be held liable or responsible for libel or slander of an employee, if committed in the course of employment. However, government, due to the English common law concept of divine rights of kings and sovereign, must first waive its sovereign immunity from liability, and consent to be sued or held liable for the tortious acts of its "servants." In the absence of specific statute, the only relief generally afforded the injured or damaged at the hands of government is by a private bill offered by a sympathetic legislator. It was President Lincoln, in his first annual message, who declared: "It is as much the duty of the government to render prompt justice against itself in favor of citizens as it is to administer the same between private individuals."

One of the more eloquent pleas for redress of those persons damaged by slander or libel of accusers protected by congressional immunity was made by then United States Senator Lester C. Hunt of Wyoming, who introduced numerous bills in Congress in the early 1950's, to terminate the demagoguery practiced with complete immunity from laws applied to all other citizens. Senator Hunt, though realizing that money will not save or restore a reputation, was desirous of giving one defamed by any member of Congress, witnesses or investigators, the right to sue the government. The intolerable abuses which resulted in total loss of job and job opportunities for persons so defamed greatly perturbed him. One of the early bills he introduced (Senate Joint Resolution 203, 81st Cong. 2d Sess.) proposed an amendment to the Constitution to repeal the provision granting immunity from suit to members of Congress for speeches and debates in their respective Houses. This constitutional amendment of Article 1, Section 6, Clause 1, i.e., deleting or repealing the last sentence thereof with respect to questioning a member of Congress for any speech or debate in any other place, required ratification within seven years by three-fourths of the several states, and was therefore not feasible. Moreover, it is not necessary to impose criminal or civil sanctions upon members of Congress, nor to deprive them of this immunity, since an adequate remedy exists in an action for monetary damages directly against the Government.

Senator Hunt subsequently introduced identical bills (S. 4113, 81st Cong., 2d Sess., and S. 782, 82d Cong., 1st Sess.) to provide for civil suits against the United States by persons suffering damage as a result of defamations committed by members of Congress in the course of their official activities:

> "Be it enacted by the Senate and House of Representatives of the United States of America in Congress assembled, That the United States district court for the district wherein the plaintiff is resident, or the United States District Court for the District of Columbia, sitting with a jury, shall have exclusive jurisdiction to hear, determine, and render judgment on any claim against the United States, for money only, accruing on and after the date of enactment of this Act, on account of loss or damage sustained as a result of any defamatory statement, con-

stituting a libel or slander, made by a member of Congress during any proceeding of either House of Congress, any committee thereof, or joint committee of the two Houses of Congress. The United States shall be liable in respect of any such claim, in the same manner, and to the same extent as the Member making any such statement would be liable, if such Member had no immunity to suit by reason of Section 6 of Article I of the Constitution of the United States. Costs shall be allowed in all courts to the successful claimant to the same extent as if the United States were a private litigant, except that such costs shall not include attorneys' fees."

This bill, in five other sections, also authorized the Attorney General "to arbitrate, compromise, or settle any claim . . . after the institution of any suit thereon, with the approval of the court." Suit had to be brought "within one year after such claim accrues." Attorney's fees exceeding 20 per cent of the amount recovered were specifically prohibited with criminal penalties. Section 6 of the bill, interestingly enough, expressly forbade, "by subpoena or otherwise, the compulsory attendance of any member of Congress in any action or proceeding," which safeguard was designed to insure against interference with the legislative process. It is presumed that the government's defense in such suits would have been a claim for qualified privilege, the right to "fair comment" like newspapers, magazines, and other publications or forums.

These bills introduced by Senator Hunt were shelved in the Senate Committee on the Judiciary. However, it does not appear that the enactment of S. 4113 or S. 782 would suffice to meet the problem: First, the language of the bills described only the defamatory statement "made by a member of Congress," whereas scurrilous, sensational accusations are also made by investigators, witnesses, and other participants in such proceedings, and all such accusers are truly agents of the particular member of Congress. The desirability of broadening the liability for the defamatory statements of other accusers is therefore evident. Also, the bills should have established a minimum sum as exemplary damages once the court had determined that the statement was in fact defamatory. This requisite is to insure against judgments for such nominal sums as six cents which obviously do not reflect the seriousness of the tortious wrong. An amendment to the Federal Tort Claims Act of 1946 (Title IV of the Reorganization Act of 1946), similarly waiving sovereign immunity for defamation "by any employee of the government while acting within the scope of his office or employment," is also necessary. The amending language should spell out the additional basis for governmental liability, i.e., having provided the very forum for the requisite publication of the defamation, the government has thereby ratified the resultant character assassination. The preamble might well recite the great need for legal protection of all citizens from irresponsible accusations and incriminations of a defamatory nature spoken during or written after a legislative proceeding, either by senators, representatives, witnesses, investigators, or others participating in such legislative proceedings.

Also, there is a feeling that the United States Court of Claims, rather than the United States District Court "for the district wherein the plaintiff is resident, or the United States District Court for the District of Columbia, sitting with a jury" should have exclusive jurisdiction to hear, determine, and render judgment on these claims for defamatory damage against the United States. The United States Court of Claims, established in 1855, is a legislative court deriving its judicial powers solely from the acts of Congress. Its jurisdiction (28 U.S.C. 1491-1505) is confined to the rendition of money judgments against the United States, deciding suits referred by Congress and the executive departments of government. While the United States Court of Claims has no equitable jurisdiction, it does apply equitable principles where applicable in suits waiving the tort for money judgment in contract (*Munsey Trust Co. v. U. S.*, 67 F. Supp. 976). However, it seems wiser to vest jurisdiction in the United States district courts, particularly since the person defamed can institute action in the district in which he resides rather than journey to Washington, or have an attorney appear in his behalf before the United States Court of Claims. However, nothing should prohibit the institution of a claim for defamatory damages against the United States in the United States Court of Claims.

While money cannot compensate the person defamed for lost reputation, the very fact of winning a judgment in a court of law would help somewhat to restore his reputation. But, by far the most important aftermath of the judgment against the United States, is the public record of defamatory utterances by members of Congress, their investigators, and their witnesses which cost the government so heavily in terms of judgments paid to persons defamed. No accuser can long stand in the public spotlight when his record reveals judgment after judgment against the United States for his defamatory conduct. It is the taxpayers' (and voters') money which is being wasted by the accuser's charges when deemed by a court of law to be defamatory and to entitle the defamed to the recovery of monetary damages against the government. Thus, the threat of liability and the public record of such judgments against the United States would be a deterrent to the unscrupulous and the conscious liars. [Criminal prosecution for perjury under Title 18 USC, Section 1621 is always likely.] But, above all, as aptly expressed by Federal District Judge Yankwich, our final hope is:

> "an elightened, vigilant and aroused public opinion which will refuse to accept 'guilt by mere accusation' in lieu of proof under the due process of the Anglo-American legal system which will actively aid those wrongfully accused and will express its disapproval of abuse by legislators of this valuable privilege. For, free as it is now of all legal restraint, if it is allowed to go unchecked by due regard for the decencies of civilized behavior, it will help undermine the legislative process."

## Group Libel and Group Slander

Protection of the individual from defamation is not always possible where that defamed individual is an *unidentified* member of a large group which is itself defamed. Such group defamations as "All doctors are quacks" or "All citizens of New Rochelle are selfish and dishonest" obviously do not require legal relief or legal remedy since such group defamation is meaningless, except perhaps to the ultra-sensitive person whose interest cannot be legally protected at the expense of freedom of speech and of press for all others. However, as the group becomes smaller in numbers, the status of the individual member becomes more important; and as a defamed, *identifiable* person he can sue for his individual damage as a member of the group which is defamed.

To the contrary was the decision of the New York Supreme Court, New York County, on October 19, 1959, in *Cohen v. Brecher*. Here, the plaintiff-employee of a corporation was addressed by the defendant officer of the corporation: "Mr. Cohen, there is a hundred-dollar bill missing, and only you three had access to it. Mr. Cohen, and I want that money returned or else I will fire you, you, and you. . . . One of you is a crook." Mr. Justice Loreto declared that "the words refer to one not specified of a group of persons. . . . The words, 'One of you is a crook' negative the claim that they apply to the plaintiff." The court concluded:

> "Where the words are used to a small or restrictive group expressly but impersonally or indefinitely refer to one or more of several memebrs thereof, one of the members in order to maintain an action must establish the application to himself."

The famous *Red Channels* case, *Julian v. American Business Consultants, Inc.* (131 N.Y.S.2d 374, and 2 NY2d 1) in 1954 delineated the potential influence in radio and television of Communism by listing names of actors and artists in a publication, published in 1950. Joe Julian, a radio actor found his name listed as a speaker at two public meetings in 1942 of the Artists' Front to Win the War. He admitted that he had then recited a roll call of various artists who had died in the struggle against Fascism. Julian was also listed in *Red Channels* as a spectator at a 1949 meeting of the National Council of the Arts, Sciences, and Professions in the Hotel Commodore, New York City, which was called to oppose the practices of the House Un-American Activities Committee. He commenced his libel action against the publication in 1954 and alleged that his yearly income, immediately after the listing of his name, had dropped from $17,000 to $11,878 to $6,710 and to $1,630 in 1953, because the defendant publishers had exposed him to public contempt, ridicule, infamy, and reproach by intentionally painting him in a false light as sympathetic to the Communist Party. Judge Saypol, however, was of the opinion that attaching Julian's name "to the coterie which surrounded him" was *not* "to impute to him their personal defects or moral turpitude." The court declared:

> "Reading *Red Channels* without the introduction and explanation heading the list which contains the plaintiff's name is less than that fair reading which the law requires as an ingredient in a determination of whether or not there is defamation."

Upon dismissal of the complaint, Julian's appeal to the New York Appellate Division, First Dept., resulted in a unanimous affirmance (139 N.Y.S.2d 903) and the New York Court of Appeal on July 11, 1956, in a five to two decision, also affirmed. Judge Burke took the occasion to write:

> "In this state and in this country, every citizen has a constitutional right to free speech. The law of libel is a limitation on the right of every citizen to write freely. Just as the constitutional right of free speech must be extended to all our citizens equally and without discrimination, so also the limitations must be based upon a rule or doctrine which does not create a preference or discrimination in favor of or against any citizen or group of citizens .... Any invasion of the freedom of the press justifies a concern about the inviolability of that great right. The protection of political comment which has been written because the circumstances are of public interest is indispensable to the exercise of freedom."

Judge Burke reminded "those who seek public acclaim and support" that they "cannot expect immunity from criticism or insist that the public remain uninformed regarding their activities":

> "To hold that this book, in light of the admissions made by the plaintiff is defamatory, is to expand the law of libel so as to violate the constitutional guarantee of free speech."

The dissenting opinion of Judge Fuld (joined in by Judge Desmond) pointed out that the court should not itself dispose of the factual issues of the case which were for the jury's determination, i.e., whether the publication *Red Channels* was defamatory of the plaintiff, and whether the publication was privileged as fair comment:

"Just as had individuals in the industry, so may a jury, reasonably find that the booklet, considered as a whole, charges plaintiff with being a Communist sympathizer, a Communist tool, or a Communist dope, and, by reason thereof, defames and disparages him in his business and profession."

Indeed, group libel is more than a legal problem; it is also political, economic, and social. It is a basic cause of prejudice and inter-group tension, and legislation cannot be expected to end group libels. In 1952, in *Beauharnais v. Illinois* (343 U.S. 250), the U. S. Supreme Court declared that the only possible justification for a group libel statute is protection of the public against breaches of the peace. It would appear that any statute giving a remedy for group libel would run afoul of the free speech guarantees under the First Amendment. Yet there is little doubt that public serenity can be seriously destroyed (and a nation placed in desperate straits) by even one vicious hate-monger who foments and exploits one minority group by libel. But the libeler of a group can only be successful in spreading his rancor if the public feels economically, socially and politically insecure and suffers from the psychological maladies of frustration and anxiety. It follows that the only true solution to group libel is a vigilant public, a democratic government, and society capable of removing the insecurity that makes bigotry possible.

The courts have a role to play in criminal libel prosecutions where public disorder results. In Quebec, Canada, in 1914, a bigot Plamondon made a violently antisemitic speech in which he charged all Jews were intent upon committing heinous crimes, and urged his audience to take action against the potential menace. A few days later, a Jewish storekeeper, Ortenberg, was assaulted and his store window smashed; in addition, his business was boycotted by the community. Judge Carroll, in finding against the defendant, noted that there were but seventy-five Jewish families among Quebec's 80,000: "This is not the case of a wrong against an entire class so large that the injury is lost in its members." (35 C.L.T. 262).

In civil suits where the defamed seeks compensation for his alleged injury to reputation the fact of group libel will preclude success unless the libel is accompanied by violence and breaches of the peace. Aside from the difficulties of proving damage either to each group member or to the group itself there is the possibility of a multiplicity of suits which could stultify our judicial system, i.e., if a single libel were to become the basis for litigation by hundreds or thousands of defamed persons. There is also the judicial reluctance to allow encroachment on free speech; and frequently the pursuit of a remedy will more likely inure to the benefit of the defamer and wrongdoer and to the further detriment of the class or group which was defamed and wronged.

## Selected Bibliography

Vol. 6 *Villanova Law Review* 525-531, 1961.
Vol. 39 *Minnesota Law Review* 180-184, 1955.
*Mencher v. Chesley*, 297 N.Y. 94.
*Hudson v. Pioneer Service Co.*, 346 P.2d 123, Oregon, 1959.
*Carlson v. Hillman Periodicals, Inc.*, 3 A.D.2d 987.
*Martin v. Johnson Pub. Co., Inc.*, 157 N.Y.S.2d 409.
*Coleman v. MacLennan*, 78 Kan. 711, 98 P. 281, 1908.
*Tracy v. Newsday, Inc.*, 5 N.Y.2d 134, 1959.
*Matter of Meyer*, 72 N.Y.Misc. 566, 1911.
*Jump v. Barnes*, 139 Md. 101, 114 A. 734, 1921.
*Macy v. New York World Telegram*, 2 N.Y.2d 416, 1957.
*Ogden v. Association of the U. S. Army*, 177 F.Supp. 498, 1959.
Vol. 49 *American Bar Association Journal* 771, August, 1963.
*Remington v. Bentley*, 88 F.Supp. 166, New York, 1949.
*Port Huron Broadcasting Co.*, 12 F.C.C. 1069, 1948.
*Murray v. Brancato*, 290 N.Y. 52, 48 N.E.2d 257.
*Kimmerle v. New York Evening Journal*, 262 N.Y. 99, 186 N.E. 217, 1933.
*State v. Klapprott*, 127 N.J.L. 395, 1941.
*Palmer v. Concord*, 48 N.H. 211, 1868.
*Drozda v. State*, 86 Tex.App. 614, 1920.

## Questions for Review

1. Why should society concern itself with protecting an individual's reputation? Is free speech and freedom of the press more or less important to the democratic process?
2. Who should judge whether an utterance or statement is defama-

tory, the victim or "a sizeable and moral segment of the community," to wit, a jury?
3. Should anyone have a "privilege" to defame another? Is malice an element of the defamation?
4. What is the right of privacy? Should privacy be protected in the absence of a libel or slander?
5. How can a person defame a person or a product if the defamer is honestly unaware of the existence of the person or product?
6. Should candidates in a political campaign be given immunity from liability for libelous and slanderous statements?
7. What is "fair comment" by a newspaper or magazine? Is it a defense to a defamation?
8. Should "embarrassment" be legally actionable for damages? Should "provocation" uttered loudly be legally actionable for damages?
9. Should society permit defamation by last will or testament? Should the decedent's estate be liable?
10. Why do courts recognize the *absolute privilege* between spouses with respect to liability for defamation?
11. When is "truth" an absolute defense to defamation? Should a newspaper be accorded special consideration in defending a libel suit based upon "errors" of its reporter?
12. Do you you sympathize with Miss Torre's plight in refusing to disclose the identity of her news informant? How could C.B.S. defend the libel suit without her testimony?
13. Should there be different legal principles applicable to defamation over radio and television? Is "equal time" for political candidates a salutary rule?
14. Why do governmental officials have absolute immunity from defamation in the performance of their official duties?
15. Why do legislators have immunity from defamation? What restraints do you suggest?
16. Is a group libel statute desirable or necessary? Is group defamation a social, political or economic problem?

## Chapter VI

# CORPORATE MERGERS AND ACQUISITIONS: PATTERNS OF ECONOMIC CONCENTRATION

### Our American Economy Generally

THE AMERICAN ECONOMY has been governed, in a large measure, and its market structure shaped, by mergers and acquisitions of corporate enterprises. Our anti-trust laws are geared to foster competition by preventing any substantial lessening of competition, any monopolization, or any tendency to monopoly. Specifically, Section 7 of the Clayton Act, as amended, has prohibited since 1914 corporate mergers or acquisitions that may produce the above adverse effects. The measurement of economic concentration is a task intimately connected with American public policy objectives of furthering and maintaining competition, and Section 7 was designed to enhance that policy: (a) competitively determined prices reflect the influences of supply and demand, and thereby guide the flow of labor, capital and other resources toward the most productive uses; (b) competition provides powerful and persuasive incentives for product innovation, product development, and cost reduction ,and (c) competitive conditions in business lead to freedom of choice and equitable diffusion of real income among consumers and the factors of production. In Attorney General Robert F. Kennedy's maiden address before the American Society of Newspaper Editors on April 2, 1961, he declared:

> "Our aim in enforcing the anti-merger law is to make sure that no enterprise has a chance to dominate or control an industry or to start in that direction."

A glance into the background of the merger movement is therefore in order.

## A Short History of the Merger Movement: "The Urge to Merge"

The history of the merger movement in the United States stems from the great combines or trusts preceding the enactment, by Congress, of the Sherman Act of 1890. From that year to 1904, American business was motivated by the development of mass production techniques which gave birth to giant corporations and to an era of corporate consolidations. Undoubtedly, these early mergers were effected through the purchase of the *stock* of the acquired company rather than of physical assets. The Sherman Act successfully brought about the dissolution of such monopolies as *Northern Securities* in 1904, and *Standard Oil* and *American Tobacco* in 1911. (In the *Standard Oil* case, eleven million words of testimony over four and one-half years of trial ended in the divestment of thirty-three Standard Oil subsidiaries as an "unreasonable" monopoly in restraint of trade; Standard Oil had then produced 30 per cent of all domestic crude oil and controlled 70 per cent of all domestic purchasing, refining, transporting and marketing of petroleum and its products.) Several years later, the *U.S. Steel* monopoly, after dragging through the courts for nine years, was exonerated despite its acquisition of competing, steel-producing companies: sheer bigness alone did *not* constitute a monopoly. It was thus recognized that the Sherman Act was unable to nip monopolies in their incipiency, and in 1914, Congress passed the Clayton Act to halt the overall monopoly growth before it reached the proportions of a Sherman Act violation. Under Section 7 of the 1914 Clayton Act, the corporate acquisition of the *stock* of a competitor which substantially lessened competition between the acquiring and the acquired companies, or which substantially restrained commerce in any area of the country, or which tended to create a monopoly in any line of commerce, were specifically prohibited.

But the 1914 Clayton Act did not abate the tremendous number of corporate mergers with their inherent monopolistic tendencies. Business promoters acquired and held *stock* control of competing companies until such time as a merger of the physical assets of the companies could be accomplished. Such a method obviously circumvented the very purposes of the 1914 Clayton Act, and the federal government was powerless to intercede, much less seek a divestiture of the physical assets thus acquired. The wave of corporate mergers in the 1920's was instigated by promoters who obtained incredible profits from such ventures. The stock market crash of 1929 saw the disintegration of these short-lived "empires," and Congress finally stepped into the breach by the enactment of the Securities and Exchange Act and the Public Utilities Holding Company Act in 1933. Yet the growth of mergers and acquisitions continued in the face of unsuccessful efforts to prevent or limit such practices through this legislation. It is estimated that between 1940 and 1947 some 2,500 independent companies of substantial size and importance disappeared as the result of mergers and acquisitions.

Finally, on December 30, 1950, Congress amended Section 7 of the Clayton Act (the Celler Amendment) by prohibiting corporations from acquiring

> "the whole or any part of the *assets* of another corporation, engaged in commerce, where in any line of commerce, in any section of the country, the effect of such acquisition may be substantially to lessen competition or tend to create a monopoly."

Thus, the defect in the 1914 Clayton Act was corrected, not only by prohibiting acquisition of *physical assets* as well as *stock,* but also by enlarging upon the measurement of the effect of such merger or acquisition by not limiting the test to the lessening of competition between the acquired and the acquiring companies, or "horizontal mergers." By deleting the words "any community" in favor of "any section of the country," the prohibition on restraint of trade was broadened. Similarly, the old test was eliminated in favor of "where the effect . . . may be substantially to lessen competition or tend to create a monopoly." The broad language of the Celler Amendment was deemed to affect all types of corporate mergers and acquisitions, i.e., *vertical, horizontal,* and *conglomerate,* as hereinafter delineated.

### The Role of the Federal Trade Commission in Mergers

The Federal Trade Commission under Section 7 of the Clayton Act, as amended, has no authority to prohibit or prevent mergers in their incipiency—in contrast to the role of the U.S. Department of Justice, discussed hereinafter. The FTC must first determine the reasonable and probable competitive effects of the specific merger or acquisition before it can enforce the law by the issuance of a complaint. It would seem that the FTC is impeded from accomplishing the avowed congressional purpose of striking down monopolistic tendencies in effective terms. The post-World War II period indeed nurtured a fantastic boom in the number of mergers: in 1951 alone, more than 750 resulted, of which more than half the acquiring companies had assets in excess of ten million dollars, and of which almost 200 companies had assets of more than fifty million dollars. In its "Report on Corporate Mergers and Acquisitions" the FTC, in May 1955, found that, during the 1948-1954 period, the largest number of acquisitions were made by firms in the non-electrical machinery and food and kindred product industries, which two industries accounted for one-fourth of the total of 1,773 mergers which occurred. The report disclosed that the most active acquiring company was Foremost Dairies with forty-eight acquisitions, followed by Borden Company with seventeen, Olin-Mathieson Chemical Corp. with sixteen, Food Machinery and Chemical Corp. with fourteen, H. K. Porter Co. with thirteen, Burlington Mills with twelve, American Marietta Co. with twelve, and American Machine and Foundry Co. with eleven. In forty per cent of all acquisitions, the competitive advantage desired was "additional capacity to supply a market already supplied by the acquirer;" in 25 per cent of the acquisitions, the reason given was "lengthened product lines and product diversification." There was a marked tendency for more and more persons representing outside interests such as legal and economic consultants, research industrial engineers, banks, investment houses, etc., to become "engaged or involved in the business of promoting or playing some other vital role in the merger formation." The most widely used method of financing such acquisitions was that of exchanging stock, not physical assets.

In November 1962, the House Select Committee on Small Business released a staff report tracing acquisitions made by the 500 largest industrial and fifty largest merchandising firms since 1951. These firms absorbed some 3,736 companies, most of which were in the following industries: dairy products (462); paper (213); petroleum (193); electrical equipment (160); industrial chemicals (204); aerospace (170); and merchandising (332). Indeed, the growth of the merger movement points up the need for constant vigilance by the federal government to see that competition is still active and healthy in the American economy.

## The Role of the U. S. Department of Justice in Mergers

The ability of the U.S. Department of Justice to nip monopolies in their incipiency is evident from an examination of three important 1955 cases which, unfortunately, were not carried out to a logical, legal conclusion but terminated by voluntary consent orders. These cases were challenges to the legality of "horizontal mergers" in the hotel, shoe, and whiskey industries.

In the *Hilton Hotels Corp.* case the acquisition of the second largest hotel chain (Statler) by the largest hotel chain (Hilton) was challenged. The U.S. Department of Justice asserted that Hilton operated fifteen hotels in eleven cities with 16,500 rooms, had assets of one hundred and five million dollars, and gross revenue of ninety-seven million dollars; and that in Washington, D.C., New York, St. Louis, and Los Angeles, the Hilton chain competed directly with the Statler chain which ran nine hotels in nine cities with 9,830 rooms, had assets of sixty-seven million dollars, and gross revenue of sixty million dollars. The government stressed the competition nationally in obtaining convention business, and charged Hilton, as the result of the Statler acquisition, with (a) elimination of actual and potential competition, including soliciting and servicing conventions; (b) enhancement of Hilton's monopolistic advantage over all other hotels, including the permanent elimination of its nearest competitor, and (c) the substantial increase, both nationally and in certain sections of the country, of economic concentration in the hotel industry. The government demanded divestiture of the acquired properties in the four cities in order to restore competitive conditions to the hotel industry. On February 6, 1956, without a finding of facts or a violation of law, the U.S. Department of Justice accepted a settlement agreement with Hilton, which decree required Hilton to dispose of one Hilton hotel in St. Louis, Washington, D.C., and

New York, and limited the number of Hilton hotels in New York City to four, in Washington, D.C., St. Louis, and Los Angeles to one per city. Thus, no divestiture was accomplished, and after 1961, Hilton was permitted to acquire additional hotels even in these three cities. Obviously, the alleged violation of Section 7 of the Clayton Act, as amended, by virtue of the settlement, did not arrest the hotel monopoly growth of the Hilton chain.

In the *General Shoe Corp.* case the government pointed to the many acquisitions by this defendant during the 1950-1955 period which had substantially lessened competition and tended to monopolize both the manufacture and retail sale of shoes in the United States. General Shoe operated thirty manufacturing plants and 500 retail shoe stores, grossed one hundred and thirty-five million dollars from sales of twenty-five million shoes, two-thirds of which were sold at wholesale. The company had acquired eighteen manufacturing and/or shoe retailing companies with total annual sales exceeding sixty-seven million dollars. The government contended that, as the result of these acquisitions, competing shoe manufacturers were foreclosed from a market of 250 retail outlets with annual sales of thirty-four million dollars. Although the court found violation of Section 7, the consent decree of February 17, 1956, resulted in a limited divestiture of only eighteen acquired companies; several general restraints, for a period of five years, were also imposed upon General Shoe, but the net effect was not to curb the monopolistic growth.

The multiple acquisition by *Schenley Industries, Inc.* of the controlling stock of Park & Tilford was also attacked in February, 1955, by the U.S. Department of Justice. Included in the government's complaint were nearly fifty similar purchases by Schenley of competing companies in the liquor industry during the 1933-1950 period. In 1953, Schenley had controlled 17 per cent of the total industry capacity for producing whiskey, and had produced 22 per cent of all whiskey after acquiring Park & Tilford, bottling therefore more whiskey than any other company. The scarcity of competition in the sale of liquor prompted the government to seek divestiture of all Park & Tilford stock. On April 3, 1957, the *Schenley* case was settled without divestiture, although, in the interim, foreign suppliers had canceled their agency agreements with Park & Tilford and this acquired company had become a mere shell. The consent decree limited Schenley for a period of ten years from acquiring any other distilling company which would substantially lessen competition or tend to create a monopoly in the distilling business.

It should be observed that the typical antitrust proceeding involves an exorbitant expense in time and money, both for the government and for the defendant. In *United States v. Henry S. Morgan, et al* (118 F. Supp. 621, 1953), for example, there were 10,640 pre-trial exhibits consisting of 43,252 pages; 6,848 pages of pre-trial depositions; 309 days of trial plus twenty-five days of off-the-record conferences between court and counsel; 23,962 pages of trial transcript; and 417 pages devoted to the court's opinion deciding the case. There can be little wonder why consent agreements are frequently reached without necessarily deciding the merits of the case.

### The Problems of Merger: "Line of Commerce," "Relevant Market," and "Competitive Impact"

The economic complexities inherent in any Section 7 case are readily apparent by reviewing briefly several illustrative cases which involve these major points: (a) the line of commerce or product; (b) the section of the country or market area, and (c) the competitive impact of the merger in that relevant market.

In 1956, Brown Shoe, the fourth largest manufacturer of shoes, acquired Kinney, the largest family shoe store operator in the United States. This "vertical merger" was attacked by the government, and the federal court in St. Louis, in November 1959, ruled that Brown must divest itself of the Kinney Company. Judge Weber agreed that "line of commerce cannot be determined by any process of logic and should be determined by the process of observation . . . In other words, determine how the industry itself and how the users, the public, treat the shoe product." Accordingly, he concluded that "men's," "women's" and "children's" were separate product lines to be considered, and so accepted the government's contention by rejecting Brown's argument that product lines had to be determined by grade, quality, price, and use. For "market area" the court stated that manufacturing must be measured in terms of the whole United States, although a single city could be taken as a unit of the market for retailing shoes. On the issue of "competitive impact," the court found that the merger would pose a serious threat:

> "What difference can it make that Brown has only 5 per cent of the shoe production and Kinney 0.5 per cent when Brown is the fourth largest firm in the U.S. and Kinney, with only 0.9 per cent of all retail shoe sales, is the largest family shoe chain retailer? The test is, what do the facts show as to the trends in the industry and the true economic impact of this particular merger, which takes place among an industry having a few very large firms that control a sizable segment of the total, with the balance divided among hundreds of others having only minute segments?"

Judge Weber noted that there was a definite trend of shoe manufacturers in buying up retail outlets; that after such acquisitions, the manufacturer's sales to that retailer jump, as did Brown's sales to Kinney from 0 to 7.9 per cent of all Kinney shoe purchases. As a result thereof, retail markets for independent manufacturers were being "seriously limited," and it had become "harder and harder" for independent retailers to compete with company-owned and company-controlled retail outlets. On June 25, 1962, the U.S. Supreme Court affirmed the lower court ruling (370 U.S. 294), and Brown was compelled to divest itself of Kinney stock and assets, and ordered to file a plan with the court for carrying the divestiture into effect. Chief Justice Warren in his opinion pointed to the "rising tide of economic concentration in the American economy."

Divestiture was ordered by the U.S. Supreme Court, on April 6, 1964, in the *El Paso Natural Gas Co.* case (376 U.S. 651). This acquiring company was the sole out-of-state supplier of natural gas to the California market when it acquired Pacific Northwest Pipeline Corp., which operated a pipeline from New Mexico to Washington, and had previously tried, without success, to enter the California market. El Paso, in May 1957, acquired 99.8 per cent of the stock of Pacific Northwest and, within two months, the U.S. Department of Justice filed suit under Section 7, charging that the acquisition substantially lessened competition in the sale of natural gas in California. Mr. Justice Douglas opined that it was irrelevant whether Pacific Northwest as an independent entity could have obtained a contract from California distributors to furnish natural gas to them, because the effect of the merger was still a substantial lessening of competition:

> "Congress used the words 'may be substantially to lessen competition' . . . . to indicate that its concern was with probabilities, not certainties . . . . Mergers with a probable anticompetitive effect were to be proscribed by this Act."

On June 1, 1964, the U.S. Supreme Court held illegal the *Aluminum Company of America's* acquisition of Rome Cable Corp., a maker of wire and cable for electrical transmission, although Rome [before the merger] had accounted for only 1.3 per cent of all alumincum-conductor production. By the six to three decision, Alcoa was ordered to divest itself of Rome which it acquired in 1959. Mr. Justice Douglas observed that Alcoa already controlled 27.8 per cent of the aluminum-conductor market, and declared that there was a growing "likelihood that parallel policies of mutual advantage, not competition, will emerge . . . " The dissent argued that the government had not proved there was a separate "line of commerce" made up of aluminum cable, that the relevant markets were made up of both aluminum and copper cable.

And on June 22, 1964, the highest court held that the acquisition of the *Hazel-Atlas Glass Co.*, the nation's third largest producer of glass containers, by Continental Can Company, the second largest producer of metal containers, was illegal, although the court conceded that the products made by the two companies were only partially competitive. Mr. Justice White, speaking for the seven to one court, found that glass and metal containers are sufficiently competitive to form "a line of commerce" within the meaning of Section 7 of the Clayton Act, as amended:

> "There may be some end uses for which glass and metal do not and could not compete, but complete inter-industry competitive overlap need not be shown . . . . We would not be true to the purpose of the Clayton Act's line-of-commerce concept as a framework within which to measure the effect of mergers on competition were we to hold that the existence of non-

competitive segments within a proposed market area precludes its being treated as a line of commerce."

The court found that after the merger Continental's percentage of the relevant market increased from 22 to 25 per cent, and reduced from five to four the number of major companies in the market.

### Types of Mergers: Horizontal, Vertical, and Conglomerate

The FTC reported that for the year 1963, the number of mergers consummated or publicly known to be in negotiation totaled 1,311, a considerable increase over previous years. The continued uptrend in mergers necessitates some analysis of the "types" of mergers and acquisitions.

"Horizontal" mergers involve competing companies; "vertical" mergers involve competing raw material suppliers and/or customers of the finished product; and "conglomerate mergers involve companies selling unrelated products or services. Generally, only the latter "type" of a merger would *logically* imply no extinguishment of competition since the relevant markets are separate and non-competitive. However, "conglomerate" or diversified mergers are not *legally* free from the ban of Section 7 because the total size of a company in all markets may tend to a monopoly. Indeed, sheer size and economic power may threaten the continued existence of small competitors in that unrelated market or industry. In February 1963, the FTC ruled that a "conglomerate merger" was illegal because the acquiring company, *Consolidated Foods Corp.*, had enough buying muscle to force its suppliers to buy dried onion and garlic from Gentry, Inc., the non-competitive company it had acquired. FTC Commissioner Elman declared that the merger was illegal because Gentry would acquire a sheltered market, i.e., a food processor who wanted to do business with Consolidated would buy from Gentry, regardless of whether Gentry's product or price was better than Gentry's competitor. In another suit the FTC ruled that *Proctor & Gamble* could not acquire Clorox because Proctor & Gamble's big size and efficient, well-financed marketing facilities would result in damage to Clorox's competitors. Thus, such "conglomerate" mergers run afoul of Section 7 of the Clayton Act, as amended; but under the Sherman Act or the unfair practice clause of Section 5 of the FTC Act, as amended, *overt* coercion by a company would be necessary to establish a violation of law.

Under Section 7, there are six express acquisitions or mergers which are *not* prohibited, even though they may result in prohibited competitive consequences: (a) acquisitions by non-corporations or individuals; (b) acquisitions from non-corporations or individuals; (c) acquisitions solely for investment purposes; (d) acquisitions under authority of federal regulatory agencies; (e) acquisitions solely for formation of corporate subsidiaries, and (f) acquisitions consummated prior to December 30, 1950, the date of passage of the Act. A corporation in a failing or bankrupt condition is not prohibited from selling its assets to a competitor.

**Selected Recent Cases: "Pillsbury" and "duPont-General Motors"**

The *Pillsbury Mills* proceeding before the FTC took almost ten years before the merger was held to be unlawful and divestiture ordered on January 5, 1961. Pillsbury, a large producer of flour and mixes, acquired the assets of two small competitors, one of which was important in the southeastern United States (Ballard) and the other was a leader throughout the country (Duff). Although Pillsbury was the second largest flour miller in the country, it argued that proof of lessening of competition in a given, relevant market area was necessary to establish a violation of law. The FTC opined that the "growth history" of Pillsbury and its cumulative movement toward monopoly power was the proper factor for violation of law without reference to a selected, relevant market.

Vertical integration (as opposed to horizontal integration in the *Pillsbury* case) was curtailed by the U.S. Supreme Court in the *duPont-General Motors* case, in 1957. In a four to two decision, the court held that duPont acquisition of the stock of General Motors, both a customer and a competitor, was illegal (353 U.S. 586). The fundamental issue was whether duPont's purchases of G.M. stock in 1917-1919 and duPont's voting of 23 per cent of G.M. stock, achieved for duPont a "commanding position" as GM's supplier of automotive fabrics and finishes, because of (a) competitive merit, or (b) the close inter-company stock relationship which allegedly channeled G.M. purchases to duPont. (G.M. is the second largest U.S. industrial concern and duPont is the fourth largest.) The court reviewed the history of the relationship between the two companies, and pointed out:

> "The fact that sticks out . . . is that the bulk of duPont's production has always supplied the largest part of the requirements of the one customer in the automobile industry connected to duPont by a stock interest. The inference is overwhelming that duPont's commanding position was promoted by its stock interest and was not gained solely on competitive merit."

Mr. Justice Brennan opined that Section 7 applied to both "horizontal" and "vertical" mergers — "whenever the reasonable likelihood appears that the acquisition will result in a restraint of commerce or in the creation of a monopoly in any line of commerce." He noted that duPont supplied about two thirds of GM's automobile finishes and about one half of GM's automobile fabrics, both of which products were readily distinguishable from other products for all other uses as a distinct "line of commerce" in the relevant market. The bounds of the relevant market were not co-extensive with the total market for all finishes and fabrics, but were deemed co-extensive only with the automobile industry.

The court also rejected the defendants' argument that Section 7 was applicable only to the acquisition, not the holding or subsequent use of such stock:

> "Its aim (Section 7) was primarily to arrest apprehended consequences of inter-corporate relationships before those relationships could work their evil, which may be at or any time after acquisition . . . . To accomplish the congressional aim the government may proceed at any time that an acquisition may be said with reasonable probability to contain a threat that it may lead to a restraint of commerce or tend to create a monopoly of a line of commerce.
> 
> "Even when the purchase is solely for investment, the plain language of Section 7 contemplates an action at any time the stock is used to bring about or in attempting to bring about the substantial lessening of competition. The test of a violation of Section 7 is whether *at the time of suit* there is a reasonable

probability that the acquisition is likely to result in the condemned restraints" (italics added).

The dissenting opinion of Mr. Justice Burton (in which Mr. Justice Frankfurter joined) declared that the language and structure of Section 7 showed that the effect of the stock acquisition on competition was to be determined as of *the time of the acquisition,* not at the time the government chose to bring suit which was some thirty years after duPont acquired the G.M. stock:—

> "The court's holding is unfair to the individuals who entered into transactions on the assumption, justified by the language of Section 7, that their actions would be judged by the facts available to them at the time they made their decision . . . . Examination of the dozen or more cases brought under Section 7 reveals that in every case the inquiry heretofore has centered on the probable anti-competitive effects of the stock acquisition at or near the time it was made."

The two dissenters opined that duPont products were used on a large scale for many other purposes in many other industries, and neither the automobile industry nor General Motors comprised a substantial share of that market: "The record does not show that the fabrics and finishes used in the manufacture of automobiles have peculiar characteristics differentiating them from the finishes and fabrics used in other industries."

[It should be observed that a seven-month trial, with a transcript of 8,283 pages dealing with a multiplicity of issues thoroughly and expertly developed by counsel and carefully appraised by the federal district court judge in an opinion of some 100 pages, was culminated in a determination by only four justices of the U.S. Supreme Court, still a minority of the full court of nine justices.]

In late September, 1957, Federal Judge LaBuy in Chicago directed the drafting of a plan for duPont to comply with the order of the U.S. Supreme Court. He outlined a method of disposal by duPont of its 63,000,000 shares of G.M. stock worth $2,700,000,000. On October 25th, the government proposed a ten-year divestment by duPont of 60 per cent of its G.M. stock to the 153,000 duPont common stockholders, excepting duPont affiliate corporations; the remaining 40 per cent of G.M. stock would be sold at public and private sale during "reasonable market conditions." In addition, the government requested other provisions to separate duPont and General Motors: a barring of duPont influence over GM by prohibiting interlocking directorates and sharing of officers; a prohibition against contracts requiring G.M. to buy any specific percentage of its needs in any product from duPont; and a restraint against G.M. granting duPont any preferential rights to make or sell G.M. chemical discoveries. The federal district court rejected, in -1959, the government's contention that absolute divestiture was a mandatory remedy, but agreed to "divest duPont of the votes on such G.M. shares and pass such votes through *pro rata* to duPont stockholders and then to enjoin the exercise of such votes as lodge in Christiana and Delaware and in officers and directors of duPont, Christiana, and Delaware, their spouses and dependents." Ancillary injunctive relief included bars against additional stock acquisitions and common officers, directors, and employees; also, included were injunctive provisions relating to trade between the two companies.

In May, 1960, the U.S. Supreme Court agreed to review the district court's determination (366 U.S. 316), and in May 1961, the highest court refused to change the ten-year deadline on duPont to dispose of its G.M. stock, remanding the case to the federal district court with instructions that (a) the proposed judgment provide for complete divestiture of GM stock be filed within sixty days; (b) divestiture begin within ninety days and terminate within ten years, and (c) the government file proposed amendments or alternative relief within thirty days after service of duPont's proposed judgment. The three dominant considerations in formulating the decree were as follows: (a) it must give effect to the prohibitions of the statute; (b) injury to the public interest must be minimized, and (c) the interests of private property, such as stock held by "innocent" shareholders, must be considered.

On March 1, 1962, Federal Judge LaBuy handed down his *final* judgment in this thirteen-year old case, the biggest antitrust case in history! By disposal of the stock, the holdings of the principal duPont family group closest to management would be reduced from 4.5 per cent to 1.85 per cent of the outstanding G.M. stock. A total of 8,575,000 shares of G.M. stock was involved in the final disposition by the duPont family, trust funds, and others close to the duPont interests.

## Other Selected Merger-Acquisition Cases

### Bethlehem Steel and Youngstown Sheet and Tube Co.

A 1954-originated merger agreement was attacked by the U.S. Department of Justice in the federal district court in New York:

> "The merger would compound the already high degree of concentration in the iron and steel industry. The combined company would have 20 per cent of the total industry capacity. It would be two and one-half times the size of the next largest company (Republic) and four times the size of either Jones & Laughlin, National, Armco, or Inland, the four next largest companies . . . . A combination of Bethlehem and Youngstown cannot be deemed necessary to enable them to compete more effectively with United States Steel. Neither Bethlehem nor Youngstown is a weak enterprise: both are among the fifty largest corporations in the country . . . . "

The two companies, on the other hand, argued that the merger "would permit a rapid, economical addition of 3,000,000 tons of capacity in the Chicago and Youngstown areas . . . . The building of new mills and the pooling of technical skills and managerial abilities of Bethlehem and Youngstown would introduce a new and strong competitive factor into the situation . . . . A merger of the two concerns would create a second steel company positioned to compete with the largest unit in the industry across the nation, instead of in certain areas only as now."

On November 20, 1958, Federal Judge Weinfeld in an eighty-eight-page opinion prohibited the merger upon the ground that there was a reasonable probability that it would violate Section 7 with respect to both the iron and steel industry as a whole and with respect to separate lines of commerce within the industry, to wit: hot rolled sheets, cold rolled sheets, hot rolled bars, buttweld pipe, electricweld pipe, seamless pipe, oil field equipment and supplies, tin plate, track spikes, and wire rope. Judge Weinfeld concluded that the merger would eliminate substantial competition, present and potential, between Bethlehem and Youngstown in substantial relevant markets; that it would eliminate a substantial, independent alternative source of supply for all steel customers; and that it would substantially increase the concentration of power among the biggest companies in the steel industry for the combined company would have assets of nearly three billion dollars and sales of three billion dollars. Thus, the court found that the merger would "substantially lessen competition in a line of commerce in a section of the country."

### Cuban-American Sugar Co.

In a private lawsuit, American Crystal Sugar Co. sought a permanent injunction against Cuban-American Sugar Co., contending that Cuban had acquired a substantial block of stock in American Crystal, in violation of Section 7 of the Clayton Act, as amended. American Crystal manufactured and sold sugar from *sugar beets;* Cuban was a holding company whose wholly-owned subsidiary, Colonial, operated a *cane sugar* refinery, imported raw cane sugar, and then marketed the refined sugar in a ten-state area in open competition with American Crystal. The federal district court, in 1957, found that Cuban was substantially lessening competition to the detriment of American Crystal, and awarded injunctive relief to American Crystal (152 F. Supp. 387). On appeal, the appellate court affirmed, holding that the two products were reasonably interchangeable, and thus part of the same line of commerce (259 F.2d 524). Judge Hincks stated that, despite the fact that cane sugar commanded a premium price and customers in placing orders often specified whether they wanted cane or beet sugar, each product was sensitive to price changes in the other, thus establishing cross-elasticity of demand. The court also noted the evidence of the eventual merger of the two competitors by stock acquisitions in face of evidence that no new sugar refiners could be anticipated in the industry, and ruled that Section 7 permitted the court to forestall activities in advance of actual violation of the statute. No divestiture of the acquired stock was deemed necessary since the court restrained Cuban from voting the stock, from acquiring more stock, and from being represented on the board of directors of American Crystal.

### Chrysler Corporation

In August 1964, an agreement by Chrysler Corp. to acquire Mack Trucks was smashed on the rocks of Section 7. Chrysler contended that the deal would enable it to compete more effectively with "bigger" makers of heavy-duty trucks. But Federal Judge Wortendyke declared that the merger would stop planned Chrysler expansion of its own truck efforts and eliminate an independent competitor. The court's ruling resulted in both parties calling off the merger.

### Federal Trade Commission Cases

In the *A. G. Spaulding* proceeding (Dkt. 6478, February 1959), the relevant product market was the bone of contention when Spaulding acquired its competitor. But the FTC found no less than nineteen lines of commerce, such as baseballs, footballs, basketballs, golf irons, and strung tennis rackets. None of the products was interchangeable with equipment used in other sports, and each had its own peculiar characteristics. The FTC ruled that the acquisition was not in violation of Section 7.

On the other hand, in the *Scott Paper* proceeding (Dkt. 6559, January 1961), the FTC ruled that Scott had unlawfully acquired three suppliers of semi-processed materials. The cumulative effect of the acquisitions in the line of commerce (nationwide production and sale of sanitary paper products and component items) was considered against the background of an already high level of market concentration in the industry and Scott's dominant position even before the acquisitions. The FTC specifically held that Scott had decisively strengthened its ability to compete by gaining needed materials and production facilities which also afforded operating economies and strategic market advantages that could be reflected in prices, profits, advertising volume, and product diversification for further enhancement of its market positions; and Scott had substantially increased its share in the market over their already high levels. The "vertical" acquisitions therefore necessitated divestiture.

In the *Union Carbide* case (Dkt. 6826, August 1956), the FTC attacked the largest manufacturer of polyethylene resin which had acquired its customer Visking, the largest producer of polyethylene film. In addition to the vertical integration, the acquisition had a "conglomerate" acquisition aspect because Visking was engaged in a wholly unrelated enterprise, the production and sale of regenerated cellulose sausage casings. The FTC examiner found that there were only three producers of such casings, that the market was substantial (over $30,000,000) and that Visking's 60 per cent share was substantial. But the FTC examiner refused to infer that the merger would result in a substantial lessening of competition:

> "All that is here essentially is that in this market, two commercial strangers have united and the product of one, sausage casings, now has the financial backing of a billion and a half dollars of assets instead of something less than one hundred million formerly, and that therefore this financial power can be used to drive everyone else out of the market. Such a forecast on this loose and spotty record calls for a temerity and clairvoyance which I do not possess. The verdict is a Scotch one —*not proved*."

### Bigness! Is It Illegal Under the Anti-trust Laws?

Professor A. A. Berle, Jr., of Columbia Law School, in a November 21, 1959 article in the *New York Times* attacked the theory that economic bigness, in itself, was illegal under the anti-trust laws. While he conceded that size in business could be dangerously anti-social, he argued that the anti-trust laws were not enacted to deal with bigness:—

> "Unquestionably the problem of bigness has to be faced. But I suggest that the federal courts are not apt instruments either for national economic decisions or for economic planning. They have neither mandate, method nor competence to lay down the basis on which such decisions or such planning should proceed. Still less they have any business to assign them-

selves that function by their own fiat. The Congress of the United States is there just for these purposes."

Professor Louis B. Schwartz, of the University of Pennsylvania Law School (in 109 *Univ. of Penna. Law Review* 31-53, November 1960), concerned himself with oligopolies which must be identified, their effects and the extent to which other market forces may counteract their monopolistic tendencies, must be studied:

> "It is remarkable that . . . our antitrust laws may permit a structural change—a unification of firms by merger or holding company control—where it would not tolerate restrictive agreements between the same firms, although market control involved in the latter arrangement is far less comprehensive and enduring and presumably, therefore, less dangerous . . . . A startling consequence of this paradox of antitrust regulation is that the enactment of a law preventing temporary combinations to replace the newly forbidden restrictive agreements. The process of consolidation will go on to the limit of the law. Where this limit is high, as it has been in the United States, major industries will typically come to be dominated by two, three, or four firms—that is, by an oligopoly. Economists tell us that oligopolies function like monopolies, or as if there were agreements among the leading firms even though no such agreements exist."

## Selected Bibliography

*FTC v. Crown Zellerbach,* —F2d —, CA9,1961.
Hale and Hale: *Market Power: Size and Shape Under the Sherman Act,* 1958.
H.R. Report No. 1191 (81st Cong., 1st Sess.).
*United States v. First National Bank and Trust Co. of Lexington,* 376 U.S. 665, April, 1964.

## Questions for Review

1. Why is an anti-merger law compatible with our economic objectives? Is it a restraint upon "freedom?"
2. Why did not the 1914 Clayton Act succeed in busting up monopolies?

3. What "loophole" did the Cellar Amendment plug? Why was this legislation necessary?
4. Discuss the basic difference in approach to a merger problem between the FTC and the U.S. Department of Justice.
5. Was divestiture the logical weapon for the government in the *Hilton Hotel* case? In *General Shoe*? In *Schenley Industries*?
6. What is a "vertical" merger? Contrast it with a "horizontal" merger, and cite examples. Does a "conglomerate" merger necessarily involve both "vertical" and "horizontal" integration? Explain.
7. List the express mergers or acquisitions which are not prohibited under Section 7 of the Clayton Act, as amended. Are these "loopholes?"
8. What was the guiding principle in the *duPont-General Motors* decision? Do you agree with the divestiture ruling?
9. Are *private* lawsuits between the acquired and the acquiring company capable of resolving merger problems? Is there a need for the government to step in and initiate the proceeding?
10. What is wrong with "bigness?" When is a corporation "big?"

## Chapter VII

# ANTI-TRUST LAW: THE BUSINESS OF SPORTS

### "Trade or Commerce" and Sports

THE FUNDAMENTAL anti-trust law, under the Sherman Act of 1890, declares to be illegal those contracts, combinations, or conspiracies in restraint of "trade or commerce" among the several states. Since the first days of enactment of the Act, the meaning of the words "trade or commerce" has been the subject of complex litigation resulting in decisions which at times, appear to limit and, at other times, appear to expand upon the content of the phrase. In the 1895 decision by the U.S. Supreme Court, in the *E. C. Knight* case (156 U.S. 1), dealing with the defendant's control of the manufacturing sugar through its purchase of the stock of three competing sugar refineries, it was held that *manufacturing alone* was *not* "trade or commerce," and the Sherman Act was *not* applicable to bar that particular restraint upon competition. Other early cases similarly held that the anti-trust statute did not apply unless it could be proved that the direct and immediate result of the contract, combination, or conspiracy was to restrain "trade or commerce" among the several states. It was not until 1947, in the *Mandeville Island Farms* case (327 U.S. 114), that the highest court broadened its interpretation of the phrase to include those contracts, combinations, and conspiracies involving *local* activities and services, if the restraint exerted a *substantial* economic effect upon interstate commerce; or, if, even in the absence of such a restraint, there was an *intent* on the part of the parties to restrain interstate commerce in some particular. Here, certain beet sugar refiners in California had agreed among themselves upon the prices they would pay to local growers. Since a substantial part of the refined sugar was later shipped into interstate commerce, the court construed the local, illegal price-fixing as, in effect, part of interstate commerce. Because an appreciable part of the interstate commerce was the subject of the restraint, such activities fell within the condemnation of the Sherman Act.

In more recent years, the U.S. Supreme Court has held that motion picture films released throughout the country (*Crescent Amusement Co.*, 323 U.S. 173); news gathered throughout the country for local dissemination (*Lorain Journal Co.*, 342 U.S. 143); and insurance policies sold in the several states (*South-Eastern Underwriters Assn.*, 322 U.S. 533) —all involved "trade or commerce" among the several states; and, if, in restraint of trade or commerce, such activities were subject to the antitrust laws. But the business of Sports has run a course which has sidestepped the ban of the anti-trust laws until stymied by relatively recent court decisions, except for the business of professional baseball.

Organized professional sports in the United States have generally operated apart from normal business considerations as affected by the anti-trust laws. Admittedly, a professional sports league is a closely-knit combination of firms or corporations, formed by an agreement which regulates the activities of individual members, and which delegates authority to a commissioner or president. This organization of owners of professional teams in a given industry necessitates the displacement of the free, competitive market. These leagues control a significant part of our national economy, directly affect the young athlete as they take over the responsibilities of one of the most important aspects of American life, i.e., the final development of physical abilities and nationwide identification with such abilities; and these professional sports leagues have, until recently, operated beyond the pale of the antitrust laws. Their rules of business conduct were not subject to governmental scrutiny, particularly their regulations on fair play and equal opportunity for those engaged in the sports business. Since such professional sports businesses were interstate in nature and operation, they were in essence another "sovereign state," uncontrolled and unregulated by any single state. Interstate monopolies in each line of sports has meant that their edicts and declarations were virtually "law," incapable of attack under the federal antitrust laws and beyond the reach of the federal government.

To grasp the significance of this anomaly, we must view in some detail the various professional team sports: baseball, football, boxing, wrestling, basketball, and even horse-racing.

### The Business of Baseball

Baseball has been described as our national pastime, part of American folklore, integrated with the entertainment industry, and a profitable business affecting millions of Americans in their daily lives. The enormous economic power of organized professional baseball today is due, in part, to the favorable decision of the U.S. Supreme Court, in 1922, in *Federal Baseball Club of Baltimore v. National League of Professional Baseball Clubs* (259 U.S. 200). The complaint therein recited the formation and attempted operation of the Federal Baseball League, the combination and conspiracy of the National League and "organized baseball" to destroy such competition, and the ultimate elimination as a competitor of the Federal Baseball League. The trial court was impressed with the evidence in support of the complaint that the anti-trust laws had been violated; and Judge Stafford held, as a matter of law, that the defendant National League had attempted to monopolize the "business" of professional baseball as a part of interstate "trade or commerce." On appeal, the U.S. Court of Appeals of the District of Columbia, however, *reversed*:

> "A game of baseball is not susceptible of being transferred . . . . Not until the players come into contact with their opponents on the baseball field and the contest opens, does the game come into existence. It is local in its beginning and in its end . . . . a game effects no exchange of things according to the meaning of 'trade or commerce' . . . "

The appellate court dismissed the reserve clause, the publication of ineligible lists of players, and other restrictive provisions and practices as "relating directly to the conservation of the personnel of the clubs," and which "did not directly affect the movement of the appellee in interstate commerce. Whatever effect, if any, they had was incidental, and therefore did not offend against the statute."

Upon writ of error the case came before the highest court and

Mr. Justice Oliver Wendell Holmes sustained the appellate court by holding that professional baseball clubs were *not* subject to the anti-trust laws, because baseball itself did not constitute "trade or commerce," although, admittedly, baseball was played professionally for money and for profit in the several states. He argued that professional baseball did not become interstate commerce merely as the result of team traveling; as an obtuse illustration he pointed out that a firm of lawyers sending a member to argue a case in another state would not be deemed to have engaged in interstate commerce! Mr. Justice Holmes ruled that the exhibition of baseball was purely intrastate, and the efforts of the players were not related to the production of "trade or commerce," nor were their efforts in any way the subject of "trade or commerce." Thus, the *immunity* of professional baseball from the federal anti-trust laws was launched; and, despite many court decisions in the past forty-odd years, the anomaly of an American business enterprise engaged in interstate commerce and immune from anti-trust prosecution, persists to this very day.

Since 1922, organized professional baseball has enjoyed a phenomenal growth as a business enterprise. Its monopolistic position has established the only market for the services of highly skilled professional baseball players; and yet the business operation centers about the so-called "reserve clause" and other restrictive rules and regulations. In the years following World War II, numerous controversies arose out of the enforcement of these restraints against various players. One of the first cases was the *Pasquel* case (187 N.Y. Misc. 230), in 1946, when the New York Yankees sought a temporary injunction to restrain officials of the Mexican League from inducing Yankee players to repudiate their contracts. Mr. Justice Miller of the New York court found ample evidence that the defendant and the Mexican League had attempted and were continuing "to entice away plaintiff's players," which conduct he deemed to be "wrongful and illegal under well-settled principles of law." The court dismissed the defendant's argument that an injunction should not be granted because baseball was a monopoly! He opined that even if it were a monopoly, it would not seem to be a combination in restraint of trade under then Section 340 of the New York General Business Law or at common law.

In 1949, Danny Gardella, a former New York Giant baseball player, "unsuccessfully" challenged the epochal decision of the *Federal Baseball Club* case, *supra*. Although under contract to the New York team, he contracted with and played for a baseball team in the Mexican League. He was thereupon placed on the ineligible list and unable to obtain employment as a professional baseball player anywhere in the United States when his Mexican venture fell through. The federal district court granted the motion of the Commissioner of Baseball to dismiss the case upon authority of the *Federal Baseball Club* case that baseball was not "trade or commerce." The U.S. Court of Appeals for the Second Circuit (172 F.2d 402) in a two to one decision, however, remanded the case for trial upon the merits, and held that professional baseball was "trade or commerce," and, therefore, subject to the laws against combinations in restraint of trade. Although the Commissioner of Baseball appealed the decision to the U.S. Supreme Court, he reinstated those ball players who had jumped to the Mexican League, and Gardella then discontinued his action for damages upon receipt of a substantial sum of money. Thus, the U.S. Supreme Court was deprived of the opportunity to rule upon the issue of baseball's immunity from the anti-trust laws.

In 1953, in *Toolson v. New York Yankees* (346 U.S. 356) the highest Court reaffirmed its 1922 ruling in the *Federal Baseball Club* case to the effect that the business of providing public baseball games for profit between clubs of professional baseball players was not "trade or commerce:"

> "If there are evils in this field which now warrant application to it of the anti-trust laws, it should be by legislation."

Thus, the U.S. Supreme Court shifted all responsibility for enforcement of the anti-trust laws against baseball, or the exemption of baseball from enforcement of such laws, to the legislative branch of government. And yet, years later, in the 1957 case of *Radovich v. National Football League* (353 U.S. 445), the court ruled "Congress had no intention of including the business of baseball within the scope of the federal antitrust laws."

The dissenting opinion of Mr. Justice Burton, in the 1953 *Toolson* case, bears careful re-reading:

> "In the light of organized baseball's well known and widely distributed capital investments used in conducting competitions between teams constantly traveling between states, its receipts and expenditures of large sums transmitted between states, its numerous purchases of materials in interstate commerce, the attendance at its local exhibitions of large audiences often traveling across state lines, its radio and television activities which expand its audience beyond state lines, its sponsorship of interstate advertising, and its highly organized 'farm system' of minor league baseball clubs, coupled with restrictive contracts and understandings between individuals and among clubs or leagues playing for profit throughout the United States . . . . it is a contradiction in terms to say that the defendants are not now engaged in interstate trade or commerce as those terms are used in the Constitution of the United States and in the Sherman Act."

The dissent concluded that Congress "has enacted no express exemption of organized baseball from the Sherman Act," nor has any court "demonstrated the existence of an implied exemption from that Act of any sport that is so highly organized as to amount to an interstate monopoly or which restrains interstate trade or commerce."

### *"Inside Baseball"*: *How It Operates*

At the head of organized professional baseball is the Commissioner of Baseball whose duties are proscribed by the major league and major-minor league agreements to include (a) the enforcement of discipline among the clubs, players and employees; (b) the determination of disputes among the parties; (c) the investigation of acts deemed detrimental to baseball, and (d) the adoption of rules of conduct for the players, the owners, and other employees. In general, each player must sign a *standard* employment contract, the only permitted variations (based upon negotiation) being compensation and special privileges. Such a contract may be terminated by the club on ten-days written notice, and generally has a one season duration. The contract may be assigned to any other club or renewed, which renewal option must be exercised by February 1st of the following year. A player must cooperate in promotional activities that, in the opinion of the club, enhance its welfare or that of professional baseball, even though such activities interfere with the player's off-the-field pursuits or interests. Clubs may impose reasonable fines or suspend a player without salary for a period not exceeding thirty days for violation of the contract.

To relieve baseball players of the hardships engendered mainly by the "reserve clause," i.e., the provision giving the club which first signs a player to a contract the continuing and exclusive right to his services, which right is respected by all organized baseball, attempts have been made from time to time, since 1885, to organize the players into labor unions which would give them stronger bargaining power and greater personal freedom. However, in practice, there seems to be little *union spirit* among professional baseball players primarily because the professional life is relatively short, and the average major league compensation of $7,500 is more than adequate for the inexperienced, young ball player whose skill, if proven, will entitle him to greater rewards in the immediate future. Nevertheless, the courts have frequently labeled the baseball player as mere "chattel," entitled to be protected from the rigors of his contractual vicissitudes, *American League Baseball Club of Chicago v. Chase* (86 N.Y. Misc. 441):

> "The quasi peonage of baseball players . . . . is contrary to the spirit of the Constitution of the United States."

## Other Baseball Problems and Practices

In February, 1959, a federal court in the *Lawrence* case ( — F.2d — ) dismissed a $250,000 damage suit brought by the president of a defunct minor league baseball club against the Commissioner of Baseball and sixteen major league teams. Lawrence contended that his Portsmouth, Va., professional baseball club had earned $50,000 per year before the radio and television industry had, without authorization, invaded his territory in 1949. He argued that under Rule 1 (a) of the Professional Baseball Rules, a major league baseball game broadcast was prohibited within fifty miles of a minor league team's territory. The failure of the Commissioner of Baseball to enforce this rule was alleged to have caused damages to Lawrence. The defendant responded that the rule precluded only *physical* invasion of the Portsmouth territory, and did not encompass radio and television broadcasting. Federal Judge Dimock dismissed the suit upon that very basis, to wit: there was no contractual committment to protect minor league baseball clubs from invasion of their territories by the broadcast of major league baseball games. On appeal, the Second U.S. Court of Appeal affirmed in May 1960:

> "No doubt radio and television have had an adverse effect on attendance at baseball games, theatres, and concerts. But this radical change in the manner in which the public chooses to be entertained cannot create contractual rights and obligations not within the fair intendment of the parties."

It should be noted that, *subsequently,* organized baseball's rule restricting broadcasts was quietly dissolved when the U.S. Dept. of Justice decided the rule was in violation of the anti-trust laws!

On August 12, 1959, the uniform player contract was the subject of a lawsuit by two professional baseball players in the International League who sued the Commissioner of Baseball, the Buffalo Bisons, and the Rochester Red Wings baseball clubs, *Blake v. Frick* (142 N.Y.L.J. No. 31). Plaintiff's, suing in behalf of all other players in the League, contended that the player contracts were void and unlawful because the defendants were monopolizing the business of baseball, were restraining competition and plaintiffs' free exercise of the conduct of their baseball skills and services. Specifically cited were the inability of ball players to bargain collectively for pension plans, welfare benefits, and improved playing conditions; in addition, there was cited the threat that defendants would "trade the players out of the International League to lower classifications, or will eliminate them from organized baseball, if the players persist in such request." Mr. Justice Loreto of the New York Supreme Court, New York County, recognized the problem:

> "There has been, in the past, strong judicial denunciation of the system of organized baseball under which the players

are required to pursue their profession . . . . The restrictive provisions of these contracts and the system under which the players are required to render their services are oppressive, and deprive them of rights and freedom usually granted to and enjoyed by employees. It may well be that the contracts should be declared illegal and void."

But Mr. Justice Loreto could not grant the relief requested, because *technically* the suit was not a representative action or a "class action." The common interest of all players was found only in the uniform contract, and, once declared void, their common interest would end; furthermore, all players of the League would be bound by the remedy selected although they were not before the court. In addition, the relief sought by the two plaintiffs "may be granted only at the behest of the Attorney General, and may not be the subject of separate suit by individual plaintiffs on behalf of others not parties thereto." In closing, Mr. Justice Loreto apologized to the plaintiffs:

"The court's attention has been called to the fact that since the submission of this motion and because of the prosecution of this suit, disciplinary action has been taken against one of the plaintiffs by his baseball club. The court expresses its regret that this has happened and unfortunately can do nothing about it."

### The Business of Football

Football as a professional team sport is today a million dollar business in the same spirit as professional, organized baseball. But the business of professional football is not treated under our anti-trust laws with the same privileges as organized baseball. It all began in 1946, when Bill Radovich, a professional football player for four years with the Detroit Lions of the National Football League, requested a transfer to the N.F.L. club on the West Coast because of the illness to his father. The Detroit Lions refused the transfer, and Radovich broke his player contract and signed with the Los Angeles Dons, a member of the competing All-American Football Conference. In 1948, the San Francisco Clippers of the competing Pacific Coast League offered him a job as player-coach, but withdrew the offer when the National Football League notified the San Francisco Clippers that Radovich was "blacklisted" and could not be employed by any organized professional football club. Whereupon, Radovich brought suit for treble damages against the N.F.L., alleging that he was damaged in the sum of $35,000, as the result of the conspiracy to monopolize interstate commerce in the business of professional football.

The federal court in California dismissed his complaint (231 F.2d 620), in 1956, on the authority of the *Federal Baseball Club* case, and held that football like baseball was not "trade or commerce" within the meaning of the Sherman Act. After the Ninth U.S. Court of Appeals had affirmed, the U.S. Supreme Court rendered its decision (352 U.S. 445) in 1957, and *reversed* the lower courts by refusing to extend the *Federal Baseball Club* case beyond the business of baseball! Mr. Justice Clark, writing for the six to three court, indicated that the *Federal Baseball Club* case was of doubtful validity today; and "the volume of interstate business involved in organized football places it within the provisions of the Sherman Act." Although aware of the anomaly in which the court's decision placed the business of football, Mr. Justice Clark felt that the orderly way to eliminate the discrimination in favor of baseball was by congressional legislation which is "more accomodative, affording the whole industry hearings and an opportunity to assist in the formulation of new legislation."

The dissenters argued that since they could not distinguish between the business of baseball and the business of football, they could not accept the rationale of the majority's decision.

The bylaws of the NFL in 1953 provided that no member football club could permit a telecast or radio broadcast of its game within seventy-five miles of another NFL city on the day that the home football club was playing *at home,* unless the home club gave its permission. The U.S. Dept. of Justice sought to enjoin such practices, and Federal District Court Judge Grim in Pennsylvania agreed that the bylaw provision was a contract in restraint of trade, an allocation of markets among competitors. But Judge Grim concluded that such a restraint was a "reasonable one," and a "legal restraint of trade" since it "promotes competition more than it restrains it, in that its immediate effect is to protect the weak teams and its ultimate effect is to preserve the League itself . . . . and also makes possible competition in the sale and purchase of television rights in situations in which the restriction does not apply." However, the restriction on telecasting in home territories, when the home team is playing *away*, Judge Grim held to be "an unreasonable and illegal restraint of trade" since he could find no factual justification or need for such restriction. He distinguished the *Federal Baseball Club* case upon the ground that the baseball case did not involve the "question of restrictions on the sale of radio and television rights."

Eight years later, Judge Grim in *U.S. v. National Football League* (196 F. Supp. 445) invalidated a $9,300,000 television contract between the NFL and the Columbia Broadcasting System. This exclusive contract to televise regular season football games by the fourteen professional football teams, in which each team would share equally in the income, was declared to violate the anti-trust laws:

> "By this agreement the member clubs . . . . have eliminated competition among themselves in the sale of television rights to their games . . . . Clearly this restricts individual clubs from determining from which areas the telecasts of their games may be made . . . . "

Just two months later, on September 30, 1961, the 87th Congress enacted Public Law 87-331 and obviated the decision of Judge Grim. The new law provided that the anti-trust laws "shall not apply to any joint agreement . . . . by which any league of clubs participating in professional football . . . sells or otherwise transfers all or any part of the rights of such league's member clubs in the sponsored telecasting of games . . . . engaged in or conducted by such clubs." The Senate Judiciary Committee Report on Public Law 87-331 pointed to the public interest in viewing professional football which warranted "some accommodation of anti-trust principles . . . . with minimal sacrifice of antitrust principles." However, this anti-trust *exemption* does not apply to a joint agreement which prohibits the telecasting of a game within any area, except within the home territory of a member club on a day when that club is playing a game *at home*. It is believed that the professional football exemption also provides greater protection for in-person attendance at *college* football contests!

In 1960, the American Football League, as a competitor of the NFL, sued the NFL, contending that the NFL had conspired to destroy the AFL. After a trial, the federal district court in Maryland, on May 21, 1961, ruled that the NFL did not have a monopoly in professional football, and had not undertaken a course of action to exclude competition or prevent competition. Judge Thomsen opined: "Neither rough competition nor unethical business conduct is sufficient (to prove monopolization). The requisite intent to monopolize must be present and predominant."

### The Business of Boxing

The multi-billion dollar pugilistic business of professional boxing has also drawn the attention of the courts to the exhibition of professional championship boxing contests, the promotion of which involve valuable rights to broadcast, televise, and film for sale in interstate commerce. The far-flung activities of the International Boxing Club of New York were attacked by the U.S. Dept. of Justice in March 1952 as a conspiracy to monopolize and a monopoly of the professional boxing business in the United States. Two corporations and two individual defendants, together with Madison Square Garden, were initially successful in getting the complaint dismissed, before the Federal District Court for the Southern District of New York, upon the basis of the *Federal Baseball Club* case that professional boxing also was *not* "trade or commerce." The government directly appealed to the U.S. Supreme Court, which on January 31, 1955, *reversed* the lower court, and held that the promotion of professional championship boxing contests on a multi-state basis, coupled with the sale of rights to televise, broadcast, and film the contests for interstate transmission constituted "trade or commerce" within the meaning of the Sherman Act (348 U.S. 236).

Chief Justice Warren declared that a boxing contest is not a local affair if the business itself is engaged in interstate commerce, to wit: negotiation of contracts with boxers, advertising agencies, seconds, referees, judges, announcers, and other personnel living in every state; arrangements and maintenance of training quarters of the boxers in every state; leasing of suitable arenas in diverse states; sale of tickets of admission across state lines; negotiation for sale of and sale of rights to broadcast and telecast boxing contests to homes through more than 3,000 radio stations and 100 television stations in the United States; and negotiation for sale of and sale of rights to telecast directly boxing contests to some 200 motion picture theatres throughout the country. (Between 1949 and 1952, all but two of the twenty-one boxing championship contests in the United States were promoted by the defendant IBC.)

The court distinguished the *Federal Baseball Club* case as not holding that "all businesses based on professional sports were outside the scope of the anti-trust laws." He stated that the proper inquiry was whether the boxing business should be granted an exemption, but this issue "is for Congress to resolve, not this court."

On March 8, 1957, the IBC was found guilty after trial of violating Sections 1 and 2 of the Sherman Act (150 F. Supp. 397). Federal Judge Ryan held that IBC's monopoly of championship fights was the "relevant market;" and remarked that "the promotion of professional championship boxing contests is a pure and simple money-making, profit-seeking business." He found that IBC had accomplished its illegal position (a) through purchasing promotional control of championship contests; (b) through acquiring the exclusive use of physical facilities for the presentation of such contests; (c) through acquiring the assets of competitors, and (d) through contracts requiring boxers who won championships to engage in future title contests exclusively for IBC for periods of three to five years. In his June 24, 1957 opinion Judge Ryan demanded "a dissolution of the combination which will permit the re-establishment of the competitive positions of the defendants and the entry of others in the market." He ordered "an immediate and complete severance of the interlocking ownership of Norris and Wirtz in Madison Square Garden," necessitating the resignation of both men as officers and directors within thirty days and divestiture of their stock within five years.

The defendants were enjoined from promoting more than two championship contests in any one year, and were ordered to open competitive leasing of Chicago Stadium and Madison Square Garden on a reasonable rental basis. He also placed certain restrictions upon IBC with respect to radio and television which would open up the boxing business to "legitimate and healthy competition."

An appeal to the U.S. Supreme Court resulted in affirmance of Judge Ryan's order on January 12, 1959. Mr. Justice Clark noted that without such stringent curbs "the government in its effort to free the professional boxing business of monopoly . . . would have won the battle, but lost the war."

Prior to the pronouncement of the U.S. Supreme Court in the IBC case, the lower federal courts had held that the boxing business was not subject to the anti-trust laws. In *Shall v. Henry* (211 F.2d 226, CA7, 1954) the court was powerless to come to the aid of a boxing manager who alleged that he was the victim of a restraint of trade in the form of a conspiracy against him by his own boxer, two co-managers, and a professional boxing club.

### The Business of Wrestling

Wrestling has been delineated as an exhibition sport bringing dollars into the pockets of its promoters. The prevalence of various restrictions on promoters and bookers of professional wrestling matches, coupled with the sale of rights to broadcast and televise, have brought the business into anti-trust difficulty. The National Wrestling Alliance, an association of bookers and promoters of professional wrestlers, was prohibited in 1956 by the federal district court in Iowa from conspiring among themselves with the purpose or effect of:

(a) Recognizing a booker or promoter as the exclusive booker or promoter in a designated territory.

(b) Preventing a booker or promoter from doing business in any other territory.

(c) Restricting promotion and booking of wrestling matches to certain arenas and to promoters or bookers who are members of the NWA.

(d) Requiring a booker to book wrestling matches only through promoter NWA members, and to discriminate in

favor of promoter NWA members.
(e) Requiring a promoter to promote wrestling matches only through the services of NWA members, and to discriminate in favor of booker NWA, members.
(f) Preventing any wrestler, booker, or promoter from participating in studio exhibitions.

Under the consent decree, the NWA cancelled all existing regulations and bylaws inconsistent with the decree. The NWA added new bylaws requiring the expulsion of any member violating the decree, and opening membership up on non-discriminatory terms to any booker or promoter with proper qualifications. Federal Judge Riley did not rule specifically whether or not the business of wrestling was "trade or commerce," but he left no doubt that the court "has jurisdiction of the subject matter of this action and of the parties thereto."

## The Business of Basketball

The business of professional basketball and the sale of broadcasting and television rights to such basketball games has been held to constitute "trade or commerce" within the anti-trust laws. In *Washington Professional Basketball Corp. v. National Basketball Assn.* (154 F. Supp. 154) the federal district court in New York, in 1956, faced the complaint by the plaintiff that the NBA, Madison Square Garden, and four professional basketball teams, were preventing plaintiff from completing an acquisition of players and assets of the defunct Baltimore Bullets professional basketball team. The court ruled that the complaint stated a cause of action under the anti-trust laws and remanded the case for trial.

Jack Molinas, a professional basketball player, was barred for life from professional basketball, in 1954, after admitting that he had bet on his own team, the Fort Wayne Pistons. In 1960, Molinas, a lawyer, started suit against the National Basketball Association, alleging a conspiracy to keep him out of professional basketball. On January 12, 1961, Federal Judge Kaufman in New York dismissed the suit: "Molinas has not established any violation of the anti-trust laws which has in any way injured him." The court held that the NBA rule against gambling was not a restrictive practice in restraint of trade, but "about as reasonable a rule as could be imagined." (In 1963, Molinas was convicted in New York of criminal charges for betting on basketball games.)

## The Business of Horse-Racing

The fact that horse-racing is subject to regulation by the several states negatives any doubt that horse-racing is a business subject to the anti-trust laws of the state and the federal government. In May 1960, the U.S. Department of Justice sued the United States Trotting Association, charging that its charter, rules, and regulations maintain a stranglehold on harness racing in the country. Specifically, the government contended that USTA rules gave the USTA the power to bar horse owners, drivers, trainers, tracks, sponsors of stakes and futurities races, and officials from the business. Judge Underwood in the Ohio federal court ruled that the government did not establish that the USTA "unreasonably, arbitrarily or capriciously excluded any person or organization from membership, or prevented any interested party from obtaining the benefits or 'products' of the USTA." In dismissing the government's suit he held that the USTA rules "are not such commercial boycotts as have been stricken down in previous cases as unlawful," and concluded that USTA activities were *reasonable* restraints that merely regulate and standardize the business of harness racing.

## Legislative Proposals for Exemption of Professional Teams from the Anti-trust Laws

From time to time, momentum has been gathered by sports enthusiasts and professional businessmen involved in sports to correct the inequity favoring baseball by exempting all professional team sports from the anti-trust laws. On the other hand, in 1957, Congressman Celler of New York authored a bill to bring baseball under anti-trust regulation. The prospects of such legislation becoming a law are very slim since "business pressures" are too great to effect any changes in the status quo. It is submitted, however, that there can be no valid reason for granting exemptions to sports and not to other unique businesses similarly engaged in interstate commerce.

## Selected Bibliography

*Griffin v. Brooklyn Baseball Club,* 68 A.D. 556.
*Egan v. Winnepeg Baseball, Ltd.,* 96 Minn. 345.
*Philadelphia Baseball Club v. Lajoie,* 202 Pa. 210.
*Peller v. IBC,* — F2d —, U.S. D.C. N.D. Illinois, 1955.
H.R. 5383, H.R. 6876 (introduced in Congress in 1957).
142 N.Y.L.J. No. 99, November 20, 1959.

## Questions for Review

1. Historically, why was the business of sports not subject to the anti-trust laws?
2. Is organized sports a monopoly? Explain.
3. Distinguish. in a business sense, between professional baseball and football. (a) In 1922, was professional baseball a game or a business? (b) Was professional football a game or a business?
4. What is baseball's "reserve clause?" It it justifiable?
5. Should the courts or Congress change the decision in the *Federal Baseball Club* case, and end baseball's immunity from the anti-trust laws?
6. Was Public Law 87-331 salutary legislation on televising of professional football games?
7. Does subjecting professional boxing to the anti-trust laws aid in eradicating the evils inherent in boxing?

## Chapter VIII

## GAMBLING — LOTTERIES, BINGO, AND THE PUBLIC INTEREST

> "There may be in every child the impulse that prompts him to take a chance, but it has been the public teaching and the public policy of the land that gambling is immoral and to be condemned. The federal government has made it a criminal offense to transport lottery tickets or to cause them to be transported in interstate commerce (18 USC Sec. 387). Lotteries used in the marketing of merchandise have long been condemned by the United States Supreme Court . . . . "
>
> *Modernistic Candies v. FTC,* (145 F.2d 454, CA7, 1953)

### The Historical Background of the Lottery

THE ABOVE STATEMENT on public policy with respect to lotteries and the sale of merchandise by lottery or lottery devices is supported, not only by state statutes, but by the federal government through its control of the mails and the mass media of radio and television communication, in addition to its basic right of taxation.

The history of lotteries shows that lotteries have been employed for many purposes other than gambling. The aristocrats of Rome used lotteries as a means of adding to the gaiety of their festivals. Kings and princes, during the feudal ages, raised revenue by means of lotteries. The various Italian republics relied upon lotteries to stimulate interest in commercial transactions; even in recent days, countries like France, Sweden, and Switzerland have raised monies for governmental welfare purposes by lotteries. The support of a charitable hospital is behind the Irish Sweepstakes. In the United States, during the Revolutionary War, the Continental Congress conducted a lottery to raise money to defray the cost of the war.

Although England, in 1698, was the first country to outlaw lotteries, many American states "legalized" their lotteries by acts of the legislature. A Louisiana statute of 1864 legalized gambling on a free-enterprise basis with license fees providing the only state revenue; a gambling syndicate headed by Charles T. Howard journeyed to New Orleans and began operating a lottery. In 1868, a heavily-bribed Louisiana legislature gave his Louisiana Lottery Co. the right to operate a state lottery for twenty-five years on an exclusive basis. The company paid the State of Louisiana $40,000 and its operations were tax-exempt. Howard's lottery was a popular and financial success; with tickets selling at 25¢ and prizes running up to $600,000, the syndicate was soon marketing its lottery all over the United States, and paying its backers enormous dividends. It was estimated that the syndicate annually collected thirty million dollars and paid out less than fifteen million dollars. Efforts by rival syndicates to get into the lucrative field ran into a stone wall in the Legislature, but by 1892, the "party" was over as reform groups, newspaper editors, and the federal government, finally prevailed. All in all, the State of Louisiana had received no more than a small fraction of the revenues generated by the lottery.

No state resuscitated the lottery for the next sixty-odd years, until April 30, 1963, when the State of New Hampshire enacted a legal sweepstakes or lottery, all receipts from which were to go to public school aid in the state. Governor King in signing the law opined that the law "represents the will of the majority of people of New Hampshire. To veto it would deny the right of the people of the state to 'embark upon a legitimate fiscal experiment' . . . . I am unwilling to set myself up as a Solomon or a Caesar in the holy assumption that my views are more intelligent or discerning or moralistic than those of our people." In September, 1964, the first of two sweepstakes races, brought to New Hampshire's public school system two and one-half million dollars, to the U.S. Treasury $570,000 in taxes, and to the 1,992 winning tickets $1,800,000. The operation of the lottery was handled by the New Hampshire Lottery Commission, headed by an ex-FBI agent, who charted a path through the maze of federal rules and regulations making state lotteries illegal. Purchasers of tickets had to go to one of the state's two race tracks or the forty-nine liquor stores, where on payment of three dollars a clerk activated a machine which exposed a ticket on which the bettor wrote his name and address. The machine thereupon "swallowed" the ticket and issued him an "acknowledgement" which presumably may be sent across a state line or through the mails (unlike a lottery ticket which cannot be mailed nor legally be transported across the state line). Winners were announced by telegram since postal regulations prohibit sending any lottery information by mail. Prize money was deposited in a New Hampshire bank for the winners to pick up by normal banking procedures.

New Hampshire's success has prompted consideration of similar lotteries in other states. Kentucky is considering a sweepstakes, and California is planning to hold a referendum in November 1964, on a proposal for a straight lottery at two dollars a ticket, with drawings every month for prizes totaling nine million dollars.

### "Lottery" Defined

The inadvertent failure of most state statutes to define "lottery" prompted the North Carolina Supreme Court (*State v. Lipkin*, 169 N.C. 265, 1915) to reason that:

> "No sooner is a lottery defined and the definition applied to a given set of facts, than ingenuity is at work to evolve some scheme of evasion which is within the mischief but not quite within the letter of the definition."

Nevertheless, a "lottery" is generally defined in terms of three elements, i.e., *prize, chance,* and *consideration*: a distribution of prizes by chance; a game or hazard or risk in which small sums are ventured for a chance of obtaining a larger sum, either in money or other valuables; or simply a scheme for the distribution of prizes by lot or chance in payment of some consideration. The elements of *prize* and *chance* (or *non-skill*) are uncomplicated and unambiguous terms, but the third element of *consideration* plagues the courts for clear-cut definition, particularly where no money or other valuables is paid in by the participant in the lottery.

In *Maughs v. Porter* (157 Va. 415), free chances were given on an automobile to all persons who attended a certain auction, whether they bid or not. The Virginia court, in 1931, ruled that the requisite attendance at the auction was sufficient *consideration* bargained for by the auctioneer, and hence the scheme was an *illegal* lottery. The decision quoted the following illustration from *Williston On Contracts* in order to distinguish between a gift (involving no *consideration*) and *consideration* itself:

> "If a benevolent man says to a tramp 'If you go around the corner to a clothing shop, there you may purchase an overcoat on my credit,' no reasonable person would understand that the short walk was requested as the consideration for the promise, but that in the event of the tramp going to the shop the promisor would make him a gift."

Indeed, in the instant case, the physical attendance at the auction was the *consideration* "paid" by the participant who thereby incurred legal detriment or a legal change in his position or status. It has thus been held that the requirement of registration or attendance in a lobby or even outside a movie theatre in order to be eligible to receive a prize, without the necessity of payment of any money, was sufficient *consideration* to constitute a lottery and therefore illegal, *Affiliated Enterprises v. Waller* (5 A.2d 257, 1939).

In New Jersey, a state statute prohibited lotteries and declared that any person who "gives, barters, sells, or otherwise disposes of or offers to give . . . a ticket in a lottery, is guilty of a misdemeanor." In *Lucky Calendar Co. v. Cohen* (19 N.J. 399), the plaintiff had contracted with a chain of supermarkets to operate its scheme whereby contestants fill out coupons or calendars mailed to them without charge, whether customers or not, and place the coupons in a receptacle in a named store, after which a drawing is held to determine the winners. The New Jersey court, in 1955, determined that the scheme was a lottery, since *consideration* existed both in the detriment to the contestant in entering the store and in the benefit to store proprietor in having the contestant enter the store to deposit the coupon or calendar.

In *California Gasoline Retailers, Inc. v. Regal Petroleum Corp.* (322 P.2d 945), a group of major-brand service station operators were successful in obtaining an injunction to stop trade-stimulating "give-aways" conducted by three independent gas station chains. The crucial point in the "give-aways" was whether there was *consideration* in some form for a *chance* to receive a *prize*. The system used involved tickets with stubs which had to be deposited at the gas stations; however, it was not necessary to go to the gas station or buy gasoline to get tickets, for the tickets were distributed under windshield wipers and in diverse ways without any detriment to the automobile owners. (In some instances, the price of gasoline was raised 1¢ per gallon to finance the merchandise prizes.) The California District Court of Appeal, in 1958, declared that the scheme was still a lottery, i.e., the *consideration* was the necessity to deposit the stub in the gas station to be eligible to win a prize.

The *minority* view that *consideration* must take the form of pecuniary valuables or money before a scheme can be deemed an illegal lottery is illustrated by an 1893 Colorado decision, *Cross v. People* (18 Colo. 321). Here there was a gratuitous distribution of business cards to all persons calling or writing for them, each card entitling the possessor to a chance of winning a piano. The court, in holding that the scheme was not a lottery, emphasized that no contestant had been induced to risk money with the hope of obtaining something of greater monetary value, which the court opined was the evil which lottery statutes seek to prevent. The Colorado court also felt that any increase in the promoter's business was a benefit too remote to constitute a *consideration* for the *chance* to win the *prize*. It is submitted that the court was in error, not only with respect to the concept of *consideration*, i.e., the legal detriment was incurred by the participant who had to come to the store to pick up his prize, it being of less concern that the promoter received any benefits from the scheme (then why did he execute the scheme?), but also the court was in error in overlooking the fact that the scheme aroused the insatiable desire in contestants to gain something for nothing, which is the evil to be prevented by lottery statutes. Lotteries are prohibited whether they are merely lotteries in the strictest sense of the term, or enterprises in the general nature of a lottery, wherein *chance* and *prize* predominate, even though the participants risk no money or property of their own.

### New York's Attack Upon Lotteries and Gambling

In New York, under Section 1370 of the Penal Law, a lottery is defined as "a scheme for the distribution of property by chance, among persons who have paid or agreed to pay a valuable consideration for the chance, whether called a lottery, raffle, or gift enterprise, or by some other name." Under Section 1372, a person who "contrives, proposes, or draws a lottery, or assists in contriving, proposing or drawing the same, is punishable by imprisonment for not more than two years or by fine of not more than $1,000 or both." And, under Section 1376 of the same Penal Law, it is a misdemeanor for a person "who offers for sale or distribution, in any way, real or personal property, or any interest therein, to be determined by lot or chance, dependent upon the drawing of a lottery within or without this state, or who sells, furnishes, or procures, or causes to be sold, furnished or procured, in any manner, a chance or share or any interest in property offered for sale or distribution, in violation of this article, or a ticket or other evidence of such chance, share, or interest." Under these three criminal statutes it was held, in December 1958, in *People v. Cadle*, that the operation of a Bingo game was in violation of law, even though the payment or consideration was in the form of a one dollar receipt for a folding chair upon which the participant sat in order to play bingo! According to the court, "the chair and the subsequently delivered (Bingo) board obviously are part of the Bingo plan and an adjunct to the game. The sale or rental is a part of the entire scheme, and without such rentals, Bingo could not go on from a financial standpoint, and probably not because of the physical inability of a large group to play while standing." (Subsequently, a New York constitutional amendment legalized bingo, as discussed hereinafter.)

In *People v. Coppo*, the New York County Court, Queens County, on March 18, 1959, convicted the defendant of violating Section 1372 of the Penal Law for operating a "policy bank" on credit. The winning numbers on policy slips were calculated from prices paid on the results of certain horse races. According to the court, "almost every jurisdiction has deemed this activity to be a lottery. And from colonial days, lottery has been prohibited or regulated by statute . . . . Lottery is both unlawful and a public nuisance." However, the New York Court of Appeals in *People v. Lalli* (5 N.Y.2d 536) held that mere possession of tip-sheets and dream books "having no integral connection with the playing of 'policy' and not used in actual policy operations" was not prohibited under the Penal Law. Only those activities of "the operators of games of policy, the entrepreneurs and their henchmen and the players" are forbidden by the statute.

Article I, Section 9, Subdivision 1, of the New York Constitution provides that "no lottery or the sale of lottery tickets, pool selling, bookmaking, or any other kind of gambling, except parimutuel betting on horse races . . . . shall hereafter be authorized or allowed within this state." In addition to the exception for pari-mutuel betting added in 1939, there was an amendment in 1957 authorizing, upon a local option basis, the conduct of games of chance commonly known as Bingo and Lotto. The constitutional prohibition on all kinds of gambling (with the two exceptions) has existed in New York since 1894. In addition, the Penal Law makes different types of gambling *criminal* offenses (*People v. Lambrix,* 204 N.Y. 261, 264). On February 26, 1963, the New York Appellate Division, First Dept., in *Intercontinental Hotels Corp. v. Golden* held that the operator of a gambling casino in Puerto Rico cannot maintain an action in New York on I.O.U.'s which a patron gave him for chips that he advanced and that the patron lost at dice. The New York Constitution which forbids gambling expresses a deep-rooted and long-standing policy of the state that a gambling debt is unenforcible in New York, notwithstanding that it was lawful in Puerto Rico where it was incurred.

### Merchandising by Lottery Devices

The Federal Trade Commission has for many years issued cease and desist orders against manufacturers, sellers, and distributors in interstate commerce of gambling or lottery devices such as punch boards and push cards which are used in making sales of merchandise to the consuming public. The gist of the typical FTC action is that the purchasing public has been wrongly induced to trade or deal with certain manufacturers, sellers, and distributors of merchandise by means of these lottery devices; and therefore substantial trade or commerce has been unfairly diverted from competitors selling similar or competitive merchandise without lottery devices. Such conduct constitutes an unfair trade practice in violation of Section 5 of the FTC Act, as amended. Thus, as a *civil* wrong, the federal government has acted to bar the use of lotteries or lottery devices in the economy.

In 1953, in *Feitler v. FTC,* the power of the FTC to prohibit interstate shipments of such gambling devices as punch boards and push cards was attacked, upon the ground that the FTC had no authority to stop interstate shipments of true gambling devices such as dice, roulette wheels, and the like. Feitler argued that persons patronizing punch boards and push cards do so not to procure merchandise, but to gamble *per se;* that punch boards and push cards are found in pool halls, taverns, and other places where people are encouraged to loiter and not to buy merchandise; and that therefore such lottery devices do not divert any sales from the ordinary channels of trade, nor are the lottery devices sales aids or sales stimulators. The Ninth U.S. Court of Appeals, however, upheld the jurisdiction of the FTC, which, it said, depends "upon the single fact that these devices, unlike most other gambling devices, are used as a means of selling or distributing merchandise, which is opposed to the public policy of the United States." Furthermore,

> "It is a fact that the interstate shipment of these devices facilitates a kind of merchandising which induces and encourages the public to gamble which makes such shipment an 'unfair trade practice.'"

If such lottery devices are transported in interstate commerce for use only in connection with the sale and distribution of merchandise in *intrastate* commerce, the jurisdiction of the FTC is still retained. Indeed, the sale of merchandise by plan or method involving the use of a game of chance, gift enterprise, or lottery is a practice contrary to the established policy of the government, whether intrastate or interstate.

In *Consolidated Manufacturing Co. v. FTC* the manufacturer of punch boards argued that since he merely sold punchboards and not the merchandise, the FTC could not prosecute. The Fourth U.S. Court of Appeals, in 1952, answered that merchandising by gambling cannot be divided into isolated acts which appear innocent when examined separately; and that the FTC has the authority to police the aiding or abetting, and the inducing or procuring of unfair trade practices.

In *Wren Sales Co. v. FTC,* the mail order business in merchandising by push cards argued that the public policy of the United States was not opposed to casual, social, non-professional adult gambling such as was involved in its operation. One witness before the FTC testified that her minor daughter, aged thirteen years, had received a push card in the mail and had sold the chances to secure one radio for herself and another for the buyer of the "lucky" chance. Wren Sales Co. described its push card operations as necessarily limited for use between friends, neighbors, relatives, and co-workers. The Seventh U.S. Court of Appeals upheld the determination of the FTC that the business was "a game of chance, gift enterprise, or lottery scheme," and the firm was guilty of supplying and placing in the hands of innocent persons the means of conducting such illegal enterprises. The court, in its November 16, 1961 decision, declared that the business practices were "contrary to the public policy of the United States."

### Trading Stamps as Gift Enterprise

Since 1891, trading stamps have occupied a place in the American economy: little pieces of gummed paper issued by retailers to customers who, in turn, accumulate them in sufficient quantities to exchange for an item of value. Trading stamps are generally sold by the same company that redeems the stamps for merchandise. At first, attempts were made in several states to bar trading stamps as lottery devices, but the courts decided that no element of chance was involved, *Commonwealth v. Sisson,* (178 Mass. 578, 60 N.E. 385, 1901). In 1954, in *Sperry & Hutchinson Co. v. Hoegh,* the Iowa "gift enterprise" statute prohibited the issuance of trading stamps, redeemable by the stamp company, instead of by the retailer himself. The Iowa Supreme Court declared the prohibition to be unconstitutional since it did not operate "alike upon all within a reasonable classification:"

> "During the past half-century, many states have enacted laws similar to our gift enterprise statutes . . . . The overwhelming weight of authority is that such statutes as ours are unconstitutional as not being within the sphere of police power . . . . Anti-trading stamp laws constitute unnecessary restrictions on the right of contract; unwarranted interference with a natural right to attract custom; prohibit contractual relations which do not affect the public health or morals or welfare; and are not within the proper exercise of police powers."

For a *contrary* view holding that state "legislation relative to coupons and stamps is not unconstitutional under the Fourteenth Amendment of the U.S. Constitution," see *Rast v. Van Deman & Lewis Co.* (240 U.S. 342), decided in 1916.

The Federal Trade Commission, on October 3, 1957, issued a press release that it did not consider "trading stamp plans in themselves to be an unfair method of competition under the laws its administers." Trading stamps in 1964 were used in every state except Kansas where they are prohibited; in Washington, Wisconsin, and Wyoming, stamps may be redeemed only for cash.

### Lotteries and the Federal Communications Commission

The Federal Communications Commission has the power of controlling lotteries and lottery devices in connection with radio and television broadcasting. Under FCC rules and regulations, based upon a *criminal* statute (18 U.S.C.A. Sec. 1304), the broadcasting of "information concerning any lottery, gift enterprise, or similar scheme, offering prizes dependent in whole or in part upon lot or chance" is banned. But, unfortunately, the FCC has not taken its responsibility seriously and acted promptly and with efficiency. In the *Caples Co.* case, the FCC, in 1957, questioned "Marko," a television bingo game over a Los Angeles television station. Viewers played at home with cards obtainable from stores selling the sponsor's products. Numbers were drawn in the studio and shown on a master card on television. Winners telephoned the television station to claim prizes of merchandise, cash, and trips. The U.S. Court of Appeals for the District of Columbia conceded that the necessity of the contestant to visit the store to pick up a "Marko" card came close to "consideration" which would make the entire entertainment program a lottery device. But the court determined that to so rule would stretch the FCC rules and regulations:

> "The undesirability of this type of program is not enough to brand those responsible for it as criminals."

The U.S. Supreme Court, in the *ABC* case (347 U.S. 284), also refused to go along with the FCC rules and regulations which had banned "give-away" shows, upon the ground that listening and watching a program was sufficient to support the element of consideration to prove a lottery. The highest Court's decision is legally not understandable in view of the innumerable court decisions that consideration need not be based upon monetary gain, may involve simply any affirmative act or participation, and need not be overt or apparent. Even absentee ownership of a lottery by an advertising company conducting it for a theatre was held to be consideration because patrons had to be present at the theatre to receive prizes, *Society Theatre v. City of Seattle,* (118 Wash. 258).

Since public policy in the field of lotteries has long been enunciated, it is obvious that some drastic overhaul of the FCC rules and regulations is necessary. Perhaps the answer lies in supplanting the *criminal* statute with a strong, civil remedy available to the FCC as well as to competitors and members of the public affected adversely by the lottery or lottery device.

## Bingo or Lotto by Referendum in New York

The people of the State of New York, in November 1957, ratified a constitutional amendment to legalize Bingo and Lotto upon a local option basis. The New York Legislature was authorized to act so that localities may choose or refuse such games in their areas. With this local option, over five hundred New York localities passed bingo licensing laws subject to the approval of their voters. On November 4, 1958, the voters of New Rochelle, N. Y., approved the following legislation:

AMUSEMENTS, EXHIBITIONS, AND PUBLIC GATHERINGS

2-14. BINGO GAMES PERMITTED. Pursuant to Chapter 854 of the Laws of 1957 any authorized organization may apply to the City Clerk of the City of New Rochelle for a license to conduct Bingo games, subject and pursuant to the rules and regulations and restrictions as contained in Chapter 854 of the Laws of 1957 as amended.

Section B. All Bingo games conducted in the City of New Rochelle shall be subject to the following restrictions:

1. No person, firm, association, corporation, or organization other than an authorized organization licensed under the provisions of this article, shall be permitted to conduct such games.

2. The entire net proceeds of any game shall be exclusively devoted to the lawful purposes of the organization permitted to conduct the same.

3. No single prize shall exceed the sum or value of two hundred fifty dollars.

4. No series of prizes on any one occasion shall aggregate more than one thousand dollars.

5. No person except a bona fide member of any such organization shall participate in the management or operation of such game.

6. No person shall receive any remuneration for participating in the management or operation of any such game.

7. The unauthorized conduct of a Bingo game and any willful violation of any provision of any such local law or ordinance shall constitute and be punishable as a misdemeanor.

Section C. It shall be lawful for any organization duly licensed under the provisions of this subdivision to conduct Bingo games in any and all zoned districts of the City of New Rochelle; any provision of the Zoning Ordinance of the City of New Rochelle to the contrary notwithstanding.

The avowed purpose and effect of this legislation was "to authorize the conduct of games of chance commonly known as Bingo or Lotto by (a) bonafide religious; (b) charitable, or (c) nonprofit organizations for veterans, volunteer firemen and similar nonprofit organizations." The entire net proceeds of the games must be devoted exclusively to the lawful purposes of such organization. A license for the conduct of such games must be obtained from the City Clerk on forms prescribed by the State Lottery Control Commission.

New York City also voted "yes," on November 4, 1958, to authorize Bingo and Lotto in the five boroughs, despite great opposition from such groups as Citizens Union, which in its *Annual Voters Directory* stated:

> "We still feel that legalized gambling is undesirable and degrading for an enlightened community . . . . Aside from questions of private morals, upon which we do not consider it our function to pass, the public and governmental consequences of this proposal would be very harmful for our city. Legalized public gambling . . . . nearly always creates unmanageable problems of law enforcement and grave dangers of official corruption."

The *New York Times* editorial of April 30, 1961, indicated that the fears of the Citizens Union were justified:

> "Last week the State Investigation Commission opened public hearings on how the law was working. There were charges that some of the 3,000 licensees were paper organizations which existed solely for the purpose of operating Bingo games; that William F. Buckner, a convicted swindler, had been paid $172,000. to run bingo games for seven organizations, largely in the form of under-the-table payments for excessive rents and illegal transportation of bingo customers. One organization reported that it had received only $15. a week from a Buckner-operated game. Payments to inspectors of the State Lottery Commission also were disclosed."

### The Status of Gambling in England

In sharp contrast to the United States, the reputation of a gambler in England is relatively untarnished by vulgarity. England has removed most restrictions on off-track horse race betting and has permitted the establishment of licensed shops at which bets may be placed. England has made gambling with cards and dice *legal*, provided that all players have an equal chance of winning, that they do not play in public places, and that all stakes wagered are returned to the players in winnings.

The *New York Times Magazine* for June 19, 1960, commented about gambling as a social custom in England:

> "In eighteenth century London, gambling was at the very heart of city life. The card games, like faro or omber, played for high stakes, gave London social life an intensity and high drama which is reflected in much of the writing of the time. The fashionable men's clubs . . . . were founded on gambling. During the Regency, with the sanction of the Prince Regent himself, the gambling fashion reached its climax. There was considered nothing disreputable in the fact that Charles Jean Fox, the most brilliant politician of his time, should lose £30,000 at the tables in one night . . . . "

Legislation attempted to curb the British passion for gambling, but without success. The first major act was passed by King Henry VIII, in 1541, to prevent gambling from ruining the archery business. ("Menfolk were spending their time at dice and backgammon and neglecting the important art of the longbow.") Such legislation as the Gaming Act of 1710, the Disorderly Houses Act of 1751, the Metropolitan Police Act of 1839, and the Ready Money Football Betting Act of 1920 never achieved much change. In 1949, a Royal Commission on Betting, Lotteries, and Gaming recommended the legalization of gambling.

## Selected Bibliography

*New York Times Magazine,* June 19, 1960, pp. 16, 41, 42.
*Gregory v. United States,* — F.2d —, C.A.5, March 12, 1958.
*People v. Burns,* — N.Y.S.2d —, Niagara County, December 16, 1959.
*State v. Eames,* 87 N.H. 477.
*State v. Shugart,* 138 Ala. 86, 35 So. 28, 1903.
*Humes v. City of Fort Smith,* 93 Fed. 857, Arkansas, 1899.
*Zitserman v. FTC,* — F.2d —, C.A.8, 1952.
*Time,* September 18, 1964, p. 59.

## Questions for Review

1. What is the vice in gambling? Is the eradication of the evil the task of government?

2. Are state-operated lotteries legal? If so, can a state license anyone to go into the lottery business?
3. Why is legal "consideration" an element of every lottery?
4. When is Bingo or Lotto *not* a lottery and illegal?
5. What is the vice in merchandising by lottery devices? Explain.
6. Are trading stamps lottery devices or gift enterprise?
7. Does England have the answer to gambling?

*Chapter IX*

## ADOPTION AND SOCIETY: THE LEGAL CREATION OF A FAMILY

### "Adoption" Defined

ADOPTION MAY BE simply defined as the creation of a family relationship, not by biological means but by means of legal authority and sanction. Under Section 110 of the New York Domestic Relations Law, for example, adoption is that "legal proceeding whereby a person takes another person into the relation of child, and thereby acquires the rights and incurs the responsibility of parent in respect of such other person." Thus, adoption is a status which exists only because a statute has said so!

The legal creation of a family demands strict adherence to the particular state statute. The relationship, its meaning and validity, is strengthened by communal social and psychological patterns of the individuals brought into the legal situation. Unfortunately, too strict conformity to the legal rules has often marred the parent-child relationship thus created.

The Surrogates Association of New York, representing the surrogates from all over the state, released on May 27, 1964, a survey of adoptions as recorded in the courts of the State of New York for the sixteen year period, 1948 to 1963. The outstanding figures in the tables, printed *below,* reveal many striking facts:

1. The largest percentage of adoption of legitimate children were by the step-parent, with adoptions by blood relatives or strangers running neck and neck, but far behind.
2. In the case of voluntary adoptions of children born out of wedlock, the percentage adopted by strangers ran ahead of that of adoptions by the husband of the mother, with blood relatives running far behind.
3. The number of voluntary adoptions of legitimate children

just about equalled the number of voluntary adoptions of illegitimate children.
4. The number of adoptions from authorized agencies was increasing steadily, so that today it is almost 50 per cent of total adoptions.
5. Of the nineteen adoptions of legitimate children "by others," sixteen were by blood relatives of the natural father of the child.
6. Of the forty-four adoptions of illegitimate children "by others," fifteen were by the natural father of the child.
7. Total adoptions have apparently begun to level off after the peak year of 1960.
8. In addition to the statistics below, four *adult* persons were adopted in 1955; six in 1961; three in 1962; and one in 1963.

In 1954, the U. S. Children's Bureau estimated that there were 90,000 adoptions in the United States (of which New York had 3,638); in 1962, there were approximately 121,000 adoptions (of which New York had 4,855). But in 1954, it is believed that there were a dozen couples waiting for each adoptable child; and in 1962, there were only three or four couples waiting for each adoptable child. Thus, the lessening of the demand with the greater supply has improved the atmosphere in the technique of adoption. The marked rise in illegitimacy and medical advances that has made it possible for many women previously considered barren to conceive, account for the phenomenon.

## Questionable Adoption Practices

In former years, when the demand for adoptable children exceeded the supply, questionable adoptive practices were commonplace. And, the courts were not always able to combat the problem, as indicated by Judge Marks of the New York City Court of General Sessions on May 17, 1960, in *People v. Issachar:*

> "I decry the method used by these defendants to obtain the legal adoption of these children. It seems that the operation of some sort of 'black market' prevailed in the placing in foster homes of unwanted infants and the operation turned into a

## NUMBERS OF ADOPTIONS

| | Voluntary Adoptions of Legitimate Children | | | | | | | Voluntary Adoptions of Illegitimate Children | | | | | | | Adoptions from Authorized Agencies | Total Adoptions | Number of Counties that Submitted Figures |
|---|---|---|---|---|---|---|---|---|---|---|---|---|---|---|---|---|---|
| Year | By Step-parent | By Blood Relative | By Relative through Marriage | By Friend of Family | By Stranger | By Others | Total | By Husband of Mother | By Blood Relative | By Relative through Marriage | By Friend of Family | By Stranger | By Others | Total | | | |
| 1948 | 571 | 132 | 31 | 51 | 146 | | 931 | 275 | 130 | 23 | 84 | 698 | | 1,210 | 1,238 | 4,289 | 46 |
| 1949 | 881 | 167 | 14 | 67 | 220 | | 1,349 | 402 | 152 | 19 | 105 | 1,024 | | 1,702 | 694 | 2,835 | 38 |
| 1950 | 697 | 150 | 11 | 32 | 144 | | 1,034 | 334 | 118 | 15 | 51 | 735 | | 1,247 | 1,091 | 3,381 | 32 |
| 1951 | 885 | 131 | 26 | 42 | 138 | | 1,222 | 505 | 129 | 9 | 78 | 608 | | 1,329 | 1,303 | 3,854 | 33 |
| 1952 | 742 | 118 | 28 | 32 | 108 | | 1,028 | 400 | 103 | 6 | 78 | 456 | | 1,043 | 1,127 | 3,198 | 32 |
| 1953 | 721 | 125 | 38 | 46 | 149 | | 1,079 | 421 | 134 | 15 | 90 | 410 | | 1,070 | 1,321 | 3,470 | 41 |
| 1954 | 802 | 127 | 75 | 52 | 113 | | 1,169 | 432 | 124 | 16 | 91 | 551 | | 1,214 | 1,255 | 3,638 | 44 |
| 1955 | 842 | 141 | 61 | 63 | 141 | | 1,248 | 480 | 144 | 15 | 111 | 599 | 2 | 1,351 | 1,240 | 3,889 | 48 |
| 1956 | 950 | 107 | 43 | 58 | 101 | | 1,259 | 446 | 131 | 22 | 131 | 463 | 1 | 1,194 | 1,318 | 3,771 | 48 |
| 1957 | 1,023 | 170 | 72 | 35 | 112 | 2 | 1,414 | 550 | 159 | 14 | 103 | 657 | | 1,483 | 1,684 | 4,581 | 49 |
| 1958 | 1,108 | 115 | 46 | 45 | 146 | 7 | 1,467 | 497 | 102 | 4 | 151 | 659 | 2 | 1,415 | 1,657 | 4,539 | 49 |
| 1959 | 1,070 | 135 | 40 | 54 | 141 | 1 | 1,441 | 575 | 136 | 10 | 131 | 635 | 7 | 1,487 | 1,641 | 4,576 | 48 |
| 1960 | 1,250 | 123 | 82 | 48 | 138 | 4 | 1,645 | 583 | 162 | 39 | 104 | 688 | 6 | 1,582 | 2,245 | 5,472 | 53 |
| 1961 | 1,213 | 137 | 48 | 51 | 132 | 5 | 1,586 | 551 | 155 | 21 | 127 | 672 | 13 | 1,539 | 2,327 | 5,452 | 56 |
| 1962 | 1,035 | 108 | 17 | 24 | 100 | | 1,284 | 512 | 143 | 6 | 88 | 628 | 10 | 1,387 | 2,184 | 4,855 | 52 |
| 1963 | 1,249 | 112 | 19 | 30 | 111 | | 1,521 | 527 | 165 | 13 | 118 | 657 | 3 | 1,483 | 2,362 | 5,366 | 48 |

flourishing business—an evil, if presently existing, that calls for supplemental legislation of a more effective remedial nature. But, so far as I, as a judge, am concerned, I, for my part, have no alternative other than to follow the law as it now is written."

Here a New York adoption agency and a Greek lawyer were charged by a New York grand jury with violating Section 487-a of the Penal Law and Sections 371 and 374 of the Social Welfare Law, in that the agency head received compensation "for the placing out of children . . . unauthorized by the law." But the *criminal* accusation pertained to the *results* of adoption proceedings instituted and completed in Greece and not in New York, and hence Judge Marks admitted that the children "had already been legally adopted in Greece by adoptive parents residing in this country." Thus, the bringing of the children into the homes of the adoptive parents in New York was not in violation of the laws of New York!

## A Capsule History of Adoption Practices

Historically, adoption was a frequent and observed practice in ancient times. The early Greeks were certainly adept at the intracacies of adoption, and in Roman times the role of the Genitor, the biological parent, and the Pater, the foster parent, were distinct, as each had his own role to play in Roman society. The history of the Caesars is a long successful practice of adoption to ensure the transmission of the family name. Under Hebrew law there was no provision for the creation of this parental relationship, but the voluntary assumption of the parental care of another's child was well known in ancient Hebrew society, i.e., Abraham took his nephew Lot as his son, and Mordecai took Esther into his home as a daughter. In Oriental societies, the objective of adoption was familial, i.e., to secure a continuity of ancestor worship.

In later periods, adoption laws were inspired by social and political motives, although in English-speaking countries adoption had been unknown at common law. Formal adoption was given legal status in England as late as 1926! The first adoption law in the United States requiring judicial determination was enacted in Massachusetts in 1851, with New York following suit in 1873. In 1940, Texas became the last state to enact statutory provisions prescribing court proceedings for adoption, although South Carolina, as recently as 1953, permitted a parent to sell his child under the age of twenty-one without court approval!

## Deficiencies in Present-day Adoption Statutes

Probably the two most salient deficiencies in modern day adoption statutes are (a) the failure to provide for immediate investigation and supervision whenever a child is placed outside its own home in some other home by an individual; and (b) the lack of comprehensive, separate procedures to terminate parental rights, whenever the well-being of the child demands it. The former shortcoming affects only the voluntary, *private* adoptions where the child is placed by his parent or by an intermediary; in contrast to the *agency* adoption, the placement is generally not made under the legal supervision of a third party. The latter shortcoming is perhaps well-illustrated by the decision of the New York Appellate Division, First Dept., on June 15, 1964, in *People ex rel Anonymous Petitioners* for a writ of *habeas corpus* to determine custody of a male child held by Louise Wise Services or Wise Adoption Services. Here, the parents of the child had been married after the child's birth, and had placed the child, at the age of five months, with an agency for adoption. Less than one month later, the day after the agency had placed the child with a couple, with a view toward adoption, the natural parents demanded the return of their child. Judge Breitel opined that there was no showing of unfitness of these parents, so that their parental rights could *not* have been terminated, and the child should be returned to them. However, Judge Breitel remarked that "it was unjust and unkind of petitioners to characterize the agency as they did. . . . It was they, after all, who created all but one of the conditions which brought about the unfortunate situation with which the court is confronted. . . . It is they who, because of their own inadequacies, will have wrought the worst kind of pain to the adoptive parents." It is submitted that termination of parental rights should be independent of any adoption proceedings and antecedent to such proceedings: the agency should have been empowered to so act in the best interests of the child.

## Aims of Adoption

The Children's Bureau of the U. S. Dept. of Health, Education and Welfare issued in 1949 a publication which set forth the following essentials to good adoption procedure:

*"To Protect the Child*—from unnecessary separation from parents who might give him a good home; . . . . from adoption by persons unfit to have responsibility for rearing a child; and from interference after he has been happily established in his adoptive home.

*"To Protect the Natural Parents*—from hurried decision to give up a child made under strain and anxiety.

*"To Protect the Adopting Parents*—from taking responsibility for children about whose heredity or capacity for physical or mental development they know nothing; from later disturbance of their relationship to the child by natural parents whose legal rights had not been given full consideration."

The welfare of the child is always paramount so that the aims of adoption should never be obfuscated.

## Classification of Adoptions and Procedures

Today, all adoptions may be classified as either (a) voluntary, non-agency or (b) voluntary, authorized social agency. In New York, agency adoptions account for only 35 per cent of all adoptions. Both classifications under New York law require the filing of a Verified Adoption Petition containing the name, date, and place of birth of the child; the religious faith of its natural parents and the religious faith of the adopting parents; and the adopting parents' occupations and income. The adopting parents must also execute an agreement which is a contractual repetition of the Petition's recitals. The written consent of the natural parents or of the mother, if the child is born out of wedlock, is required. If the child had been surrendered for adoption to an authorized social agency, no parental consent is necessary before adoption.

### Religious Groupings Under the New York Statute

Under the New York Domestic Relations Law the religious faith of the child and the religious faith of the adopting parents must be the same. This legal requirement is allegedly founded upon a logical concern for the child's spiritual welfare, so that adopting parents may adopt a child only of their religion "when practicable." This unrealistic, statutory mandate was delineated in an article in the *New York Times* (October 11, 1959, p. 82) which identified a New York City organization composed predominantly of Jewish couples and a small number of Catholic and Protestant members who have adopted babies, its chief aim being to help other couples who want to adopt babies:—

> "From the Jewish point of view we have a very half-hearted attitude about trying to adopt, because there are so few so-called Jewish babies and no agency that will place a baby in a home of another religion . . . More and more childless Jewish couples are turning away from the agencies and to private adoption . . . . The committee has found, in polling its 500 adoptive parents, that judges or surrogates handling private adoption cases are more willing than are the agencies to approve the placement of children across religious lines and with couples of mixed faiths . . . . "

The *New York Times* article, *supra*, interviewed a Catholic mother on the committee: "She thought it was important for a child to have religion, but more important to have loving parents who would provide a home that was emotionally, morally, and ethically satisfying. . . . We are working for a place on the adoption form where a natural mother, if she wishes, can state that she has no preference concerning the religion of her child."

Indeed, the religious-grouping requirement in the adoption law has held firm because of the increasing influence of the Roman Catholic Church in matters of legislation. In New Jersey, the law parallels closely the New York statute. Connecticut, which forbids private adoptions, requires merely that the religious affiliation of the child and all parties to the adoption be listed; but in practice, Connecticut adoption agencies place the child in the same faith as its natural parentage. Practices outside the Northeast are generally less rigid about the religious factor.

### The True Foundling: What Religion?

Suppose a baby to be placed for adoption is a true foundling, perhaps one left on the steps of the police station with no identification as to its religion. The New York City Child Welfare, Foster Home Care and Adoption Service solves the problem of religion on a *rotation* basis: first, Protestant, then Catholic, and then Jewish. The children are turned over to the appropriate sectarian agency in that sequence. A child left on the steps of a Protestant church will however, be designated Protestant; such indication of the child's religion will be respected, even though the church may have been simply more convenient to the natural parent in abandoning the child. One can conjure up all sorts of complex problems stemming from so arbitrary a procedure; but then only the religious factor in the adoption law is to blame!

### The Constitutional Issue of Religious-grouping

As reported in the *New York Times, supra,* a constitutional issue or question has been raised concerning the religious-grouping requirement of the New York adoption law. Domestic Relations Court Justice Polier was quoted as follows:

> "Any attempt by the state, through overzealous employees in our courts, public departments or hospitals to infringe upon the parent's religious freedom or right to choose adherence or nonadherence to any faith, violates the Constitution and its guarantee of freedom of conscience and freedom of religion."

To the contrary is the warning by Rev. Edward Head, director of social research of the Catholic Charities of the Archdiocese of New York, as quoted in the *New York Times:*

> "It would be prejudicing the rights of religious people if they knocked this clause out of the law. This is a religious nation, and we have a right to exercise our belief in God. And, this should be recognized in law."

The *New York Times* concluded:

> "Whether the adoption agencies could change their approach without a change in the law is debatable. New York surrogates apply the religious provision rigorously. They believe the agencies would be violating the spirit, and perhaps the letter of the law if they interpreted the 'when practicable' clause to mean 'whenever they want to.'"

## *Enforcement of Pre-nuptial Agreements to Rear Child in Particular Religion*

Perhaps tangential to the problem of the religious-grouping requirement in adoption proceedings is the question of enforcement of pre-nuptial agreements to rear children in a particular faith or religion. But, upon reflection, it is evident that the identical question is raised in both instances: shall the religious faith of some person determine the religious faith of the child? In *Diemer v. Diemer,* the New York Appellate Division, Second Dept., on June 24, 1958, dismissed a husband's action for separation wherein he had specifically charged his Catholic wife with violating the pre-nuptial agreement that their child would be raised in the Protestant faith. A strong *dissent* by Judge Wenzel raises interesting issues:

> "(They) have the moral and legal right to worship as they please . . . . Her conduct and the resulting disputes between the parties over the religious issue, which included attempts to convert him to her faith, do not constitute cruel and inhuman treatment within the meaning of Sec. 1161 of the New York Civil Practice Act . . . . (But) a wife's refusal to have marital intercourse should have some just cause or excuse . . . . (There was no basis for) a finding that he was so insensitive as not to suffer mental anguish at the defection of his wife and the scorn of his only child who, as a result of her training, was openly prejudiced against her father's religious faith . . . ."

In *Begley v. Begley,* the New York Appellate Division, Second Dept., on June 6, 1961, ruled that three small children could remain with their Protestant mother, even though she had made a pre-wedding agreement with her husband to rear them as

Roman Catholics. It seems clear that the courts are reluctant to enforce such agreements upon grounds of public policy which demand that, in matters of religion and antipathy toward the enforcement of moral obligations, courts should not intervene. It is submitted that courts should declare antenuptial agreements providing for the religious upbringing of children in a particular faith to be null and void and of no legal effect.

### *The Religious Choice in Adoptions*

The highest New York court in, *In Re Maxwell's Adoption* (4 N.Y.2d 429), in 1958, by a four to three decision refused to upset an adoption because the child born of a Catholic mother was adopted by a Protestant couple. The natural mother, married but separated, claimed that the child was that of her paramour. Prior to the birth, she told her doctor that she did not want the child and asked him to make arrangements for a placement. Shortly after the delivery, she executed a consent in which she declared that she "does not at the present time embrace any religious faith." A year later, however, when she appeared to object to the foster parents' petition of adoption, she declared that she was a Catholic, that she did not know that her child would be placed in a Protestant home, and that she wanted her child back. The adoption court turned down her protests.

On appeal, she contended that her consent was not effective because the New York statute required foster parents to be of the same religious faith as that of the child. The New York Court of Appeals ruled that whether or not the consent was good was immaterial, since the natural mother had abandoned the child by virtue of the arrangements made at the time of birth. The court also noted that the statute provided for religion-matching "when practicable," a phrase which the court found was designed to accord the trial judge "a discretion" in exceptional circumstances. Accordingly, the "settled policy" of the state would not deny custody to the foster parents "where a child has been accepted by (adoptive parents) following a declaration or representation by the mother, which may or may not be true, that she does not embrace any religious faith."

The three dissenting opinions called the natural mother's consent "completely illegal" and declared that the religion-matching statute had been violated because there had been no fact-finding and that would take the case from the "when practicable" category.

In contrast to the *Maxwell* case, *supra*, was the later decision by Mr. Justice Beckinella in *Doe v. Doe* (New York Supreme Court, Kings County, June 14, 1960) which gave custody of children to a Roman Catholic husband as against his Baptist wife from whom he sought separation. It seems that the wife had signed a pre-nuptial agreement that she would rear the children as Catholics; she now contended that she was forced to sign it under the duress of her pregnancy. Defendant wife also argued that the subsequent marital rift was due to plaintiff's habitual drunkenness, although the court rejected this issue as "calculatingly injected by defendant to obviate the effect of the antenuptial agreement." Mr. Justice Beckinella surprisingly upheld the enforceability of the pre-nuptial agreement, in the support of which he made the following "characterizations" of the defendant wife:

"This (raising children in the Baptist religion) . . . . she feels is the most important mission in her life . . .
"She shamelessly deceived the Catholic priest into performing the marriage . . .
"She duped the plaintiff into marrying her by appearing to agree to the terms imposed by him . . . .
" (The priest) considered her motive for marrying so unworthy from a religious point of view that he told her that under the circumstances he would not perform the ceremony even if she were a Catholic . . . . "

Although, under Section 81 of the New York Domestic Relations Law, "the mother and father are deemed to have equal rights in the control of their offspring," Mr. Justice Beckinella held firm, and concluded that "in addition to the antenuptial agreement, the infants by baptism have been initiated into the Catholic faith," and therefore:

"They should be permitted to continue in that faith without interference until such time as they are old enough to make a choice of their own."

Mr. Justice Beckinella refused to award the custody of the children to the defendant Baptist wife, because she "is so uncompromising on the religious question that such a course would be ineffectual."

This problem of religious differences was focused by Mr. Justice J. I. Shapiro of the New York Supreme Court, Queens County, in *Hehman v. Hehman,* decided on August 28, 1958:

> "No court can fail to be distressed by broken marriages and ruptured homes. These cases of deep unhappiness are rendered all the more tragic when diversity of religion is one of the causes which aids in destroying what should be the most joyous human relationship, and one of the most sacred of human relationships. . . . To add to these the great strain of difference in religion is to tempt fate. Religious intermarriage too frequently brings disagreement in its train . . . . Religious differences may cause damage to the children that is well nigh incalculable . . . "

The court pointed out that "in cases of broken homes, the interest of the child is paramount. The child is the ward of the court, and the court must look to his welfare and his rights before all else." However, Mr. Justice Shapiro concluded:

> "Arbitrarily to assign different religious upbringing to children of the same household is certainly not leaving them unmolested . . . . "

And, therefore, the "choice" of the thirteen-year-old's religion "should be left to him, and such choice should be ascertained under circumstances that will make certain that it is his wish, and not alone that of either parent, that the court is carrying out."

## Adoption Procedures in New York

### Investigation of Prospective Parents

Under the New York statute, an investigation is made only when the prospective adoptive parents present their petition in the adoption proceedings. At the earliest, this occasion is after the completion of the six-month waiting period required by the statute. Since the initiation of adoption proceedings is dependent entirely on the wishes of the adoptive parents, a child may remain in a strange home in which he has been placed, good or bad, for years or even permanently, without any investigation of the home and without any supervision of his well-being! Until the adoptive parents act, no court nor any other public agency may even have cognizance of the child's whereabouts!

The purposes of the requisite waiting period are to protect adoptive parents from receiving an unsuitable child, to protect the natural parent from a hasty decision, and to protect the child from an undesirable placement. But, without supervision beginning at the initial placement, the waiting period does not accomplish its avowed objectives. New York can well review the good adoption procedures found in Wisconsin, Tennessee, New Jersey, and California, where early investigations by professionally trained personnel is required.

## Initial Placement of Child in Private Adoptions

It is indeed self-evident that the initial placement of the child for adoption is of great importance. Uprooting a child once placed is often tragic and marked with grave consequences. Indeed, the agency must consider the adoptive parents psychologically, economically, and socially, and endeavor to match child and parent from the point of view of background and intelligence and prospective happiness.

In New York, there is no statute requiring investigation of the initial *private,* non-agency placement of the child with the prospective adopting parents, as previously indicated. There is no obligation on the part of the recipient to start adoption proceedings, and so the child may remain where he is for years or even permanently in the undesired placement. In Kentucky, Maryland, Massachusetts, Michigan, Missouri, Nebraska, Ohio, and Rhode Island, for example, the vital placement regulations calling for initial investigation are written into the statute.

In *State of New York v. Anonymous,* decided by the New York Court of Appeals on November 30, 1961, the problem of supervision over children placed with foster parents and with prospective adopting parents through an authorized social agency was delineated. When the natural mother was fourteen years of age and unmarried, she gave birth to a son, who was turned over to the foster parents at the age of four days. The identity of the child's father was uncertain, since she had had sexual relations with three boys when she was thirteen. Subsequently, she married one of these boys but he was definitely not the father of the child. Three years after the child's birth, she brought the present habeas corpus proceedings to obtain custody of the child. The trial court dismissed the writ upon the ground that she had abandoned the child, and is now unfit to assume the care and welfare of the child. The intermediate court reversed, but the highest New York court *reversed* the intermediate court, holding that the girl was *not* entitled to the child's custody:

1. During the three years, she had made not the slightest inquiry about the child's welfare.
2. Her conduct had been such that she must be deemed unfit to raise the child.

The court ruled that the presumption that it is in a child's best interest to be brought up by his natural mother was overcome, particularly in view of the callous disregard and complete indifference she exhibited as to where the child was or how the child was faring, all of which show a repudiation of motherhood and an abandonment of maternal rights and responsibilities. It thus appears that by virtue of the timely writ of *habeas corpus* the court was able to exercise the vital supervision over the child placed in a foster home. Although the natural mother did not obtain custody of her child, she did, at least, insure that the child's welfare was supervised by the court at the early date.

In 1961, New York State Senator Janet Hill Gordon sought to amend the statute by setting up a plan calling for earlier and stricter court investigation and supervision of non-agency adoptions. But numerous social agencies in New York urged the

Governor to veto the bill because the bill could be interpreted as depriving the courts of the power to approve a non-agency adoption solely because the adoptive family was of a different religion from that of the natural parent, even though the natural parent desired and consented to the adoption by the family, and even though the court was satisfied that the adoption was in the best interests of the child.

## The Inheritance Rights of the Adopted Child in New York

Effective March 1, 1964, Section 117 of the New York Domestic Relations Law was amended to clarify the rights of adopted children in wills, trusts and estates. The right of a foster child to inherit from and through his natural parents will terminate upon the making of the order of adoption, *except* that when a natural or foster parent, having lawful custody of a child, remarries and consents that the step-parent may adopt the child, neither such consent nor the order of adoption shall affect the rights of the consenting parent and the foster child to inherit from and through each other. The foster parents and the foster child shall have all the rights of inheritance from and through each other and the natural and adopted kindred of the foster parent.

In addition, the fourth and eighth paragraphs of Section 117 dealing with the passing of and limitation over property depending on a foster parent dying without heirs or a foster child dying without surviving brother and sisters, have been repealed.

Also, by virtue of a new Section 49 of the New York Decedent Estate Law, a class gift under a will or trust agreement to issue, lawful issue, children, grandchildren, descendants, heirs, heirs-at-law, next of kin, distributees, or words of like import, will *include* adopted children, unless the will or trust agreement specifically provides to the contrary.

## The Statistics of Adoption

It has often been said that statistics are revealing: there are about 250,000 babies born out of wedlock in the United States each year, of which 75,000 babies are born to teenage girls, including 5,000 to girls less than fifteen years of age. The stigma attached to such illegitimate or bastard children raises a distinct problem which, at least in New York, was partly overcome by Section 59 of the New York General Construction Law which strikes out and deletes from all New York statutes the terms "bastard" and "illegitimate."

It is estimated that one half of children adopted by voluntary, non-agency means are born out of wedlock, and this fact places a great emotional burden upon well-meaning doctors, lawyers, and laymen who serve as intermediaries between the highly emotional natural mother and the avid foster parents. The unwed mother is frequently subject to exploitation by the unscrupulous, and the consent to adoption is often obtained under the pressure of emotional shock. See *Matter of Anonymous,* (10 N.Y. Misc.2d 1076).

### The "Black Market" for Adoption of Babies

Under Section 487-a of the New York Penal Law, it is a crime for a person or firm or agency to receive *compensation* for the permanent placement of a child in an adopted home. This statute, together with the great demand for children by barren marriages, has placed a premium upon babies eligible for adoption. The payment of money to effect transfer of a child gives rise therefore to the "black market." It is estimated that perhaps 15 per cent of all infants born to unwed mothers are sold on the "black market," which is devoid of the necessary investigation of both the natural parent and the child. The typical procedure was outlined by the 1954 Kefauver Committee:

> "The couple who has procured an out-of-state baby returns with the child to New York where they initiate adoption proceedings based on written consents already obtained in other jurisdictions. These consents have frequently been irregularly obtained. Often it is a consent procured from the natural mother immediately after delivery of the child, an 'ether' consent. Indeed, it is usually the paid intermediary who actually secures the consent document. Although the mother is required to come to New York by many of the judges, and to appear personally, this expedient is not always proof against deception or

intimidation. Sometimes it is a 'stand-in' arrangement by the original intermediary who pretends to be the mother; at other times the mother herself, frequently a teen-ager does appear, but she is so intimidated by court atmosphere and by a sense of guilt that her pretended consent is meaningless."

A full-scale investigation of every child placed privately in a home not his own, just as soon as he is placed, would obviously impede the success of the "black market." It should further be noted that 40 per cent of children placed are under two years of age, and generally no reliable tests as to physical and mental normality have been conducted.

### Termination of Parental Rights Over the Child

Prior to the 1959 amendments to the New York statute, a termination of parental rights in *agency* adoptions took place when a social agency had been designated as the guardian of the child. Such a designation was made only when the parent was legally declared insane or mentally defective, or where the parent had indeed abandoned the child. Obviously such procedure left much to be desired, particularly where there were other overriding reasons for terminating the parental rights over the child. New York courts sought to plug the hole by ruling that a "presumptive termination" took place when the natural parent surrendered the child for adoption to an authorized social agency, by signing and executing a written instrument giving up the child, as provided in Section 384 of the New York Social Welfare Law. Yet a revocation of the surrender for adoption was often permitted, provided the natural parent brought an action to annul the surrender within a reasonable time thereafter.

The 1959 amendment in New York set up an *additional* procedure applicable to agency adoptions, whereby the parental rights of the natural parent may be terminated by a petition in the Domestic Relations Court or the Children's Court (now the Family Court) filed by the social agency seeking to adjudicate the child as "permanently neglected" by the natural parent. Such an adjudication depends upon the failure of the natural parent for more than a year to maintain contact with the child and to plan for his future, and upon the failure of efforts by the agency to bring the family back together. When the child has been so adjudicated, its custody is awarded to the social agency, and the consent of the natural parent is no longer required in any subsequent adoption proceedings.

But, these 1959 amendments in New York pertain only to *agency* adoptions which constitute only 35 per cent of all adoption in New York. There are no procedures for termination of parental rights over children placed *privately* or in 65 per cent of all adoptions! Voluntary, *private* adoptions permit termination of parental rights only at the time of the adoption proceedings, which can be years afterwards or in fact never at all, despite the mental incompetency of the foster parents or the undesirability of the home for the child. Until the time the adoption becomes final in the private adoption, the natural parent can change her mind and even arbitrarily repossess the child. If the natural parent in a private adoption is not available to consent to the adoption or has disappeared, there is no procedure whereby the parental right can be terminated and proceed to complete the adoption, unless the court finds that the child has been "abandoned."

### *Termination of Parental Rights by Foster Parents*

On occasion, the foster parents may seek to terminate their parental rights or seek to abrogate a previous adoption. In *Matter of Abrogation, etc.* (167 N.Y.S.2d 472), the foster parents had adopted a boy at the age of four, and some thirteen years later, sought to abrogate the adoption upon the ground that the boy was incorrigible. The New York Supreme Court, Westchester County, in 1957, permitted the abrogation, despite the fact that natural parents do not enjoy such a luxury! It seems that the statutory right to abrogate should be amended to include a reasonable statute of limitations after which the right would be lost. There is indeed an area of responsibility belonging to even a foster parent which should not be shed so lightly simply because the foster parent had failed in his obligation toward his seventeen-year-old son who is now cast adrift in society!

## Judicial Determination of Termination of Parental Rights

The courts have been plagued with fact situations involving effort to terminate parental rights over an adopted child. One complicated fact-picture is found in *Matter of Adoption of Linda Marie Porras,* decided by the New York Appellate Division, Second Dept., on May 31, 1961. The parents were married in Nicaragua in 1951. Within four months, the mother left the father and returned to New York City, and shortly thereafter the father obtained a divorce in Nicaragua upon the ground of abandonment. Upon arrival in New York City, the mother discovered she was pregnant and notified the father. She received no reply until June, 1952, when he sent her $600. After the daughter was born, the mother received about $800 more. In August 1953, the mother re-married, and she and her present husband seek to adopt the daughter. The court observed:

> "While we do not condone the father's apparent indifference to his daughter's welfare, we must, nevertheless, on the question of abandonment give considerable weight to the unusual circumstances disclosed in this case . . . . On the record we cannot find that he abandoned his wife when they separated in Nicaragua or that he deserted his wife or child thereafter . . . "

Accordingly, the court could not find that the first husband had severed his relationship as parent to the child, and therefore the court disallowed the adoption petition by the natural mother and her present husband. In effect, the court refused to declare a determination of the parental rights over the child.

On June 26, 1961, the same New York court, however, in an *Anonymous* case declared that a mother may not be held to have abandoned a child, unless she may be said to have renounced the child positively as established by clear and certain proof. A finding of abandonment was not warranted when it appeared that (a) the child, born when the mother was under fifteen years of age, was given (when four days old) to a couple with a view to adoption; (b) this arrangement was insisted on by the mother's father over her strong protests; (c) her father gave her no information as to who the couple was and she did not know how to go about finding the child; (d) her first information as to the child's whereabouts came two and one-half years later when [her father having meanwhile died] her mother received letters from an attorney concerning consent to an adoption and (e) soon thereafter she instituted a *habeas corpus* proceeding to obtain custody of her child. Three months after the child's birth, she married and today, she and her present husband maintain a proper home and attend church regularly; furthermore, her present husband is steadily employed and wants to treat the child as his own. The court determined that it may well have a harmful effect on the child to let him remain with the couple to whom he was given, and therefore awarded custody of the child to its natural mother. Thus, there was no termination of parental rights because (a) the foster parents had at no time reason to believe the mother would consent to adoption, and (b) the foster parents could not adopt the child unless the natural mother consented, which she obviously would not do.

In May 1961, the U. S. Children's Bureau issued guidelines to the states under which the rights of *neglectful parents* may be terminated for the welfare of the child. These guidelines were in response to the growing feeling that the perpetuation of the rights of neglectful parents may keep a child in the permanent limbo of foster care with no hope of returning to its own home or of finding a suitable adoptive home. The following grounds for involuntary termination of parental rights were suggested:—"abandonment, substantial and continuous or repeated neglect, and parental incapacity to discharge parental responsibilities."

The New York Appellate Division, Second Dept. in the *Vasta* case on June 27, 1961, upheld the right of an unwed mother to regain custody of her child, who had been in the custody of foster parents for more than four years. Testimony showed that the foster parents had been given the child at the age of four days, the child having been born to a fourteen-year-old girl. Mr. Justice Cone ruled that the foster parents "had failed to sustain their burden that the mother had shown present or prospective unfitness to have her child." The unwed mother had married three months after the birth of the child, and the court felt that parental rights over the child should not have been terminated.

### Selected Bibliography

*New York Times Magazine,* August 23, 1964, pp. 48 *et seq.*
*New York Law Journal,* May 27, 1964, p. 1.
*People ex rel Anonymous v. New York Hospital,* 17 A.D.2d 122, aff. 12 N.Y.2d 863.
*Matter of Reep,* New York Supreme Court, Queens County, June 15, 1961.
*New York Herald Tribune,* November 2, 1959, p. 1.
*Matter of Anonymous,* 10 N.Y.Misc.2d 1076.
*In Re Knapp,* 156 N.Y.S.2d 668.
*People v. New York Foundling Hospital,* — AD2d — (First Dept., Oct. 4, 1962).

### Questions for Review

1. Why is "adoption" a *legal* relationship in the sense that a common law marriage is not? Is "adoption" a necessary tool of society?
2. Statistically, is it important to differentiate between adoptions of legitimate and illegitimate children? Explain.
3. Why is the demand for adoptable children less acute today?
4. Why is termination of parental rights over the child so vital? Who should be empowered to terminate?
5. How is a child's "spiritual welfare" enhanced by religious-grouping adoption statutes?
6. Are religious-grouping adoption statutes constitutional? Explain.
7. Are pre-nuptial agreements to rear a child in a stated religion enforceable? Why?
8. How would you explain Mr. Justice Beckinella's decision in *Doe v. Doe?*
9. Explain the importance of mandatory investigation of prospective adopting parents.
10. Are children of unwed mothers more or less eligible for adoption? Explain.
11. How can a "black market" in adoptable babies best be controlled?
12. List the arguments, pro and con, for *not* terminating parental rights over a child and returning the child to its natural parent.

## Chapter X

# THE RIGHT TO TRAVEL: PASSPORTS, DEPORTATION, AND FREEDOM

### Travel: A Constitutional Right?

THE "RIGHT TO TRAVEL" naturally embraces all those rights which are entitled to be respected in the issuance, the limitation of use, the denial, and the revocation of an American passport necessary for travel abroad. (Excluded by definition herein is travel *within* the United States and its possessions). International locomotion has been for some time the battleground between those championing the supremacy of the freedom of the individual, and those setting themselves up as guardians of our national security. Today it is illegal for a citizen to depart from the United States for a destination outside of the Western Hemisphere (or Cuba) without having a valid passport!

An individual's quest for a passport depends very much on how the law characterizes it, i.e., if the petition is accorded the status of a "privilege," the path may be strewn with impediments; on the other hand, if the petition is accorded the status of a "right," the government assumes the burden of proof when it seeks to deprive the petitioner of his right. Since the federal government has, in twentieth century practice, determined that the possession of a passport is a privilege, it is difficult to delineate and uphold violations of either procedural or substantive due process of law. Yet, during most of the nineteenth century, visas and/or passports were not necessary to leave the United States and to enter most countries abroad, or to re-enter the United States. The argument still centers about whether the "right to travel" is part of the liberty guaranteed by the First Amendment, or the "right to travel" is part of the foreign affairs of the United States not subject to judicial review.

The Secretary of State is empowered by law to conduct foreign relations which include the issuance and withholding of passports for international travel. In times of stress and strain, the national security may demand that unreliable citizens not leave the United States; in *Kent v. Dulles* (357 U.S. 116), however, the highest court solemnly ruled that the Secretary of State had not been given authority by existing legislation to withhold passports from citizens simply because of their beliefs and associations, or their ideologies and memberships in even subversive organizations. After numerous court decisions it has become evident that the conduct of foreign relations is not outside the pale of constitutional protection, so that the Secretary of State's discretion to issue, deny, or revoke passports is subject to judicial review.

To be differentiated from the unlawful discrimination on the basis of membership in any organization or association holding unpopular views or critical opinions of U.S. policy is the valid discretion of the Secretary of State to impose area restrictions on the travel of all citizens in exceptionally grave circumstances. In *Worthy v. Dulles* (270 F.2d 905) the U.S. Court of Appeals in 1959 found no constitutional issue in upholding the right of the Secretary of State to impose the travel ban to certain specific countries of the world, including Communist China.

It would seem that constitutional rights implicit in the First Amendment, Fourteenth Amendment, and Ninth Amendment, as delineated hereinafter, are protected in the realm of international travel. But individual passports may be denied where the Secretary of State finds reasonable grounds for believing that the activities of the passport applicant would endanger the national security of the United States, as by (a) transmitting without proper authority security information; (b) inciting hostilities or conflicts which might involve the United States, or (c) inciting attacks by force upon the United States or inciting attempts to overthrow the government by force or violence.

## A Short History of the Right to Travel

Historically the right to travel did not involve the modern document of a passport, for the simple reason that there was in antiquity no international traffic of travelers nor laws to govern that traffic. With the growth of the Roman Empire, and improvement in means of communication, travel was ameliorated, and occasionally a traveler would cover hundreds of miles on a business journey. The barbarian conquests and the resulting disruption of communications, together with the development of intense national feelings, again put the damper on travel beyond the limits of one's birthplace.

About three hundred years ago, the modern passport was introduced as a repressive measure to control the movement of undesirable peoples. By the end of the eighteenth century the obligatory passport was in force practically everywhere in Europe. France abolished the device from time to time, only to reinstate the obligatory passport even more restrictively after the French Revolution. The advent of World War I made the passport more obligatory, and today a majority of the nations of the world require passports of both nationals and foreigners. In the United States, the issuance of passports was not regulated comprehensively by law until the Act of August 14, 1956, when Congress placed the issuance of passports in the hands of the Secretary of State "under such rules as the President shall designate and prescribe." Every President in recent times has taken the position that the issuance of passports should be "permissive" or privileged, subject, however, to judiciary review of the act in accord with constitutional protections.

The first clear affirmation of the "right to travel" is found in *Bauer v. Acheson* (106 F. Supp. 445), decided by the Federal District Court for the District of Columbia in 1952. Here the court declared that freedom to travel outside the United States was "an attribute of personal liberty," and decreed that Miss Bauer's passport allowing her to return from France should not have been revoked *without a hearing*. (Under a 1941 Presidential proclamation, citizens were unable to leave *or* enter the United States without a passport).

The *Universal Declaration of Human Rights*, adopted by the General Assembly of the United Nations on December 10, 1948, states, in part, that "everyone has the right to leave any country, including his own, and to return to his country."

## Some Problems with Passports

The refusal of a passport impliedly denies to a citizen the economic and cultural benefits of travel abroad. As the world is brought closer together by ultra-speed jet aircraft, the inability of a citizen to travel abroad may involve irreparable, personal losses and disadvantages. Prior to 1958, the Secretary of State exercised the utmost of discretion in denying (or even delaying) passports to citizens whose names were involved with allegedly subversive activities. In *Dulles v. Nathan* (225 F.2d 29) the executor of the last will and testament of Albert Einstein was refused a passport in 1952 after waiting nearly two years without approval. Suit was brought against the Secretary of State in the federal court some two years later to direct Dulles to "promptly afford plaintiff an appropriate hearing." After a favorable decision and ten weeks additional waiting for a hearing, the court ordered Dulles to "forthwith issue to the plaintiff a passport." Dulles appealed and petitioned the court for a stay; again the court directed that Dulles hold a hearing for Dr. Nathan. Finally, almost five years after application had been made, Dulles issued the passport *without* affording Dr. Nathan a hearing! (The travails of Dr. Nathan were later experienced by Dr. Linus Pauling, winner of the Nobel Prize and recipient of the Medal of Merit, the highest award given to a civilian by the U.S. Government.)

In the same year, 1955, the chairman of the Independent Socialists League, an organization listed as subversive on the Attorney General's list, sued to obtain a passport, *Shactman v. Dulles* (225 F.2d 938). Although Shactman spent six years challenging the listing of the ISL as a subversive organization, his efforts went for nil. But the Chief Judge of the U.S. Court of Appeal for the District of Columbia declared that the denial of a passport solely because of the inclusion of the ISL on the Attorney General's list, was "arbitrary . . . . and causes a deprivation of liberty that a citizen otherwise would have." The court ruled that the Secretary of State may not "in his discretion deprive a citizen of liberty without due process of law." Indeed, a citizen's "freedom to leave a country or a hemisphere is as much a part of his liberty as freedom to leave a state." Again, a full hearing on the issue was deemed essential to the passport procedure.

## The Rockwell Kent Case

Rockwell Kent, one of America's foremost artists, had long been a stormy petrel of the art world. In 1957, he was refused a passport to visit England and attend a meeting of an organization known as the World Council of Peace, in Helsinki, Finland. According to the U.S. Supreme Court, "the director of the U.S. Passport Office informed Kent that the issuance of a passport was precluded by Section 51.135 of the regulations promulgated by the Secretary of State on two grounds: (a) that he was a Communist, and (b) that he had a 'consistent and prolonged adherence to the Communist party line.'" Kent was told that he was entitled to an informal hearing, but before a passport could be issued, he must submit an affidavit as to whether he was then or ever had been a Communist. He did not ask for a hearing, but instead filed a new passport application listing the several European countries he desired to visit. The attorney for Kent stated that Kent would not file an affidavit concerning Communist party membership, because Kent deemed the affidavit "unlawful" and in conflict with his "conscience." At the informal hearing, the principal evidence against Kent was taken from his book, *It's Me, O Lord*, but since Kent had filed no affidavit, the U.S. Passport Office informed him that no passport would issue.

In the federal district court Kent's action for declaratory relief was denied; and the U.S. Court of Appeals affirmed (248 F.2d 561). But on June 17, 1958, the U.S. Supreme Court *reversed* by a five to four vote in which Mr. Justice Douglas was joined by Chief Justice Warren and Justices Black, Frankfurter, and Brennan (The minority views was upheld by Justices Clark, Burton, Harlan, and Whittaker). The majority opinion voiding the passport denials declared:

> "The right to travel is part of the 'liberty' of which the citizen cannot be deprived without the due process of law . . . Freedom of movement across frontiers in either direction, and inside frontiers as well, is a part of our heritage. Travel abroad, like travel within the country, may be necessary for a

livelihood. It may be as close to the heart of the individual as the choice of what he eats, or wears, or reads . . . . Freedom of movement also has large social values . . . . "

Mr. Justice Douglas then noted that the discretion of the Secretary of State in refusing passports fell into two categories: (a) "questions pertaining to the citizenship of the applicant and his allegiance to the United States," and (b) "the question whether the applicant was participating in illegal conduct, trying to escape the toils of the law, promoting passport frauds, or otherwise engaging in conduct which would violate the laws of the United States." Mr. Justice Douglas concluded that "the grounds for refusal asserted here do not relate to citizenship or allegiance on the one hand, or to criminal or unlawful conduct on the other." Accordingly, the Secretary of State was not given by Congress "unbridled discretion to grant or withhold a passport from a citizen for any substantive reason he may choose."

The dissenting opinion of Mr. Justice Clark traced the Secretary of State's broad discretion over passport issuance back to 1856, and found no limits on that authority in such legislative history. It is of *historical interest* to compare Mr. Justice Clark's conclusion with the following historical summary found in Mr. Justice Douglas' majority opinion:

> "Prior to 1952 there were numerous laws enacted by Congress regulating passports and many decisions, ruling and regulations by the Executive Department concerning them. Thus, in 1803, Congress made it unlawful for an official knowingly to issue a passport to an alien certifying that he is a citizen. 2 Stat. 205. In 1815, just prior to the termination of the War of 1812, it made it illegal for a citizen to 'cross the frontier' into enemy territory, to board vessels of the enemy on waters of the United States or to visit any of his camps within the limits of the United States, 'without a passport first obtained' from the Secretary of State or other designated official. 3 Stat. 199-200. The Secretary of State took similar steps during the Civil War. See Department of State, *The American Passport (1898) 50*. In 1850 Congress ratified a treaty with Switzerland requiring passports from citizens of the two nations. 11 Stat. 587, 589-590. Finally, in 1856, Congress enacted what remains today as our basic pass-

port statute. Prior to that time various Federal officials, state and local officials, and notaries public had undertaken to issue either certificates of citizenship or other documents in the nature of letters of introduction to foreign officials requesting treatment according to the usages of international law. By the Act of Aug. 18, 1856, 11 Stat. 52, 60-61, 22 U.S.C. section 211A, Congress put an end to those practices. This provision, as codified by the Act of July 3, 1926, 44 Stat., Part 2, 887, reads, 'The Secretary of State may grant and issue passports .... under such rules as the President shall designate and prescribe for and on behalf of the United States, and no other person shall grant, issue, or verify such passports.' Thus for most of our history, a passport was not a condition to entry or exit.

"It is true that, at intervals, a passport has been required for travel. Mention has already been made of the restrictions imposed during the War of 1812 and during the Civil War. A like restriction, which was the forerunner of that contained in the 1952 act, was imposed by Congress in 1988.

"The Act of May 22, 1918, 40 Stat. 559, made it unlawful, while a Presidential proclamation was in force, for a citizen to leave or enter the United States "unless he bears a valid passport." See H.R.Rep. No. 485, 65th Congr., 2d Sess. That statute was invoked by Presidential proclamation on Aug. 8, 1918, 40 Stat. 1829, which continued in effect until March 3, 1921, 41 Stat. 1359. The 1918 act was effective only in wartime. It was amended in 1941 so that it could be invoked in the then-existing emergency. 55 Stat. 252. See S. Rep. No. 444, 77th Cong., 1st Sess. It was invoked by Presidential proclamation. Proc. No. 2523, Nov. 14, 1941, 55 Stat. 1696. That emergency continued until April 28, 1952. Proc. No. 2974, 66 Stat. C 31. Congress extended the statutory provisions until April 1, 1953. 66 Stat. 54, 57, 96, 137, 330, 333. It was during this extension period that the Secretary of State issued the regulations here complained of."

"Under the 1926 act and its predecessor a large body of precedents grew up which repeat over and over again that the issuance of passports is a 'discretionary act' on the part of the Secretary of State .... This long continued executive construction should be enough, it is said, to warrant the inference that Congress had adopted it .... But the key to that problem, as we shall see, is in the manner in which the Secretary's discretion was exercised, not in the bare fact that he had discretion . . . . "

"A passport not only is of great value — indeed necessary — abroad; it is also an aid in establishing citizenship for purpose of re-entry into the United States. See *Browder v. United States,* 312 U.S. 335, 339; 3 Moore, International Law Digest (1906); Section 512. But throughout most of our history — until indeed quite recently — a passport, though a great convenience in foreign travel, was not a legal requirement for leaving or entering the United States. See Jaffee, The Right to Travel, *35 Foreign Affairs 17.* Apart from minor exceptions to be noted, it was first made a requirement by Section 215 of the Act of June 27, 1952, 66 Stat. 190, 8 U.S.C. Section 1185, which states that after a prescribed proclamation by the President, it is "unlawful for any citizen of the United States to depart from or enter, or attempt to depart from or enter, the United States unless he bears a valid passport." And the proclamation necessary to make the restrictions of this applicable and in force has been made."

On the same day in 1958 that the U.S. Supreme Court decided the *Kent* case (357 U.S. 116) the passport case of Dr. Walter Briehl, a psychiatrist, was also determined. When Dr. Briehl applied for a passport, he was asked to supply the affidavit concerning Communist party membership. Briehl, like Kent, refused, contending that (a) his political affiliations with the Los Angeles County Communist Party, the Bookshop Association of St. Louis, etc. etc. were irrelevant to his right to a passport; (b) "every American citizen has the right to travel regardless of politics," and (c) the burden was on the Secretary of State to prove illegal activities in which he was allegedly engaged. In voiding the passport denial Mr. Justice Douglas opined:

> "We deal with beliefs, with association, with ideological matter. We must remember that we are dealing here with citizens who have neither been accused of crimes nor found guilty. They are being denied their freedom of movement solely because of their refusal to be subjected to inquiry into their beliefs and associations. They do not seek to escape the law nor to violate it. They may or may not be Communists. But, assum-

ing they are, the only law which Congress has passed expressly curtailing the movement of Communists across our borders has not yet become effective, it would therefore be strange to infer that, pending the effectiveness of that law, the Secretary has been silently granted by Congress the larger, the more pervasive power to curtail in his discretion the free movement of citizens in order to satisfy himself about their beliefs or associations."

Again, on June 17, 1958, the highest court also acted on the passport denial case of a Mr. Dayton who wanted a passport to take a job at the Tata Institute of Physics in Bombay, India. He was accused of association with Communist espionage agents, which charges he denied under oath; but the Secretary of State refused to issue a passport. The court (357 U.S. 144) simply ruled that the reasons of the Secretary of State for withholding the Dayton passport were not authorized by Congress.

### The 1958 Legislative Attack Upon the Right to Travel

The determinations in the *Kent, Briehl,* and *Dayton* cases were not universally liked and, in July 1958, the Eisenhower Administration sent to Congress a bill specifically restricting the constitutional right to travel, clearly intending that the legislation would overcome the effect of the U.S. Supreme Court decisions. President Eisenhower's message reaffirmed his belief that travel control vests in the hands of the Secretary of State who must have the power "to prevent Americans from using passports . . . . where their presence would conflict with our foreign policy objectives . . . . Each day and week that passes without it exposes us to great danger." The bill also intended to give legislative support to the position of Secretary of State Dulles to withhold passports to American newsmen desiring to go to Communist China. Congress, however, did not act favorably upon this bill, thereby not confusing the conduct of a specific foreign policy with the right of citizens to travel abroad.

### The "Worthy" Chronicle: Area Travel Restrictions

The misadventures of newspaperman William Worthy, Jr., describe an important chapter on the right to travel. Mr. Worthy, a correspondent for the Baltimore Afro-American, a writer for the *New York Post* and a CBS correspondent, applied in 1957 for a renewal of his passport. The Secretary of State denied his request upon the ground that Worthy's "activities abroad, at this time, would be prejudicial to the orderly conduct of the foreign relations of the United States." The State Department determination contained the following:

> "Mr. Worthy's passport renewal application was denied under the provisions of Sec. 51.136 (2) of the passport regulations. As indicated by the findings the Secretary made in the case, Mr. Worthy traveled to and in Communist China and Hungary during the period December 1956 to February 1957 in violation of the limiting and restricting endorsements contained in his passport and in willful disregard of declared United States foreign policy. He used his passport in connection with such travel, and it is clear from his testimony that he would have no hesitancy in again using a United States passport in a similar manner. In fact, he has refused to give the Department a statement that he would not again travel in violation of the restrictions contained in any passport issued to him . . . . "

The State Department in 1957 had placed restrictive travel endorsements on all passports, and Worthy commenced his suit to obtain an *unrestricted* passport to visit Communist China. On June 9, 1959, Chief Judge Prettyman in *Worthy v. Herter* (270 F.2d 905) upheld the power of the State Department to impose travel restrictions on the use of a passport. Judge Prettyman stated that the refusal of an unrestricted passport to Worthy rested in no way upon "beliefs, associations, or personal characteristics," but upon the general, non-discriminatory policy of forbidding travel in China and certain other Communist-controlled areas. Such State Department foreign policy was beyond judicial inquiry: if the Executive branch of government foresaw the possibility of diplomatic or military clashes with a foreign government because of Americans' travel there, the Executive branch had the power to prevent such travel. To hold otherwise, said Judge Prettyman, would be "illogical and unrealistic:"

> "In foreign affairs, especially . . . . in today's world of jets, radio and atomic power, an individual's yen to go and to in-

quire may be circumscribed. A blustering inquisitor avowing his own freedom to go and do as he pleases can throw the whole international neighborhood into turmoil."

The court therefore found the reasons given for denial of the passport to Worthy to be reasonable and supported by foreign policy considerations. Worthy's argument that travel by Americans in China would help rather than hurt foreign relations was poignantly answered by Judge Prettyman:

> "This is an argument he should make (not to the court, but) to the President or the Congress."

Whereupon the Court concluded:

> "The right to travel is a part of the right to liberty, and a newspaperman's right to travel is part of the freedom of the press. But these valid generalizations do not support unrestrained conclusions. For the maintenance and preservation of liberty, individual rights must be restricted for various reasons from time to time. Merely because a newsman has a right to travel does not mean he can go anywhere he wishes. He cannot attend conclusions. For the maintenance and preservation of liberty, Cabinet, or executive sessions of committees of Congress. He cannot come into my house without my permission, or enter a ball park without a ticket of admission from the management, or cross a public street downtown between crosswalks. He cannot pass a police cordon thrown about an accident, unless he has a pass from the police. A newsman's freedom to travel is a restricted thing subject to myriad limitations."

Indeed, area restrictions on American travel have been imposed for these many years by the Secretaries of State. At present, travel is generally banned to Cuba, Communist China, North Korea, North Vietnam, and Albania. After William Worthy, Jr. sought to re-enter the United States from a Cuban trip in 1961 made without a passport, he was arrested under legislation making it a crime to do so. He drew a three-month jail sentence which the Fifth U.S. Court of Appeals in New Orleans set aside in February 1964:

> "The citizen, culpable though he may have been in leaving his country without a passport which he could not obtain, and

subject as he probably was to a criminal penalty for departing without a passport, cannot, we think, be required to choose between banishment or expatriation on the one hand, or crossing the border on the other hand, being faced with criminal punishment."

Judge Jones drew a distinction between two clauses of the statute, one forbidding departure from the country without a valid passport for a trip where one is required, and the other penalizing return after such a trip. Prosecution for leaving the country without the necessary passport obviously presents "a less difficult problem." Accordingly, "a citizen at an airport or pier without a passport can refrain from a violation of the statute by remaining in the country. So doing, the citizen can continue to enjoy all the rights and privileges of citizenship." The court held that section of the statute to be *unconstitutional,* and thus cast present day doubt upon the government's general power to declare areas of the world out-of-bounds for American travel. It is surmised that Congress will soon remedy the loophole by enacting legislation which makes it a specific crime to travel in areas prohibited by the President without specially validated passports.

## The Ban on Communist Travel Abroad

Under a 1950 statute, "Communist action" and "Communist front" groups are required to register with the Government, if so found by the Subversive Activities Control Board. Various penalties are imposed on members of such groups, including a passport ban. Mr. Herbert Aptheker, editor of the Communist party's theoretical journal, "Political Affairs" and Miss Elizabeth Gurley Flynn, chairman of the party, were denied passports and therefore could not travel outside the Western Hemisphere. On June 22, 1964, the U.S. Supreme Court struck down the provision of the Internal Security Act of 1950, which denied passports to members of the Communist party. Mr. Justice Goldberg writing for the six to three majority of the court declared that the 1950 Act swept too broadly in preventing all travel; that Congress had not dealt specifically enough with the real danger that concerned it, to wit: Communist espionage or other criminal activity. While Congress does have ample power to protect the national security, it cannot condemn innocent activity along with evil:

> "Under the statute it is a crime to apply for a passport to travel abroad to visit a sick relative, to receive medical treatment, or for any other wholly innocent purpose."

Mr. Justice Goldberg cited the example of a Communist wanting to "read rare manuscripts in the Bodleian Library of Oxford," and concluded that the national security could be and must constitutionally be protected by means "more discriminately tailored to the constitutional liberties of individuals."

The three dissenters in the *Aptheker* case objected to the majority's reading the statute on its face instead of applying it specifically to the two plaintiffs who are clearly active, leading Communist Party members: "We have no 'innocent members' before us." (N.B.—Miss Flynn subsequently died while in Soviet Russia.)

### A Report of a Bar Association on Freedom to Travel

On November 24, 1958, the Association of the Bar of the City of New York issued a public statement that "U.S. citizens should be free to travel abroad with a minimum of restraint by their government." The report criticized certain regulations and practices of the Secretary of State which denied passports for a variety of reasons which were "inadequate to support the deprivation of such an important right as the citizen's right to travel abroad." The report proposed that travel should not be restrained and passports should not be denied solely on the basis of membership in any organization, association with any individual or group, adherence to unpopular views, or criticism of the U.S. or its domestic or foreign policies:

> "Each inroad upon the freedom of travel weakens the base upon which a free society necessarily depends . . . . Great difficulty with area restrictions is that they are self-defeating in too many instances . . . . U.S. reporters are in many cases subjected to the ban — possibly to the detriment of the United States by depriving its citizens of information and news gathered by U.S. reporters."

This 50-page report of the Association of the Bar of the City of New York set forth the following principles as a guide to a more intelligent solution of the problem:

"1. Area Restraints: Travel abroad by all United States citizens may be prohibited in areas where the Secretary of State determines that such prohibitions should be imposed in the national interest, but only in situations of *exceptional gravity*. The imposition of area restrictions should be accompanied by a statement by the Secretary of State setting forth the reasons therefor. Exceptions to general area prohibitions, permitting travel by particular individuals or groups, may be made by the Secretary of State in his discretion.

"2. Individual Restraints Upon National Security Grounds: Travel abroad by individual United States citizens may be restrained and passports may be denied to citizens as to whom the Secretary finds reasonable grounds to believe that their activities abroad would endanger the national security of the United States by (a) transmitting, without proper authority, security information of the United States; (b) inciting hostilities or conflicts which might involve the United States; (c) inciting attacks by force upon the United States or attempts to overthrow its government by force and violence."

This 1958 report also favored continuation of the United States policy of letting its citizens leave for Western Hemisphere countries without passports. However, it stated that it hardly seemed right to let United States citizens living in Mexico, for example, go to Europe without passports, as the present law seems to do, when citizens living here must have them:

"A nonresident citizen should be subject to the same restrictions as a resident. From Western Hemisphere countries it is often possible to arrange travel to Iron Curtain countries, which do not require a United States passport."

The report stated that this "loophole" could be closed if Congressional legislation provided punishment for any travel outside the Western Hemisphere during war or declared emergencies.

These liberal views of the Association of the Bar of the City of New York were challenged by the American Bar Association

Committee on Communist Tactics, Strategy and Objectives, which took the view that authorization to travel abroad is not a right of the same character as that granted by the Bill of Rights, but is a *privilege* subject to discretion of the government. This A.B.A. Committee urged that Congress enact legislation that would "restore to the executive branch of the government the right to deny passports to persons knowingly engaged in subversive activities, and to deny passports on the basis of confidential information." (The A.B.A. Communist Tactics Committee was headed by Peter Campbell Brown, former corporation counsel of New York City, and former chairman of the federal Subversive Activities Control Board.) While in general agreement with the objective of encouraging travel abroad for peaceful purposes and of protecting the right of freedom of travel, this A.B.A. Committee was concerned about the maintenance of a proper balance between freedom to travel and national security:

> "Any legislation should empower the Secretary of State to restrict travel outside the country if there is reasonable basis for belief that such travel conflicts with national security.
>
> "After a passport is granted, it is obviously too late to protect the country against the acts of the recipient. This Committee is of the firm opinion that the right to travel outside the United States is not an individual right of the nature and character of those guaranteed by the Bill of Rights, but partakes more of the nature of a privilege. The duty of the government to protect itself in those few cases, from those who would destroy it, is vital, not only in times of war and emergency, but at all times."

The A.B.A. Communist Tactics Committee pointed out that standards and criteria for passport denials and government employee dismissals were contained in the Report of the A.B.A. Commission on Government Security which was headed by Loyd Wright, former president of the A.B.A. The official A.B.A. Report adopted at the 1959 annual meeting took the form of the following resolutions:

> 1. RESOLVED, That the American Bar Association recommend to the Congress the enactment of legislation containing the following principles with respect to the control of travel abroad by United States citizens:

(a) The Secretary of State should be authorized to refuse to issue a passport to any person or to restrict or revoke a passport of any person as to whom it is determined on substantial grounds by a preponderance of the evidence that he knowingly engages in activities calculated to further the International Communist movement and having a tendency to endanger the national security or tending seriously to impair the conduct of the foreign relations of the United States.

(b) If a passport is denied, revoked or restricted for any reason stated in paragraph (a) hereof, the applicant or holder should be informed in writing of the reason, as specifically as is consistent with considerations of national security and the conduct of foreign relations, and shall have and be informed in writing of the right to a hearing before the Passport Hearing Board.

(c) The Secretary should be required to establish within the Department of State a Passport Hearing Board, at least one member of which shall be a lawyer, to review the denial, revocation or restriction of a passport. The member of said Board shall be independent of and have no responsibility related to the issuance, denial, revocation or restriction of passports other than their duties as members of said Board.

(d) In proceedings before the Passport Hearing Board, the Secretary should be required to establish and enunciate publicly the procedural safeguards available whereby the rights accorded to an individual are protected. In such proceedings, the individual shall have the following rights which shall be included in the rules which the Secretary shall make public:

> (1) To appear in person and to be represented by counsel.
> (2) To testify in his own behalf, present witnesses and offer other evidence.
> (3) To cross-examine witnesses appearing against him at any hearing at which he or his counsel is present and to examine all other evidence which is made a part of the open record.
> (4) To examine a copy of the transcript of the open record and upon request to be furnished a copy thereof.

(e) The right to confront and cross-examine all witnesses and to examine all documentary evidence considered by the

Board shall be accorded, except where the Secretary of State or Acting Secretary of State, personally, shall certify that information, or the sources of information, or the investigative methods pertaining to the individual is believed by him to be reliable and cannot be disclosed without serious damage to national security or the conduct of foreign relations. The Secretary or Acting Secretary shall furnish to the individual during the course of the proceedings a fair written resume of such information certified by him to be as complete as consistent with national security or the conduct of foreign relations.

(f) The Board shall take into consideration the individual's inability to challenge information of which he has not been advised in full or in detail or the individual's inability to attack the credibility of sources that have not been disclosed to him.

(g) Review procedure in the United States District Court for the District of Columbia shall be provided. In such review the court shall determine whether the decision of the Secretary is based on substantial evidence in the record and that procedural requirements have been met.

2. RESOLVED, That the American Bar Association authorize the chairmen of the said special committees jointly to appear before the committees of the Congress to state the position of the Association in conformity with the foregoing Resolution."

### Travel by Aliens: Deportation and/or Detention

The right to travel also involves (a) the deportation of aliens who do not seek to leave the U.S., and (b) the detention of aliens who wish to leave the U.S. and return to their native lands. A typical deportation case was *Bonetti v. Rogers* (356 U.S. 691), decided by the U.S. Supreme Court in 1958. Here an alien entered the United States in 1923, was a member of the Communist party from 1932 through 1936, left the United States in 1937, returned in 1938 as a "quota immigrant" and was admitted "for permanent residence," and in 1939 again "entered" the United States following a one-day Mexican visit. Bonetti was held *not deportable* under Section 22 of the Internal Security Act as an "alien who had been, after entering . . . . a member of the Communist party." The court explained that he was not a Communist party member at the time of the 1938 or 1939 entries or at any time thereafter. Mr. Justice Whittaker, writing for the six-man majority of the United States Supreme Court, pointed out that the statute "does not enable an alien resident to evade the deportation laws by leaving the country and returning after a brief period, for, if at the time of his return he is within an excluded class, he would be excludable, or, if he nevertheless enters, he would be deportable. It is admitted that when petitioner returned from Mexico after his one-day trip in September, 1939, he was not excludable under then current exclusionary laws. That entry, being lawful, can only support our conclusion in this case."

The dissent of Mr. Justice Clark (joined in by Justices Harlan and Frankfurter) declared that the majority opinion "cripples the effectiveness of the act, permitting aliens to escape deportation solely because they happen to leave and then re-enter the country":—

> "It is conceded by the court that had petitioner remained here he would have been deportable. Hence, the construction of the court restrict the literal sence of the 1950 act to aliens who have continuously remained in the United States. This innovation is contrary to decades of uninterrupted administrative interpretation and practice, and also to prior cases of this court. The Immigration and Naturalization Service has always construed 'entry' as meaning any coming of an alien from a foreign country to the United States. The Congress recognized this interpretation when considering the Immigration and Nationality Act of 1952. The court, however, sidesteps this authority by saying that 'the novel circumstances here' preclude our consideration of the 1923 entry because 'petitioner had abandoned all rights of residence under that entry.' But that is not the question. True, petitioner makes no claim under the 1923 entry, and the 1938 admission is not dependent on the former but was a regular 'quota immigrant' entry. Nevertheless, petitioner is an alien who entered and 'thereafter' was a member of the Communist Party while in the United States. Any number of additional entries - in 1938 or otherwise - cannot wipe out that fact."

## Deportation: Travel Away From the U.S.

In *Rowoldt v. Perfetto* (355 U.S. 115) the U.S. Supreme Court by a five to four vote found that an alien who joined the

Communist Party in the United States in 1935 "to fight for something to eat and clothes and shelter," rather than in "dissatisfaction with living under democracy," had not established a meaningful, political association subjecting him to deportation under Section 22 of the Internal Security Act of 1950. An amendment to the Act had directed the Attorney General not to include Communist membership or affiliation "which is or was solely . . . for purposes of obtaining employment, food rations, or other essentials of living, and where necessary for such purposes." According to the court, the government had failed to show that there was "a substantial basis for finding that an alien committed himself to the Communist party in consciousness that he was joining an organization known as the Communist party."

And, in *U.S. ex rel Fong Foo v. Shaughnessy* the Second U.S. Court of Appeal, in July 1956, refused to deport an alien to Communist China, because the court had taken judicial notice of the ruthless behavior of the Communist government in China, and of the near certainty that a Chinese known to have allied himself with the Formosan Government would be tortured and exterminated if found on the mainland of China.

On the other hand, in *U.S. v. Solazzo* the same court on January 13, 1961, found no difficulty in deporting an alien who pleaded guilty to a charge of bribery of a participant in an amateur sport and who was sentenced to a term of imprisonment. Since the New York statute makes bribery a felony, Solazzo was convicted of a crime involving "moral turpitude" within the meaning of Section 19-a of the Immigration Act of 1917. Chief Judge Lombard opined:

> "The crime of bribing a participant in an amateur sport is one which in light of contemporary standards inherently involves moral turpitude."

The Hungarian refugees who arrived in the United States in 1956 without visas were held by the United States Supreme Court *not* to be subject to deportation without a hearing. (Normally, aliens residing here are in the technical custody of the Attorney General and may be deported by revoking their parole.) The majority of the Second U.S. Court of Appeals had held that the case of the Hungarian refugees was different because they had been *invited* here under the foreign policy of the United States, as announced by President Eisenhower. The case before the court involved *Gyula Paktorovics,* a forty-four-year-old Hungarian army captain, who then lived in Baltimore with his wife, and their two daughters. The Paktorovics were among 30,000 Hungarians who fled to Austria from Hungary at the time of the uprising in 1956. In Salzburg, the family successfully applied for admission to the United States as parolees, and they arrived at Camp Kilmer, N. J., on Dec. 24, 1956. Three months later U.S. Immigration officials began interrogating Mr. Paktorovics concerning his activities in Hungary. They learned that he had been a member of the Communist Party after his release from a concentration camp in 1953. On Aug. 14, 1957, U.S. Immigration officials revoked his parole on the basis of his alleged concealment of Communist party membership. The entire family was ordered deported to Austria, and they sought a writ of *habeas corpus* to stop their deportation. The matter was brought before Federal District Court Judge Kaufman, who granted a writ to Mrs. Paktorovics and her children, enabling them to remain here; but he ruled that the Attorney General had the right to revoke the husband's parole. The decision of the Second U.S. Court of Appeals, in effect, returned the matter to the U.S. Immigration and Naturalization Service for a full hearing, because, "It is difficult to see how the statute, interpreted to authorize deportation of appellant without a hearing on the merits, could satisfy the requirements of due process. We do not say that the discretion of the courts should be substituted for the discretion to be exercised by the Attorney General as provided by law. We do say that there must be a hearing which will give assurance that the discretion of the Attorney General shall be exercised against a background of facts fairly contested in the open."

In a vigorous dissent, Judge Moore of the Second U.S. Court of Appeal upheld the lower court ruling of Judge Kaufman, who had denied a writ of *habeas corpus* to the father. Judge Moore held that the majority decision had overridden the intent of Congress, had substituted the court's judgment for the opinion of the Executive Branch of the Government, and had overruled a long line of consistent decisions of the Supreme Court:

"The effect of the decision is to remove such aliens from the parole of the Attorney General and without Congressional sanction to place it in the courts. The creation and administration of international policies including the admission of citizens of other lands to our shores have been vested in the legislative and executive branches of the Government. Wisely so. Chaos would result were international policy to be set ad hoc by individual courts throughout the country."

The U.S. Supreme Court affirmed that the Paktorovics were entitled to a hearing before deportation.

### Detention: "No Travel"

A resident alien has the same constitutional right to procedural due process of law as a citizen, and therefore detention of an alien in this country must be preceded by notice and the opportunity to be heard. In *Han-Lee-Mao v. Brownell* (207 F.2d 142, 1953), the plaintiff, a Chinese alien, desired to return to his native country in 1951. He has studied for four years in the United States and earned a master's degree in oceanography. Although he received no hearing other than a brief interrogation by an immigration inspector, plaintiff was denied an exit permit on the ground that if he returned to Communist China his scientific training and knowledge might be used to impede the national defense efforts of the United States. A three-judge district court held that the pertinent provision of the McCarran Act was constitutional!

The refusal to permit aliens to return to their native lands has been one of the practices employed by the United States in the effort to deal with the novel international problems which have arisen in the present era of indefinite national emergency. Although there are apparently no settled principles of international law to guide action in a period which cannot be termed either "wartime" or "peacetime," one can predict with some assurance that international law does not condone wholesale detention. The administration of the standard "prejudicial to the interests of the United States" must be accomplished always with the thought that detention, in the absence of a declared war, is a harsh, unprecedented method. However, since the detention policy is a discretionary, political one, the judiciary should intervene only to test the constitutionality of the applicable statute and to insure that action under the statute is neither arbitrary nor outside the authority delegated to the administrator by Congress.

**Visas and the "Right to Exclude" Aliens**

The sovereign "right to exclude" is exercised through the denial of travel visas. A visa, unlike a passport which is a travel authorization and identification document of the state of nationality, is a document taking the form of a stamp of approval of the state to be entered. The use of a visa as a means of restricting immigration to the United States commenced in 1917, when it was instituted temporarily as a wartime restriction. Instructions of the Department of State, dated April 17, 1917, and a joint order of the Department of Labor, dated July 26, 1917, required that all aliens proceeding to the United States in time of war must have passports issued by the government to which they owe allegiance and must bear evidence that the passports were inspected, settled and visaed by the American consular officials abroad. This procedure was first given legislative sanction by the Act of May 22, 1918 (22 U.S.C. 223-26 (b)), and has since become a general requirement applicable to all aliens seeking admission to the United States.

In order to supervise the issuance of consular visas, the Visa Office was organized under the direction of the Administrator of the Bureau of Security and Consular Affairs of the Department of State. The Visa Office prepares regulations to implement the immigration laws, issues instructions to its consular officers, controls the issuance of quota numbers and renders advisory opinions to consular officials in individual cases. The powers and duties respecting the admission of aliens to the United States are divided between two government agencies, (a) the U.S. Immigration and Naturalization Service, headed by the Attorney-General, and (b) the U.S. State Department. The prospective immigrant must undergo two procedural hurdles before being admitted to the United States. His first contact with United States authority is at an American consulate abroad, under the State Department, where he undergoes physical examination and files the necessary application forms. His second contact, at a United States port of entry, is with the U.S. Immigration and Naturalization Service. The United States thus reserves a double check on the grant of a visa, and the alien in possession of a visa has no assurance of entry to the United States. This double check is explicit in the Immigration and Nationality Act, which provides:

> "Nothing in this Act shall be construed to entitle any alien, to whom a visa or other documentation has been issued, to enter the United States, if, upon arrival at a Port of Entry in the United States, he is found to be inadmissible under this Act, or any other provision of law."

In both cases, the applicant must bear the burden of proof to establish that he is eligible to receive a visa and to be admitted.

*The alien, however, is not accorded similar protections upon the denial of a visa.* By virtue of an intentional quirk of the immigration law, sole and exclusive authority to grant or deny visas is vested in United States consular officers stationed abroad. No judicial review on the denial of visas to aliens seeking entry into the U.S. is required. In the leading case of *Ulrich v. Kellogg,* (30 F.2d 984, 1929) it was held that the issuance of a visa is a *discretionary function* which cannot be compelled by a court through mandamus. The rationale of the court was that since the immigration laws of the United States do not provide for review of the action of consular officers in issuing visas, Congress intended to deny judicial review.

The first and most fundamental protection available to the alien who applies for admission is the fact that the jurisdiction of consular officers to deny visas is defined by statute. No alien can be denied a visa except upon a ground specified in the Immigration and Nationality Act, which provides that:

> "No visa or other documentation shall be issued to an alien if (1) it appears to the consular officer, from statements in the application, or in the papers submitted therewith, that such alien is ineligible to receive a visa or such other documentation under section 212, or any other provision of law, (2) the application fails to comply with the provisions of this Act, or the regulations issued thereunder, or (3) the consular officer knows

or has reason to believe that such alien is ineligible to receive a visa or such other documentation under section 212, or any other provision of law . . . . "

There is no requirement that a visa applicant be confronted with the evidence upon which he is denied a visa. Nevertheless, consuls are restricted in the denial of visas to cases falling within the above classifications, the theory being that consular officers are authorized to deny visas only upon the grounds set forth in the Immigration and Nationality Act as causes for exclusion. There are approximately thirty-one such grounds of excludability and ineligibility to receive visas specified in the Act. Since, the consul is obliged to advise the applicant of the section number under which the visa was denied, the applicant is in a position to know the ground or grounds of his exclusion and can submit further explanatory evidence.

Further protections are to be found in the regulations which prescribe a procedure to be followed by consular officers in the refusal of immigrant visas. These regulations require that a memorandum of refusal be prepared on a specified form by the consular officer whenever an immigrant visa is refused. This form is retained in the appropriate consular file. The refusal must then be reviewed by the consular officer in charge of visa work at the post and, if he concurs in the refusal, he must countersign the memorandum. On the other hand, if he does not concur in the refusal, published regulations require that the case be submitted to the State Department (Visa Office) for an advisory opinion. The advisory opinions of the Visa Office conform with court decisions, opinions of the Attorney-General and decisions of the Board of Immigration Appeals.

During the pendency of a case before a consular officer, or following a visa denial, the applicant, his attorney, relative, friend or any other person with a legitimate interest, may directly approach the consular officer for clarification. In addition, such persons may address inquiries to the Visa Office, which will review the consular decision upon the contention "that the denial of a visa was in error or that the procedures followed were not consistent with established standards." In such cases, the State Department will request a report from the consular officer and, if necessary, will require the entire visa file be submitted for review. Based upon this review, the department will render an advisory opinion, which will either concur in the consul's action or point out to him that his decision was in error.

Probably the only case in which recovery was granted for a wrongful consular visa denial was *American Surety Co. v. Sullivan* (7 F.2d 605, 1925). Here the United States consul was under State Department instructions to decline to render services to persons who were involved in transferring ships against United States' interests. The consul zealously interpreted these instructions as meaning that he should deny a visa to an American seaman who served as captain of a ship which was suspected of being so involved. The U.S. Court of Appeals held that this misinterpretation of instructions entailed liability on the part of the consul and stated that this "was not an error in the discharge of his duties, but an error in understanding what they were, and for that he is liable." The court further stated:

> "The case is a hard one, but a public officer, while not chargeable for the mistaken exercise of his actual powers, is responsible for keeping within them. He may not use his authorization to excuse action which it does not justify."

## Selected Bibliography

Senate Document No. 126, 85th Congress, 2nd Session, 1958.
*Kwong Hai Chew v. Colding,* 344 U.S. 590, 1953.
*Edwards v. California,* 314 U.S. 160, 1940.
*New York Times,* June 17, 1958, p. 1 *et seq.*
Vol. 40 *Virginia Law Review,* 1954.
Vol. 41 *Iowa Law Review* 6, 1955.
*Foreign Affairs,* October, 1956.
Vol. 70 *Harvard Law Review* 193, 1956.

## Questions for Review

1. Is the "right" to travel a "right" or merely a privilege?
2. Explain why "foreign affairs" are not subject to judicial review.
3. What is the effect upon the United States of the U.N. Universal Declaration of Human Rights on freedom of travel?

4. Why should the Secretary of State be required to hold a hearing whenever a passport application is denied or revoked?
5. Do you agree with the U.S. Supreme Court's determination in the *Rockwell Kent* case? Explain.
6. Did the court's decision in the *Briehl* case add anything to its determination in the *Kent* case? Explain.
7. Does a newspaperman have a right to travel over and above that of an ordinary citizen?
8. Why are area restrictions in passports considered part and part and parcel of foreign policy? What is the significance of William Worthy's court victory in February 1964?
9. Criticize the 1959 A.B.A. resolutions on passport control.
10. Does the alien have a right to travel? State the grounds for "detention" and the grounds for "deportation."

*Chapter XI*

# SELECTED CRIMES AGAINST INSTITUTIONS: SOCIAL AND CRIMINAL WRONGS

IT CAN BE LOGICALLY argued that the "crimes against institutions," some of which are delineated herein, are not the crimes of passion and notoriety which mark the criminal as a necessary outcast from society. For the most part, these selected crimes against society are committed not by the hardened, criminal mind capable of causing his victim grievous bodily injury, but by the sophisticated gentleman whose cunning approach to crime is one of challenge. The crime is no less a crime simply because the social animal does not pursue observable criminal conduct but leaves these crimes to the "one-shot" gambler, the Casper Milquetoast who desperately needs money, or to the frightened husband who wants to support his wife in the style to which she has not yet grown accustomed! An understanding of what constitutes these "social crimes" or social wrongs of Extortion and Blackmail, Perjury, Forgery and Plagiarism, and deceptive practices in broadcasting, will enable the reader to ask and perhaps answer the question of whether society is sufficiently protected from the evil engendered by such "social crimes." Indeed, what other challenges are presented by the "social crimes" to our present attitudes toward criminal behavior and society?

## Extortion

The crime of extortion involves the element of threat or fear in obtaining property from a victim with the victim's consent. In New York, under Section 850 of the Penal Law, extortion is defined as "the obtaining of property from another, or obtaining the property of a corporation from an officer, agent or employee thereof, with his consent, induced by a wrongful use of force or fear, or under color of official right." The term "property" is not limited to tangible goods or real property, but includes money, a man's job, or in fact, anything of value or worth.

The element of "consent" distinguishes the crime of extortion from the crime of robbery, for in the case of robbery the taking is against the will of the victim. Robbery also is limited to the taking of personal property in the presence of the victim. In the crime of extortion the victim's consent to the taking is necessary; even though the victim may be unwilling to part with the property, the requisite consent is not vitiated.

The willing victim of extortion must consent to the taking of his property because his consent was induced by the wrongful use of force or fear. Even where payment was made in cooperation with the police and for the purpose of entrapping the defendant, the Utah Supreme Court held that the crime of extortion was committed, for the payment was actuated by fear, *State v. Prince* (284 P. 108, 1930). In New York, under Section 851 of the Penal Law, six specific oral or written threats are set forth:

1. To do an unlawful injury to the person or property of the individual threatened, or to any relative of his or to any member of his family or to a corporation of which he shall be an officer, stockholder, employee, or agent.
2. To accuse him or any relative of his or any member of his family, of any crime.
3. To expose, or impute to him, or any of them, any deformity or disgrace.
4. To expose any secret affecting him or any of them.
5. To kidnap him or any relative of his or member of his family.
6. To injure his person or property or that of any relative of his or member of his family by the use of weapons or explosives.

These threats need not be express, nor need the conduct of the wrongdoer be overt. It is sufficient if the attitude assumed by the defendant is intimidating, as shown by the circumstances of the case. In *People v. Dioguardi* (8 N.Y.2d 260), in 1960, the highest

New York court held that as long as the defendant created the fear existing in the mind of his victim, and the victim willingly parted with his money as tribute, the crime of extortion has been committed. The point is simply that the defendant made use of the fear to extort money or property.

In extortion a specific intent to commit the crime is an essential element of the crime. Intoxication or ignorance of the law may be shown to negative that specific intent. In *People v. Learman* (28 N.Y.S.2d 360), in 1941, the defendant was a police officer charged with taking the sum of eighty dollars from a motorist, and with threatening to report certain facts to the Bureau of Motor Vehicles which could result in the revocation of the victim's driver's license. The victim was intoxicated at the time of the alleged extortion. The New York court dismissed the indictment for extortion because if the defendant did report the true facts to the Bureau of Motor Vehicles, it would warrant revocation of the victim's driver's license! Thus, where the defendant has an absolute legal right to do what he threatened to do, he cannot be held to have intended to do an unlawful injury, even though his motive in making the threat was to obtain money to which he was not entitled.

The threat to prosecute for an alleged offense connected with the creation of a debt, when the motive of the threat is merely to secure the payment of the debt due from the victim, does not constitute the crime of extortion.

## Blackmail

Blackmail, like extortion, is a crime involving the element of threat or fear. It is defined generally as intentionally sending a writing to a victim with the knowledge of the contents of the writing and with the specific intent therein of making certain defined threats or fears, for the purpose of extorting or gaining money or other property. In New York, Section 856 of the Penal Law defines the "blackmailer" as

> "A person who, knowing the contents thereof, and with intent, by means thereof, to extort or gain any money or other property, or to do, abet, or procure any illegal or wrongful act,

sends, delivers, or in any manner causes to be forwarded or received or makes and parts with for the purpose that there may be sent or delivered, any letter or writing threatening:
1. To accuse any person of a crime; or
2. To do any injury to any person or to any property; or
3. To publish or connive at publishing any libel; or
4. To expose or impute to any person any deformity or disgrace,

is punishable by imprisonment for not more than fifteen years."

Thus, blackmail involves the sending of a writing with an unlawful purpose acknowledged by the blackmailer. One who merely delivers a threatening letter to another as an intermediary has obviously not committed the crime. In California in *People v. Davis* (318 P.2d 129) the defendant went into a bank and handed the manager an envelope, and said that he was told to deliver it. The envelope contained a note that the manager was to put $20,000 in a package and take it across the street to a certain luncheonette. The bank manager made a false package containing four marked bills and took it to the luncheonette where it was received by a man named Weber, who was thereupon immediately arrested. The only evidence against the defendant was as stated above, and the testimony of the policeman that the defendant at first denied and later admitted delivering the envelope and knowing Weber. The court in 1957 affirmed the conviction for blackmail, statments were evidence of guilty knowledge, and that his failure to take the witness stand was an indication of the truth of the evidence against him. Admittedly, this California decision leaves much to be desired, for failure to take a witness stand is flimsy evidence of guilt and contrary to ordinary rules of criminal procedure!

The New York statute on blackmail prescribes that the threat or fear must be made with specific intent to extort or gain, although it need not be express. Parole evidence may be offered to prove that by use of the language and phrases employed, the defendant intended and the victim understood, that the threat was in fact being made. But, unlike extortion, blackmail does not require that the threat inspire fear in the victim, nor need it succeed in obtaining money or property for the person making the threat. If the threat made is of the kind set forth in the statute, as in New York, and is made with specific intent to extort or gain, the crime of blackmail has been committed.

## Perjury

The crime of perjury involves the making of a statement under oath which the maker does not believe to be true. The false statement under oath must be *material,* in that it must support directly the main or principal fact. Testimony at a trial is always material, but under other circumstances such as an appearance before a grand jury or a congressional committee, the false swearing may relate to irrelevant or immaterial matter, and the crime of perjury would not be committed. However, by specific statute in several states "materiality" is a requisite only for perjury in the first degree. In *People v. Perna,* the New York Appellate Division, Fourth Dept., on February 20, 1964, ruled that an indictment for perjury in the first degree should not have been dismissed on the ground that the perjurer's statements as to his wife's being in Florida were as a matter of law, immaterial. It was for the jury to determine, if they found there was false swearing, whether the testimony related to a material or to an immaterial matter. Testimony relating to a collateral or possibly remote subject may be material if it has a legitimate tendency to prove a fact that is material.

A perjury statute cannot guarantee to stop witnesses from lying anymore than one can legislate good morals or deterrence to crime. However, a perjury statute, broad enough to prohibit all false swearing and graded to permit adjustment of the degree of punishment to the seriousness of the offense, would probably serve to increase veracity of witnesses. A definitive statute with gradations of punishment would also stop prosecution of alleged misconduct not falling within the scope of other crimes.

## Forgery

The crime of forgery may involve almost any type of written instrument, i.e., checks, wills, deeds, bills of sale, etc. Forgery is the "alteration" falsely, or the false making of a written instrument, with intent to defraud, the written instrument, if genuine, being of legal efficacy. In New York, the only statutory definition of forgery is found in the criminal law (Section 880 of the Penal Law); the specific intent to defraud is the essential element of the crime, which is also delineated in terms of counterfeiting, erasure, or obliteration of a genuine written instrument, in whole or in part.

Section 23 of the New York Negotiable Instruments Law declares that "when a signature is forged or made without the authority of the person whose signature it purports to be, it is wholly inoperative." If a check is drawn payable to the bearer or to a fictitious person known to the maker, such a circumstance would preclude the maker from setting up the defense of forgery; it would also excuse the payee from criminal liability for forgery should he sign the check as the fictitious person. Similarly, where a check is delivered to an imposter as a payee, and the drawer of the check believes that the imposter is the person upon whose indorsement it will be paid, the indorsement by such imposter in the name which he is using to impersonate another is not a forgery, *Schweitzer v. Bank of America* (109 P.2d 441). In the *Atlantic National Bank* case (250 F.2d 114) the Fifth U. S. Court of Appeal in 1957 faced a rather ingenious swindle perpetrated against the Internal Revenue Department by a person who filed a series of purported income tax returns in behalf of nonexistent taxpayers, with a request for a refund of taxes supposedly withheld by employers. In each instance, the person would intercept the checks issued to the fictitious taxpayers, and would proceed to collect by indorsing the names of the fictitious payees. The court ruled that "when the drawer or issuer of the check intends that it shall go to the person falsely pretending to be another who is in fact non-existent, the endorsement in the fictitious payee's name by the pretender is not a forgery." The court also ruled that the collecting banks were not liable to the federal government for the collection of the checks!

In *Russell v. Second National Bank of Paterson* (55A.2d 211), the New Jersey court squared off with another imposter swindle.

A charitably-minded woman received a phone call from someone who identified himself as a well-known person of excellent reputation; he solicited her contribution to a worthy charity. The woman agreed to make a contribution; the imposter said that he did not want his own name to appear and asked that her check be made payable to his "secretary" who would shortly call upon her. Shortly thereafter a man called at her home, gave the name of the "secretary" and received a check payable to that name. Later, the same charitably-minded woman was again victimized, but this time the messenger who picked up the check was not described to her as a person of the name to which the check was to be made payable. As to the first check payable to the "secretary," the court ruled that no forgery had occurred; but, as to the latter check payable to a name other than that assumed by the person who called for it, there was a forgery—and the drawee bank was liable.

Some states provide by statute that a drawee bank shall not be liable to its depositors for payment of a forged or raised check, unless the depositor has given notice of the forgery within one year after return of the canceled check as a voucher of such payment. A drawee bank pays at its peril so far as forgery of the maker's name is concerned, and generally has no right of recourse against the bank or banks by or through which the check was presented for collection.

One who endorses a government check by signing the name of the payee and then his own, as agent, when in fact he has no such authority, is not guilty of forgery under Section 495 of the federal Criminal Code. No forgery is committed where the falsity lies in the representation of fact, not in the genuineness of execution. See *Gilbert v. United States* (370 U.S. 650).

## Plagiarism

Originality lies in the method of expressing an idea, rather than in the idea as such. The law of plagiarism protects not the general pattern, but its expression, i.e., the methods of expressing the pattern or idea. Our copyright laws unfortunately do not contain a definition of plagiarism, except by reference to the rights conferred by the copyright. Generally, it has been held to imply that as the copyright gives the owner the exclusive right to print, reprint, publish, copy, and vend the copyrighted work, the doing of any of these acts by one not authorized by the owner is an infringement of the copyright, or plagiarism.

Conscious plagiarism describes a common situation where a person may have retained in his mind the essence of an idea or composition he had seen or heard before, to such an extent that, although at the time of composing his own work he actually was not copying from it, in reality he was. Unconscious plagiarism is a more difficult concept, and liability is fastened upon the answer to the question of whether or not the plagiarer had "access" to the idea or composition. Obviously, similarities can arise from the use of similar materials which are in the public domain, or because the situation with which the work deals called for development along particular lines.

However, in the final analysis, it is submitted that recovery in plagiarism suits should be limited to "intentional" cases. Those who may innocently plagiarize should not be punished in the form of heavy damages, if at all.

### Bribery

The crime of bribery, as construed, for example, under Section 378 of the New York Penal, seeks to deter corruption in the public service. The bribery of a public officer was delineated in *People v. Chapman* (13 N.Y.2d 97). It appeared that a police officer had been offered money by the defendant to release a prisoner he had arrested and to drop all charges against him. The offer was made after the prisoner had been booked and while awaiting arraignment. In defense, it was contended that the officer then had no power to release the prisoner, hence the purpose for which the money was offered was not within the police officer's official duties. But the New York Court of Appeals, in 1963, affirmed the conviction, pointing out that the crime of bribery covers even matters over which the officer may be *assumed* to have power, regardless of whether he actually is authorized by law to execute it. In other words, it is not necessary for the police officer to actually have jurisdiction if he has colorable authority to perform the desired act. A firm stand on bribery convictions effectuates the best deterrent to public corruption.

### Unlawful Detention of Person by an Institution

In *Schlachet v. Alexander's Department Store* the New York Supreme Court, Bronx County, on April 5, 1963, examined the problem of unlawful detention of a person by a commercial institution. Unlawful detention can also be a crime, but in the context of this case, it involved a civil action by a disgruntled customer against the department store. It was alleged that the plaintiff was detained in an unreasonable manner and for more than a reasonable time to permit investigation and questioning. She was accused of committing or attempting to commit the crime of larceny by stealing a lady's gold-colored sweater valued at $4.99. She testified that the day before she had purchased a number of items from the store, including the sweater; at home that evening, she noted a dirt spot on the sweater and the next day, she went to the same counter where she had purchased the sweater, but was unable to exchange it for there was no sweater of the same color and size. Placing the gold-colored sweater in her handbag she left the counter, and proceeded to another part of the store where she bought a grey sweater for $1.99. A little later she purchased an $11 dress, and then left the store. As she was about to enter a nearby entrance to the subway, she was stopped by a store detective who accused her of stealing the gold-colored sweater. Plaintiff testified that she was grabbed by two other store detectives and dragged back into the store where she was detained, except for a short visit to the nurse's office. During the period of detention, she was asked to sign a statement confessing to the larceny of the sweater, but she refused to do so. Four hours later, she was permitted to leave the store as her husband arrived; both husband and wife thereupon signed a general release in exchange for one dollar.

The store detective testified that she saw the plaintiff remove the price tags from the gold-colored sweater and place the sweater in her handbag. When apprehended the plaintiff allegedly agreed to and did voluntarily walk back into the store.

Upon this evidence the Court determined that the plaintiff was unlawfully detained on the premises for almost four hours, and that the defendant department store had "failed to establish by a fair preponderance of the credible evidence that the detention of the plaintiff was reasonable or that it was accomplished in a reasonable manner, or that the defendant had reasonable grounds to believe that plaintiff had committed or attempted to commit the crime of larceny in defendant's store." The New York court found it "significant that despite the plaintiff's many requests during her four hours detention, the city police were never summoned, nor was a formal charge of larceny ever made against the plaintiff in any criminal proceedings." For her mental anguish, the court thereupon awarded her the sum of $4,000, the sum of $500 for her medical injuries, and $4.99 which sum represents the purchase price of the gold-colored sweater which was never returned to her!

In contrast, an Oregon court in 1964 in *Delp v. Zapp's Drug and Variety Store* (395 P.2d 137) ruled that detention of a suspected shoplifter for 30 minutes for the purpose of learning her name was reasonable detention under the specific Oregon statute which authorized a merchant to do so.

The Ohio appellate court in *Isaiah v. Great A & P Tea Co.* (174 N.E.2d 128) decided, in December 1959, that the merchant has the burden of proof of probable cause to stop a customer:

> "Where a plaintiff shows that he has been subjected to false imprisonment by an employee of a mercantile establishment, and the establishment seeks to justify such conduct . . . . the burden of proof is upon it to show probable cause for believing that the items offered for sale by the mercantile establishment have been unlawfully taken by the plantiff."

However, the various state statutes on unlawful detention and false imprisonment have generally broadened the powers of the merchant in defending himself against "shoplifting" and the resulting detention. The merchant may offer certain facts, among them that the detention was on reasonable grounds and in a reasonable manner for a reasonable length of time, plus the fact that the purpose of the detention was for investigation or questioning on the ownership of the property involved. But no merchant should place his property interests above the personal dignity of his customers when the temptation to detain arises.

### Deceptive Practices in the Broadcasting Industries

Again bordering close to the criminal act and in a few instances actually culminating in criminal indictment of certain individuals, are various deceptive practices which plagued the broadcasting industries in the years immediately preceding 1959. Sensational exposes about "fixed" quiz shows on television and radio were so scandalous and against the public interest as to merit a Special Report of the Attorney General of the United States to the President of the United States, dated December 30, 1959. The fantastic picture of the deceptive and corrupt practices employed to gain business expectancies is seen in the following excerpts from this official document:

> "There can be no question as to the great impact of the broadcasting industry, particularly of television, upon this nation. Industry sources indicate that as of March 1959, 44,462,000 of the 51,500,000 households in the United States contained at least one television set . . . . The operation of broadcasting stations cannot be left to the uncontrolled interplay of individual initiative and economic forces . . . .
>
> "The corruption largely relates to deceptive programs, deceptive advertising, and to matter broadcast as a result of undercover payments to employees of broadcasting stations—colloquially called 'payola' . . . . "

It was not until 1957 that rumors began to circulate that various television quiz shows were not unrehearsed as represented, that contestants were provided with answers to questions, and that undercover payments were made to enhance the public image of these commercial programs designed to sell the sponsor's products. In September 1958, a New York grand jury heard testimony that contestants were intensely briefed before each appearance on the quiz show, or were told the questions beforehand and what answers to give, together with a "script" of how to answer dramatically. In some cases, a technique more subtle was used to "control" the program: the producers would question the contestants in advance of the show so that the scope of their knowledge about a particular subject was well understood both by the producer and the contestant. The producer's ability to gauge the contestant's knowledge made it possible for them to frame questions so as to keep a contestant who was attractive and would gather a larger audience on the air, and to dispose of contestants who did not have such popular qualifications. The bank vault paraphernalia was meaningless, for the specific questions were merely taken to the bank vault and then produced on the program as planned.

The Attorney General's report found that "school teachers, infants, clergymen, and other from many walks of life had been drawn into a gigantic hoax perpetrated upon a nation through the medium of television. . . . . The disclosures have been accompanied by a sense of public shock and disgust . . . " Shortly thereafter, the National Association of Broadcasters issued an amended Television Code, which provided: (a) that no program shall be presented in a manner which would mislead the audience as to any material fact; (b) that quiz and similar programs presented as legitimate contests must in fact be genuine, and the results not controlled by collusion or other action which will favor one contestant against another; (c) that the acceptance by a producer, talent or other personnel, of cash or other consideration for including deceptive material in a program is forbidden, and (d) that broadcasters are required to use extreme care to prevent false and misleading advertising in programs.

The result of such disclosures was the demise of television and radio quiz programs. In February 1960, the U.S. Senate Subcommittee on Legislative Oversight recommended that the Federal Communications Commission be empowered to seek restraining orders in all types of unfair or deceptive business practices over the air. As the public furor subsided, new and less provocative radio and television programs replaced the old format.

A few individual contestants received suspended sentences for their role in the great conspiracy when they had not given truthful statements before grand juries investigating the situation. Such "social" crimes against institutions like the public at large, have gone unnoticed, and they have taken different forms and varied shapes since these days of 1959.

## Selected Bibliography

New York Penal Law, Section 1620 *et seq.*
*People v. Clark,* 242 N.Y. 313, 1926.
*Sheldon v. Metro-Goldwyn Pictures Corp.,* 81 F.2d 49 C.A.2, 1936.
*Time,* April 1 22, 1957.
*Look,* August 20, 1957.
*New York Times,* Editorial, November 3, 1959.
*FTC v. Radio Corporation of America,* Consent Order 7676, December 15, 1959.
*People v. Moris,* 155 A.D. 711.
Vol. 3 *Wharton's Criminal Law & Procedure,* Sec. 1311.
*Davis v. Nadell,* 138 N.Y.S.2d 50.

## Questions for Review

1. Are "social crimes" deterred by criminal penalties? Should they be deemed "crimes?"
2. Is consent of the victim a necessary ingredient of the crime of extortion? How is extortion distinguished from blackmail?
3. Can a Western Union messenger be guilty of blackmail? Explain.
4. What is a false statement under oath? Why is it a crime?
5. Are swindles deterred by prosecutions for the crime of forgery? Is Plagiarism a crime?
6. Is the crime of bribery a deterrent to corruption in public office? Why?
7. Should unreasonable detention be made a crime even when committed by a department store? Is unreasonable detention by police a crime?
8. Can deceptive practices in radio and television be curbed by making such practices criminal?

*Chapter XII*

# GOVERNMENTAL REGULATION OF THE INSURANCE INDUSTRY

## The Nature of the Business of Insurance

INSURANCE IS A BUSINESS ENTERPRISE based upon contracts of indemnity; and, like all contracts, these "tools" of the insurance business must contain the following elements: (1) there must be an agreement resulting from an offer by the insured and an acceptance by the insurer; (2) the agreement must be in a form required by law; (3) the payment of a premium is the valuable consideration supporting the agreement; (4) the purpose of the contract of insurance must be legal and not contrary to public policy, and (5) the contract must be made fairly, the consent of each of the parties being given upon a full knowledge of all natural and relevant facts known to the other party. The contract of insurance is further distinguishable from other contracts on at least these grounds, to wit: the insured possesses an interest of some kind susceptible of pecuniary estimation (insurable interest); the insured is subject to a risk of loss through the destruction or impairment of that interest by the happening of designated perils beyond the control of the parties (insured event); the insurer assumes that risk of loss; such assumption of risk by the insurer is part of a general scheme to distribute and shift actual losses among a large group of persons bearing similar risks; and, as consideration for the insurer's promise to pay upon the occurrence of the event, the insured makes his ratable contribution to the general fund, or pays a premium.

The importance of the insurance business to the nation's economy has been noted in every economic treatise and perhaps in every State of the Union message by the President of the United

States. In *Richards on Insurance* (4 vol., 1952) the author Warren Freedman describes the nature of the insurance industry in these words:

> "The largest accumulation of private capital in the history of the world is today found in the history of one insurance company, the Metropolitan Life Insurance Co. This power is held for its policyholders who number one-fifth of the population of the United States and Canada. It is therefore no wonder that understanding the nature of the insurance business is generally the concern of every person of intellect or reason, whether in the business or social role."

Mr. Justice Robert Jackson of the United States Supreme Court in 1944, in the famed *South Eastern Underwriters* case [332 U.S. 533], took occasion to remark:

> "The modern insurance business holds a commanding position in the trade and commerce of our nation. Built upon the sale of contracts of indemnity, it has become one of the largest and most important branches of commerce. Its total assets exceed thirty-seven billion dollars or the approximate equivalent of the value of all the farm lands in the United States. Its annual premium receipts exceed six billion dollars more than the average annual revenue receipts of the United States government during the last decade. Included in the labor force of insurance are 524,000 experienced workers, almost as many as seek their living in coal mining or automobile manufacturing. Perhaps no commercial enterprise directly affects so many persons in all walks of life as does the insurance business. Insurance touches the home, the family, and the occupation or business of almost every person in the United States."

Today, after an era of very rapid insurance growth, total assets of all types of insurance organizations greatly exceed $200 billion. Today the insurance industry represents perhaps 30 per cent of the total assets among all main groups of financial institutions. In the field of *life* insurance—the largest category of insurance—admitted assets exceed $120 billion.

The business of insurance is admittedly a vast industry, its branches are multiform, its ramifications are infinitely complex. As a risk-spreading mechanism for millions of people, the insurance business has been properly termed a business affected with a public interest. In view of the magnitude and interstate operation of the insurance business [as well as the public interest involved], regulation by government authority has been necessary so as to place the insurance business within reasonable limits and on such a substantial basis as would afford adequate protection to citizens and their property. Specifically, the principal causes of regulation have been: (1) the unduly high premium rates which did not result from bargaining in the open competitive market; the rate-making or price-fixing function had been responsible for widespread, predatory abuses and other unlawful practices; (2) the inadequate reserves and general financial unsoundness, which have prevented some insurers from performing their promises to pay in the future; (3) the slow, difficult and expensive judicial remedies available to an insured in an action against the insurer and (4) the technical and legalistic language of the insurance policy which has been an easy trap for the unwary.

The cudgel of governmental regulation in the United States over the insurance industry has traditionally been swung by state regulatory bodies; every insurance carrier is domiciled in a state and is deemed to be "doing business" in a state or states. State regulation, initially, takes the form of the granting, or refusing to grant, a license or certificate of authority stating that the insurance company has complied with state laws and is authorized by the state to negotiate the kind of insurance business specified in the license. The extent of control over the insurance carrier's business thereafter varies with each state regulatory body. Throughout the years there has traditionally been much criticism of the effectiveness of state regulation, such as: (1) lack of uniform enforcement of insurance statutes; (2) political influence in the state insurance departments; (3) exorbitant public expense of maintaining fifty separate state insurance regulatory bodies, and (4) the inability of a state to regulate effectively insurance carriers engaged in *interstate* commerce.

## Insurance Is or Is Not "Commerce" (1868-1944)

The U. S. Supreme Court in *Paul v. Virginia* (8 Wall (U.S.) 168) firmly established the principle that the insurance business was *not* "commerce" within the meaning of the third clause of Section 8, Article I of the U. S. Constitution, and therefore the federal government could not concern itself with the allegedly unfair trade activities of a Virginia insurance agent for several fire insurance companies incorporated in the State of New York. The highest court, in 1868, held that insurance policies were not articles of commerce nor subjects of trade and barter, nor commodities shipped or forwarded for sale from one state to another, and hence were not interstate transactions subject to regulation by Congress. In 1913, the highest court in *New York Life Insurance Co. v. Deer Lodge County* (231 U.S. 495) reaffirmed the decision that insurance contracts were like personal contracts between the parties over which the federal government could not exercise supervision. The principle that *exclusive* jurisdiction over the business of insurance existed in the states was therefore generally accepted. Even the Temporary National Economic Committee (TNEC) Report in 1938-1941 recommended the continuation of improved state supervision "without interjecting the federal government into the field of insurance regulation."

## A Short History of Rate-making or Price-fixing

Cooperative rate-making or price-fixing is characteristic of the insurance industry, and particularly of property insurance. Joint making of fire insurance rates in the United States began as early as 1806, but predatory rate-cutting up to the Civil War resulted in numerous company failures. The disastrous losses following the Civil War led the companies in 1866 to organize the National Board of Fire Underwriters as a nationwide cooperative rate-making bureau. But again rate-cutting resulted, and local and regional rating bureaus futilely endeavored to perform the rate-making functions. The great Chicago fire led to cooperative rate-making on a more comprehensive scale, and such activities tended to stabilize the industry. In the early 1880's, several States in the

South and West unsuccessfully attempted to apply their antitrust statutes to the insurance rate-making combinations; Iowa, Kansas, and Mississippi were successful. After specific "anti-compact" statutes had been enacted in some twenty states, the fire insurance companies abandoned their formal rating bureaus and joint organizations in favor of "private rating services" to which member companies simply "subscribed." Although the employees of these organizations were former employees of the rating bureaus, and old rate books were still used, the new rates were deemed "advisory" only; but the members still faithfully observed the rates. Where state anti-trust laws were successful, the companies retaliated by simply withdrawing from the state and writing the business from across the state line.

The legal assaults upon rating bureaus continued. Shortly after 1911, the State of New York reversed the trend by specifically authorizing the fixing of fire insurance rates by rating bureaus, provided that the State Insurance Department exercised general supervision over such activities. After the Lockwood Committee Report, in 1922, the New York law was amended to provide for closer state control over rating bureaus and for regular review of all rates proposed. The New York statutory scheme was soon adopted by other states, and the disruption of normal insurance services to the general public abated. But insurance companies operating across state lines were frequently subject to no regulation for the simple reason that many states had no regulation whatsoever. To close the "loophole" some resort to federal antitrust principles was necessary.

### Insurance Is "Commerce" (1944)

On June 5, 1944, the entire insurance world, policyholders, investors, carriers, and the general public, received a catastrophic shock, precipitating an avalanche of fear and uncertainty that the business of insurance had been singled out by governmental bureaucracy for special application of the federal antitrust laws. On that momentous day, the United States Supreme Court handed down an epochal decision in the *South Eastern Underwriters Association case* (322 U.S. 533). A federal grand jury in

Georgia had returned an indictment against nearly 200 fire insurance companies in six southeastern states, alleging a conspiracy to restrain interstate trade and commerce by fixing and maintaining arbitrary, "noncompetitive" premium rates and arbitrary agents' commissions. In a four to three decision, the highest Court sustained the indictment with Justice Hugo Black, establishing a wholly new premise, to wit: an insurance business conducting a substantial part of its business across state lines is engaged in "commerce among the several states":

> "Premiums collected from policyholders in every part of the United States flow into these companies for investment. As policies become payable, checks and drafts flow back to the many states where the policyholders live. The result is a continuous and indivisible stream of intercourse among the states."

The Court defined as a primary test for regulation "whether, in each case, the competing demands of the state and national interests involved can be accommodated," and declared that the local contract or policy of insurance was but part of the entire interstate transaction:

> "A nationwide business is not deprived of its interstate (or national) character merely because it is built upon sales contracts which are local in nature. . . . No commercial enterprise of any kind which conducts its activities across state lines has been held to be wholly beyond the regulatory power of Congress under the Commerce Clause. We cannot make an exception of the business of insurance. . . ."

The dissenting opinion of Mr. Justice Frankfurter feared the far-reaching dislocations in the insurance industry which the application of the Sherman Act and other antitrust legislation would bring. Chief Justice Stone's dissent also cautioned that overturning the precedents of seventy-five years governing the insurance business "cannot fail to be the occasion for loosening a flood of litigation and of legislation . . . during which a great business and the regulatory officers of every state must be harassed. . . ." On the other hand, the dissent of Mr. Justice Jackson admitted that the transaction was interstate commerce, but contended that the

Court ought not reverse the trend of history and set the nation's feet on a new path of policy which the Congress has not yet determined: "We have not a hint from Congress that it concurs in the plan to federalize responsibility for insurance supervision. Indeed every indication is to the contrary."

Thus, the four to three *South Eastern Underwriters Association* decision of 1944 clearly placed upon the states the obligation to re-examine their insurance laws and to rewrite many statutes for better enforcement. It opened the door to federal administrative agencies to investigate and to the Congress to legislate on practically every phase of the insurance business. The *South Eastern Underwriters Association* decision also placed in jeopardy the large revenues derived by the states from the taxation of insurance companies doing business within the state.

## Aftermath of the South Eastern Underwriters Association Case

The dire consequences of this court decision extending the Commerce Clause were incompatible with the will of Congress, and on March 9, 1945, Congress passed the McCarran-Ferguson Act, [Public Law 15, 15 U.S. Code, Sec. 1011-1015] declaring that "the continued regulation and taxation by the several states of the business of insurance is in the public interest." The federal anti-trust laws were deemed, after a moratorium period to July 30, 1948, applicable to the business of insurance only "to the extent that such business is not regulated by state law." In addition, the Act made clear that "Nothing contained in this Act shall render the . . . Sherman Act inapplicable to any agreement to boycott, coerce, or intimidate, or act of boycott, coercion, or intimidation."

In response to the Congressional invitation, all states enacted laws regulating insurance. Such legislation was precipitated by the model laws of the National Association of Insurance Commissioners and the All-Industry Committee. While these laws vary from state to state, all states regulate life, fire and casualty insurance, including fidelity and surety lines, and inland marine insurance. Cooperative rate-making through licensed rating bureaus was encouraged. Unfair trade practices prohibiting false advertising, defamation of competitors, rebates, and deceptive acts, became the subject of legislation in all states. However, less than half of the states passed laws designed to deal with mergers and interlocking directorates forbidden by the Clayton Act:—Section 67 of the New York Insurance Law is typical in permitting insurance companies to acquire controlling stock interest in another insurance company and to have interlocking directors, as long as the effect is not to lessen competition. The "loophole" has never been "plugged" by state regulatory bodies.

In fairness to the insurance industry, it should be observed that "big business" in the industrial sense, i.e., high productivity and distributive greatness, are not relevant in terms of the operation of the insurance business. The hazards of "big business" such as the danger of concentration or over-centralization of economic power, are not similarly present. Insurance has become a *social* institution with proven capabilities for promoting human freedom and individualism. Thus, the stringent requisites of federal antitrust laws as applied to large-scale industrial undertakings, may be incompatible with the insurance business. The effectiveness of *state* regulation of insurance is one of the brightest anomalies of American business life today. To the policyholder and investor any change from the present system of state regulation could mean increased policy cost, conflicting and expensive administration supervision, and lower yield on investments generally. Federal regulation would probably require additional taxation upon insurance premiums, and necessitate severe restrictions upon life insurance as a capital investment pool which has been responsive to the needs of business, government, farm, and home. Life insurance with such investment features as safety of principal, avoidance of managerial care and reinvestment, liquidity, and fair rate of return could be put in jeopardy. Indeed, the very stability of life insurance, its ability to adapt to economic and social changes, would be tested against the background of governmental bureaucracy, and the result could be unfortunate for the American economy.

## Jurisdiction of the Federal Trade Commission

The Federal Trade Commission stepped into the picture of federal regulation of the insurance business on October 19, 1954,

## Governmental Regulation of The Insurance Industry 301

when the Commission issued seventeen complaints against accident and health (and hospitalization) insurance companies, charging them with false and misleading advertising in interstate commerce. Less than two years later, on June 15, 1956, the Commission set up a code of fair trade practice rules for the accident and health insurance industry, in the preamble of which the Commission declared that

> "Congress, in enacting the McCarran Act, contemplated a division between the Federal Trade Commission and the several states, of the regulatory responsibility concerning the advertising practices found in the business of insurance."

These rules embodied the Commission's policy, as modified by court decisions, with respect to the broad field of misrepresentation and of deception of the buying public in the sale of insurance policies. The rules, in general, ban sales representations or promotions in any form which have the capacity and tendency or effect of misleading or deceiving purchasers with respect to coverage, losses insured, causes of loss, premiums payable, benefits receivable, and the like.

Typical of the many proceedings brought by the Federal Trade Commission since October 1954 are the actions brought against *Federal Life and Casualty Company* (Dkt. 6312), *Commercial Travelers Mutual Accident Association* (Dkt. 6242), and *Liberty Mutual Insurance Co.* (Dkt. 6451). The complaint against *Federal Life* alleged that respondent's advertising misrepresented: (1) the extent of coverage of the policy generally; (2) that its policies were renewable indefinitely or until the insured reached an advanced age; (3) that actual surgical fees up to a specified maximum amount were payable, and (4) that its disability policy provided for a lump-sum payment in case of dismemberment, in addition to a monthly disability payment. Federal Life denied these alleged misrepresentations, and declared that the allegedly unlawful practices were only subject to the primary jurisdiction of the State of Michigan where Federal Life was licensed to do business, and to the secondary jurisdiction of the other forty-five states in which Federal Life was licensed to do business. Federal Life pointed out in its Answer that some of the statements cited in the complaint, were taken out of context and were not, when read in context, deceptive and misleading; also that many of the statements charged as misrepresentations had been discontinued "long before the issuance of the complaint." A hearing was held before FTC Examiner Frank Hier who granted respondent's motion, in November 1955, limiting FTC jurisdiction over the insurer's advertising to such practices only in Rhode Island, Mississippi and the District of Columbia which had no state laws on the subject. In granting the motion, FTC Examiner Hier stated that all other states have laws which "adequately prohibit false, misleading by deception advertising. . . ." However, the Examiner refused to dismiss the complaint entirely since obviously "no state can exercise its police power beyond its borders, on other than its own citizens for acts . . . done within its borders." Furthermore, the mere fact that the complained-of-advertising had been abandoned did not require dismissal of the complaint, because "the public interest is immortal whereas respondent's officials are not." Examiner Hier held that there is a sanction for "state control of the business of insurance and every phase thereof except where such state regulation is either as a matter of fact or of law impossible or clearly ineffective." Subsequently, he issued an order prohibiting Federal Life in these three states from so misrepresenting the unlimited benefits of its accident and health insurance policies. His initial decision, however, resulted in an FTC three to two decision reversing him, and instructing him to proceed with the case on the basis that the FTC has authority to regulate the advertising of Federal Life in all states in interstate commerce, regardless of certain state regulations covering intrastate advertising. The majority of the FTC contended that it was not the purpose of the McCarran-Ferguson Act to substitute exclusive state power for the FTC's jurisdiction over the interstate aspects of the insurance business. The minority of two commissioners was inclined to believe that "there *may* be an area of insurance advertising activity in commerce—for example, radio or TV—within the peculiar aegis of the federal government and effectively beyond the reach of state regulation."

An FTC Examiner, in June 1957, ordered the *Commercial*

*Travelers Mutual Accident Association of Utica, New York,* to stop making certain false claims for its policies, following a hearing in which the evidence showed that the company had misrepresented: (1) the duration of coverage of its policies; (2) the extent of coverage, and (3) the amount paid for medical, surgical and hospital service. According to FTC Examiner Laughlin, the Insurance Department of the State of New York "cannot and does not regulate the unfair or deceptive acts or practices of insurers who owe their very corporate life to it," and therefore "the FTC has been obliged to step into this void and regulate" the company's advertising. The examiner pointed out that New York acted only after complaints were received from policyholders, a practice like "locking the barn after the horse is stolen." Thus, FTC jurisdiction was clearly warranted and established.

In November 1955, *Liberty Mutual Insurance Co.,* the nation's largest mutual casualty insurance company, and the largest writer of workmen's compensation insurance among private carriers, was charged by the FTC with misrepresentations in advertising concerning: (1) the renewability of its policies; (2) the weekly income benefits for sickness disability regardless of preexisting conditions, and (3) the payment of weekly cash benefits for a disabling accident or sickness. After a hearing, FTC Examiner Laughlin issued an order dismissing the complaint for lack of proof. He pointed out that Liberty Mutual did not even advertise by direct mail, radio, television or periodicals, but merely published certain leaflets directed to executives and businessmen: "Certainly the very intelligent segments of the public to which these advertisements appeal and are expressly directed would not in any way be deceived thereby." Examiner Laughlin found no merit in the alleged misrepresentations which might still fall into the hands of persons without the requisite education and background to avoid deception.

### The American Hospital Case

The asserted jurisdiction of the FTC over insurance companies in matters involving false and misleading advertising was also delineated in *American Hospital and Life Insurance Co. v.*

*FTC* (CA5, 1957).This company, operating in fourteen states, had allegedly misrepresented in advertising its health and accident policies with respect to: (1) illnesses covered; (2) dollar amounts paid for each illness, and (3) maternity benefits generally. On October 17, 1954, the Commission issued a complaint (Dkt. 6237) against this insurer (and against sixteen other health and accident insurance companies). FTC Hearing Examiner Cox, in December 1955, ruled that the charges of misleading advertising were not proven, and that the FTC had jurisdiction only in Mississippi which State did not then have an insurance code. By a three to two decision, the FTC itself, in April 1956, reversed its hearing examiner, and held that Congress did not deprive the FTC of the power to regulate the interstate activities of insurance carriers. The majority opinion of the Federal Trade Commission declared that the McCarran-Ferguson Act—

> "was not designed to permit insurance companies to secure new business by false and misleading advertising in interstate commerce, nor was it intended as an abdication of federal jurisdiction. . . . It surely could not have been the congressional intent to create a legal vacuum wherein an insurance company would have been enabled to escape regulation of the interstate aspects of its business in cases in which the federal and state laws did not conflict."

The moratorium clause in the Act which suspended the application of the antitrust laws to insurance from 1945 to 1948, according to the FTC,—

> "gave the states about three years in which to define a reasonable area of state police power. Beyond that reasonable area states could not go. Regardless of whether a state regulated insurance during this time, after 1948 the FTC was expressly authorized to regulate it on different grounds, namely, regulating the use of interstate channels of commerce."

The minority view of FTC Commissioners Gwynne and Mason responded that the Act itself warned that

> "the continued regulation by the several states of the business of insurance is in the public interest. . . . There is nothing in the

entire Act which justifies the interpretation that the regulation was to continue only by the grace of the FTC."

The majority of the FTC opined that both FTC and state laws are designed to suppress such deception in advertising, and "the Commission's action in the instant matter aids the states in their own local procedures to protect the citizenry. . . ."

Specifically, the FTC order required American Hospital and Life Insurance Co. to cease and desist from representing, either directly or indirectly, by advertising that any of its accident and health policies—

"may be continued in effect by the insured upon payment of stipulated premiums, indefinitely or for any stated time, unless full disclosure of any other provision or condition of termination contained in the policy is made conspicuously, prominently, and in sufficiently close conjunction with the representation as will fully relieve it of all capacity to deceive. That said policy provides for payment in full or in any specified amount or for payment up to any specified amount for any medical, surgical or hospital service, unless the policy provides that the actual cost to the insured for that service will be paid in all cases up to the amount represented, or unless full disclosure of the schedule of payments for which the policy provides is made conspicuously, prominently and in sufficiently close conjunction with said representation as will fully relieve it of all capacity to deceive. That said policy provides for indemnification against losses due to sickness or accident, unless a statement of all the conditions, exceptions, restrictions and limitations affecting the indemnification actually provided are set forth conspicuously, prominently, and in sufficiently close conjunction with said representations as will fully relieve it of all capacity to deceive. That said policy provides for a stipulated sum to be paid upon the accidental death of the insured unless full disclosure of the conditions, exceptions, restrictions and limitations affecting the indemnifications actually provided is set forth conspicuously, prominently, and in sufficiently close conjunction with the representation as will fully relieve it of all capacity to deceive."

The Fifth U. S. Court of Appeals in later reversing this FTC decision in *American Hospital and Life Ins. Co. v. FTC* (243 F2d

719) referred to the extensive judicial and Congressional history applicable to the regulation of insurance, and held that since the FTC hearing examiner found effective regulation of insurance advertising in all states where the company did business, the FTC had no jurisdiction over the matter. Furthermore, the advertising practices complained of had been abandoned by the insurer. In laconic style, Circuit Judge Jones opined, "If there is an 'irreducible area' of Commission jurisdiction, we are of the firm conviction that the matter presented by the record before us is not within it." The Court thus affirmed that, under the McCarran-Ferguson Act, the anti-trust laws applied to interstate insurance only to the extent that the insurance business is not regulated by state law! The U. S. Supreme Court affirmed in 1958 [357 U.S. 560]. [Similar rulings were made by the United States Court of Appeals for the 6th Circuit (245 F. 2d 883) in *National Casualty Co.* (Dkt. 6311), which was affirmed by the U. S. Supreme Court also.]

### F.T.C. Conflict Resolved—1958 and 1960

The resolution of the conflict seemingly occurred on June 30, 1958, when the United States Supreme Court in a *per curiam* decision (355 U.S. 867) in *FTC v. National Casualty Co.* and in *FTC v. American Hospital and Life Insurance Co.* held that the FTC did *not* have jurisdiction to regulate insurer's *intrastate* advertising practices in states which regulate under state laws. But the ambiguity was not finally resolved until March 28, 1960, when the *Travelers Health Assn.* case was decided.

In 1958 the Solicitor General, in support of the FTC had contended it—

> "is not attempting to apply a federal statute which conflicts with state legislation. Nor is the Commission here asserting that a federal statute supersedes or invalidates state legislation in any way. Instead, all that the Commission contends is that Congress has not divested it of authority under the Federal Trade Commission Act to join with the states in order to provide full protection to the public."

But in analyzing these two cases, the United States Supreme Court had pointed out that National Casualty was licensed to sell accident and health insurance in all states including Hawaii and the District of Columbia, and American Hospital was licensed in fourteen states. Solicitation of business was carried on by independent local agents who operated on commission: "Only an insubstantial amount of any advertising (material) goes directly by mail from the companies to the public." The U. S. Supreme Court therefore concluded:

> "Whatever may have been the intent of Congress with regard to interstate insurance practices which the states cannot for constitutional reasons regulate effectively, that intent is irrelevant in the cases before us. Respondents' advertising programs require distribution by their local agents, and there is no question but that *the states possess ample means to regulate this advertising within their respective boundaries.*" (italics added).

In those instances where the states have not regulated, the FTC still cannot regulate, and the Court refused to make a distinction between "legislation" and "regulation"—if the state has legislated, it has regulated, even though not "effectively regulated." The Court found that:

> "Each state in question has enacted prohibitory legislation which proscribes unfair insurance advertising and authorizes enforcement through a scheme of administrative supervision. Petitioner does not argue that the statutory provisions here under review were mere pretense. Rather, it urges that a general prohibition designed to guarantee certain standards of conduct is too 'inchoate' to be 'regulation' until that prohibition has been crystalized into 'administrative elaboration of these standards and application in individual cases'."

The Court found no support in the legislative history of the McCarran-Ferguson Act for the Government's argument. However, the Court failed to decide whether the FTC would have jurisdiction over matters involving purely interstate business, such as the mail order insurance business.

### The Travelers Health Association Case

In *Travelers Health Assn. v. F.T.C.*, the U. S. Court of Appeals for the Eighth Circuit, on January 13, 1959 (262 F.2d 241), specifically held that the FTC is [and was at all times pertinent to the decision] without authority to regulate the direct mail order business practices of Travelers in advertising and soliciting insurance. The Attorney General of Nebraska had filed an amicus curiae brief in support of Travelers, which brief was concurred in by the attorney generals of twenty additional states. Another brief amicus curiae was filed by The Health Insurance Assn. of America, a trade association comprising more than 260 companies writing accident and sickness insurance. The Court decision answered the FTC contention of "dual regulation," i.e., both by state and federal government:—"The Commission is clearly without authority to do any additional or supplemental regulating of petitioner's advertising practices." The Court added that Nebraska law was adequate to enable its insurance department to deal effectively with unfair advertising practices of a Nebraska-domiciled company. The fact that the Nebraska statute, at the time the FTC entered its cease and desist order, did not expressly authorize the Nebraska Director of Insurance to deal with unfair practices "in other states" by a company domiciled in Nebraska, was "of no substantial consequence," since the gap in the Nebraska statute was closed by a 1957 amendment. The Court concluded:

> "With every activity of the petitioner, in the conduct of its business, subject to the supervision and control of the Director of Insurance of Nebraska, we think that the petitioner's practices in the solicitation of insurance by mail in Nebraska or elsewhere, reasonably and realistically cannot be held to be unregulated by State law. . . . We think that the advertising practices of the petitioner are regulated by State law within the letter and spirit of the McCarran-Ferguson Act, and that the Act has placed such practices beyond the regulatory power of the Commission."

The two to one decision of the Court included an able dissent of Judge Vogel who declared that he did not believe the 1957 Nebraska amendment to include deceptive practices "in any other state" is the kind of regulation by state law that Congress had in mind. Judge Vogel added that to force citizens of other states to rely upon Nebraska's regulation is impractical and ineffective, and therefore he would sustain the FTC order.

Finally, on March 28, 1960, the U. S. Supreme Court *reversed* the lower court, and by a six to three decision settled the issue of FTC jurisdiction over insurance carriers doing interstate business by mail. *(FTC v. Travelers Health Association of Omaha*, 362 U.S. 293). Mr. Justice Stewart solemnly declared that, while the insurance business, to the extent that it is "regulated" by state law, is exempted from the FTC Act by the McCarran-Ferguson Act, nevertheless an insurance company domiciled in Nebraska but doing an *interstate* mail order business in every state in the United States, is *not* insulated from FTC regulation by a Nebraska statute prohibiting any person "domiciled" there from engaging in "unfair or deceptive acts or practices in the conduct of the business of insurance in any other state. . . ." According to the Court, this was "not the protective legislation of the states whose citizens are the targets of the advertising practices in question," but "a single state's attempted regulation of its domiciliary's extraterritorial activities." Mr. Justice Stewart also pointed out that the State of Nebraska here was not "in a better position to regulate that business than the Federal Government," since no one state should have "the sole legislative and administrative control of the practices of any insurance business affecting the residents of every other State in the Union."

The dissent of Mr. Justice Harlan simply refused to make new law: "The temptation is strong, no doubt, to ask the Court to innovate with respect to the McCarran-Ferguson Act when state regulation may be thought to have fallen short. . . . I think it unwise for us now to yield to this encore on the part of the Commission. One innovation with the Act is apt to lead to another, and may ultimately result in a hybrid scheme of insurance regulation, bringing about uncertainties and possible duplications which should be avoided. . . . If innovations in the policy of McCarran-Ferguson Act are thought desirable, they should be made by Congress, not by us."

To counteract the jurisdiction of the F.T.C., the insurance industry proposed a model bill known as the Unauthorized Insurers False Advertising Process Act. The purpose of this proposed legislation is to strengthen state regulation by authorizing the insurance commissioner of non-domicillary states into which advertising is sent by mail, to hold hearings, issue cease and desist orders, and through court judgments follow an offender to its state of domicile for enforcement purposes.

### Aviation Insurance

Shortly thereafter, on April 14, 1960, in the U. S. District Court for the Southern District of New York, Judge Cashin in *In Re Grand Jury Investigation of the Aviation Insurance Industry,* [183 F.Supp. 374] declared that, even though it is assumed that New York regulates aviation insurance and that relevant insurance contracts were executed in New York, those contracts would have impact in all states, many of which do not regulate aviation insurance—and therefore government subpoenas duces tecum issued by the grand jury were valid. The Court pointed out that perhaps forty-five states expressly exempted aviation insurance from rate regulation, and that the aviation insurance industry was not exempt from the anti-trust laws, because of the following factors:

> "The first of these factors is the failure of many states to regulate at all the fixing of rates for aircraft hull insurance and aircraft personal injury and death and property liability insurance. The second factor is the recent decision of the U. S. Supreme Court in *FTC v. Travelers Health Assn.* . . ."

### Boycotts and Restraints: Jurisdiction of the U. S. Department of Justice

Following its initial victory in the *S.E.U.A.* case, in 1944, the U. S. Department of Justice brought numerous proceedings against insurance associations charging boycotts and similar restraining actions in violation of the antitrust laws. One such action was directed against the Insurance Board of Cleveland, Ohio (144 F. Supp. 684, 1955), alleging that the Board (established in 1846) had combined and conspired with its officers to restrain and monopolize interstate commerce in the business of selling and writing fire insurance in Cuyahoga County, and had also attempted to monopolize such trade and commerce in violation of Sections 1 and 2 of the Sherman Act. The government claimed that rules of this county association of 452 independent fire insurance agents (accounting for 85 per cent of all fire insurance coverage in the Cleveland area), excluded from membership agents who represented insurance companies that sell through branch offices, the effect of which rule also subjected to expulsion a member of the association who violated rules. The government therefore contended that the operation of the rules constituted an agreement among the Board members to refuse to deal with or boycott insurance companies who sell insurance directly to policyholders. The Board argued that the rules were justified as reasonable and as necessary to protect insurance agents against insurance company domination.

The federal court, at the outset, sustained the jurisdiction of the U. S. Department of Justice:

> "The Supreme Court's opinion in *South Eastern Underwriters Association* leaves no room for doubt that the business of these foreign corporations conducted by their local agents is interstate commerce."

District Court Judge McNamee granted the government's request for an injunction restraining the Insurance Board of Cleveland from enforcing the rules, upon the ground that such a practice by such an association which occupied a dominant position in the local market, constituted a boycott and unreasonably restrained competition. The Court, having refused to concur with the government's contention that an agreement to boycott or to refuse to deal was illegal *per se,* applied the Rule of Reason to these "direct writer rules":

> "When an agent goes beyond his personal right and combines with others of like purposes in a concerted refusal to deal with insurance companies, 'such action brings him and those acting with him within the condemnation' of the Sherman Act. . . . Such a boycott is illegal."

The Court in thus granting summary judgment, held that the prohibitions of the Sherman Act against boycotts, coercion or intimidation was applicable to the business of insurance. In contrast, however, to the "direct writer rules" the Court observed that another Board rule limiting membership in the organization to agents representing stock fire companies, did not adversely affect those agents representing mutual fire companies. [On appeal, the decision was affirmed in October 1960, 188 F.Supp. 949].

In another United States District Court, the government charged on substantially similar facts that the *New Orleans Insurance Exchange* (148 F. Supp. 915, 1957) engaged in an unlawful combination and conspiracy to restrain interstate commerce in insurance and to acquire a monopoly in its area of operations by maintaining a group boycott, all in violation of Sections 1 and 2 of the Sherman Act. A group of 130 independent insurance agencies, controlling approximately three-fourths of the fire, casualty and surety insurance business in New Orleans, boycotted all non-member insurance agencies as well as all insurance companies which did not place insurance exclusively through members of the New Orleans Insurance Exchange. District Judge Wright upheld the jurisdiction of the Department of Justice over such insurance activities in interstate commerce:

> "The defenses of the Exchange regarding interstate commerce and the McCarran Act may be quickly disposed of. . . . The business of insurance when conducted across state lines is interstate commerce."

The Court also found the requisite intent to monopolize under Section 2 of the Sherman Act from the unlawful effects of the unreasonable restraints: "This record depicts a nascent, if not an accomplished, monopoly, nurtured by group boycott." But District Judge Wright was unwilling to rule that group boycotts were unreasonable per se. He stated that such a declaration was "not necessary," since—

> "The rule of reason dictates that this illegal combination must be destroyed. . . . The group boycott in suit not only had the potential unreasonably to coerce, restrain and control interstate commerce in insurance in the New Orleans area, but it actually did. . . . Group boycotts and concerted refusals to deal flout the Sherman Act's command that competition rule the market place."

The U. S. Supreme Court later affirmed. [355 U.S. 22].

## The Future of Regulation

Federal regulation of the insurance industry is indeed a reality in the areas occupied by such other federal statutes as the National Labor Relations Act, the Fair Labor Standards Act, the postal laws (including the mail-fraud provisions), the Securities and Exchange Act of 1933 and the Investment Company Act of 1940, to name but a few. While these federal regulations apply to the insurance business only incidentally, they constitute federal regulation to the same extent as other industries transacting business in interstate commerce or affecting interstate commerce. Public Law 15 may always be amended by Congress at any time, and increased Federal anti-trust activity in the field of insurance is always a possibility. Continued state regulation of the insurance carrier, however, will not be jeopardized in those areas where States have *effectively* regulated.

To restore general competition to the insurance industry by compelling rate or premium competition may not necessarily constitute the *summum bonum*. Competition may be destructive because of the unusual characteristics of the insurance contract: (1) inpossibility to determine value received due to its financial complexity; (2) inability of insurance carrier to know its costs in advance; (3) necessity for carrier to maintain continued ability to meet contractual obligations and (4) reliable rate-making necessitates combining the experience of many insurance carriers.

## Selected Bibliography

Vol 56 *Michigan Law Review* 545 (1958).
*Pacific Fire Rating Bureau v. Insurance Co. of North America*, 321 P.2d 1030 (Ariz., 1958).
Feb. 1960 *Insurance Law Journal* pp. 75-103.
*Allstate Ins. Co. v. Commonwealth of Virginia*, 100 S.E.2d 31 (1957).
*S.E.C. v. Variable Annuity Co.*, 359 U.S.65 (1959).
*Professional & B. M. Life Ins. Co. v. Bankers Life Ins. Co.*, 362 U.S. 293 (1960).
1954 *Insurance Law Journal* 192.

## Questions for Review

1. Distinguish between commercial contracts and the contracts or policies of insurance. Why regulate one and not the other?
2. Do you believe that a decision like *S.E.U.A.* was inevitable? Is the sale of insurance policies "trade or commerce?"
3. What did the McCarran-Ferguson Act hope to accomplish in 1945? Was it a successful statute?
4. What jurisdiction does the Federal Trade Commission have over the insurance industry?
5. What was the significance of the 1952 *Federal Life* case brought by the FTC?
6. What was the significance of the *American Hospital & Life Ins. Co.* case? When was the conflict over FTC jurisdiction resolved?
7. What was the significance of the U. S. Supreme Court's 1960 decision in the *Travelers Health Assn.* case?
8. Do you favor federal or state regulation of the insurance carrier? Explain your views.

# INDEX

## A

ABA Committee on Communist Tactics, strategy and objectives, 267-270
Abandonment of maternal rights, 246-247
Abel, Rudolph, 154
Abolition of action for alienation of affections, 38-39
Abolition of action for breach of promise to marry, 38-39
Abolition of action for criminal conversation, 38-39
Abolition of action for seduction, 38-39
Abolition of "family immunity" doctrine, 56-57
Abortion, criminal, 75
Abraham, 48, 236
Abrogation of adoption, 250
Absolute privilege to defame, 150-152
Abuse of privileged defamation, 146-147
"Academic freedom," 98-101
Acquisitions and mergers, corporate, 181-199
Adjusting business, insurance, 151
"Admirer," 154
Admission to bar, 108-112
Adopted child, inheritance rights of, 247
Adopting parents, religious faith of, 238-244
Adoption agency, 236-253
Adoption, aims of, 238
"Adoption," defined, 233-234
Adoption practices, 233-253
  history of, 236-237
  questionable, 234-236
  statistics of, 247-248
Adoption statutes, deficiencies in, 237-238
Adoptions
  agency, 237-238, 244-250
  classification of, 238
  placement for, 237-238
  private, 237-238, 245-247, 250
  religious choice in, 242-244
  religious groupings in, 239-244
  survey of, 233-235
  tabulation of numbers of, 235
Adrenocortical mechanism, 74
Adultery, imputation of, 143
Advertising, false and misleading, 300-310
Aeronautical engineer, 93
"Affair with a married man," 141
Affections, alienation of, 31-62
Affidavits
  "loyalty oath," 81-83
  non-Communist, 115-117
Agency adoptions, 237-238, 244-250
Agency, sectarian, 240
Agreements, prenuptial, 241-242
Aircraft hull insurance, 310
Aircraft personal injuries insurance, 310
Albania, 264
Albany, N. H., 100
Albinism, 47
Alcoa, 189
Alden, John, 38
Alienation of affections, 31-62
Aliens
  deportation of, 270-274
  detention of, 274-278
  generally, 112-114
  travel by, 270-278

315

## 316 Societal Behavior

All-American Football Conference, 209
"All doctors are quacks," 175
"Alteration," 284-286
Aluminum Company of America, 189
AMA Consent Forms, 24-26
Amateur sport, 272
American Bar Association, 268-270
American Crystal Sugar Company, 196-197
American Football League, 212
*American Hospital* case, 303-307
American Machine and Foundry Company, 184
American Marietta Company, 184
American Medical Association, 23-26, 74
American POW's, 167
American Society of Newspaper Editors, 181
*American Tobacco* case, 182
Amnesty or pardon, 107, 121
Amputation, traumatic, 50
Amusements, generally, 229
*Anastaplo* case, 110-111
Ancestor worship, 236
"Annual Voters Directory," 230
Annulment of marriage, 45-46
"Anti-compact" statutes, 297
Anti-merger laws, 181-199
Anti-semitism, 178
Anti-trust laws
  and business sports, 201-217
  and mergers, 181-199
  applicability to insurance, 297-313
  exemption from, 206
Aptheker, Herbert, 265
Archdiocese of New York, Catholic Charities, 240
Archery, 231
Area restrictions on travel, 255, 262-265
Aristotle, 75
Armco Steel Company, 195
Arrest, privilege from, 164-165
Article I of U. S. Constitution, 164-165
Artists' Front to Win the War, 176
"Assasination of character," 164-175
Assault
  generally, 132
  sexual, 54
Assets and stock, divestiture of, 188

Assets, purchase of, of competitors, 182-183
Association of the Bar of the City of New York, 266-270
Asylum, insane, 50
Atelactasis, 72
Attainder, bill of, 88, 96
Attendance at auction sale, 221
Attendance, required, 221
Attorney General's list, 257
Auction, attendance at, 221
Aunt-nephew marriage, 48
Austria, 273
Authority To Admit Observers Form, 24
Automobile, operation of, 48-58
Automotive fabrics and finishes, 191-195
Autopsy and right of privacy, 26-27
Aversion, exposure to, 135
Aviation insurance, 310

## B

Babies, "black market" for, 234-236, 248-249
Babies born out of wedlock, 247-248
Backgammon, 231
Baldness, 47
Ballard Company, 191
"Baltimore Afro-American," 263
"Baltimore Bullets," 215
Baltimore, Maryland, 273
Banishment or expatriation, 265
Bank manager, 283
Bank robbery, 129
Ban on Communist travel abroad, 265-266
Baptist wife, 243
Bar, admission to, 108-112
Bar association report on freedom to travel, 266-270
Bar associations, 108-112
*Barenblatt* case, 88-90
Bar Examiners, California State Committee of, 109-110
Barr, William G., 161
*Bartkus* case, 129-130
Baseball
  business of, 203-209
  Commissioner of, 205-209
  "farm system," 206

Basketball, business of, 215-216
Bastards, 248
Beckinella, Mr. Justice, 243-244
Beet sugar, refining of, 196-197, 201-202
Berle, Professor A. A., Jr., 198-199
*Bethlehem Steel* case, 195-196
Betting
   generally, 215
   off-track, horse racing, 230
   pari-mutuel, 224
Bigamy, 46
"Bigness," 198
Bills of attainder, 88
Bingo
   by referendum, 228-230
   licensing laws, 228-230
   operation of, 218-231
   television, 227
Birthmarks, 72
Birth, premature, 69
"Black-listed," 210
Blackmail, crime of, 282-284
"Black market" for babies, 234-236, 248-249
Blood sample, 128-129
Blood-testing, 128-129
Board of Immigration Appeals, 114
Boards, punch, 224-227
Bodleian Library of Oxford, 266
Bok, Justice Curtis, 68
Bombay, India, 262
Bookers of professional wrestling, 214-215
Bookmaking, 224
Books, heretical and seditious, 77
Bookshop Association of St. Louis, 261
Booth, Shirley, 11-12
Borden Company, 184
Boston Naval Shipyard, 162-163
Boxing, business of, 212-214
Boxing manager, 214
Boycotts, 299- 310-313
*Braden* case, 91-92
Brain, deformed, 67
Brain-wave recordings, 28
Brandeis, Louis D., 3
*Brawner* case, 94-95
Breach of promise to marry, 38-39
*Breithaupt* case, 128-129

Bribery, crime of, 124, 125, 272, 287-288
Briehl, Dr. Walter, 261-262
Broadcasting
   censorship over, 159-161
   deceptive practices in, 290-291
   "equal opportunities," 159-161
Brokerage, insurance, 152
Brooklyn College, 85
"Brooklyn Dodgers," 144-145
Brother-sister marriage, 48
*Brown* case, 123-124
Brown, Peter Campbell, 268
Brown Shoe Company, 187-188
Buckner, William F., 230
"Buffalo Bisons," 208
Bureau of Internal Revenue, 165
Bureau of Motor Vehicles, 282
Burlington Mills, 184
Burr, Aaron, 78
Business cards, 222
Business, mail order, 226
Business of baseball, 203-209
Business of basketball, 215-216
Business of boxing, 212-214
Business of football, 209-212
Business of horse racing, 216
Business of insurance, 151, 293-295
Business of wrestling, 214-215
Buttweld pipe, 195-196

## C

Cable and wire industry, 189
Caesar, 219, 236
Calendars, 221
California Legislative Committee on Un-American Activities, 166
California State Committee of Bar Examiners, 109-110
California Uniform Reciprocal Enforcement of Support Act, 44
Campaigns, political, 143-144
Campanella, Roy, 144-145
Camp Kilmer, New Jersey, 273
Camp, summer, 100
Canada, 294
Cane sugar industry, 196-197
Cardozo, Mr. Justice, 78-79, 139
Cards, push, 224-227
Card games, 231

Catholic Charities of Archdiocese of New York, 240
Catholic mother or wife, 239, 241, 242
Causal relation between injury and negligence, 71-73
C. B. S., 156-158, 211, 263
Cease and desist orders, 224-227
Celler Amendment, 183
Celler, Congressman Emanuel, 216
Cellulose, sausage casings, 198
Censorship over broadcasting, 159-161
Chair, folding, 223
Chance, element of lottery, 220-223
Character and Fitness Committee of Illinois Supreme Court, 110-111
"Character assasination," 164-175
Charitably-minded person, 286
Charter of City of New York, 85
Check
 drawer of, 285-286
 erasure or obliteration of, 285
Chicago fire, 296
Chicago Stadium, 214
Child
 initial placement of, for adoption, 245-247
 Mongoloid, 67
 "permanently neglected," 249
 sale of, 237
 separability of, from moment of conception, 73-74
 suit against parent, 50-53
 termination of parental rights over, 249-253
 unemancipated, 48-58
Child-parent relationship, 233-253
Child Welfare Foster Home Care and Adoption Service of New York City, 240
Children
 born out of wedlock, 233
 harms to unborn, 63-76
 illegitimate, 142-143, 233, 235
 legitimatizing of, 47
 parent's liability for misconduct of, 59-61
 "placing out" of, 236-253
 reared in a particular religion, 241-244
Child's loss of consortium, 37

China, forbidden travel in, 263-265
Chinese alien, 274
Chiropodist, 151
Chopin Cultural Center, 113
Chrysler Corporation, 197
Cigarette lighter, 60
*Cioffi and Stein* case, 125
Citizens Union of New York City, 230
City Clerk of New Rochelle, New York, 229
Civil Practice Act of New York, 241
Civil Rights Congress, 91
Civil Rights Laws of New York, 5-8
Civil Service Commission of New York, 103
Civil Suits and the Fifth Amendment, 107-108
Civil War, 260, 296
Claims, fictitious, 63
Class action, 208-209
"Classical" cases of alienation of affections, 37-38
Classification of adoptions, 238
Clayton Act, 181-199, 300
Clearance, security, 93-98
"Clear and present danger" rule, 89-90
Cleopatra, 48
Cleveland Insurance Board, 310
Clorox, 190-191
*Cohen* case, 111-112
Cold rolled sheets, 195
Collection by credit bureaus, 140
College professors, 85-86, 104-105
Collusion between spouses, 56-57
Columbia Broadcasting System, 156-158, 211, 263
Columbia Law School, 198
Columbia Pictures Corporation, 151-152
"Commentaries on the Constitution of the United States," 164
"Commerce" and insurance, 296-297
Commerce, interstate, restraint on, 201-202
*Commercial Travelers* case, 302-303
Commissioner of Baseball, 205-209
Common law marriage, 47
"Common Sense and the Fifth Amendment," 79-80
Communication, privileged, 39-42

Communism, generally, 176-178
"Communist," as libel or slander, 138
Communist China, 255, 262
"Communist Farmers Union," 159
Communist oath requirement, 82
Communist Party, 96, 103-105, 109-112, 113-114, 117-118, 118-120, 122, 145-146, 148, 176-178, 258-262, 270-278
Communist Party membership, 85-86
*Communist Party* cases, 95-98
Communist Political Association, 114
Communist Tactics, Strategy and Objectives Committee of the A.B.A., 267-270
Communist travel abroad, ban on, 265-266
Compelled testimony, 39-42
Competition in hotel industry, 185-186
Competition in liquor industry, 186-187
Competition, lessening of, 181-199
"Competitive impact," 187-190
Competitors
 purchase of physical assets of, 182-183
 purchase of stock of, 182-183
Compulsion, testimonial, 39-42
Computer processing, 28
Concentration, patterns of economic, 181-199
Conception, separability of child from, 73-74
Conditional privilege to defame, 150-152
Conduct, disorderly, 132
Confidential communications between spouses, 150-151
Confidential disclosure, 42
*"Confidential"* magazine, 9-10
Conflict of laws, 57-58
Confrontation of witnesses, 93-98
Congenital defects, 73
"Conglomerate mergers," 183, 190-191, 198
Congressional committees and the Fifth Amendment, 84-92
"Congressional Record," 108, 169-170
Consanguineous marriages, 47-48
"Conscious plagiarism," 287
Conscription, resistance to, 89-90
"Consent," 281

Consent agreements in antitrust law, 185-187
Consent, "ether," 248
Consent of patient generally, 24-26
Consent to Publication of Photographs, AMA Form, 25
Consent to Taking of Motion Pictures of Operation, AMA Form, 26
Consent to Taking of Photographs, AMA Form, 25
Consent to Televising of Operation, AMA Form, 26
Consideration and gift distinguished, 221
Consideration, element of lottery, 220-223
Consolidated Foods Corporation, 190
Conspiracy, 124, 125, 131-132
Consortium
 defined, 34
 loss of, 34-37
Constitutionality of religious-group adoption statutes, 240-241
Consular officials, 275-278
Containers industry, glass and metal, 189-190
Contempt
 criminal, 156-158
 exposure to, 135
 federal statute, 87-88
"Contemptible informer," 100
Continental Can Company, 189-190
Continental Congress, 218
Contract of marriage, 45-48
"Contumacious," 138
Conviction for narcotics, 107
Cooperative rate-making insurance, 296-297
Copyright laws, 286
Coroner's role, 27
Corporate entity and the Fifth Amendment, 120-121
Corporate mergers and acquisitions, 181-199
Corruption in public service, 287-288
Counterfeiting, 285
"Country Girl," 15
Couzens, U. S. Senator James, 165
Creation of family by law, 233-253

Credit bureau collections, 140
Creditor, harassment by, 22-23
Crimes against institutions, 280-291
Crimes involving moral turpitude, 113-114
Criminal abortion, 75
Criminal contempt, 156-158
Criminal conversation, action for, 38-39
Criminal, habitual, statute, 129-130
Criminal libel, definition of, 135
Criminal portrayals and right of privacy, 18-19
"Cross Creek," 12
Cross-examination, right of, 93
Crude oil, 182
Cuba, 264
*Cuban-American Sugar Company* case, 196-197
*Curcio* case, 106
Customer, detention of, 288-290
Cuyahoga County, 310
Cyst, rupture of, 54

## D

Dahl, Arlene, 10
Damages
  monetary, for defamation, 136-139
  speculative, 63
Daniel Singers, 136
Darwin, Charles, 48
Deaf-mutism, 47
Death, wrongful, 71
Debt collection and right of privacy, 18-19, 22-23
Debtor, harassment of, 22-23
Debtor, refusal, to testify, 107-108
Decedent Estate Law of New York, 247
Deceptive practices in broadcasting, 290-291
Defamation
  abuse of privilege of, 146-147
  and the right of privacy, 12-13, 141
  by innuendo, 147-149
  by radio and television, 159-161
  husband-wife, 150-151
  immunity of legislators from liability for, 164-175
  immunity of public officials from liability for, 161-175
  legal remedy for, 136-139
  libel and slander, 135-179
  monetary damages for, 136-139
  of a group, 175-179
  of personality, 142-147
  of product, 141-142
  truth as a defense, 151-152
Defame, the privilege to, 150-152
Defects
  congenital, 73
  teratogenic, 74
Defense and security, national, 122
Deformed brain, 67
Defraud, intent to, 152
Delinquency, juvenile, 59
Demand and supply, 181
Democratic Farmers Union, 159
Demogoguery, 168-171
Denial of passport, 257-262
Denaturalization proceedings, 118-119
Department store, 288
Dependents, support of, 43-45
Deportation hearings and the Fifth Amendment, 112-114
Deportation of aliens, 270-274
Detention
  defined, 274-275
  of aliens, 274-278
  of customer by store, 288-290
  of the person, unlawful, 288-290
"Detroit Lions," 209
Devices, lottery and the Federal Communications Commission, 227-228
Dice, 225, 230
Dice-game raid by police, 153
Directorates, interlocking, 194, 300
"Direct writer rules" in insurance, 311
Disbarment proceedings and the Fifth Amendment, 108-112
Disclaimer affidavits, 82
Disclosure, confidential, 42
Discovery of reports, 116-117
Diseases, loathesome, 137
Dishonor, exposure to, 135-136
Disloyalty in government employment, 93-98
Disney, Walt, 8
Disorderly conduct, 132
Disorderly Houses Act of 1751, 231

*Index* 321

Disrespect, exposure to, 135-136
Dissemination of news and the right of privacy, 9-12
Dissolution of monopolies, 182
Divestiture
   generally, 182-183
   of General Motors stock, 193-195
   of stock and assets, 188
Divorce, generally, 138
Documents, incriminating, 128
Domestic Relations Law of New York, 233, 239, 243, 247
Domestic tranquility in England, 42-43
Domicile, 57-58
Double jeopardy and the Fifth Amendment, 129-132
Drawer of check, 285-286
"Dream books," 224
Dried onion industry, 190
Driver's license, 282
Drunkenness, 243
Drunkometers, 129
Duff Company, 191
Dulles, John Foster, 257, 262
*du Pont-General Motors case*, 191-195

### E

Economic "bigness," 198-199
Economic concentration, patterns of, 181-199
Egypt, Pharaohs of, 48
Einstein, Albert, 257
Eisenhower, Administration, 262
Eisenhower, President Dwight D., 79, 93, 273
Electricweld pipe, 196
Elevator shaft, 65
El Paso Natural Gas Company, 188-189
Embezzlement, 79
Employees
   public, 82-83, 104-105
   subway, 103
Employer, suit against, 55
Employment by Federal Government and the Fifth Amendment, 93-98
Employment opportunities under attack, 139-141
Employment of teachers, 85-86
Endanger national security, 255, 265-266

Enforcement of support order, 44-45
England, 258
   gambling in, 230-231
"Entity" defined, 63, 75
"Entrapment," 126
"Entry" defined, 112-114, 271
"En ventra sa mere," 69
Environmental stress as cause of prenatal injury, 74-75
Epilepsy, 72
"Equal opportunities" for broadcasting, 159-161
"Equal time" in broadcasting, 159-161
Erasure or obliteration of check, 285
Espionage, 122
Esther, 236
"Ether" consent, 248
Ettore, Al, 22
Evasion of federal income tax, 131-132
Evidence
   inspection of, 115-117
   judicial torture to elicit, 77-78
   parole, 283
   scientific, and the Fifth Amendment, 128-129
Executive Order 10450, 93
Exclusion, selectivity by, 146
Exemption from antitrust laws, 206, 216
Exhibitions, 229
"Exodus, Chapter 21, 22-26," 75
Expatriation or banishment, 265
Exposeés, sensational, 147
Extortion
   generally, 124
   the crime of, 280-282
Extra-uterine survival, 64

### F

Fabrics and finishes, automotive, 191-195
"Fair comment," 144-146, 152-156
Fair Labor Standards Act, 313
False and misleading advertising, 300-310
False imprisonment, 288-290
"False labor," 72
False statement under oath, 284
Familial peace, 31-62
Family
   as a group, 31

legal creation of a, 233-253
negligently-caused injuries within the, 48-58
personal injuries within the, 48-58
"Family car," 48-58
Family Court, 249
Family immunity doctrine, 48-58
Farmers' Educational and Cooperative Union, 159
"Farm system" in baseball, 206
Faro, 231
Father Corridan, 10
Father, intoxicated, 50, 55-56
F. B. I., 116, 139, 170-171
*Federal Baseball Club* case, 203-209
Federal Bureau of Investigation, 116, 139, 170-171
Federal Communications Commission, 159-161, 227-228, 291
Federal contempt statue, 87-88
Federal Employees Veterans Association, 162-163
Federal government employment and the Fifth Amendment, 93-98
Federal immunity statutes and the Fifth Amendment, 12-124
Federal immunity-state immunity under the Fifth Amendment, 126-127
Federal income tax, evasion of, 13-132
*Federal Life Insurance* case, 301-302
Federal Tort Claims Act, 171, 174
Federal Trade Commission, 183-185, 224-227, 300-310
Federal witnesses, state prosecution of, 121-124
Fetus, 64, 68-69
Fictionalization and the right of privacy, 19-30
Fictitious claims, 63
Fictitious payee, 285
Fictitious product, 142
Fifth Amendment
and civil suits, 107-108
and congressional committees, 84-92
and corporate entity, 120-121
and deportation hearings, 112-114
and disbarment proceedings, 108-112
and double jeopardy, 129-132
and federal governmental employment, 93-98
and federal immunity statutes, 121-124
and grand jury proceedings, 105-107
and lawyers, 108-112
and local government investigations, 103-105
and school board hearings, 114-115
and scientific evidence, 128-129
and self-incrimination, generally, 77-134
and state immunity statutes, 124-126
and state legislative inquiries, 98-103
waiver of the privilege of the, 118-120
Films, motion picture, 202
Fingerprinting, 128
Finishes and fabrics, automotive, 191-195
Finland, 258
Firemen, volunteer, 229
First Amendment, 82, 96, 135, 158-159, 178, 254-255
First cousin marriages, 47-48
Fisher, Eddie, 142-143
Flour and mixes industry, 191
Flynn, Elizabeth Gurley, 265-266
Foetus, 64, 68-69
Folding chair, 223
Food Machinery and Chemical Corporation, 184
Football, business of, 209-212
Forceps, 72
Foreign affairs, judicial review of, 254-255
Ford Motor Company, 165
Foremost Dairies, 184
Forgery, crime of, 284-286
*Forman* case, 131-132
Forms
  Authority to Admit Observers, 24
  Consent to Publication of Photographs, 25
  Consent to Taking of Motion Pictures of Operation, 26
  Consent to Taking of Photographs, 25
  Consent to Televising of Operation, 26
Formosan government, 272
Fort Monmouth, New Jersey, 168
"Fort Wayne Pistons," 215

Foster homes, 234, 242, 246-247, 252
Foster parents, 236
    termination of rights of, 250
Foundling, true, 240
Fourteenth Amendment, 79, 85-86, 102, 126, 130, 166, 227, 255
Fourth Amendment, 8, 121
Fox, Charles Jean, 231
France, 256
Fraser, Dr. N., 74
Fraud, income tax, 163-164
Free chances, 220-223
Freedman, Warren, 294
Freedom of movement, 254-278
Freedom of the press, 156-158
French Revolution, 256
"From Here to Eternity," 19-20
"Front Page Detective" magazine, 11, 17
F. T. C., 183-185, 224-227, 300-310
Future of insurance regulation, 313

## G

Gambling,
    and lotteries, New York's attack upon, 223-224
    generally, 218-231
    in England, 230-231
    legalization of, 231
Gambuzza, Ralph, 154
Gaming Act of 171, 231
Gardella, Danny, 205
Garland, Judy, 156-158
Garlic industry, 190
Gas stations, 222
General Construction Law of New York, 248
"General Corrigan," 141
*General Motors-du Pont* case, 191-195
General Motors stock purchases, 191-195
*General Shoe Corporation* case, 186
Genes, recessive, 48
Genitor, role of, 236
Gentry, Inc., 190
Georgia, 298
German measles, 73
Gestation, 64
Gift and consideration distinguished, 221
"Gift enterprise," 223-227
"Give-aways," 228

Glasnik, Narodni, 113
Glass container industry, 189-190
Goelet, Robert, 9-10
"Good moral character," 109-112, 114
Gordon, Janet Hill, 246
Gospel group, 136
Gossip, "retailer" of, 158
Government employment and the Fifth Amendment, 93-98
Government, overthrow of, 81, 98-99, 109-112
Governmental regulation of the insurance industry, 293-313
Grand jury proceedings and the Fifth Amendment, 105-107
Gratuitous lottery tickets, 218-222
Greece, 236
Greek lawyer, 236
*Greene* case, 93-94
Griswold, A. Whitney, 81-82
Griswold, Dean Erwin, 80-81
Group Health Insurance, Inc., 139
Group libel, 175-179
Group slander, 175-179
"Guilt by accusation," 168-175
Guilt, presumption of, 79-80
"Guilty of insubordination," 86-87
Guliver's mad scientist, 83
Gummed paper, 226
Gun, 59

## H

Habeas corpus, writ of, 237, 246, 252, 273
Habitual criminal statute, 129-130
*Halperin* case, 106-107
Handwriting samples, 128
Harassment by creditor, 22-23
Harms to unborn children, 63-76
Harness racing, 216
Hartford County, Conn., 101
"Harvard Law Review," 3, 4
Harvard Law School, 81
Harvard University, 20, 82
Hate-mongers, 178-179
Hatred, exposure to, 135
Hazel-Atlas Glass Company, 189-190
Head, Rev. Edward, 240-241
Hearing, requirement of, 93-98
Hearst's "Journal American," 148-149

"Heartbreak House," 11
Hebrew law, 236
Helsinki, Finland, 258
Hemophelia, 47
Henry VIII, 231
Hereditary influences, as a cause of prenatal injury, 74-75
Heretical books, 77
Heroin, 131
"Hidden libels," 147-149
*Hilton Hotels Corporation* case, 185-186
Hippocratic Oath, 23
History of adoption practices, 236-237
History of corporate mergers, 182-183
History of rate-making in insurance, 296-297
History of the right to travel, 255-256
H. K. Porter Company, 184
Hoboken, New Jersey, 127
"Holiday" magazine, 11-12
Holmes, Mr. Justice Oliver Wendell, 64, 89-90, 137, 204
Homes, foster, 234, 242, 246-247, 252
Homicide, 75
Hook, Professor Sidney, 79-80
"Horizontal mergers," 183, 190-191
Horse race betting, off-track, 230
Horse racing, 216, 224
Hotel Commodore, New York City, 176
Hotel industry, competition in, 185-186
Hot rolled bars and sheets, 195
House Committee on Un-American Activities, 86, 91, 92, 145, 167, 176
House Select Committee on Small Business, 184-185
Howard, Admiral W. E., Jr., 162-163
Howard, Charles T., 219
Hungarian refugees, 272-274
Hungary, 263
Hunt, U. S. Senator Lester C., 172-174
Husband, wife as witness against, 39-42
Husband-wife defamation, 150-151
Hypoxia, 74

# I

Identification, voice, 128
Idiocy, 47
"If I Should Die," 7
Illegal lottery, 218-231

"Illegitimate" defined, 248
Illegitimacy, imputation of, 143
Illegitimate children, 142-143, 233-235
Illinois Supreme Court Character and Fitness Committee, 110-111
Imbecility, 46
Immigration and Nationality Act of 1917, 272, 276
Immigration and Naturalization Service, 271-278
Immigration Appeals, Board of, 114
Immoral portrayals and the right of privacy, 18-19
Immunities and privileges clause of U. S. Constitution, 45, 79
Immunity
  for defamation by legislators, 164-175
  for defamation by public officials, 161-175
  of witnesses, generally, 105
  state and federal, 126-127
Immunity doctrine
  family, 49-58
  abolition of, 56-57
Immunity statutes
  federal, 121-124
  generally, 84
  state, 124-126
Imposter, 285
Imprisonment, false, 288-290
Incest, 47-48
"Incompetent teachers," 114-115
Income tax evasion, federal, 116, 125, 131-132
Income tax fraud, 163-164
Incriminating document, 128
Incrimination, privilege against, 78-134
Indemnity policy of insurance, 54
Independent Socialists League, 257
India, 262
Indiana resident, 146
Individual's interest in his reputation, 135-179
Ineligible lists of players, 203, 205
Information, refusal to divulge source of, 156-158
Informers, paid, 116-117
Ingalls, Dr. Theodore H., 74-75
Inheritance rights of adopted child, 247

Initial placement of adopted child, 245-247
Injuries
  personal, within family, 48-58
  prenatal, 63-76
  recovery for prenatal, 66-71
Injuries and negligence, causal relation between, 71-73
Injury
  prenatal
    environmental stress as cause of, 74-75
    hereditary influences as cause of, 74-75
Inland Steel Company, 195
Innocence, presumption of, 80-81
Innuendoes and defamation, 147-149
Insane asylum, 50
Insanity, 47
Insinuations, 147
Inspection of evidence, 115-117
Institutions, crimes against, 280-291
"Insurable interest," 293
Insurance
  adjusting, 151
  aircraft hull, 310
  aircraft personal injury, 310
  and "commerce," 296-297
  applicability of antitrust laws to, 297-313
  as "big business," 300
  aviation, 310
  boycotts, 299, 310-313
  brokerage, 152
  carrier, state regulation of, 295-297
  "dilemma" in New York, 58-59
  industry, regulation of, 293-313
  liability, 49-50, 54-55, 58-59
  nature of the business, 293-295
  policies, generally, 202
  regulation and the Federal Trade Commission, 300-310
  regulation, future of, 313
  solicitation of, by mail, 308
"Insured event," 293
I. O. U.'s, 224
Integration of racial groups, 126
Intentional tort, 54
Intent to defraud, 152

Intercourse, sexual, 47
Interference with relational interests, 31-62
Interior Department, U. S. Government, 94
Interlocking directorates, 194, 300
Intermarriage, religious, 244
Internal Revenue Service, 116, 125
Internal Security Act of 1950, 95-98, 265-266, 270-278
International Boxing Club, 212-214
International League, 208
International Longshoreman's Association, 127
International travel, 254-278
Interstate Commerce Commission, 123
Interstate commerce, restraint on, 201-202
Intoxicated father, 50, 55-56
Intoxication, 128, 282
Intra-family suits, 48-58
"Intrastate commerce," 204
Investigation of prospective parent for adoption, 244-245
Investment Company Act, 313
Irish Sweepstakes, 218
Iron and steel industry, 195-196
"Iron Curtain," 155, 267
Irony, 147
"It's Me, O Lord," 258

# J

Jacob, 48
James, Jesse, 20
*Jencks* case, 115-117
Jenner, U. S. Senator, 87
Jeopardy, double, 129-132
Jewish couples, adoption by, 239
Joke, practical, 60
Jones and Laughlin Steel Company, 195
"Journal American," 148-149
Journalist's confidential source of information, 156-158
"Journal of the American Medical Association," 74
Judicial review of foreign affairs, 254-255
Judicial torture to elicit evidence, 77-78
Juke box hit, 136

Julian, Joe, 176-178
Justice of the peace, 46
Juvenile delinquency, 59

## K

Kefauver Committee, 248-249
Kefauver, U. S. Senator Estes, 170
Kennedy, Attorney General Robert F., 181
Kent, Rockwell, 258-261
Kerby, Marian, 15
"Keystone Comedy," 153-154
King, Governor (N. H.), 219
Kinsey Shoe Company, 187-188
*Knapp* case, 124, 126
*Konigsberg* case, 109-110
Korea, 114, 141
Korea, North, 264
"Kukla, Fran and Ollie," 155

## L

Labor leader, 87-88, 106
Labor organizer, New Mexico, 115-116
Labor union, unincorporated, 121
Lahr, Bert, 5-6
Laius, 37
Larceny, crime of, 288
Laser beams, 27
Law and social science, 31
Lawn mower, power, 60
"Law of Evidence" by Wigmore, 80
Laws, conflict of, 57-58
Lawson, Diana, 146
Lawyers and the Fifth Amendment, 108-112
League, professional sports, 202
Leah, 48
Legal detriment incurred, 220-223
"Legal existence," 63
"Legal" vs "medical" cause of injury, 71-73
"Legalized gambling," 230
Legislative attack upon right to travel, 262-266
Legislative inquiry, power of, 98-103
Legislators, immunity from liability for defamation, 164-175
Legitimizing children, 47
*Lerner* case, 103-104

Lessening of competition, 181-199
Lewis, Fulton, Jr., 145
Liability for defamation, protection of public officials from, 161-164
Liability insurance, 49-50, 54-55, 58-59
Liability, vicarious, 59-61
"Liability without fault," 63
Libel
  and slander law, 135-179
  by will or testament, 147
  definition of, 135
  of a group, 175-179
"Libel per se," 137
*Liberty Mutual Insurance* case, 303
License, driver's, 282
Licensing laws for bingo and lotto, 228-230
Lie detector tests, 27, 128
Lilburne, John, 77
Lincoln, Abraham, 48, 171
"Line of commerce," 187-190
Liquor industry, competition in, 186-187
Liquor stores, 219
Loan funds for needy students, 81-82
Loathesome disease, 137
Local government investigations and the Fifth Amendment, 103-105
"Local option basis," 224, 228-230
Lockwood Committee Report, 297
"Locus standi," 64
London, 231
Long Parliament, 77
Long, U. S. Senator Huey P., 165
Los Angeles County Communist Association, 261
"Los Angeles Dons," 209
Loss of society, companionship and consortium, 31-37
Loss, ovary, 54
Loss, risk of, 293
Lot, nephew of Abraham, 236
Lotteries
  and gambling, New York's attack upon, 223-224
  and the Federal Communications Commission, 227-228
  defined, 220-223

## Index

devices, sales of merchandise by, 218-231
  generally, 218-231
  history of, 218-220
Lotto by referendum, 228-230
Lotto licensing laws, 228-230
Louise Wise Services, 237
Louisiana gambling syndicate, 219
Louisiana Lottery Company, 219
Louis, Joe, 22
Loyalty oath, 104
Loyalty oath affidavits, 81-83
Luncheonette, 283

## M

Mack trucks, 197
"Mad Bomber," 148-149
Madison, James, 78
Madison Square Garden, 212-214
Magazines, sensational, 155-156
Mail, fraud, 142
Mail order business, 226
Mail, solicitation of insurance by, 308
Malice, generally, 152-156
Malice in defamation, 137, 140-141
*Mallay* case, 101-103
Mandamus, writ of, 276
Mann Act, 39-41
"Marionettes," 155
Marital intercourse, refusal to have, 241
"Marko," 227-228
Marriage
  annulment of, 45-46
  by minors, 46
  common law, 47
  consanguineous, 47-48
  contract, 45-48
  dissolution of, 45-46
  first cousin, 47-48
Married Women's Property Acts, 34, 48, 53
Marshall, Chief Justice John, 78, 127
Mason, George, 77
Matches, 59
"Materiality," 284
Maternal rights, abandonment of, 246-247
Matusow, Harvey, 116
McCarran-Ferguson Act, 299

McCarran Immigration Act, 274
"McCarthyism," 168
*McPhaul* case, 91
Medal of Merit, 257
"Medical" cause of injury, 71-73
Medical services rendered, defamation relating to, 139
"Men without faces," 170
Merchandising by lottery devices, 224-227
Merchandising sales through lottery devices, 218-231
Merger movement, history of, 182-183
Mergers and acquisitions, corporate, 181-199
Mergers and insurance, 300
Mergers, types of, 190-191
Metal containers industry, 189-190
Metropolitan Life Insurance Company, 294
Metropolitan Police Act of 1839, 231
Mexican League, 204-206
Mexico, 267, 270-271
*Mills* case, 125
Milquetoast, Casper, 280
Minerich, Anton, 113
Minor child, suit against parent by, 50-53
Minor league baseball club, 207-208
Minority groups, 178-179
Minors, marriage by, 46
Minox cameras, 8
"Misappropriation," 152
Misconduct of children, parent's liability for, 59-61
Mistrial, 132
"Modern Screen" magazine, 142
Molinas, Jack, 215-216
Monetary damages for defamation, 136-139
Mongoloid child, 67
Monopolies, dissolution of, 182
Monopolization, 181-199
Monopoly
  insurance, 312
  tendency to, 181-199
Moral turpitude, 272
  crimes involving, 113-114

Moratorium on enforcement of statute, 299
Modecai, 236
Moses, 48
Motion picture films, 202
Motives for "taking the Fifth," 117-118
Motive, proof of good, 151
Movement, freedom of, 254-278
Movie theatre, 221
Mower, power lawn, 60

## N

N. B. C., 142
Name, use of, for advertising purposes, 5-8
Narcotics conviction, 107
Narcotics, pills and capsules, 129
Narcotics, sale of, 131
Nathan, Doctor, 257
National Association of Broadcasters, 291
National Association of Insurance Commissioners, 299
National Basketball Association, 215-216
National Board of Fire Underwriters, 296
National Broadcasting Company, 142
*National Casualty* case, 306-307
National Council of Arts, Sciences, and Professions, 176
National Defense Education Act, 81
National Football League, 209-212
National Labor Relations Act, 313
National League (baseball), 203
National security and defense, 122
National security endangered, 255, 265-266
National Steel Company, 195
National Wrestling Alliance, 214-215
Natural gas industry, 188-190
Natural parents, 237-238, 242, 250
Nazi S S men, 167
Needy students, loan funds for, 81-82
Neglectful parents, 252
Negligence and injury, causal relation between, 71-73
Negligently-caused injuries within family, 48-58
Negotiable Instruments Law of New York, 285
Nephew-aunt marriage, 48
New Hampshire Attorney General, 98-99
New Hampshire Lottery Commission, 219
New Hampshire World Friendship Center, 99-101
New Mexico labor organizer, 115-116
New Orleans, Louisiana, 219
New Orleans Insurance Exchange, 312
New Rochelle, New York, 175, 229-230
New York, Charter of City of, 85
New York Child Welfare Foster Home Care and Adoption Service, 240
New York City Commissioner of Investigation, 103
New York City referendum on gambling, 230
New York Civil Practice Act, 241
New York Civil Rights Law, 5-8
New York Civil Service Commission, 103
New York Constitution, 105, 224
New York Decedent Estates Law, 247
New York Domestic Relations Law, 46, 58-59, 233, 239, 243, 247
New York General Construction Law, 248
"New York Giants," 205
New York Herald-Tribune, 156-158
New York insurance "dilemma," 58-59
New York Insurance Law, 58-59
New York Negotiable Instruments Law, 285
New York Penal Law, 75, 105, 223-224, 236, 248, 280, 282, 285, 287
New York Post, 263
New York, right of privacy in, 5-8
New York Social Welfare Law, 236, 249
New York State Insurance Department, 297
New York Times, 33-34, 81-82, 87, 101, 154-154, 198-199, 230, 239, 240, 241
New York Times Magazines Section, 231
New York Transit Authority, 103
New York Waterfront Commission, 127
"New York Yankees," 204-206
New York's attack upon lotteries and gambling, 223-224
News dissemination and privacy, 9-12

News gathering services, 202
Newsman's right to travel, 262-265
Newspaper reporter, privileged communication of, 156-159
Newspapers, privilege of fair comment, 152-156
N. F. L., 209-212
Nicaragua, 251
Ninth Amendment, 255
Nobel Prize, 257
Non-Communist affidavit, 115-117
Non-existent taxpayers, 285
Non-skill, element of lottery, 220-223
Nonviable fetus, 64-65
Norris and Wirtz, 213
North Carolina Law School, University of, 117
North Korea, 264
North Vietnam, 264
*Northern Securities* case, 182
*Nostrand* case, 104-105
Notice, requirement of, 93-98
"No travel," 274
Numbers, winning, 223-224

## O

Oath, false statement under, 284
Oath, loyalty, 81-83, 104
Oath requirement, Communist, 82
Oath, teacher's, 82-83
Obliteration of erasure of check, 285
Oceanography, 274
Oedipus, 37
Office of Rent Stabilization, 161
Off-track horse race betting, 230
Oil, crude, 182
Oil field equipment, 196
Old news and the right of privacy, 20-22
Oligopolies, 199
Olin-Mathieson Corporation, 184
Oma, Lee, 16
O'Malley, Walter, 144-145
Omber, 231
"One-shot" gambler, 280
Onion, dried, industry, 190
Orders, cease and desist, 224-227
"Organized baseball," 203-209

Organized professional sports, generally, 202
Oriental societies, 236
Originality of idea, 286-287
Ortenburg, 178
Orthopedic surgeon, 151
Outlawry, act of, 96
Ovary, loss of, 54
"Overt coercion" of competitor, 191
Overthrow of government, 81, 98-99, 109-112
Oxford, Bodleian Library, 266
Oxygen, lack of, 67

## P

Paar, Jack, 142
Pacific Coast League, 209
Pacific Northwest Pipeline Corporation, 188-189
Packard, Vance, 28
"Pageant" magazine, 16
Paid informers, 116-117
Paktorovics, Gyula, 273
Pandering, 41
Paper, gummed, 226
Paper industry, sanitary, 197-198
Parakeet smuggling, 41
Pardon or amnesty, 107
Parental rights of foster parents, termination of, 250
Parental rights, termination of, 237, 249-253
Parent-child relationship, 233-253
Parent
   foster, 236
   investigation of prospective, 244-245
Parents
   liability for misconduct of children, 59-61
   natural, 237-238, 242, 250
   neglectful, 252
   suit by minor child against, 50-53
Pari-mutuel betting, 224
Park and Tilford Company, 186-187
Parole evidence, 283
Passport Hearing Board, 268-270
Passport, refusal or denial of, 257-262
Passports, generally, 254-278
Pater, role of, 236

Patient's right of privacy, 23-26
Patterns of economic concentration, 181-199
Pauling, Dr. Linus, 257
Payee, fictitious, 285
Payments under-the table, 230
"Payola," 290-291
"Pecuniary loss," 156
Pegler, Westbrook, 145
Penal Law of New York, 236, 248, 280, 282, 285, 287
Pennsylvania Death Statute, 52
"Pennsylvania Law Review," 117-118
Pennsylvania Public School Code, 114
Perjury, crime of, 175, 284
"Permanently neglected" child, 249
Personal injuries within the family, 48-58
Personality, defamation of, 142-147
Personality under attack, 139-141
Personal right of privacy, 13-14
"Per verba praesenti," 47
Petroleum, 182
Pharaohs of Egypt, 48
Photographs and the right of privacy, 16-18
Photographs, use of, for advertising, 5-8
Physical assets of competitors, purchase of, 182-183
Physician-patient relationship, 23-26
Piano, 222
*Pillsbury Mills* case, 191
Pitts, Connie, 136
Placement for adoption, 237-238
Placement, initial, of child of adoption, 245-247
Placental disruption, 71
Place of wrong, 58
"Placing out" of children for adoption, 236-253
Plagiarism, 286-287
Plamondon, 178
Plato, 75
Players, list of ineligible, 203, 205
Police, railroad, 146
Police station, 240
Policies of indemnity, 54
"Policy bank," 223-224
"Policy," playing of, 223-224

Polier, Justine, 240
"Political Affairs," 265
Political campaigns, 143-144
"Political privacy," 99
Pollitt, Professor Daniel H., 117-118
Polyethylene resin, 198
Pool halls, 225
"Pool-selling," 224
Population limitation, 75
Portsmouth, Virginia, 207
Postal laws, generally, 313
Power lawn mowers, 60
Power of legislative inquiry, 98-103
Practical joke, 60
Pregnant woman, 63
Premature birth, 69
Premium for insurance, 293
Prenatal injuries
 generally, 63-76
 recovery for, 66-71
Prenatal injury
 environmental stress as a cause of, 74-75
 hereditary influences as a cause of, 74-75
Prenuptial agreements, 241-242
Prenuptial torts or wrongs, 53
*Presser* case, 90-91
Press
 freedom of, 156-158
 privilege of fair comment, 152-156
"Presumptive guilt" theory, 79-80
"Presumptive innocence" theory, 80-81
Price-fixing, illegality of, 201-202
Prince Regent, 231
Priscilla, 38
Privacy
 and autopsy, 26-27
 and criminal portrayals, 18-19
 and debt collection, 18-19, 22-23
 and defamation, 12-13, 141
 and dissemination of news, 9-12
 and "fair comment," 152-156
 and fictionalization, 19-20
 and immoral portrayals, 18-19
 and old news, 20-22
 and photographs, 16-18
 and public figures, 9-12
 and scientific developments, 27-28

## Index

and signatures, 14-16
and the United Nations, 28-29
as a personal right, 13-14
defined, 3-5
in the absence of statute, 8-9
of the patient, 23-26
right of, 3-30
    and defamation, 12-13, 141
Private adoptions, 237-238, 245-247, 250
Privilege against self-incrimination, 77-134
Privilege against self-incrimination
qualifications of, 83-84
waiver of, 118-120
Privilege from arrest, 164-165
Privilege to defame, 150-152
qualifications of, 140-141
"Privilege to travel," 254-255
Privileged communication, 39-42
of newspaper reporter, 156-159
Privileged defamation, abuse of, 146-147
Privileges and immunities clause of U. S. Constitution, 79
Prize, element of lottery, 220-223
Proceedings, denaturalization, 118-119
Procter and Gamble Company, 190-191
Product defamation, 141-142
Product, fictitious, 142
Product innovation, 181
"Professional Baseball Rules," 207-208
Professional basketball, 215-216
Professional boxing, 212-214
Professional football, 209-212
Professional, organized sports, 202
Professional wrestling, 214-215
Professor, college, 85-86, 104-105
Progressive Party, 98
Promoter of professional wrestling, 214-215
Proof of good motives, 151
"Property," 281
Property rights under attack, 139-141
Prospective parents, investigation of, 244-245
Prostitution, 39-41
Protestant, 146
Protestant Church, 240
Protestant mother, 241
Public domain, 287
Public employees, 82-83, 104-105
Public figures and right of privacy, 9-12
Public gatherings, 229
Public Law 15, 299
Public Law 87-331, 211
Public Law 269, 116
Public officer, bribery of, 287
Public officials, absolute immunity from liability for defamation, 161-175
Public service, corruption in, 287-288
Public Utilities Holding Company Act, 183
Puerto Rico, 224
Pugilistic sports, 212-214
Punch boards, 224-227
Purchase of physical assets of competitors, 182-183
Purchase of stock of competitors, 182-183
Pusey, Nathan M., 82
Push cards, 224-227

## Q

Qualifications of the privilege against self-incrimination, 83-84
Qualified privilege to defame, 140-141, 150-152
Quebec, 178
Questions for Review
  I, 29-30
  II, 61-62
  III, 76
  IV, 133-134
  V, 179-180
  VI, 199-200
  VII, 217
  VIII, 231-232
  IX, 253
  X, 278-279
  XI, 292
  XII, 314
Quiz shows, 146, 290
"Quota immigrant," 270

## R

Race tracks, 219
Rachel, 48

Racial integration groups, 216
Radar speed-detection devices, 128
Radiation, 73
Radio, defamation by, 159-161
Radio transmitters, miniaturized, 27
Radovich, Bill, 205, 209-210
Raffles, 223
Railroad police, 146
*Raley* case, 126
Rape, crime of, 51
Rapp-Coudert Committee, 85
Rasputin, 7
Rate-making bureau, 296
Rate-making, history of, 296-297
Rate-making in the insurance industry, 295
Rating bureau, 296-297
Ready Money Football Betting Act of 1920, 231
Rearing children in particular religion, 241-244
Recessive genes, 48
Reciprocal enforcement of support orders, 44-45
Recording
  voice, 128
  wiretap, 128
Records
  required, doctrine of, 121
  union, 106
Recovery for prenatal injuries, 66-71
"Red Channels," 176-178
Redemption of trading stamps, 226-227
Referendum, bingo and lotto by, 228-230
Refined sugar industry, 196-197
Refusal to answer, 77-134
Refusal to divulge source of information, 156-158
Refusal to have marital intercourse, 241
Refusal to issue passport, 257-262
Refusal to testify against oneself, 77-134
Regulation of insurance, the future of, 313
Regulation of the insurance industry, 293-313
*Reina* case, 107
Relational interests, interference with, 31-62

"Relevant market," 187-190
Religion, children reared in particular, 241-244
Religion-matching, 239-244
Religious choice in adoptions, 242-244
Religious faith of adopting parents, 238-244
Religious groupings in adoptions, 239-244
Religious grouping statues, 240-241
Religious intermarriage, 244
Remedy for defamation, legal, 136-139
Required attendance, 221
Required records doctrine, 121
Reporter, privileged communication of, 156-159
"Report on Corporate Mergers and Acquisitions," 184
Reports, discovery of, 116-117
Representative or class action, 208-209
Republic Steel Company, 195
Reputation, individual's interest in, 135-179
"Reserve clause," 203, 204, 206-207
Resin, polyethylene, 198
Respondeat superior doctrine, 171-175
"Restatement of Conflict of Laws," 57
Restraint on interstate commerce, 201-202
Restrictions on travel, 255, 262-265
Restaurant waiter, 146
"Retailer of gossip," 158
Revolutionary War, 218
Reynolds, Quentin, 145
"Richards On Insurance" (by Warren Freedman), 294
Rifle, 61
"Right" against self-incrimination, 84
Right of cross-examination, 93
Right of privacy, 3-30
Right of privacy and defamation, 141
"Right-thinking people," 148
"Right to exclude," 275-278
"Right to travel," 254-278
Risk of loss, 293
Robbery distinguished from extortion, 281
Robbery of bank, 129
"Rochester Red Wings," 208

*Rockwell Kent* case, 258-261
Rogge, O. John, 81
Roman Catholic Church, 239
Roman Catholic husband, 243
Roman Empire, 256
Rome Cable Corporation, 189
"Rotation basis," 240
Roulette wheels, 225
Rousseau, 75
Royal Commission on Betting, Lotteries, and Gaming, 231
Runyan, Damon, 14
Rupture of cyst, 54
Russian spy, 154
Ryan, Judge Sylvester, 156-158

## S

*Sabella and La Cascia* case, 130-131
Salacious titles to publications, 156
Sale of child, 237
Sale of merchandise by lottery devices, 218-231
Salzburg, 273
"Sam Cooke," 136
Samples of blood, 128-129
Samples of handwriting, 128
"San Francisco Clippers," 209
Sanitary paper products, 197-198
Sarah, 48
Sarcasm, 147
"Saturday Evening Post," 17
Sausage casings, 198
Schemes, gambling, 218-231
*Schenley Industries* case, 186-187
School board hearings and the Fifth Amendment, 114-115
Schumann, Robert, 13
Schwartz, Professor Louis B., 199
Scientific developments and the right of privacy, 27-28
Scientific evidence and the Fifth Amendment, 128-129
*Scott Paper* case, 197-198
Scripps-Howard's "World Telegram," 148-149
Seamless pipe, 196
Secretary of State, 255-262, 263-265, 266-278

Sectarian adoption agency, 240
Securities and Exchange Act, 183, 313
"Security agency," 103
Security and defense, national, 122
Security clearance, 93-98
Seditious books, 77
Seduction, action for, 38-39
Selected Bibliography
  I, 29
  II, 61
  III, 76
  IV, 132-133
  V, 179
  VI, 199
  VII, 217
  VIII, 231
  IX, 253
  X, 278
  XI, 292
  XII, 313
Select Committee on Improper Activities in Labor or Management Field, 90
Selectivity by exclusion, 146
Self-incrimination
  and the Fifth Amendment, 77-134
  qualifications of privilege against, 83-84
  "right" against, 84
  waiver of privilege against, 118-120
Sensational exposeés, 147
Sensational exposé magazines, 155-156
Separability of child from moment of conception, 73-74
Sex pervert, 148
Sexual assault, 54
Sexual intercourse, 47
  refusal to have, 241
Sexual relations, 142, 150-151
Sherman Act of 1890, 182-199, 201-202, 298, 312
Shoe manufacturing industry, 186
"Shoplifting," 288-290
Signatures
  and the right of privacy, 14-16
  forged, 284-286
  of voters, 143-144
Silent, the privilege to remain, 77-134
Sister-brother union or marriage, 48

Slander
and libel law, 135-179
definition of, 135
of a group, 175-179
"Slander per se," 137
Slochower, Harry, 85-86
Smith Act of 1940, 82, 84, 95-98
Smith, U. S. Senator Margaret, 164
"Snooze," 142
Social agency adoption, 237-238
"Social crimes," 280-291
Social science and the law, 31
Social Welfare Law of New York, 236, 249
Solomon, 219
Source of information, refusal to divulge, 156-158
*South Eastern Underwriters Association* case, 294, 297-300
Sovereign immunity, waiver of, 171-175
Soviet Russia, 266
*Spaulding* case, 197
Speculative damages, 63
Speed-detection devices, 128
Speedometers, 128
Sperry and Hutchinson Company, 226
Sporting goods industry, 197
Sports
amateur, 272
and antitrust law, 201-217
professional organized, 202
telecasting of, 210-212
Spouses
collusion between, 56-57
confidential communications between, 150-151
suits between, 53-55
Stamford, Conn., 153
Stamps, trading, 226-227
Standard Oil Company subsidiaries, 182
"Stand in" arrangements, 249
Standish, Miles, 38
Star Chamber, 77, 155
Starnes, Richard, 149
State immunity and federal immunity under the Fifth Amendment, 126-127
State immunity statutes and the Fifth Amendment, 124-126
State Insurance Department of New York, 297
State Investigation Commission of New York, 230
State legislative inquiries and the Fifth Amendment, 98-103
State lotteries, 219
State Lottery Control Commission, 230
State prosecution of federal witnesses, 121-124
State regulation of the insurance industry, 295-297
State, visitorial powers of, 120
Statistics of adoption, 247-248
Statler Hotels, 185-186
Statutes
"anti-compact," 297
deficiency in adoption, 237-238
exemption, from antitrust laws, 216
federal immunity, 121-124
gift enterprise, 226-227
group libel, 178-179
habitual criminal, 129-130
immunity, generally, 84
lottery, 218-231
on adoption practices, 233-253
religious-grouping adoption, 239-244
state immunity, 124-126
Statutory right of privacy, 5-8
Steel and iron industry, 195-196
Step-parents, 233, 247
Sterility, 47
*Steuding* case, 105
Stock and assets, divestiture of, 188
Stock, purchase of, of competitors, 182-183
Stomach pump, 129
"Stone cold dead," 143
"Stork Restaurant," 146-147
Story, Mr. Justice Joseph, 164
Strains, as cause of prenatal injury, 74-75
Strayer, Martha, 21
Stress, environmental, as cause of prenatal injury, 74-75
Students, loan funds for needy, 81-82
Subcommittee on Legislative Oversight, 291
Subcommittee on Privileges and Elections, 168

Subpoena, grand jury, 106
Subversive Activities Control Board, 95-98, 265
"Subversive organization," 257-262
"Subversive person," 82
Subway employee, 103
Sugar beet refining industry, 196-197, 201-202
Sugar cane industry, 196-197
Suicide, 51, 152
Suits against employers, 55
Suits between spouses, 53-55
Summer camp, 100
Supermarkets, 221
Supply and demand, law of, 181
Support of dependents, 43-45
Support order, reciprocal enforcement of, 44-45
Surgeon, orthopedic, 151
Surrogates Association of New York, 233
Survey of adoptions in New York, 233-235
Swearing, false, 284
Sweater, ladies', 288
Sweepstakes, 218-231
*Sweezy* case, 98-99, 100
Swindle, 285
Swindler, convicted, 230
Switzerland, 259
Syndicate, lottery, 219

# T

Tabulation of number of adoptions, 235
Taft-Hartley Act, 115
Taking of property without due process of law, 280-282
"Taking the Fifth," motives for, 117-118
Tata Institute of Physics, 262
Taverns, 225
Tax, evasion of federal income, 131-132
Tax fraud, 116, 125, 163-164
Taxpayers, non-existent, 285
Taylor, Elizabeth, 142-143
Teacher, "incompetent," 114-115
Teachers' employment, 85-86
Teachers' oath, 82-83
Teamster official, 90-91
Teen-ager, 249

Telecasting, "equal opportunities" in, 159-161
Telecasting of sports, 210-212
Television
  deceptive practices in, 290-291
  defamation by, 159-161
  surveillance by, 27
Television bingo game, 227
Temporary National Economic Committee, 296
Tenney Committee, 166
Tenure rights, 105
Teratogenic defects, 74
Termination of foster parents rights over child, 250
Termination of parental rights over child, 237, 249-253
Testament, libel by, 147
Testimony against oneself, refusal to give, 77-134
Testimony, compelled, 39-42
Testing, blood, 128-129
Testing for intoxication, 128
"The American Passport," 259
"The Big Story," (NBC), 21
"The Desperate Hours," 7
"The Fifth Amendment Today," 81
"The First and the Fifth," 81
"The Naked Society," 28
"The Night in the Forest," 8
"The New Yorker" magazine, 20
"The Red Kimono," 21-22
"The urge to merge," 182-183
Theatre, movie, 221
Threatening letter, 283
Tickets, lottery, 218-231
"Time" magazine, 148-149, 154
"Tin-horn cop," 138
Tin plate, 196
Tip sheets, 224
T.N.E.C. Report, 296
Torre, Marie, 156-158
Track spikes, 196
"Trade or commerce," 201-202
Trade practices, unfair, 224-227
Trading stamps, 226-227
Tramp, 221
Transit Authority of New York City, 103

Traumatic amputation, 50
Travel, area restrictions on, 255, 262-265
"Travel ban," 254-255
Travel by aliens, 270-278
*Travelers Health Association* case, 307-310
Travel
  history of right to, 255-256
  legislative attack upon right to, 262-266
  right to, 254-278
Treason, trial for, 78
Treble damage suits, 210
Truth as a defense to defamation, 151-152
Twenty-Second Amendment, 83

**U**

*Ullmann* case, 122-123
Un-American Activities Committee, 86, 91, 92
Unauthorized Insurers False Advertising Process Act, 309-310
Unborn children, harms to, 63-76
Unchastity, 137
Under-the-table payments, 230
Unemancipated child, 48-58
Unfair trade practices, 224-227
Uniform Reciprocal Enforcement of Support Act, 44
Uniform Support of Dependents Act, 43-45
Unincorporated labor union, 121
*Union Carbide* case, 198
Union membership lists, 88
Union records, 106
United Nations, 256
  and the right of privacy, 28-29
U. S. Children's Bureau, 234, 238, 252
U. S. Court of Claims, 174
U. S. Department of Health, Education and Welfare, 238
U. S. Department of Justice, 185-187
  and the insurance carrier, 310-313
U. S. Passport Office, 258-278
U. S. Senate Internal Security Subcommittee, 85
U. S. Senate Select Committee on Improper Activities in the Labor or Management Field, 90
U. S. State Department Visa Office, 275
*U. S. Steel* case, 182
U. S. Steel Company, 195
U. S. Treasury, 219
U. S. Trotting Association, 216
Universal Declaration of Human Rights, 256
University of New Hampshire, 98-99
University of North Carolina Law School, 117
"University of Pennsylvania Law Review," 171, 199
University of Washington, 82, 104-105
Unlawful detention of persons, 288-290
*Uphaus* case, 99-101
Urinary analysis, 129

**V**

Vassar College, 88
Veracity of witnesses, 284
Verified Adoption Petition, 238
"Vertical mergers," 183, 187-188, 190-191, 197-198
Viable fetus, 64-65
Vicarious liability, 59-61
Vietnam, North, 264
Virginia insurance agent, 296
Visa Office of U. S. State Department, 275
Visas
  denial of, 275-278
  generally, 254-278
Visitorial powers of state, 120
Visking Company, 198
*Vitarelli* case, 94
Voice identification, 128
Voice recording, 128
Voltaire, 75
Volunteer firemen, 229
Voters, signatures of, 143-144

**W**

Wagering, 218-231
Waiter in restaurant, 146
Waiver of privilege against self-incrimination, 91, 118-120
Waiver of sovereign immunity, 171-175

Wanamaker, Pearl, 145
Warren, Samuel, 3
War of 1812, 260
"Washington Daily News," 21
Washington, Superintendent of Public Instruction, 145
Washington, University of, 82, 104-105
Waterfront Commission of New York, 127
"Waterfront Priest," 10
*Watkins* case, 87-88
WDAY television station, 159
Wedlock, children born out of, 233, 247-248
Weight-reducing pills, 142
Wheels, roulette, 225
"When practicable," 239-244
White House Conference on Education, 145
"White slavery," 41
Wife, as witness against husband, 39-42
Wife-husband defamation, 150-151
"Wife trouble," 138
Wigmore, Professor John, 80
*Wilkinson* case, 91-92
Will, libel by, 147
"Williston On Contracts," 221
Windshield wipers, 222
Winning numbers, 223-224
Wipers, windshield, 222
Wire and cable industry, 189
Wireless receiver, 154
Wire rope, 196
Wire-tap recording, 128
Wirtz and Norris, 213

Wise Adoption Services, 237
Witnesses
  availability of Fifth Amendment privilege for, 78-79
  confrontation of, 93-98
  federal, state prosecution of, 121-124
  immunity of, generally, 105
  veracity of, 284
Woman, pregnant, 63
Workman's compensation insurance, 303
World Council of Peace, 258
"World Telegram," 148-149
Worship, ancestor, 236
Worthy, William, Jr., 262-265
Wrestling, business of, 214-215
Wright, Loyd, 268
Writing exemplars, 128
Writ of habeas corpus, 237, 246, 252, 273
Writ of mandamus, 276
Wren Sales Company, 226
Wrongful death, 71

## X

X-rays, 72

## Y

Yale University, 81-82
Yankwich, Judge Leon R., 171, 175
Yonkers, New York, Police Department, 143
Young Communist League, 119
*Youngstown Sheet and Tube* case, 195-196
"You Send Me," 136